INDUSTRIAL POLICY
IN OECD COUNTRIES

ANNUAL REVIEW

1992

ORGANISATION FOR ECONOMIC CO-OPERATION AND DEVELOPMENT

ORGANISATION FOR ECONOMIC CO-OPERATION AND DEVELOPMENT

Pursuant to Article 1 of the Convention signed in Paris on 14th December 1960, and which came into force on 30th September 1961, the Organisation for Economic Co-operation and Development (OECD) shall promote policies designed:

- to achieve the highest sustainable economic growth and employment and a rising standard of living in Member countries, while maintaining financial stability, and thus to contribute to the development of the world economy;
- to contribute to sound economic expansion in Member as well as non-member countries in the process of economic development; and
- to contribute to the expansion of world trade on a multilateral, non-discriminatory basis in accordance with international obligations.

The original Member countries of the OECD are Austria, Belgium, Canada, Denmark, France, Germany, Greece, Iceland, Ireland, Italy, Luxembourg, the Netherlands, Norway, Portugal, Spain, Sweden, Switzerland, Turkey, the United Kingdom and the United States. The following countries became Members subsequently through accession at the dates indicated hereafter: Japan (28th April 1964), Finland (28th January 1969), Australia (7th June 1971) and New Zealand (29th May 1973). The Commission of the European Communities takes part in the work of the OECD (Article 13 of the OECD Convention).

Publié en français sous le titre :
POLITIQUES INDUSTRIELLES
DANS LES PAYS DE L'OCDE
Tour d'horizon annuel 1992

© OECD 1992
Applications for permission to reproduce or translate all or part of this publication should be made to:
Head of Publications Service, OECD
2, rue André-Pascal, 75775 PARIS CEDEX 16, France

FOREWORD

Every year the OECD Industry Committee holds an exchange of views on the situation in industry in Member countries and reviews the main industrial policy measures. The outcome of this review is an annual OECD publication.

This report presents the general industrial policy orientations and synthesises the information on the main industrial policy measures implemented or soon to be applied in OECD countries. It covers measures to promote physical and intangible investment in industry (R&D, training, consultancy services), policies directed at industrial sectors, measures to support small and medium-sized enterprises, regulatory reform and competition policy in industry, regional development policies, industry-related environmental and energy policies, measures related to international investment and trade, and policies for co-operation with central and eastern European countries.

The report also reviews the situation in industry in OECD countries, on the basis of quantitative indicators which illustrate recent trends and enable international comparisons. It examines the macroeconomic environment within which industry operates and trends in industrial production, trends in factor inputs (employment, physical investment, capacity utilisation, costs and prices, industrial R&D, international investment), and trends in performance (productivity, profitability, competitiveness and international trade).

In addition to recent trends and policies, the report also examines some longer-term structural issues and processes under way which are of particular importance. A special part is devoted this year to the evolution of performance and structural change in seven large OECD countries since before the first oil shock. The structural shifts that have occurred in their industrial composition during the last fifteen years are analysed by decomposing growth during this period into its underlying factors: domestic demand, trade, and changes in the technology of production.

Another part discusses the emergence and policy implications of the globaglisation of industrial activities under way, by focusing both on quantitative developments (through indicators such as foreign investments, the international sourcing of inputs, intra-industry and intra-firm trade, and international co-operation agreements), and on the domestic and international policy issues that arise from this process.

In addition to the examination of trends and policies in OECD Member countries, the report also reviews industrial policy measures and examines the situation in industry in the four newly industrialised Asian economies (Korea, Taiwan, Hong Kong, Singapore) and in the three countries of central and eastern Europe (the Czech and Slovak Federal Republic, Hungary and Poland) which participate in the OECD Partners in Transition Programme.

The report was prepared in the Industry Division of the Directorate for Science, Technology and Industry of the OECD with contributions from staff in the Industry Division and in the Economic Analysis and Statistics Division, and with the help of outside consultants; its preparation was co-ordinated by George Papaconstantinou. In September 1992, the Industry Committee recommended that the report be made available to the public. It is published on the responsibility of the Secretary-General of the OECD.

ALSO AVAILABLE

Government Policies and the Diffusion of Microelectronics (1989)
(70 88 04 1) ISBN 92-64-13161-2   FF125   £15.00   US$27.50   DM54

Industrial Policy in OECD Countries: Annual Review 1991 (1991)
(70 91 03 1) ISBN 92-64-13571-5   FF145   £20.00   US$35.00   DM58

Industrial Revival through Technology (1988)
(70 88 02 1) ISBN 92-64-13103-5   FF100   £12.00   US$22.00   DM43

Prices charged at the OECD Bookshop.
THE OECD CATALOGUE OF PUBLICATIONS and supplements will be sent free of charge
on request addressed either to OECD Publications Service,
or to the OECD Distributor in your country.

TABLE OF CONTENTS

Part 1
INDUSTRIAL POLICY ISSUES AND INITIATIVES

A. Introduction and overview — 11
B. Structural changes and evolution in industrial policy — 13
C. Main industrial policy orientations in OECD countries — 18
Notes and references — 27

Part 2
RECENT INDUSTRIAL POLICY MEASURES

A. Measures to promote industrial investment — 31
  (i) Measures affecting physical investment (including tax-related measures and other measures of a general nature) — 33
  (ii) Measures affecting intangible investment (covering R&D, advisory services, labour-related measures) — 37
B. Policies directed at industrial sectors — 48
C. Measures to support small and medium-sized enterprises — 53
D. Regulatory reform and competition policy in industry — 57
E. Regional development policies — 66
F. Industry-related environmental and energy policies — 68
G. Measures related to international investment and trade — 72
H. International co-operation with central and eastern European countries (CEECs) — 78
Notes and references — 81

Part 3
TRENDS IN INDUSTRY

Chapter I. The macroeconomic environment and trends in production — 85
A. The macroeconomic background — 85
B. Trends in industrial production — 88

Chapter II. Trends in factor inputs — 95
A. Employment — 95
B. Investment — 101
C. Capacity utilisation — 107
D. Costs and prices — 109
E. Industrial research and development — 113
F. International investment — 120

Chapter III. Trends in performance — 135
A. Productivity — 135
B. Profitability — 139
C. Trade and competitiveness — 142
Notes and references — 164

Part 4
STRUCTURAL CHANGE AND INDUSTRIAL PERFORMANCE: GROWTH DECOMPOSITION IN SEVEN OECD ECONOMIES

A. Introduction	167
B. Analytical framework	167
C. Results of the growth decomposition	171
D. Conclusions and policy implications	185
Notes and references	191

Part 5
GLOBALISATION: DEVELOPMENTS AND POLICY ISSUES

Chapter I. Recent developments	195
A. Introduction	195
B. Globalisation of firms	196
C. The patterns of foreign direct investment	197
D. Acquisitions, mergers and green-field investments	198
E. Minority investments, joint ventures, inter-firm agreements and networking	198
F. Foreign investment, R&D and technology generation	200
G. Impacts of globalisation	201
H. International sourcing for final production	210
I. Competition and concentration	211
Chapter II. Industry policy issues	213
Notes and references	215

Part 6
TRENDS IN INDUSTRY AND POLICY MEASURES IN NON-MEMBER COUNTRIES

Chapter I. Recent trends and policy measures in the newly industrialised economies of Asia	219
A. Recent trends in manufacturing industry	219
B. Recent industrial policy measures	223
Chapter II. Recent trends and policy measures in the countries of central and eastern Europe	229
A. Introduction	229
B. Recent trends	230
C. Recent industrial policy measures	233
Notes and references	242

LIST OF TABLES

1. Reported expenditures for industrial support	17
2. Policy objectives of reported expenditures	17
3. Policy objectives and main instruments of investment support	32
4. Proposed federal R&D budget in the United States	38
5. Federal initiatives in applied R&D in the US	38
6. Financing pattern of reported sectoral policies	49
7. Distribution of public enterprises by industry, 1989	58
8. Growth of real GNP/GDP and of domestic demand	86
9. Inflation and unemployment	86
10. Internal and external balances	87
11. Trade and current balances	87
12. Manufacturing production	88
13. Manufacturing production by industry	90
14. United States computer industry	94
15. Manufacturing employment	95

#	Title	Page
16.	Unemployment rates in some "white collar" regions	101
17.	Growth of gross private non-residential fixed capital formation	101
18.	Investment as a percentage of business sector value added	102
19.	Capacity utilisation in manufacturing	107
20.	Capacity utilisation in the United States	108
21.	Capacity utilisation in Japan	108
22.	Capacity utilisation in the European Community	109
23.	Producer prices in manufacturing	110
24.	Producer prices in main manufacturing industries	111
25.	Import unit values in local currency	112
26.	Export unit values in local currency	112
27.	R&D expenditures in the business enterprise sector	114
28.	Country shares in total OECD BERD and contribution to its growth	114
29.	Contribution of different sources of funds to growth in industrial R&D	115
30.	Shares of OECD industrial R&D by industry group	117
31.	Ten biggest R&D performers in eight OECD countries	118
32.	Outward direct investment flows from OECD countries	126
33.	Inward direct investment flows to OECD countries	127
34.	Breakdown of US inward direct investments by geographical origin	129
35.	Breakdown of US outward direct investments by geographical destination	129
36.	Sectoral breakdown of US investments in the EC	129
37.	Foreign direct investment in Japan by geographical origin	130
38.	Japanese foreign direct investment by geographical destination	131
39.	Shares of EC countries and of Europe in foreign direct investments originating in the US and in Japan	131
40.	Joint venture projects in central and eastern Europe and in the CIS	132
41.	Inward foreign direct investment to the Asian NIEs by origin	133
42.	Outward foreign direct investments by Asian NIEs	134
43.	Apparent labour productivity in manufacturing	135
44.	Productivity in the business sector	136
45.	Profitability in the business sector	140
46.	Trade in manufactured goods	143
47.	Trade in manufactured goods: export market growth and relative export performance	144
48.	Competitive positions	145
49.	Export market shares by type of industry	150
50.	Revealed comparative advantage in manufacturing exports	158
51.	Sources of growth in real output for manufacturing	171
52.	Ten highest output growth industries and dominant factor	178
53.	Sources of change in real output shares for manufacturing	179
54.	Ten lowest output growth industries and dominant factor	181
55.	Index of structural change of output	182
56.	Primary sources of change for the ten fastest and the ten slowest output growth industries	184
57.	World stocks of inward direct investment	197
58.	Industrial deals of the 1000 largest firms in the European Community	199
59.	Share of R&D expenditures of foreign-controlled firms in total business enterprise R&D expenditures	201
60.	Share of foreign enterprises in manufacturing employment	202
61.	Share of foreign enterprises in manufacturing turnover	202
62.	Sales, employment, capital expenditure and R&D by US majority-owned foreign affiliates as a percentage of US parent firm totals	203
63.	Research and development expenditures of foreign affiliates of US MNEs as a percentage of total MNE group expenditures	203
64.	Industrial sectors with the highest share of production by foreign enterprises	204
65.	Employment in foreign affiliates	204
66.	Trade intensity of foreign affiliates in manufacturing	205
67.	Bilateral intra-industry trade indices, total products	209
68.	Intra-industry trade in the G-7 countries by product group	210
69.	GNP growth rate and consumer price inflation in the Asian NIEs	219
70.	Trade and current balances in Asian NIEs	220
71.	Production indices in Asian NIEs	221
72.	Trade balances in Asian NIEs	222
73.	Science and technology investment plans in Korea	223
74.	Output of central and eastern European countries	229
75.	Inflation and unemployment in central and eastern European countries	230
76.	Export growth and current balances in central and eastern European countries	231
77.	Industrial production in Hungary	232
78.	Budgetary subsidies in the CSFR, 1985-91	233
79.	Summary of progress in privatisation in Poland	234

LIST OF GRAPHS

1. Productivity, investment and R&D growth — 31
2. Japan's import promotion budget — 74
3. Real GNP/GDP — 85
4. Manufacturing production in selected industries — 91
5. Motor vehicle production — 93
6. Manufacturing employment — 97
7. Investment by industry — 103
8. Gross fixed capital formation — 106
9. Industrial research and GDP in the OECD area — 113
10. Sectoral composition of business R&D — 116
11. R&D intensities — 119
12. R&D intensity profiles — 121
13. Outward and inward direct investment flows — 128
14. Manufacturing productivity — 138
15. Rates of return in the business sector — 141
16. Bilateral trade balances: United States, Japan, EC — 147
17. Export prices and exchange rate movements — 149
18. Export market shares — 154
19. Revealed comparative advantage — 160
20. Changes in share of real output — 173
21. Decomposition of total structural change — 183
22. Performance comparisons by industry group — 186
23. Intra-industry trade indices, all products — 208

LIST OF BOXES

1. OECD industrial support programmes database — 16
2. Ireland: "A Time for Change: Industrial Policy in the 1990s" — 22
3. "Building a Competitive Australia" industry statement — 26
4. Germany: Economic support measures for industrial investment in the new Länder — 34
5. The subcontracting and outsourcing programme in the Netherlands — 41
6. Spain: Technological Action Plan — 42
7. Productivity in Sweden: Restoring the growth potential — 46
8. Small and medium-sized enterprises in Turkey — 57
9. Industrial structure in Japan: efficient or exclusionist? — 60
10. Italy: the new anti-trust law — 64
11. Foreign direct investment in Portugal — 76
12. Identifying high, medium and low technology industries — 124
13. Productivity: Can we trust the numbers? — 137
14. Classifying international trade — 152
15. Revealed comparative advantage in manufacturing — 157
16. Gross output and value-added measures of structural change — 168
17. Capturing the indirect effects of structural change: US steel — 169
18. Technical change in input-output analysis — 170
19. The blurred lines between manufacturing and services — 189
20. Globalisation and intra-industry trade — 206
21. International sourcing and the "nationality" of products — 211

Part 1

INDUSTRIAL POLICY ISSUES AND INITIATIVES

A. Introduction and overview

The policy challenge

Industrial policy in the OECD countries is at a crossroads. It has gradually moved away from the philosophy and practices that prevailed in past decades, when it mainly consisted of measures in support of industries in decline or aimed at stimulating promising activities by "picking winners". A certain convergence has now been reached around a set of principles that broadly favour policy measures which do not interfere with the market process directly and instead attempt to improve its mechanisms. Such policies tend to be of a horizontal nature; they are market-correcting or market-enhancing, aimed directly at specific and known market flaws, or at promoting industry generally, and in particular the (labour and infrastructural) inputs available to industry.

Yet despite the existence of a consensus around such policies, it is also true that the practice of policy has often lagged behind the rhetoric, and that there are many different, and sometimes contradictory, interpretations of the same basic guiding principles. It is thus the case that important differences remain in practice about such issues as the appropriate role of government in assisting the restructuring of declining industries, the desirability of a strong competition policy, or the scope for programmes to support "strategic" industries or technologies.

Many of these differences can be traced to the ongoing globalisation of economic activities and the intensified international competition that results from it. Globalisation is a new stage in economic interdependence which arises from the strategies that multinational enterprises adopt in order to cope with rapid technological change and to compete effectively. It is characterised by the development of international networks of collaborating firms, the pivotal role of foreign direct investment, new patterns of international sourcing of inputs, and by the wide geographical dispersal of activities. In this environment, the objectives of global firms and that of national governments do not always coincide. The citizenship of companies often becomes "blurred" as ownership, assets and production is spread across countries, while products become multinational composites whose origins are often difficult to determine.

Globalisation raises a number of issues for policy makers. Some of these relate to the possible divergence of the global strategies of firms from "national interests". The issues have practical implications for the choice of policy instruments and the targeting of policy measures, as for example when choosing between supporting the production or R&D activities of particular firms versus assisting the development of less mobile factors such as labour through measures for training. Other issues relate to the intensified international competition arisising from globalisation. This has led to a greater use of protectionist measures in many countries which, in addition to their doubtful effectiveness, has resulted in increased international frictions. The development of multilateral disciplines that limit such behaviour remains a priority area for policy.

Another important development raising new issues for policy makers is the far-reaching programme for the establishment of economic and political union between the countries of the European Community. During the process, the growing importance of an industrial policy at the Community level has been demonstrated by the adoption of a relevant article into the European Community Treaty. In areas such as competition policy and the setting of standards, countries are increasingly delegating part of their national authority to the European Commission, while in areas such as technology policy, regional assistance, or industrial support for particular industries there is a growing number of initiatives at Community level alongside national programmes.

The European integration process provides unique opportunities for the EC Member states and for the OECD area as a whole, while at the same time raising a number of concerns. The opportunities lie with the elaboration of an industrial policy for a truly open single market. Most EC initiatives in industry-related matters are in this spirit, and seek to create a competitive environment for the development of European industry. Competition policy at the Community level is increasingly active, industrial subsidies are coming under increasing scrutiny, while a host of technology and infrastructural programmes are aimed at upgrading the capabilities of firms to compete. At the same time, there are concerns over other initiatives of a sectoral or regional nature, or about "grey-area" measures of border protection. These are aimed at easing the adjustment of industries or regions in difficulty, but may potentially annul some of the benefits of the creation of the single market and lead to increased international frictions. The concerns which relate to trade measures are akin with those that arise in the context of the creation of other regional trade blocs around the world. It is important for the emerging industrial policy at the Community level to ensure that such initiatives do not detract from the goal of creating an open and competitive market.

In addition to issues related to the globalisation of economic activity and to European economic integration, industrial policy in the OECD countries has to take into account the problems in the economic transformation of the countries in central and eastern Europe. Their transition to a market economy is proving far more difficult and protracted than originally anticipated. Reform programmes have come under considerable strain, and there are dangers that if the emerging new production and trade structures are too slow in demonstrating their effectiveness for the enhancement of welfare, an erosion of social support for the reform programme could occur, especially as the employment situation worsens.

The issues facing OECD policy makers in this respect revolve to a large extent around trade and investment. It is important to ensure that current trade and industrial policies in the OECD do not hinder the access to western markets of central and eastern European producers. To the extent that they do, they need to be reformed in the direction of more openness. With respect to foreign investment, the insufficient flows from OECD countries into the region are to a large extent due to transitional domestic factors such as the economic and legal uncertainties involved when investing in the area. More global factors however, such as the competition for world savings and for attracting scarce private resources, are also partly responsible, which would call for greater international involvement in promoting investment in the region.

Policy makers are also responding to the need for integrating industry and environmental concerns. Pressure on industry to improve its environmental performance has steadily increased in recent years. As a response, business is increasingly incorporating pollution concerns and natural resource conservation into enterprise strategy. For policy makers, it has become clear that industrial policy decisions cannot be dissociated from environmental considerations. Both industrial activity and environmental effects are areas of inherently international scope so that effective policies often cannot be formulated on a domestic basis.

Most environmental problems arise because environmental services are not properly priced. Cost-effective policies should therefore aim at internalising the external costs associated with the environment, by giving the right incentives to change patterns of production and consumption and for developing better technologies [1]. In order to achieve this goal, policy-makers have until now relied on regulatory instruments. Economic instruments such as emission trading procedures, charges or taxes for environmental management purposes, are however increasingly used [2]. Apart from utilising the efficiency of market signals to allow economic agents to decide upon the best way to reduce pollution, economic instruments can also act as incentives for the development of "clean" technologies.

Aside from these policy issues that are related to the structural changes and processes under way in the international economic environment, policy makers are faced with certain acute problems as a result of the economic slowdown in the OECD area. Member countries are currently experiencing significant job losses in industry, and in particular in manufacturing. Unlike in previous recessions, employment in services is not acting as a buffer for job losses in manufacturing. The decline in employment seems to be more evenly spread, with regions and industries previously unaffected recording sharp employment declines. In addition, structural unemployment has continued to increase, while long-term and youth unemployment are very high in many OECD countries. In some countries, this has coincided with skilled labour shortages, pointing to a mismatch problem in labour markets which has defied government policies.

In addition, industrial investment rates have been seriously affected by the general economic slowdown and by high real interest rates in many countries and do not seem to be recovering despite recent interest rate declines. These developments have induced many governments to take exceptional measures aimed at containing employment losses and at boosting investment. This has been chiefly in order to stimulate industry, but also in an attempt to maintain the levels of public investment, in areas ranging from infrastructure to spending on health, education and training. It is particularly important in this context to ensure that such support measures do not detract from the structural reform of labour markets and of the tax systems that are under way in most countries.

An outline of the report

The report consists of six parts. Part 1 presents an overview of evolutions in industry-related policy and examines some of the issues that policy-makers are currently facing. It is structured in two sections. The first section examines the industrial policy issues emanating from the structural transformations taking place in the international economic environment, as well as evolutions in the public support of industry. The second section then examines the broad thrust of industrial policy in OECD Member countries.

Part 2 reviews recent government initiatives in OECD Member countries to promote industrial development and adjustment. These are grouped under eight headings: support of physical and intangible investment (including R&D, consultancy services and labour-related measures); measures directed at industrial sectors; support of small and medium-sized enterprises; regional policy initiatives; privatisation, regulatory reform and competition policy in industry; measures related to international investment and trade; industry-related environmental and energy policies; and international co-operation initiatives with central and eastern European countries.

Part 3 of the report reviews the industrial performance of OECD countries. It examines the macroeconomic environment within which industry operates and trends in industrial production; trends in factor inputs (employment, investment, capacity utilisation, costs and prices, industrial research and development, international investment); and in industrial performance (productivity, profitability, competitiveness and international trade).

Part 4 examines more closely the performance and the structural change in seven large OECD economies since the first oil shock. The structural shifts that have occurred in the industrial composition of these countries during the last fifteen years are analysed by decomposing their growth during that period to its underlying factors: domestic demand, trade, and changes in the technology of production.

Part 5 discusses the emergence and policy implications of the globalisation process that is under way, by focusing both on quantitative developments (through indicators such as foreign investments, the international sourcing of inputs, intra-industry and intra-firm trade, and international co-operation agreements) and on the policy issues that emerge from this process.

Finally, Part 6 of the report examines the trends in industry and industrial policy measures of two groups of non-OECD Member countries: the newly industrialised economies of Asia (Korea, Hong Kong, Singapore, and Taiwan), and three of the economies of central and eastern Europe (the Czech and Slovak Federal Republic, Hungary and Poland).

B. Structural changes and evolution in industrial policy

The changing nature of industrial policy

The international economic environment is changing constantly under the influence of the ongoing globalisation process, the formation of regional economic and trading blocs, the new challenges posed by the transition of central and eastern European economies to market economies and the increasing integration of environmental issues into economic policy. Industrial policy is also continuously evolving, sometimes in an attempt to respond to the new problems and take advantage of the new opportunities, and sometimes in a defensive fashion, trying to preserve certain industries or firms in the face of shifts in comparative advantage.

In the context of such changes, policy makers need to constantly re-examine and evaluate their choices. The type of questions that need to be addressed include the broad policy approach to take, the level of authority with which the design and delivery of industrial policy measures should reside, the issue of whom and where to support, of which instruments to use, and the institutional mechanisms necessary for assessing the success or failure of particular policy choices.

Broadly speaking, it is possible to identify three different approaches to industrial policy, reflecting three different types of market economies, of which most OECD markets are variants [3]. In the first type of economy, resources are directed by short-term market signals, extensive markets exist, and there are strong links between short-term effort and reward. Policy tends to be hands-off, with a strong emphasis on measures and administrative frameworks which increase competition. In the second type of economy, resources are directed by market transactions conducted within long-term relationships and on the basis of implicit contracts, while there is a strong competitive ethos centred on long-term strategic variables. Governments here tend to be more actively involved in industrial development, sometimes by explicitly targeting particular industries, but more often through implicit agreements on common objectives with industry. Finally, in the third type, resources are sometimes directed by short-term market signals, sometimes by longer-term strategic variables, and sometimes by government. Policy tends to reflect this mix of objectives, with active support of certain industries, a number of horizontal initiatives, and a distinctive concern for employment preservation, even at high cost.

The debate about which broad approach to take in industrial policy matters is essentially political. It goes to the heart of fundamental systemic differences between countries and the kind of policy structures and stance that follow. There is nevertheless little doubt that in recent years OECD countries have genuinely converged to a set of principles that broadly favour policy measures which do not interfere with the market process and instead attempt to improve its mechanisms. This convergence is for example apparent in the European Community document on industrial policy [4].

There are two types of policy measures that could be identified as together constituting a consensus of what is a market-oriented industrial policy which does not distort the allocation of productive resources. The first type is directly aimed at correcting specific and known market flaws or indirectly at improving the market's functioning. Such market-correcting or market-enhancing policies include those to counter disincentives to R&D activities because of inappropriability problems, to counter environmental or training externalities, alleviate the problem of information asymmetries, prevent monopoly, or enforce property rights.

A second type of policies are those which promote industry generally, without targeted support, and in particular which aim to improve the inputs available to industry. They include measures such as investment tax allowances, general R&D subsidies, measures to upgrade skills, improve the infrastructure, and the provision of consulting services that furnish economic players with information. These two type of policies often overlap; they both however contrast with protectionist measures whose result is to raise output prices, or with subsidies that reduce costs to particular activities or firms.

Despite these areas of convergence and agreement, important differences remain. These tend to centre around issues such as the appropriate role and nature of government intervention in the restructuring of declining industries, the scope of policy measures to support particular industries or technologies considered to have growth potential, and the desirability of a strong competition policy. Such differences are to a certain extent unavoidable, reflecting as they do fundamental societal choices about the type of economic model to follow within the framework of market-oriented economies. They do however in many instances imply certain types of actions that create friction in international economic relations. It is therefore necessary to find the type of mechanisms that enhance international policy co-ordination and minimise frictions.

One avenue that is promising in this respect is suggested by the application in the field of industrial policy of a debate that has long existed in macroeconomic policy. This is the desirability of *rules vs. discretion* in the conduct of policy. Internationally accepted rules guiding the behaviour of governments provide transparency and discipline, which facilitates monitoring. They also involve the necessary predictability in government actions that allows economic agents, both industry and consumers, to make economically rational decisions based on expectations about the future. Rules for the evolution of the money supply have for example reduced the uncertainty about future investments, moderated wage claims, etc. Discretionary action instead in areas such as industrial subsidies, trade policies or competition policy often leads to international disputes. The elaboration of such "rules" or "codes of behaviour" may help improve the broad framework for industrial activity.

Globalisation and competition

The globalisation of economic activities raises a variety of issues which require new responses from policy makers in order to attain the economic benefits involved and to minimise potential costs and international frictions (see also Part 5 of the report). These issues were examined in detail in the context of the recently completed OECD Technology-Economy Programme (TEP)[5]. One set of issues centres on the possible divergence between the global strategies of firms and national interests as defined by governments and on the associated "stateless" nature of many firms. Firm strategies are expanding and evolving far more rapidly than related government policy which often tends to lag behind developments in industry. Furthermore, the design of industrial policy measures is still largely based on the assumption that national firms can be meaningfully identified and that the interests of the firms and of public policy coincide. The growing role of foreign direct investment and of cross-border alliances and other phenomena associated with globalisation make this assumption increasingly questionable.

There are important implications from this process for the general thrust of policies pursued by Member countries. In particular, they raise a number of policy dilemmas. One is the choice of *general vs. selective* policy measures[6]. General policy measures such as subsidies to labour training, favourable tax treatment of non-tradeable services, or tax concessions on certain types of investments would benefit all firms, national or foreign, operating within a given market. They therefore have the potential to benefit foreign investors as much as domestic firms. In contrast, selective measures which target particular firms or activities could in principle ensure that foreign firms benefit only to the extent that they become involved with the domestic economy. These potential benefits are however outweighed by the efficiency costs associated with choosing the firms or activities with the highest potential.

Another policy dilemma exists with respect to measures aimed at *mobile vs. immobile* factors of production. The choice here can be formulated as that of supporting firms vs. location, and of supporting location vs. activity. Policies which do not discriminate between firms in a given location are less competition-distorting and have the added advantage that they may attract firms from other locations. Policies that target activities rather than attempting to make particular locations attractive however have additional advantages. The support of activities inadequately provided by the market (such as R&D, training or infrastructure) is the least discriminatory approach, the one that gets closer to the sources of market failure and the one least likely to lead to international frictions. Unlike firms, which are mobile and may move operations to other countries, such activities represent factors of production that are relatively immobile. Their support and upgrading is therefore more likely to improve the competitiveness of the economy in the medium and the longer term.

A second set of issues is related to the intensified international competition that is associated with the globalisation process. The research and production activities of firms in many industries have become dispersed internationally while the markets for their products have become truly global. International markets are increasingly characterised by the strategic behaviour of large companies, rapid technological change and short life-cycles of products. The resulting intensified competition on a world scale has seriously hurt less efficient producers, often concentrated in certain geographic regions. This has led governments in many cases to attempt to support whole industries in crisis, often through the use of "grey-area" trade instruments such as voluntary export agreements, anti-dumping measures or other practices that limit foreign access to domestic markets.

The interest of governments is motivated by a host of reasons, some more justified than others. These range from possible externality effects, concern about the high entry costs or access to markets and technologies, to the perceived strategic importance of certain industries as suppliers of inputs to other industries, concerns of overdependence on foreign suppliers, or the need for an indigenous capability [7]. Reflecting the increased interdependence of trade and industrial policies, these concerns have led them to increase border and non-border protection measures. In the process they have imposed significant costs on consumers and on individual economies, without in most cases achieving the goals of promoting restructuring and fostering the development of internationally competitive industries. While tariff protection has overall declined, non-tariff measures have increased and have been imposed on an even broader range of activities, including industries where current and prospective growth is strong. In addition, this increasing sectoral spread of trade restricting measures has been accompanied by a shift towards instruments such as voluntary export agreements that are highly selective and targeted in their impacts and are in general less transparent than tariffs and quotas [8].

There are two recurring themes to these trade-distorting measures: easing the adjustment of industries facing severe difficulties; and helping domestic firms become internationally competitive in industries with strong growth prospects. It is however questionable whether the policies in place have actually helped advance these goals, or have done so at a reasonable cost [9]. One question that arises in this respect is to what extent the "grey-area" measures currently used by many OECD countries is symptomatic of the lack of "rules" (in e.g. industrial support, technology or competition policy). The elaboration of such "rules of the game" could in effect be used in order to reduce unilateral actions and bilateral arrangements and to minimise international disputes around "friction-prone" industries.

Public support to industry

Industrial subsidies, recognised as having a role in promoting national policy, have also been recognised as having the potential for distorting competition, both domestically and internationally. Current concerns about their level and composition arise to a large extent from the belief that increasing globalisation of economies will be sustainable only if competition is perceived as fair. Under prevailing economic circumstances, support to industry may increasingly result in frictions, as highlighted by their continued existence in a small number of specific industries or even product lines (mostly in high-technology areas).

The recently completed phase of the OECD project on industrial subsidies is aimed at increasing the level of transparency of Government support measures and programmes in order to help developing stronger international guidelines in the area. It provides an important analytical tool for analysing patterns and trends of these policies and for developing international co-operation to reduce the potential for trade frictions (see Box 1) [10].

Two broad conclusions can be drawn from this first compilation of data. First, the programmes reported to the OECD exercise represent a sum that is significant at the macroeconomic level; and secondly, the total amount of reported public support has been decreasing for the OECD area as a whole over the period 1986-89. This last trend does not exclude the possibility of contrasted evolution for different sorts of programmes.

The net cost to government of the programmes reported accounted for an average of $66 billion yearly between 1986-89. From the point of view of beneficiary manufacturing industries, total public support received via all these reported schemes is considerable, since the ratio of reported subsidies to total manufacturing value-added in OECD has been 2.5 per cent on average. However, this ratio of total reported net cost to government (NCG) to value added in manufacturing is not a representative indicator of subsidisation rates at this stage. Improvement in data coverage and in reporting methodologies should be expected to increase this rate.

Total amount of reported public support across OECD shows a decrease during the period. As shown in Table 1, this is reflected in the indexed real (deflated) growth of total reported NCG throughout the period, which declined from 100 in 1986, to 89 in 1987, 84 in 1988, and 64 in 1989 (from $75 billion current value in 1986 to $55 billion current value in 1989). However, the impact of a small number of large-sized tax programmes is primarily responsible for this decrease -- largely due to tax reforms diminishing expenditures. If this special development is left aside, the evolution of total reported expenditures becomes less straightforward, the trend being one of stagnation or slight increase in total net expenditures for the remaining group of programmes.

Analysis of the database by policy objective indicates a relative shift away from general-purpose policies such as general investment aids (general capital cost subsidies) to more focused support measures such as aid to R&D, regional development, and export-promotion. Within the total of net expenditures reported, the share of general investment support moved from 55 per cent in 1986 to 28 per cent in 1989, while the share of R&D support, regional development support and export-related support increased respectively from 9 per cent to 12 per cent, from 14 per cent to 22 per cent and from 8 per cent to 20 per cent (Table 2).

Box 1. OECD industrial support programmes database

In the framework of its "Subsidies and Structural Adjustment" project, the OECD Industry Committee has created an information data base describing industrial support schemes implemented by 22 Member countries and the Commission of the European Communities [1]. On the basis of a commonly agreed questionnaire, detailed technical information and quantitative expenditure data has been collected on the basis of a "net cost to government" methodology.

As of May 1992, the database consists of 879 programmes for the period 1986-89. A minimum amount of quantitative information (Net Cost to Government data for at least one year) was available for 739 of these programmes. Programmes are described according to three criteria: policy objectives; financing instruments; and according to the economic costs subsidised. Each programme is also described with some detail as to its administrative workings; i.e. eligible companies to benefit from the measures, awards rates, reimbursement conditions of aids etc.

The 879 programmes analysed cover a wide variety of policy objectives. These were classified under eight groups:

- 130 were sectoral programmes aimed at improving a country's competitiveness in a given sector;

- 37 were schemes of exceptional recourse for bailing-out companies in difficulty (crisis aid);

- 159 were programmes dedicated to the strengthening of R&D expenditures and capabilities;

- 123 were dedicated to improving general investment behaviour by diminishing general capital costs;

- 162 were supporting regional development in areas with adjustment difficulties and remoteness handicaps;

- 117 were to support small and medium-sized enterprises;

- 60 aided employment and training activities inside companies;

- 91 supported exports and international investment.

The 879 programmes surveyed use one of six financing instruments. Direct grants are used in 468 programmes. Subsidised loans are the financing instrument for 61 programmes, and government guarantees for 57 programmes. Equity capital infusions are used in 24 support schemes. Tax concessions are the financing tool for 145 programmes. Finally, 115 remaining schemes utilise simultaneously two or more of the above-mentioned instruments, and are classified as mixed instruments.

Programmes differ also according to the economic costs they target and reduce. Among the 879 programmes, 126 diminish current production costs, 147 schemes specifically reduce research and development costs, and 144 focus on costs of acquisition of specific tangible and intangible assets. 88 programmes reduce export and international investment costs. Finally, 46 programmes subsidise not company costs, but the operating costs of non-profit industry organisations.

The management structures administering support programmes in different countries also differ and can be grouped into four categories. 627 programmes are directly funded and administered by central governments. 88 programmes are funded and managed by regional and local authorities, and 46 under the joint action of central and regional bodies. 109 programmes are conducted by partially off-budget intermediary institutions.

Although this information database is probably the most systematic and extensive information source available internationally, a number of important shortcomings still remain with respect to data coverage and to the methodology used. Support schemes by sub-central authorities and quantitative measurement of tax concessions to manufacturing are especially two areas where reporting remains uneven. The OECD Industry Committee intends to update this data base regularly with an improved coverage and methodology.

1. OECD (1992), "Subsidies and Structural Adjustment", Report to the OECD Council at Ministerial level, Paris.

Table 1. **Reported expenditures for industrial support**[1]
1986-89

	1986	1987	1988	1989
Total Net Cost to Government (NCG) of reported programmes (million current US$)	74 590	68 140	66 870	53 130
Total reported NCG of programmes using direct financing tools (million current US$)	25 318	28 880	36 061	27 420
Total reported NCG of programmes using tax expenditures (million current US$)	49 272	39 260	30 809	25 710
Indexed real (deflated) growth of total NCG for reported programmes 1986 = 100[2]	100	89	84	64
Ratio of total NCG reported to OECD value added in manufacturing (percentages)	3.3	2.6	2.3	1.8

1. Total Net Cost figures represent an approximation of net subsidies distributed via reported programmes, but fall short of the total actual amount of subsidisation because of the remaining data coverage and methodology-related shortcomings.
2. For the deflation of national expenditures annual GDP deflators have been used. For the deflation of cross-country expenditures, national net costs converted to current US$ have been deflated by the annual US GDP deflator.
Source: OECD, Industrial Subsidies Database, March 1992.

Table 2. **Policy objectives of reported expenditures**

Policy objectives	Programmes			NCG (Billion current $)				NCG (percentages)			
	Number	NCG[1] avail.	Aver. NCG[2]	1986	1987	1988	1989	1986	1987	1988	1989
Sectoral programmes	130	118	44	4.4	6.3	5.8	4.1	5.9	9.2	8.6	7.7
Crisis aid	37	29	45	1.8	2.0	0.7	0.7	2.4	2.9	1.1	1.3
R&D support	159	144	46	6.7	7.4	6.2	6.1	9.0	10.9	9.4	11.5
Regional development	162	136	84	10.2	11.7	11.9	11.8	13.7	17.2	17.8	22.2
General investment aid	123	91	290	40.9	25.2	24.4	15.0	54.7	37.0	36.6	28.3
SME programmes	117	87	33	2.5	3.1	3.2	2.8	3.3	4.6	4.8	5.2
Employment and training support	60	54	44	1.9	2.0	3.6	2.0	2.6	2.9	5.4	3.8
Export-related aids	91	80	119	6.3	10.3	10.9	10.5	8.4	15.2	16.4	19.9
Total	879	739	89	74.6	68.1	66.9	53.1	100.0	100.0	100.0	100.0

1. NCG avail. indicates the number of programmes for which the Net Cost to Government data is available for at least one year.
2. Average Net Cost to Government of reported programmes in million $US.
Source: OECD, Industrial Subsidies Database, March 1992.

The data regarding financing instruments used and economic costs subsidised also indicate a shift from generally available to more focused support. The relative importance of tax concessions declined while that of direct grants and government guarantees rose. Instead of general capital costs, which at the outset represented the most frequently subsidised economic cost category, more recent support programmes tended to target current production costs, export-related costs and R&D investment costs.

In the area of sectoral policies, programmes supporting sectors which face intense international competition are predominant. At this stage in the database, sectoral policies do not generally include specific R&D programmes for high-technology industries, which are generally reported under R&D support. Even within this restrictive coverage, sectoral measures seem to be attracting relatively constant resources across the OECD area.

In the area of support to industrial R&D, several types of programmes are often applied simultaneously. Programmes supporting general private sector R&D efforts coexist with those supporting certain types of technologies, sectors or enterprises. Disaggregated analysis of R&D programmes in this project should allow a more refined identification of support provided by various types of R&D schemes in the future.

Export-related supports seem also to have increased, in spite of the international efforts to contain them. This growth should become even more apparent if the contingent risks and actualised costs of the export-credit guarantees are taken more fully into consideration with a more refined measurement methodology.

Overall, while substantial progress has been made towards international transparency of Government support to industry covering 22 Member countries and the CEC, for the period 1986-89, important gaps remain in the information. They vary from country to country and still hamper international comparability of absolute levels, trends and structures of support by governments. These are largely due to uneven coverage in data reporting and to specific methodological problems. The next phase of the exercise will update the database, as well as attempt to fill in the existing data gaps and address some of the methodological problems.

C. Main industrial policy orientations in OECD countries

This section briefly reviews the main orientation and thrust of industry-related policy in OECD Member countries. More detailed information on recent policy measures in the field is in Part 2 of the report.

Against the background of a slowdown that has proved longer than expected, the main recent industry-related policy measures in the *United States* fall mainly under three headings: microeconomic and structural reform; trade-related measures; and technology policies. Measures aimed at structural adjustment focused mainly on the reform of financial institutions (savings and loans, commercial banking) and on efforts to reduce the cost and increase the cost-effectiveness of new regulation, including the recent moratorium on new regulations. Trade-related policy developments include the new US-Japan semiconductor arrangement, slow progress in the Structural Impediments Initiative (SII) talks with Japan, the conclusion of negotiations for a North America Free Trade Agreement (NAFTA), and a host of programs to assist the restructuring of central and eastern European countries, especially the former Soviet Union. Funding of technology policies increased, focused primarily on support for the development of pre-competitive, generic technologies, but including also assistance for the development of certain technology programmes in areas that are considered promising (such as in fibre optics or in flat-panel computer screens). Structural reform efforts also focused on education and training, including the Administration's America 2000 and Job Training 2000 initiatives.

In the United States policies towards industry at the federal level are consistent with the government's attitude that a hands-off policy is the most effective approach. Fears over the loss of international competitiveness have however recently prompted a wide-ranging debate over the need for developing an explicit strategy and a more co-ordinated approach to industry-related matters. The debate focuses on the necessary structural reforms which would address some of the problems that are considered responsible for the country's eroding competitiveness: shorter-term horizons than its international competitors in investment decisions, a host of perverse incentives that favour consumption over investment and lead to low savings rates, and the problems related to technical infrastructure, education or training. Assistance to particular industries is also being discussed, through well-placed, modest investments in certain emerging technologies, funded jointly by the government and the private sector, rather than through protectionist measures aimed at shielding them from international competition.

In *Canada*, the concern about the competitiveness of the Canadian economy and its low productivity growth is reflected in the importance given by the authorities to such policy areas as technological innovation and diffusion, consultancy services, the designing of new approaches to human resource development, the strengthening of SMEs and the promotion of entrepreneurship. In the pursuit of its mainly horizontal approach to industry-related policy, the government continues to take steps in order to improve the regulatory environment for business, with a large recent initiative for regulatory reform in the transport sector, as well as to pursue the process of privatising those activities that can most efficiently be carried out by the private sector.

Trade liberalisation has been an important part of Canadian policy since the mid-1980s, with the negotiation and implementation of the Free Trade Agreement with the United States, the recent conclusion of a free trade agreement with the US and Mexico, and the strong support given to a successful conclusion of the present round of GATT negotiations. In addition, and in the context of the country's federal structure, negotiations among provincial governments have been under way for several years to strengthen Canada's internal markets through the development of comprehensive federal-provincial arrangements to remove the trade barriers existing between the provinces and thus ensure that the domestic economy is sufficiently open and efficient to contribute to the competitiveness of Canadian industry.

Recent industry-related policy measures in *Japan* have focused on answering the often-voiced criticisms about its persistent trade surplus and the alleged barriers to inward direct foreign investment. The government has introduced a number of measures aimed at the expansion of imports (an allocation of 10 billion yen in the 1992 fiscal budget) and the promotion of foreign direct investment in Japan. Among the former, notable are tax incentives for manufactured products, low-interest loans for imports, the setting up of "foreign access zones" to improve import infrastructure and facilitate market access, as well as amendments to the existing procedures for government procurement to facilitate bids by foreign companies. Among the latter, the most important are preferential tax treatment to foreign affiliates meeting certain requirements, low-interest loans and loan guarantees to foreign affiliates establishing manufacturing and R&D facilities in high technology areas, as well as an increased budget for information dissemination about investment opportunities in Japan.

In addition, the government is pursuing actively some of its long-standing interests in technology and the environment. Measures to promote industrial R&D, innovation, and the diffusion of technology were recently strengthened, as were a number of policies aimed at the promotion of energy conservation, the introduction of clean energy sources and the development of innovative environment-friendly technologies.

In the *European Community*, the most significant recent development was the modifications to the EC Treaty agreed upon by the Council of Ministers in Maastricht, the Netherlands, in December 1991. Subject to their approval by the national parliaments of EC Member States, the modifications will facilitate the on-going process of European integration beyond the completion of the single market by the end of 1992. The most important achievements of the Maastricht meeting were the signing of an accord on European Monetary Union (EMU) and on issues related to political union (EPU). Within the context of the chapter on political union, an agreement was reached on several industry-related matters. A new article was adopted that anticipates changes to the European social fund to facilitate industrial restructuring. A new article on trans-European networks was agreed upon, aimed at ensuring the implementation of energy, telecommunications and transport networks that are necessary for the proper functioning of the single market. Furthermore, a new article was adopted explicitly incorporating industrial competitiveness amongst the priority objectives of the Treaty.

The article on industrial competitiveness provides for the first time a specific legal basis upon which the Member States can take co-ordinated action to achieve a number of industry-related objectives, within the context of an open and competitive market. Such objectives include improving the response of industry to structural change; encouraging an environment which is favourable to industry's own initiative and to the development of enterprises, in particular that of small and medium-sized enterprises; encouraging an environment which supports co-operation between enterprises; and encouraging the best exploitation of the industrial potential of innovation, research and development policies.

The EC Commission has made proposals for the period 1991-93 for certain actions to strenghen industrial competitiveness through measures of a horizontal nature in the fields of training, technology and infrastructure (trans-European networks).

Recent policy initiatives aimed at Community industry follow from the Commission's general industrial policy approach as presented in the communication on *Industrial Policy in an Open and Competitive Environment*, issued in November 1990, and endorsed by industry ministers. Ensuing communications, that appeared during the course of 1991, have addressed specific industrial sectors or activities, like the electronics and information technology industry, biotechnology-based activities, maritime industries, and the textile and clothing industry (see Part 2 of this report). A communication regarding the automobile industry was recently presented.

The design and implementation of industry-related policies at the European Community level is a relatively recent phenomenon. It has been prompted by concern about the performance of EC-based industries in comparison to that in other OECD countries, especially in high-technology areas like segments of the electronics and information technology industry. In addition, it is the result of continuing problems in industries like textiles and clothing, shipbuilding, and automobiles, where structural adjustment programmes at the national level have not produced the expected results.

Recent industrial-related policy measures in *Belgium* are concentrated in four areas: labour-related initiatives aimed at retraining and other assistance to workers in difficulty; competition policy, with a new law on restrictive business practices in 1991, accompanied with administrative changes to facilitate its operation; industry-related environmental policy, with a number of initiatives for waste management; and trade-related measures, in particular modifications in the basic legislation governing the activities of the official export credit agency.

Over the medium-term, the national government has reduced its aid to industry, a decline which within the manufacturing sector can be attributed almost entirely to steel and shipbuilding [11]. In terms of aid to industry by regional bodies, recently both Wallonia and Flanders announced revisions to their assistance programmes, in order to make them more effective in terms of job creation.

In *Denmark*, recent industrial policy initiatives have focused on intangible investment, with a host of programmes for the promotion of R&D activities, the support of technological and other services to business (and in particular to small and medium-sized enterprises), and the improvement of vocational education. At the same time, regulatory and competition policy reform attempt to improve the efficiency of both the public and private sectors; new initiatives aim at reconciling environmental and industry concerns and priorities; and an extensive programme of technical assistance to the economies of central and eastern Europe is in place.

Underlying these type of measures is a wide-ranging debate on defining a new and broader way for viewing industrial policy. This would involve coordinating government policy in relation to industry by taking into account issues relating to areas as disparate as taxation, research, education, environment, employment and transport. An interministerial committee has been established in this respect with the task to set up procedures for an assessment system of the economic and administrative impact on business of new rules and regulations. The establishment of the Danish Industry and Trade Development Council is a step in the same direction, as its main task will be to gain an insight into the conditions in the Danish business sector, analyse business areas that cut across traditional industries, map out strategic key problems, and offer policy advice.

In *France*, the approach to industrial policy has changed significantly since the early 1980s. There was a marked increase in state involvement in industry during the 1981-83 period, with the nationalisation of major industrial groups, closer control of industrial financing and with the elaboration of sectoral plans for steel, chemicals, information technology, machine tools and textiles. This was followed by a reduction in public sector involvement in the ensuing years. State control on prices was relaxed from 1985, the financial sector was liberalised, and a number of industrial groups were privatised [12].

Current initiatives in industrial policy range over a number of areas. Extensive programmes exist for the support of innovative activities and for the diffusion of technology, many through international collaboration in the context of EC projects. A plan for the support for small and medium-sized enterprises was announced in 1991, comprising a number of fiscal stimuli for their development. Measures for training and re-training are also in place, often focused on SMEs. In terms of direct support to industry, the public sector has remained active in areas permitted by EC directives, as for example in the case of the subsidies for shipbuilding and in regional support. Finally, in 1991 also private firms, national or foreign, were allowed to take minority stakes as strategic investors in nationalised companies, a departure from the previous policy.

In *Germany*, policies are currently dominated by an overriding concern: assisting the rapid adjustment of the economy in the new *Länder* to the needs of a market economy. The federal government has put in place three major sets of market-oriented industrial and structural policies with the following main features: the establishment of diversified and efficient SMEs together with investment in new and competitive jobs in both manufacturing industry and services; the on-going privatisation of the former nation-owned firms under the guidance of the *Treuhandanstalt* to re-organise industry in the eastern part of Germany; and the labour market and social policy measures necessary to facilitate the period of adjustment and to assist in the restructuring process (see Box 4 in Part 2 of the report).

The funding of this process has taken on a variety of forms. The direct financial contribution by the federal government through the Upswing East project (*Gemeinschaftswerk Aufschwung Ost*) amounts to a total of DM 24 billion in 1991 and 1992. In 1991 also a total of more than DM 110 billion in loans was applied for under various schemes: the Joint Scheme Regional Economic Support, the European Recovery Programme (ERP) for business start-ups and equity capital as well as the local-authority infrastructure programmes. At the same time, the federal government intends to soften the impact of the additional burden for the other parts of the economy by continuing its policy to relieve trade and industry through reforms of various aspects of company taxation. In order to enhance the attraction of Germany as an industrial location, it is considered particularly important to stabilise non-wage labour costs, which are at present, by international standards, at relatively high levels.

In *Greece*, industrial policy initiatives fall mainly in three areas: sectoral measures to assist industries facing structural adjustment, in particular in textiles and clothing; measures to support small and medium-sized enterprises which form the backbone of the economy; and the ongoing privatisation plan of nationalised "ailing" enterprises. The programme of privatisation, started two years ago, is proceeding very slowly and is far from attaining its targets. New measures in 1992 are aimed at reinforcing the legal and institutional framework and accelerate the process.

In addition, the Greek government is in the process of preparing a multi-faceted industrial development umbrella programme (HELPEID) along the lines of the Portuguese PEDIP. This 5-year plan will have a horizontal character, concentrating on the modernisation of technological infrastructure, on productivity improvements through skills upgrading, on upgrading product quality and industrial design, and on the promotion of SME activities, while at the same time including some sectoral initiatives, mainly aimed at the restructuring of the textiles, clothing and fertilisers sectors. The plan comes at a time when Greek industry is facing serious problems related to falling manufacturing production, eroding competitiveness, stagnant investment, and an increasing number of bankruptcies.

Changes in industrial policy in *Ireland* in recent years have included: strengthened procedures for linking grant assistance to employment or other performance criteria; increased focus on advisory services, marketing, product development, and the S&T infrastructure through the set-up of the new International Financial Services Centre in Dublin, and through services offered by Coras Trachtala (CTT) -- the Irish export agency -- such as the Marketing Consultancy Programme or the Special Trading House Scheme; further movement away from fixed asset support and towards non-fixed assets (such as training or R&D); greater emphasis on repayable forms of aid; extension of the employment grant mechanism in small industry to foster start-ups and incremental expansions; and introduction of a major S&T programme emphasising the development of national centres of expertise in key technology areas such as biotechnology, optoelectronics and advanced manufacturing technologies, the use made of skills available in the higher education sector, and the creation of dynamic linkages between higher education and industry.

In addition, a report commissioned by the Irish government on the country's industrial policy (*A Time for Change: Industrial Policy for the 1990s*), was presented in January 1992 (see Box 2). The Industrial Policy Review Group (IPRG) addressed in particular the internationally trading indigenous sector and concluded that, in spite of the large contribution of foreign inward investment to the Irish economy over the past thirty years, future competitiveness and industrial performance depend on increasing the contribution to the economy from home managed firms. In this sense, if industrial policy is to be successful in helping to generate a competitive industrial structure which can sustain long-term employment growth and living standards, the focus must shift decisively to indigenous companies. Recognising that industrial policy had to go beyond traditional demarcation lines to take account of all relevant factors, the report made a number of recommendations on reforming the tax system, for infrastructure development, for education, enterprise and technology, for direct support to industry, as well as for strengthening the institutions responsible for industrial policy.

In *Italy*, recent policy initiatives in the area of industrial policy reflect the growing attention paid by the government to the functioning of markets and the costs of market imperfections. This is in sharp contrast to the previous approach to industry, dominated by public interventions, and extensive subsidies to protect ailing public sector companies. A major part of the recent regulatory activity related to industrial policy is derived from the necessity to conform the Italian legal system to EC directives. In addition to special laws adopted for state-controlled banks and for the securities markets, legislation in 1990 established a legal framework for promoting competition. This late introduction of formal competition policy (Italy was until recently the only major OECD country without an antitrust provision) is due to the weight of state-controlled firms and their use as instruments of industrial policy[13].

The Italian authorities recognise privatisation as a useful means of raising economic efficiency, developing capital markets and reducing public debt, although progress in this area has been slow, with full privatisation limited to a few firms only. Other areas where there are recent industrial policy initiatives are in the promotion of intangible investment (in particular in R&D and in training and labour mobility activities), in small and medium-sized enterprises, and in the energy and environment field.

The recent economic slowdown in the *Netherlands* has had repercussions on the government's budgetary situation and on the conduct of industrial policy. In the harsher economic climate, it has become more difficult to achieve a reduction of the budget deficit, the overriding government objective since already a number of years. During 1991, a new set of measures was announced resulting in expenditure reductions and revenue increases. In its attempts to cut back expenses, the government has given priority to reductions in the amounts of subsidies, and to improved efficiency and effectiveness of government. An exception has been made for public investment in infrastructure, since a high quality infrastructure is deemed an important element of the business environment. The government has decided to set aside a part of the profits on exports of natural gas for investment in infrastructure.

The decision to invest in infrastructure can be seen in light of the main objective of industrial policy in the Netherlands, aiming at the improvement of general conditions that determine the competitiveness of industry. This objective, although somewhat restrained by the above-mentioned budgetary cuts, is above all pursued by stimulating technological innovation. Other, but related, elements of industrial policy are the encouragement of collaboration between business, universities and R&D facilities, and the creation of a favourable business environment in general. Also, in its special concern for the physical environment, the government encourages the development of new technologies that are necessary to tackle environmental problems.

In *Portugal*, the period since entry to the EC has been marked by a significant effort to tackle a number of the structural problems facing the economy. Progress has been made, to different degrees, in bringing about a greater reliance on market mechanisms, in effecting rationalisation and privatisation, and in upgrading the country's stock of physical and human capital. Assistance from various Community programmes has proved to be a valuable support for the adjustment which is necessary if Portugal is to attain full integration into the economy of the EC area. EC membership has also provided an important stimulus to the inflow of foreign direct investment that comprises a major driving force for the economy.

With specific reference to the development of industrial structures responsive to the demands emanating from the evolving European and, more broadly, international context, the Portuguese authorities are placing emphasis on a number of objectives. These include (i) the improvement in the operation of financial markets, with special emphasis on access by SMEs and new innovative

Box 2. Ireland: "A Time for Change: Industrial Policy for the 1990s"

Report of the Industrial Policy Review Group

The Irish government commissioned a review of the country's industrial policy with a view to instituting reforms and preparing Ireland for the changing economic environment of the 1990s. The outcome of the review process was a report, published in January 1992, and making detailed recommendations in a number of areas. Its main proposals are outlined below.

Taxation. The report recommends a fundamental reform of the tax system. This would involve a broadening of the tax base through the reduction or abolition of many of the reliefs, exemptions, deductions and other tax expenditures; an extension of the standard-rate band to reduce the numbers paying higher marginal rates; and an overhaul of the taxation of savings to remove distortions. With respect to business tax, no indication should be given of any continuation of the 10 per cent corporation tax rate beyond 2010, while also not extending the range of activities to which it applies.

Infrastructure. The report recommends maintaining the increased investment momentum on road improvements, changing the institutional framework and ownership of Irish ports, greater competition in air services, telecoms and energy supply, and a restructuring of the postal system. With respect to energy, proposals are aimed at a more efficient electricity and gas production through the reduction of subsidies and of price discrimination practices. In relation to environmental issues, the report urges the government to make a definite decision on providing for the safe disposal of hazardous industrial waste.

Education, enterprise and technology. For the education system, recommendations include attaching a higher priority to the acquisition of usable and marketable skills in order to meet the requirements of industrial development, as well as developing a new curriculum with industry involvement. For training, the report advocates increased funding for general training with additional emphasis on enterprise, productive systems and technology application. Recommendations are also made for stronger management and evaluation systems in the Department of Industry and Commerce and implementing agencies in order to ensure that resources from the EC Structural Funds are applied as effectively as possible to the needs of industry.

Direct support for industry. In terms of direct support to industry, the report recommends that the grant-aid budget for internally mobile industry should be squeezed further and advocates a decisive shift from grants for home-managed industry to the use of equity to meet gaps in financial markets for venture capital and seed capital. The reduced grant-aid budget would then be focused on fostering industrial clusters around industrial segments and niches of national competitive advantage. The government is also urged to actively promote more effective EC restrictions on State aids for industry in the more developed Member States.

Institutional strengthening. A number of recommendations focus on institutional changes. The Department of Industry and Commerce should redefine its role as being predominantly one of policy determination for industrial development and the supervision of its implementation, with a number of its regulatory and administrative functions removed and established as self-financing, para-statal organisations. The setting up of an Advisory Board on industrial policy is suggested, as well as a widening of the 3-yearly review of industrial performance to include a review of industrial policy. In addition, the report considers that a regrouping of institutional functions is necessary in order to attract foreign investment to Ireland.

The food industry. The report concludes with an analysis of the problems faced and some recommendations for the food industry, the only industrial sector thus singled out. The promotion of a greater and selective involvement in the industry by multinational food companies with access to markets and best industry practices is recommended, including joint ventures and partnership arrangements with Irish food firms. In addition, environmental and hygiene related legislation and regulations should promote the "green" image of Irish food products. Finally, an expert group, comprising farmers, manufacturers and retailers should be asked to prepare, in co-operation with the State sector, and within six months, a national food development plan.

start-up initiatives; (ii) the modernisation and restructuring of traditional industries, notably textiles, where the implementation of major, and difficult, adjustment seems imperative; (iii) the raising of industry's technological levels and a deeper business commitment to quality and design as factors of competitiveness; (iv) the cultivation of an "enterprise culture" and the intensification of training; (v) the development of service and information activities linked to, e.g., microelectronics, optoelectronics and robotics; and (vi) the internationalisation of industry through the encouragement of inward foreign investment, Portuguese investment abroad and the creation of joint ventures with foreign partners.

In *Spain*, early in 1992, the Ministry of Economic and Financial Affairs was drawing up a set of measures to be presented to the European Commission in March with a view to accelerating the alignment of the Spanish economy with that of the country's more advanced European partners. In this context, it should be noted that the move towards complete integration with the European Community, underway since 1990, has been aimed mainly at preparation for the full opening up to EC competition of industries where restructuring plans had been extended beyond 1986 and at full compliance, in those industries, with EC restrictions on state aid. A second objective has been to integrate specific national instruments used in the restructuring process with EC rules (in connection, e.g., with government promotion of Spanish enterprises participating in EC technology projects, state controls on energy prices, regional incentives in the reindustrialisation areas, and promotion of SMEs).

At present, the Ministry of Industry, Trade and Tourism is preparing an industrial strategy for boosting competitiveness through both cost and non-cost factors. This strategy involves: the firming-up of traditional industrial sectors and the restructuring of state-owned firms so that they may operate in accordance with market criteria; the stimulation of business services with a view to enhancing productivity and product differentiation as well as the promotion of better industrial quality and design, with particular reference to SMEs; the bolstering of the technological infrastructure and the development and diffusion of new production technologies; the encouragement of economies of scale and the internationalisation of Spanish enterprises, through their own expansion or through co-operation agreements; and the improvement of management and technical training.

At the same time, new legislation approved by Parliament in July 1992 sets out criteria for government action in the field of industry (with repect to promotional activities, security and quality), for the different policy measures to be used, and determines procedures for co-ordinating the work of the various administrative bodies concerned.

Industrial policy in the *United Kingdom* has since 1979 attempted to influence the development of industry through privatisation, deregulation, and the exposure of firms to market discipline by the phasing-out of subsidies. The deregulation of markets was aimed at freeing them from restrictions such as controls on exchange rates, wages, dividends and credit, while increasing competition by removing barriers to entry (such as those existing previously in telecommunications and financial services). Privatisation was far-reaching, covering industrial sectors such as utilities and transport, while the phasing-out of subsidies has led to a situation where only two sectors continue to receive direct financial assistance: aerospace, as part of EC initiatives, and shipbuilding, in line with international (EC and OECD) norms.

The supply-side structural reforms during the 1980s have made the UK product market one of the most open, liberal and competitive among OECD countries under criteria such as tariff levels, the prevalence of non-tariff barriers, industrial subsidies, restrictions on foreign direct investment and administrative barriers to entry [14]. Policy has nevertheless continued to evolve, reflecting the experience of the reforms. Thus, much greater effort is being put today in the design of efficient regulatory control, while encouraging productivity gains in privatised industries. At the same time, policy towards foreign direct investment is moving towards attracting higher value-added activities, by for example encouraging foreign companies established in the UK to undertake the full spectrum of activities, from R&D and design to production and marketing.

The industrial policy areas receiving major attention, as well as the choice of instruments, follow from this general horizontal approach and have not changed in the last few years. Support for training and the upgrading of skills remains very prominent as a focal point of policy concern, through programmes such as "Investors in People". Small and medium enterprises and new start-ups are the beneficiaries of a very extensive range of policy measures, while support is given for consultancy and advisory services for firms. Regional policy is pursued both directly (by the support of regional development authorities) and indirectly through other instruments (such as industrial development grants). These four policy threads (training, SMEs, advisory services and regional policy) have been brought together in 1991 in Technical or Local "Enterprise Councils", managed by the local business community under the direction of regional development agencies and the Department of Employment.

In addition, scientific research and technological development are actively encouraged through programmes such as LINK (often through international collaboration). While the principal emphasis is on pre-competitive collaborative research, a number of initiatives are aimed at providing opportunities for small firms to participate in R&D. Finally, one should underline a salient point that emerges from the current UK industrial policy initiatives: the significantly increased stress currently being placed on industry-related environmental policies.

The recent evolution of industrial policy in *Austria* has largely been characterised by an endeavour to implement reforms and structural adjustments in the context of Austria's candidacy for membership in the European Community and its participation in the European Economic Area, which is expected to be established in 1993. This effort is exemplified by policy action in numerous fields -- e.g., the shift in investment support from physical to intangible investment, the liberalisation of export and price controls, the restructuring of the nationalised industries, and the removal of non-tariff barriers by the adoption of the right to provide cross-border services and by mutual recognition of standards.

With respect to privatisation, federal participation in important companies (the national airline and financial institutions) has been allowed to decline below the 51 per cent threshold as the state did not participate in recent increases in share capital. It is also envisaged to reduce the federal participation in the two biggest Austrian banks. Proceeds from privatisation are estimated at Sch 6 billion [15].

In *Finland*, the economy has fallen into the deepest recession in two generations, with significant decreases in GDP and in industrial output for a second consecutive year in 1991 and a rising unemployment rate. Partly due to the collapse of exports to the former Soviet Union, its external deficit has widened and Finland's indebtedness is currently one of the highest among OECD countries. Against this background, the government's room for manoeuvre is limited by a fast increasing deficit in public finances. As a consequence, its programme reflects the necessity of adjustment to the completely changed environment facing the Finnish economy and to the need for rectifying its structural defects while not imposing a heavy burden on public finances. The integration of Finland in the EC, through the European Economic Area agreement in the first place, but also through a formal application for EC membership in March 1992 is essential in this respect. The government considers that membership would diminish uncertainty about rates of exchange and interest rates, reduce international exchange costs and border obstacles, and thus lead to growth in foreign trade, enhance competition, and promote investment.

In addition, the government's industry-related policy targets include curbing public expenditures and shrinking the public sector's share of the economy through the privatisation of state-owned companies, stricter competition rules and deregulation, and a reform of the taxation system bringing it more in line with that of the EC. Decreases in social charges for employers, an agreement on low wage increases reached with trade unions and a devaluation of the Finnish markka by 14 per cent in November 1991 were all aimed at increasing the price competitiveness of Finnish industry.

In *Norway*, industrial policy measures aim at strengthening the mainland economy, particularly the export-oriented and import-competing sectors, in order to reduce the current high rates of unemployment without increasing the dependence on oil revenues. Attempts are made also to improve productivity and cost efficiency in the sheltered sectors, and in particular in the public sector. In 1992, in addition to efforts towards increased employment, large budget allocations are channelled towards investments in infrastructure, and increased efforts are made for R&D. A major tax reform aims at bringing about a more efficient allocation of investments and prevent tax-motivated behaviour in capital markets. Regional policy measures continue to be an important part of overall industrial policy, often focused on small and medium enterprises and on improving the quality of inputs into the production process.

The government gives also high priority to environmental policy. It considers that clear signals need to be given to industry regarding long-run environmental choices and strategies and believes that, although costly, stringent environmental standards can act in the medium term as a basis for a comparative advantage. The signing of the agreement on a European Economic Area is seen is an important step for the Norwegian industry, widening access to EC markets.

In *Sweden*, the gradual reorientation of industrial policy towards minimising political intervention in market mechanisms during the 1980s has involved the dismantling of support for branches in crisis. The government estimates that this has appreciably reduced net costs for firm-specific and industry-specific support in the 1980s. Support has been reduced for some time and is now concentrated on the promotion of R&D and of small and medium-sized enterprises. A growing share of the support for technological development is devoted to various technology programs. Furthermore, to promote a more effective administrative structure in matters relating to industrial policy, a number of state agencies were merged in mid-1991 into the National Board for Industrial and Technical development. The new government, elected in October 1991, perceives the main role of industrial policy as creating efficient markets, being complementary with market forces, and providing, broadly speaking, the infrastructure for manufacturing. As such, it is committed to deregulation in a large number of areas to increase competition and to the privatisation of state-owned companies. A broad privatisation programme has started, aimed at the privatisation of 35 state-owned companies.

The government is also concerned about lagging Swedish productivity. A recently released report commissioned by the government examined the macroeconomic and structural causes for the lagging rates of productivity in Sweden and outlined a strategy for future higher productivity, with initiatives aimed at both government and industry (see Box 7 in Part 2 of the report).

Industrial policy in *Switzerland* has recently evolved against a background of mild recession in 1991, marked by large-scale declines of production in construction and certain industrial branches. The recession, with its differential sectoral incidence, brought more clearly to light the effect of the previous years' boom in engendering an unbalanced development of the real estate sector and in masking the structural weaknesses of some low value-added branches and firms. Similarly, the unemployment levels generated by the recession have had a particularly sharp impact, socially and politically, on the economically weaker geographical regions.

This domestic background as well as a number of international developments -- the general economic sluggishness, with its negative impact on export markets, and the progress towards economic integration in Europe, marked by both a greater reliance on market forces and a more strategic approach to industrial promotion -- have led to a rethinking of Swiss industrial policy. In the past, industrial policy mainly focused on building infrastructure for transport and telecommunications, on training, research, support of SMEs and regional policy measures. Recently, this policy has taken two major new directions: on the one hand, an inquiry into means to create a more market-oriented framework for economic activity with respect, e.g., to competition, standards, legislative controls, taxation and restrictions on the employment of foreigners, and, on the other hand, a strengthening of government support for training and oriented scientific research. The Swiss authorities stress in particular the competition-enhancing pillar of this new strategy: while external economic policy has always been liberal in Switzerland, too many restrictions on internal competition still remain.

This more active and more sharply defined industrial policy is intended to integrate Swiss industry into the broad European internal market now being developed and to improve Swiss competitiveness through technological upgrading. An important condition for meeting the latter objective is seen to be the opening up of the labour market within the European framework so as to enable Swiss firms to cope with the skilled manpower shortages that continue to beset them. Paradoxically, this integration process implies that Swiss industrial policy will lose some of its autonomy while gaining in importance in overall economic policy.

Two obstacles stand in the way of attaining the aims of present industrial policy. One of these is, in the medium term, the shrinking financial resources of the Confederation, the first victims of which are likely to be areas benefiting from discretionary grants, such as the encouragement of research, innovation and training. The other obstacle, of a short-term nature, involves the difficulties to be encountered in absorbing the impact of structural adjustment in a period of economic sluggishness. But the Swiss authorities consider that the slowdown in growth offers an opportunity to put in place a domestic economy more consonant with the country's real strengths and more resistant to the imponderables of the business cycle, while providing for greater job security.

Industrial policy in *Turkey* is structured around three broad lines of approach which are, to a considerable extent, linked to each other: (i) strengthening of investment; (ii) expansion of exports, with emphasis on manufactured products; and (iii) support for the less-developed regions of the country.

An increasingly important thrust in government action to stimulate investment is the support given to industrialisation throughout the country, particularly in the less-developed regions. This is linked to SME policies aimed, for example, at the encouragement of industrial estates, including measures to promote the development of the necessary industrial infrastructure. At the same time, in the area of trade policy, the government is refocusing export promotion towards a greater emphasis on assistance to exporting industries at the investment and production stages; this is in line with the reductions under way in direct support for exports.

Finally, considerable attention is accorded to the role of technology as a determinant of international competitiveness. The aim of the authorities is to increase the R&D potential and to improve manpower knowledge and skills sufficiently to permit the development of a capacity to produce new technologies. At the same time, through instruments such as the Small and Medium-sized Industry Development Organisation (SMIDO), the government seeks to raise technological levels and foster technology diffusion in the smaller firms located in regions throughout the country.

It is within the context of a sharp decline in economic activity that the *Australian* government continues to give a high priority to policies aimed at increasing the international orientation of its industry. In March 1991, the government launched the major Industry Statement *Building a Competitive Australia* (see Box 3). In this statement, a number of policy initiatives designed to accelerate the development of internationally-competitive industries were announced. Amongst these are the further reduction of import tariffs, the indefinite extension of R&D support through tax concessions, and the introduction of an Advanced Manufacturing Technology Strategy. The Industry Statement underlines Australia's intentions to move away from dependence on agriculture and raw materials towards a greater reliance on adding value to natural resources and developing new industries in the tradeable sector.

A range of horizontal programmes are in place to improve the flexibility of industry to meet areas of market failure, to make industry more export-oriented and to

> **Box 3. "Building a Competitive Australia" industry statement**
>
> In March 1991 the Australian government announced a number of policy initiatives in a major Industry Statement -- Building a Competitive Australia -- designed to accelerate the development of internationally competitive industries. These include:
>
> - phased reductions in the general rate of tariffs from 10 per cent and 15 per cent in 1992 to a general rate of 5 per cent by 1996;
>
> - new policy arrangements to cover the automobile industry through to the year 2000. The arrangements reinforce the previous plan and continue tariff reductions at the previous rate;
>
> - significant reform of the assistance arrangements for the textiles, clothing and footwear (TCF) industries, including the termination of quotas, the continued phase down of tariffs, and the abolition of bounties;
>
> - the indefinite extension of the tax concession to R&D after June 1993 at 125 per cent;
>
> - the introduction of an Advanced Manufacturing Technnology (AMT) Strategy, to encourage the development, production and use of advanced manufacturing technologies. Two elements of the AMT Strategy are the extension of the bounty scheme for the machine tools and robots industry with effect from 1 July 1991, and the introduction of the Advanced Manufacturing Technnology Development Programme;
>
> - the establishment of the Small to Medium Sized Enterprise (SME) Development Programme which aims to increase the international competititveness of Australia's SMEs by improving their access to information and to overseas markets;
>
> - the updating of Australia's information industries (II) strategy to take advantage of the rapidly growing domestic and world market for II goods (particularly software) and services; and
>
> - new legislation introduced in December 1991 extending the range of inputs to manufacturing which are exempt from sales tax, thereby reducing the cost burden on inputs for goods producers. New legislation was also introduced to simplify the operations of the income tax law and to allow taxation depreciation rates to be set objectively by reference to a statutory definition of effective life.

improve worker training. These include the Management and Investment Companies Program; the 125 per cent tax concession and other arrangements for R&D activities; the National Industry Extension service network; the Investment Promotion Scheme; and the Partnerships for Development Scheme. At the same time, there are also specific industry programs directed at facilitating industry restructuring in mature industries and fostering the development of new industries. Mature industry programs include the Passenger Motor Vehicle plan and the Metals-Based Engineering Program. New industry programs cover the pharmaceuticals, biotechnology and information industries.

Proposals currently under consideration aim at adopting a more active role for industrial policy. They involve providing depreciation concessions and investment allowances selectively to industries (pulp and paper, food processing, waste management, areas of mining) that commit themselves to a plan to boost investment in areas that would increase value-added exports. These proposals have received considerable support from State authorities but are a source of debate within the government. If adopted, they would shift the current policy away from providing across-the-board measures such as accelerated depreciation or investment allowances and towards a more sectoral approach.

NOTES AND REFERENCES

1. OECD (1992), *Progress in Structural Reform*, Paris.
2. OECD (1991), *Environmental Policy: How to Apply Economic Instruments*, Paris.
3. Davis, E. (1992), "Industrial Policy in an Integrated European Economy", paper presented at the "Workshop on Industrial Policy: Challenge for the 1990s", European Institute of Public Administration, March 1992, Maastricht, the Netherlands.
4. See OECD (1991), *Industrial Policy in OECD Countries: Annual Review*, Paris.
5. OECD (1992), *Technology and the Economy: The Key Relationships*, Paris.
6. Nicolaides, P. (1992), "Industrial Policy and Foreign Direct Investment", paper presented at the "Workshop on Industrial Policy: Challenge for the 1990s", European Institute of Public Administration, March 1992, Maastricht, the Netherlands.
7. For a discussion of these issues see OECD (1991), *Industrial Policy in OECD Countries: Annual Review*, *op.cit.*, Part 4. See also Krugman, P. (1987), "Is Free Trade Passé?", *Economic Perspectives*, Vol.1; and Bhagwati, J. (1991), *The World Trading System at Risk*, Harvester Wheatsheaf.
8. OECD (1992), *Progress in Structural Reform*, *op.cit.*
9. OECD (1992), *Progress in Structural Reform*, *op.cit.*
10. OECD (1992), "Subsidies and Structural Adjustment", Report to the OECD Council at Ministerial level, Paris.
11. OECD (1991), *OECD Economic Surveys : Belgium*, Paris.
12. OECD (1991), *OECD Economic Surveys: France*, Paris.
13. OECD (1991), *OECD Economic Surveys: Italy*, Paris.
14. OECD (1991), *OECD Economic Surveys: United Kingdom*, Paris.
15. OECD (1992), *OECD Economic Surveys: Austria*, Paris.

Part 2

RECENT INDUSTRIAL POLICY MEASURES

The information on industry-related policy measures in this part of the report relates to initiatives during 1991 and during the first quarter of 1992. For a limited number of countries, updated information has allowed the inclusion of some initiatives up to August 1992.

A. Measures to promote industrial investment

Investment in tangible assets declined in the OECD area in the beginning of the 1990s, following very rapid growth at the end of the 1980s (see Graph 1, showing investment, R&D, productivity growth for total OECD). In 1991 investment declined most sharply in the United States and the United Kingdom, and declined by more modest amounts in France and Italy. Of the major OECD countries only Germany, with unification, and Japan maintained positive growth in tangible investment, and in these two countries there was a very marked slowdown. Investment remained flat in early 1992 in all major countries, with Japan expected to record a fall in business investment in 1992. However, over the longer period since 1970, tangible investment by the business sector has grown steadily despite cyclical fluctuations, and taken a slowly increasing share of business value added.

Intangible investment in R&D and technology development, training, software and marketing has grown rapidly, and total industrial intangible investment probably outstripped expenditures on tangible investment by the mid-1980s [1]. But growth in business sector R&D slowed in the second half of the 1980s and into the 1990s, led by the slow-down in business R&D expenditures in the United States. Rapid growth in R&D continued only in Japan, some of the smaller OECD economies, and in economies that are still undergoing "catch-up" from a position of relatively low R&D expenditures (Australia, Denmark, Ireland, Italy, Spain), but even in these countries the rate of growth slackened. The lack of regular statistics for other intangibles makes it difficult to assess their growth or inter-country differences, but it has probably slowed along with the general slump in physical investment and R&D in most OECD countries.

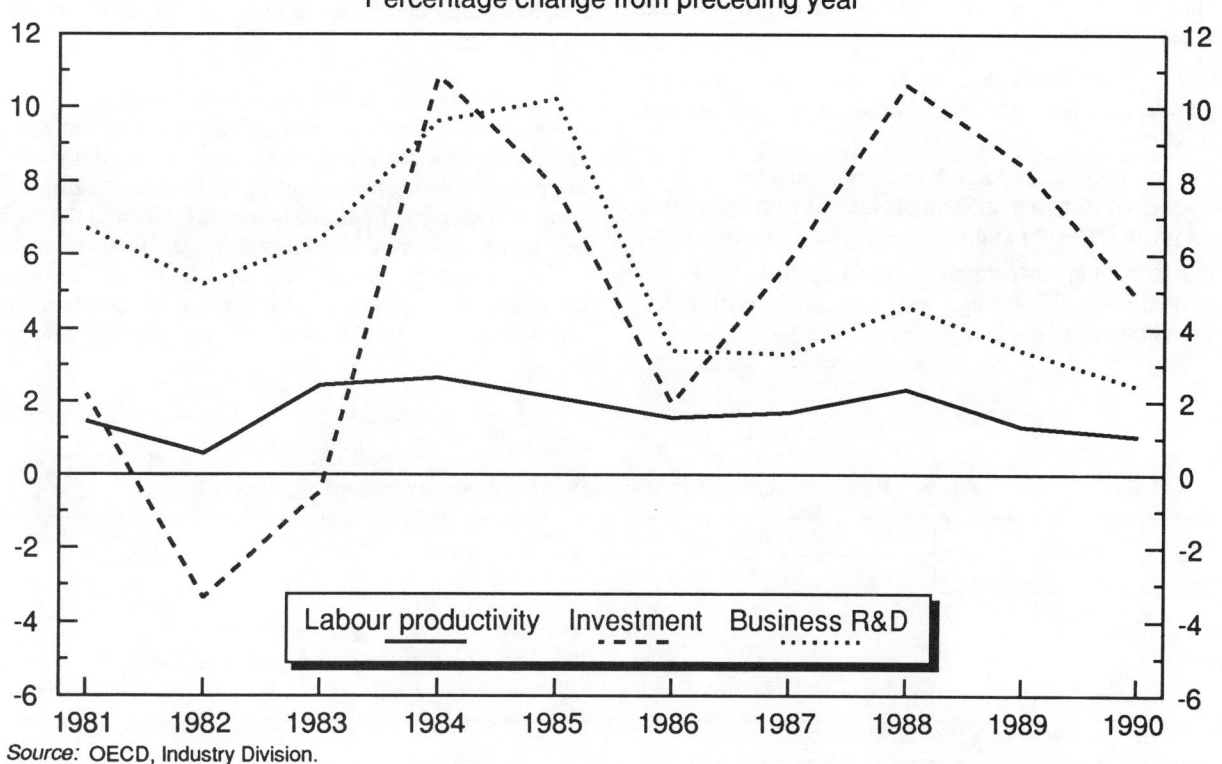

Graph 1. **Productivity, investment and R&D growth**
OECD total
Percentage change from preceding year

Source: OECD, Industry Division.

The good performance of tangible and intangible investment until the late 1980s was driven by rapid expansion of the world economy, increased opportunities in new markets, the search for competitiveness by established producers in leading OECD countries faced with competition from Japanese and other Asian producers, and investment from these countries as they developed global strategies. It has also been driven by the increasing importance that firms of all sizes are attaching to technology, quality and flexibility in an increasingly competitive environment. Investment in a wide range of intangible assets (from new product development and innovation through to training, software and organisational investments accompanying new production methods) has become of central importance in firm strategies. Intangibles are necessary complements to physical investment to achieve productivity growth and competitiveness [2].

The downturn in investment has been partly cyclical due to the recession, but it is also symptomatic of underlying structural weaknesses and differences in performance among OECD countries. There are major differences among OECD countries in investment performance -- in tangible assets and, even more importantly, in intangibles. Japan, Germany and some of the smaller OECD countries have a better overall investment record than the US and the UK. These differences in investment performance are ultimately reflected in productivity performance. The current period of retrenchment and restructuring is heightening these national differences in investment performance.

Three sets of policy issues are of key importance in shaping future investment, productivity growth and industrial performance:

- How to overcome the wide differences between countries in investment, savings and productivity growth;
- How to improve productivity performance and competitiveness if these are not being achieved with the current mix of investment in tangible and intangible assets;
- How to meet the investment needs of central and eastern Europe, without starving funds to capital-short developing countries.

To meet the first two of these challenges OECD governments have been changing the structure of their investment incentives. Tax reforms, initially in the United Kingdom and the United States but subsequently in all OECD countries, have reduced or eliminated deductions from corporate taxable income, broadened the tax base and lowered corporate tax rates. Reform has been part of government strategies to drop interventionist and directive approaches to industry and corporate behaviour, and to adopt an approach to investment and asset creation designed to remove distortions and allow businesses to determine their investment strategies in a more neutral environment. One major result of reform has been a significant reduction in the value of tax incentives (government tax expenditures, which are reductions in tax revenues due to tax incentives) to invest in tangible assets. This trend is apparent in the comprehensive data on government support of the OECD industrial subsidies database. These data show that with tax reform, tangible investment has become much less important in terms of total support to industry (Table 3). The relative importance of tax expenditures has also declined markedly.

Support to intangible investment has become a more important part of government support to industry. R&D incentives through grants and the tax system have increased in relative importance. More emphasis is being given to training and skill formation through direct assistance and encouragement to the private sector to expand training efforts. Small firms are another area of greater focus for investment policy. Increased assistance is designed to improve their functioning by expanding intangible inputs of R&D and skills, and improving their flexibility and access to external technical and management resources.

Improving the technological and commercial environment for firms has been another area for investment policy. A broader array of intangibles is of increasing importance for improved firm performance, and in many countries increased emphasis is being given to the supply of input services (management and technological expertise, quality and design inputs, special services to complement investment in advanced manufacturing technology) to extend and increase the efficiency of

Table 3. **Policy objectives and main instruments of investment support**

Policy objectives	Share of all programmes (percentages)				Main instruments (approximate percentage distribution)
	1986	1987	1988	1989	
Tangible investment	55	37	37	28	Tax incentives (90), grants (10)
R&D	9	11	9	12	Grants (50), tax incentives (40)
Employment, training	3	3	5	4	Grants (60), tax incentives (40)

Source: OECD, Industrial Subsidies Database, March 1992.

internal intangible investments. A broad range of intermediate institutions, intermediaries and consultants have been mobilised to provide input services, often on a non-profit basis, but supplying services through extensive use of commercial consultancy and technical services provided on a subsidised basis.

The main questions to be addressed in the design of investment policy are: (i) whether the current economic downturn combined with high interest rates and a strong anti-inflationary stance have depressed investment to the point where further pro-investment measures are needed; (ii) whether the current mix of different kinds of tangible and intangible investment is adequate to improve long-term performance and reverse low productivity growth; (iii) whether there is room for improvement in the treatment of some intangible investments, by allowing them to be depreciated and written off against income over several years, as for physical investment, rather than treating them as current expenditures to be cut during down-turns in the business cycle.

Some recent policy measures aimed at promoting investment in physical and intangible assets are indicated below.

(i) Measures affecting physical investment (including tax-related measures and other measures of a general nature)

In *Canada*, the government has completed the implementation of its tax reform, designed to introduce a simpler, fairer and more effective system with a broader base and lower corporate tax rates. The first phase of the revision was terminated with an additional 1 per cent reduction in the tax on manufacturing and processing profits, effective on 1 July 1991. The second phase, consisting of the introduction of a 7 per cent value-added goods and services tax (GST), went into effect on 1 January 1991; this levy replaces the federal manufacturers' sales tax, which was considered to have been burdened with anomalies and competitive distortions.

In *Belgium*, the provisions of the European Commission directive of July 1990 on the establishment of a common tax system relating to parent companies and subsidiaries have been carried over to Belgian national law. The legislation distinguishes between two situations with respect to taxation: (i) where income is distributed by a Belgian subsidiary to a parent company established in an EC country other than Belgium and (ii) where such income is distributed to a parent company situated in Belgium.

In *Germany*, in addition to measures concerning general framework conditions for the financing of investment referred to in the 1991 *Annual Review*[3] (e.g. the abolition of state authorisation to issue bearer bonds and of the exchange turnover tax or the enlargement of the investment range for insurers), a number of new measures have been announced or entered into force, including a package of measures for the new *Länder* (see Box 4).

Since the beginning of 1992, home loan associations are allowed to acquire interests in foreign companies within the EC, thus facilitating access by companies to equity and outside capital. Both the Banking Law (*Kreditwesengesetz*) and the Stock Exchange Law (*Börsengesetz*) are in the process of being further adjusted to implement the EC banking directive and to improve market supervision as well as to implement the EC insider trading directive. In addition, it is planned to improve access by SMEs to the Stock Exchange. In the tax policy area also, a number of measures had been referred to in the 1991 *Annual Review* concerning, in general, a reduction of taxation that is not earnings-related; and, for the new *Länder*, an exemption from the trading capital tax and the net worth tax from 1991 to 1994. Both these measures are important for firms starting in business and not yet making a profit.

In addition, new measures contained in the 1992 Tax Amendment Law aim at facilitating administrative procedures (e.g. in the new *Länder* there is a first prolongation until June 1992 of the 12 per cent investment allowance; the rate is to fall to 8 per cent afterwards), at abolishing special rules (with the introduction in 1993 of a 25 per cent withholding tax on interest-bearing investments) or at harmonising German laws with EC legislation (the raising of consumer taxes i.e. mineral oil tax, taxes on tobacco and alcoholic beverages, insurance tax, and of the VAT rate from 14 to 15 per cent).

In *Greece*, efforts have been made for the modernisation of the stock market in line with EC directives in this area, while banking reforms are underway. The government expects that the new legislation will facilitate the financing of industry from the stock market and will thus partly offset the poor investment performance of Greek industry due to the high cost of borrowing, itself a result of the large public sector deficits and the restrictive monetary policy pursued. The unfavourable interest rates, together with persistently high inflation levels, are also blamed for the inability of the business community to pursue long-term investment strategies through the Investment Law passed in 1990 (see the 1991 *Annual Review*).

In addition, the government has established a working group to prepare a multi-faceted industrial development programme (HELPEID -- Hellenic Programme for Economic and Industrial Development). The programme will have a horizontal character, with some sectoral initiatives, and will be designed along the lines of the Portuguese PEDIP. Measures will concentrate on the following aspects of industrial policy: (i) modernisation of technological infrastructure, creation of "technology parcs"; (ii) productivity improvement through skills upgrading; (iii) improved financial incentives for investment, and for more

Box 4. Germany: Economic support measures for industrial investment in the new Länder

In order to assist the restructuring of the economy in the new German *Länder*, the German government has instituted a number of economic support measures like the Upswing East project (*Gemeinschaftswerk Aufschwung Ost*) and others. These initiatives cover tax benefits, regional assistance, investment loans, European Recovery Programmes (ERP), equity capital assistance programmes; and loan guarantees. They are outlined below.

Tax benefits

Investment allowances. For the purchase and production of movable assets in the new *Länder*, a 12 per cent allowance of purchase and production costs is in place where the purchase or production occurs between 1 July 1990 and 30 June 1992. The rate falls to 8 per cent where the purchase or production occurs between 1 July 1992 and 30 June 1994. Between 1 July 1994 and 31 December 1996 the rate is 5 per cent. The investments have to be concluded up to 31 December 1996.

Special depreciation allowances. These are instituted for the purchase and production of depreciable movable and fixed assets, and for extensions and alterations to buildings which form part of the assets in the new *Länder*. The applicable rate is 50 per cent of the purchase/production costs if the purchase/production occurs before 1 January 1995. Under certain conditions, a tax-free investment reserve may be established amounting to the special depreciation allowed in future.

Further tax aids. These amount to conditional relief from the trading capital tax and the net worth tax until 31 December 1992, differential rates in the case of the trade tax on earnings, and a tax-free amount of DM 600/1 200 annually in the case of the income tax.

Regional assistance

Measures here consist of investment grants within the framework of the joint federal government/*Länder* programme "Improving the regional economic structures". Grants for private investors of up to 23 per cent are possible (cumulation with other programmes can bring this to a maximum of 35 percentage points); assistance for industry-related infrastructure is also included. The programme also includes funds totalling DM 5.7 billion in earmarked funds and commitment authorisations (the same amount from the *Länder*) within the Joint Federal Government/*Länder* Programme State, as well as additional aid from the European Regional Fund (a total of DM 3 billion in the 1991-93 period). Finally, a special programme is in place entitled "Improving the regional economic structures" with the aim of supplementing the Joint Federal Government/*Länder* Programme in regions that are particularly affected by structural change; it involves another DM 1.2 billion in 1992 (50 per cent State and *Länder* funds each).

Investment loans

Measures include the investment programme of the KfW (*Kreditanstalt für Wiederaufbau*) totalling DM 12 billion for investment by German and foreign companies in the new *Länder*. Additional investment loans for small and medium-sized businesses are available from funds of the KfW, the *Deutsche Augleichsbank* (Dta-Bank) and the *Berliner Industriebank* (BIB). Investment loans are also available from the KfW to companies that are (still) public.

ERP programmes

In the context of the European Recovery Programme (ERP), there is provision for loans totalling DM 10 billion in 1992 for business start-ups and other investment in the new *Länder*.

Equity capital assistance programmes

The equity capital assistance programme promotes independent businesses in the new *Länder* by providing funds for interest rate subsidies etc. amounting to DM 3.5 billion in 1992 (earmarked funds and commitment authorisations). In addition, in the context of the promotion of savings to increase equity capital (promotion of business start-ups), assistance is provided for up to 20 per cent of the savings, a maximum of DM 10 000.

Loan guarantees

A three-stage programme to provide security for loans is in place, set according to the volume of finance needed. It involves bank guarantees for people setting up in business and for small and medium-sized businesses and collateralisation of loans up to DM 1 million; deficiency guarantees of the *Berliner Industriebank* for small and medium-sized enterprises and collateralisation of loans between DM 1 million and DM 20 million; and Federal Government guarantees for projects totalling more than DM 20 million, whose promotion is in the public interest. Finally, a 40 per cent release from liability for the financing banks by the three major banks (KfW, BIB, Dta-Bank) for loans amounting to a maximum of DM 1 million is also available.

efficient use of energy; (iv) assistance to some traditional industries (in particular the textiles, clothing, leather and fertilisers industries); (v) measures for the promotion of activities of SMEs; (vi) a programme for the upgrading of product quality and industrial design; (vii) measures for the protection of the environment; (viii) measures for ensuring the implementation of the programme as well as administrative mechanisms for its assessment. The Greek government estimates that the total cost of the programme will be 4 billion ECUs, to be financed jointly by the EC, the Greek government and the banking sector.

In *Ireland*, following the Review of Industrial Performance which evaluated activity from 1986 to 1990, and in line with the agreement reached between government, employers and unions and articulated in the Programme for Economic and Social Progress, the overall goal was to create 60 000 new jobs in manufacturing industry in the period 1991-93. Development of indigenous industry was set as a priority, with an emphasis on areas of perceived weakness such as innovation, marketing, technology and management development. New measures to facilitate achievement of the jobs target included the wider use of employment grants; the evaluation of the job potential of new segments in the internationally traded services sector (audio visual services, entertainment services and education and training); the provision of additional University places in specific areas such as applied computing; the development of land suitable for industrial development currently owned by local authorities; and the maintenance of pressure on the EC Commission to carry out a rigorous examination of State aid schemes throughout the Community.

As regards industrial incentives, these would be related to the jobs created rather than to capital spending. There would also be a reduction in capital grants; a shift from capital grants to employment grants, marketing and other forms of support; all grant supports would be related to performance, with jobs as the normal trigger for payment of capital grants; the industrial promotion agencies would step up their initial counselling service to prospective new project promoters; and, by 1993, 50 per cent of supports for medium to large indigenous industry would be in equity or other repayable forms.

Following the publication of the Review of Industrial Performance in 1990, the government set up the Industrial Policy Review Group (IPRG) in order to undertake a fundamental examination of Ireland's industrial policy. In its report, published in January 1992 (see Box 2 in Part 1 of this report), the IPRG strategy for industrial promotion recommended changes in a number of areas:

- A decisive shift from grants towards equity, taking account of the requirements for attracting the more mobile firms for which Ireland is competing with industrial promotion agencies abroad. This shift aims to reduce the unhealthy dependence mentality on the part of many indigenous firms, as well as the distortions to the market for industrial finance which inhibit the spontaneous development of commercial support for grant-aided firms. It would be accompanied by a refocussing of the target for industrial promotion in favour of promoting industrial clusters around sources of national competitive advantage.

- A rationalisation and simplification of the state development agencies to ensure that programmes be better targeted to the needs of firms. The IPRG recommended that there should be a new, single, integrated agency which would combine marketing, technological and other developmental and financial support to promote the development of Irish-managed, indigenous firms. Additionally, the IPRG recommended that there should also be a separate organisation to promote internationally mobile investment by overseas interest in Ireland in all fields of commercial activity, including manufacturing and internationally trade services.

In *Austria*, general-purpose investment aid continued to decline in 1991, giving way to the promotion of intangible investments (see subheading (ii) below on measures promoting intangible investment). The second stage of the tax reform programme was announced with the formation of the present government. Plans include a reform of company taxation to reduce administrative costs and to strengthen the capital base of small and medium-sized enterprises and a stronger orientation of the tax system towards environmental protection [4].

In *Finland*, industrial investment decreased by one fifth in 1991, and the downward trend is projected to continue in 1992. Improvement of investment activity is prevented by the markedly deteriorated financial situation in the business sector and the high rates of interest. Worries of a worsening credit crunch are growing as banks have made heavy losses and have been forced to tighten their loan terms. In response to this situation, the Finnish authorities unveiled in March 1992 a 29.4 billion markka support package for the nation's banking industry, aimed at sustaining investors confidence. Concerning the Finnish tax regime, the present turnover tax is to be turned into a pure value added tax in 1994. This tax reform will make the construction and service industries, exempted under the current system, subject to taxation. A reform of capital income taxation, lowering the corporate tax rate from 23 to 19 per cent, is being prepared along the lines of that in other Nordic countries.

In *Norway*, a major reform of taxation of firms and of capital taxation, with consequences also for personal taxation, was implemented on 1 January 1992. Overall, the reform has brought about reduced rates, a broadening of the tax base and equal treatment of different forms of capital revenues. The new tax system is more neutral, aims to allocate investments more efficiently, and prevents tax-motivated behaviour in capital markets that might have hampered structural adjustment in the past years.

Industrial investment has also been affected by the precarious situation of the Norwegian banking sector. A broad deregulation of financial markets in recent years has led to a situation in which private banks have incurred serious credit losses. The Norwegian government has initiated measures to restore the creditworthiness and stability of the banking sector and has approved the establishment of a Bank Security Fund, which, together with the Norwegian central bank, acts to secure the deposits of private savers and investors. In addition, a merger has taken place between the four governmental institutions that have traditionally met a substantial part of the financial needs of Norwegian industry and constituted the main instruments for loans, grants and guarantees for investments (the Industry Bank, the Regional Development Fund, the Norwegian Industrial Fund, and the Small Business Fund). The role of these state institutions has, however, declined in line with the deregulation in the banking sector, but still remains significant. The new, merged institution, the Norwegian Industrial and Regional Development Fund, will be operative by 1 January 1993, the total amount allocated for the fund and the guidelines being outlined in autumn 1992.

In *Sweden*, the newly-elected government is implementing a policy aimed at encouraging entrepreneurial initiative and investment. The aim of industrial policy is, broadly speaking, to establish efficent markets, to complement the market mechanism (market correction), to promote productivity growth in industry, and to provide the infrastructure required to ensure a sustained industrial growth. In practice, this means that industrial policy shall improve the conditions for new ventures to be started, promote the development and diffusion of new technology, promote the renewal of mature industries, deregulate markets, improve competition, privatise state-owned companies, and, together with labour market policy, improve the supply of skilled labour. Measures are gradually shifted away from direct intervention, e.g. in the from of support to industry, to more general measures, e.g. to improve the skills and competence of the work force and to improve the transportation and communications networks.

In *Switzerland*, the downturn in the employment situation led the Federal Public Economy Department at the end of 1991 to release the tax-free reserves which firms may build up as a contribution to job stability or with a view to the long-term strengthening of their competitiveness. The unfreezing of these funds will make available to some 700 enterprises about SF400 million for investment up to the end of 1993.

In a referendum held in June 1991, government proposals for revising the financial system were rejected. The proposed modifications called for adjustments to the turnover tax, reductions in the tax burden on investments (elimination of hidden taxation), levies on energy-related services and activities and introduction of an added value tax.

In *Australia*, reforms to the tax system continued with the introduction in December 1991 of new sales tax legislation providing relief from taxes on inputs to manufactured goods, thus avoiding double taxation. This is expected to reduce the costs of manufacturing inputs, especially in equipment for R&D and materials handling. Depreciation arrangements were also altered to account for changing technology and new environmental standards and to allow taxation depreciation rates to be set by reference to a statutory definition of "effective life" of investment goods.

One of the pillars of the recent (1991) Industry Statement is the elaboration of an Advanced Manufacturing Technology (AMT) Strategy aimed at encouraging the development, production and use of advanced production techniques. The introduction of this strategy is connected to the increasing pressure on Australian industry to improve productivity and to become more internationalised, now that tariff protection as well as input costs are being reduced. Two elements of the AMT strategy have so far been announced. First, the bounty scheme for the machine tools and robots industry has been extended with effect from July 1991 to cover equipment used in processing advanced materials. The rates of bounty will be phased down over time so as to align with the level of assistance provided to other industries. Secondly, an Advanced Manufacturing Technology Development Program was introduced, with the aim of encouraging more local development, production and use of innovative Australian AMT products and services. It is a discretionary grants based scheme aimed at private sector users where the federal government will commit A$20 million over the next four financial years, with taxable grants of up to 50 per cent of eligible project costs being available for approved projects.

Developments in two institutional mechanisms for financing industrial investment should also be noted. The lending operations of the Australian Industry Development Corporation (AIDC), established in 1970 to help finance projects in the mineral and manufacturing sectors, recorded an after tax loss of A$8.8 million in (financial) 1991, while the development investment side of the business generated a larger profit than in the previous year. New funding commitments for the year ended June 1991 totalled approximately A$612 million. The Management and Investment Companies (MIC) Programme was wound up in 1991 after spanning eight financial years. The Programme was introduced in order to play a catalytic role in the establishment of a venture capital industry in Australia. Over its life it raised A$373 million in capital at a cost (by way of tax revenue foregone) to the federal government of A$160 million. Venture capital funds under management by the industry in June 1991 were estimated at A$794 million.

(ii) Measures affecting intangible investment (covering R&D, advisory services, labour-related measures)

In the *United States* the federal government has traditionally been the primary funding source for basic scientific research, as well as funding mission-oriented research, development, testing and evaluation activities for federal departments serving key "national need" areas (e.g. defense, health, energy, environment and space). This strong support for scientific research and the advancement of new technologies was maintained in 1991 and 1992, despite the sluggish state of the economy and the severe constraints on the national budget. Federal funding in this area is estimated to have grown by nearly 7 per cent between fiscal years 1991 and 1992 (in terms of budget authority) to reach almost US$75 billion, allowing for some 4 per cent in inflation. For fiscal 1993, the proposed budget would raise federal funding of R&D and research facilities to US$77 billion (see Tables 4 and 5).

Technology development-oriented agencies and programmes that have received significant attention in the last two budget years include:

- The National Science Foundation (NSF), which in addition to its core funding for basic research at universities supports education programmes in the sciences and engineering; university-based science and technology centres of fundamental research that contribute to US competitiveness; and the Engineering Research Center Programme to develop fundamental knowledge in engineering fields.

- Interagency programmes for the development of "precompetitive, generic technologies" with broad defense and civilian applications in areas such as advanced manufacturing and robotics, communications, semiconductors, new materials and biomedicine.

- Department of Transporation programmes aimed at increased use of satellites for aviation navigation and communications systems; Department of Energy programmes that promote alternative sources of energy.

- Joint industry projects on precompetitive technologies and on manufacturing engineering, computer systems and technology assistance to firms under the Department of Commerce National institute of Standards and Technology (NIST).

This growing array of programmes is buttressed by a complementary set of policies. These include making permanent the R&D tax credit; expanding the National Cooperative Research act to permit joint production ventures and the proposed reduction of the tax rate on capital gains; and vigorous international efforts to strengthen the protection of intellectual property. Other policy changes in this direction are the liberalisation of controls on the export of high technology products, following changes in the eastern European security environment, reforming the federal procurement process in order to reduce its complexity and provide contractors with incentives to reduce costs, and the fostering of advanced manufacturing technologies and management practices in firms. In addition, the commercialisation of technologies developed through government funding and the encouragement of partnerships between firms for collaborative R&D, are seen as important recent policy initiatives.

In *Canada*, a number of initiatives have been taken to reinforce the government's wide-ranging effort to stimulate R&D and technological innovation as well as to broaden the scope of technical and management information and consultancy assistance available to firms.

One recent development is the creation of the Japan Science and Technology Fund to enhance Canada's scientific and technological base by expanding mutually beneficial collaboration with Japan. This project is intended to: increase the participation of Canadian scientists and engineers in world-class Japanese research and technology development programmes; train highly qualified personnel in state-of-the-art Japanese research facilities; improve access to Japanese technologies and industrial laboratories; and promote collaboration in research, standards setting and similar initiatives to facilitate exports to Japan.

A recently established "diSTCovery" service, designed to increase Canadian firms' awareness of the worldwide supply of transferable technology available through licensing and joint ventures, provides information on more than 25 000 manufacturing licensing opportunities. Canadian companies can also use diSTCovery to promote their own products or processes for licensing internationally.

At the same time, a Technology Opportunity Showcase scheme has been created in order to provide more face-to-face interaction by the Canadian business and technical communities with Canadian and foreign technology specialists and organisations, and to heighten awareness of the need to exploit technology in order to be globally competitive. Under this programme, regional offices of the Department of Industry, Science and Technology co-sponsor technology showcase events with private and public sector organisations.

In order to help individual enterprises improve productivity and competitiveness, an Interfirm Comparison Program is offered to groups of manufacturing and service companies having similar operating characteristics. Government support for information and advisory assistance to companies also includes a number of activities reported upon previously, such as: the Business Service Centres, the Free Trade Agreement (FTA) Strategic Planning Initiatives, the Manufacturing Visits Program, and the Workshops on Informatics for Senior Executives (see the 1991 *Annual Review*).

Table 4. **Proposed federal R&D budget in the United States**
Million dollars

	Budget Autority					Outlays				
				Change					Change	
	1989 Actual	1992 Enacted	1993 Proposed	Dollar: 1992-93	Percentage: 1992-93	1989 Actual	1992 Enacted	1993 Proposed	Dollar: 1992-93	Percentage: 1992-93
Government-wide totals:										
Conduct of R&D:										
Basic research	10 615	13 254	14 322	+1 068	+8	10 255	12 491	13 405	+914	+7
Civilian	9 650	12 053	13 086	+1 034	+9	9 312	11 325	12 142	+817	+7
Defense	965	1 201	1 236	35	+3	943	1 166	1 263	+97	+8
Applied research and development	51 298	57 839	59 302	1 463	+3	50 626	53 890	56 253	+2 363	+4
Civilian	11 620	16 257	17 313	1 056	+6	11 030	15 132	15 958	+826	+5
Defense[1]	39 678	41 582	41 988	406	+1	39 758	38 758	40 295	+1 538	+4
Subtotal:										
Conduct of R&D	61 913	71 093	73 624	+2 531	+4	60 881	66 381	69 658	+3 277	+5
R&D facilities	2 293	3 498	2 933	−565	−16	2 054	3 286	3 189	−96	−3
Total[2]	64 206	74 592	76 557	+1 965	+3	62 935	69 666	72 847	+3 181	+5

1. Includes the military-related programs of the Departments of Defense and Energy.
2. Components may not add to totals because of rounding.
Source: Budget of the United States, Fiscal Year 1993.

Table 5. **Federal initiatives in applied R&D in the US**
Million dollars

Initiative	1989 Actual	1992 Enacted	1993 Proposed	Change Dollar: 1992-93	Change Pourcent: 1992-93
High performance computing and communications	..	655	803	+148	+23
Advanced materials and processing	..	1 659	1 821	+162	+10
Biotechnology research	..	3 759	4 030	+271	+7
Energy R&D	397	774	914	+140	+18
Moving fusion energy from a science to engineering	347	337	360	+23	+7
Advanced manufacturing R&D (non-defense)	..	252	321	+69	+27
Improving the efficiency of the transportation sector through technology	802	1 224	1 433	+209	+17
Protecting the public health: health research and disease prevention	3 482	4 757	4 849	+92	+2
Expanding R&D at the National Institutes of Standards and Technology	159	247	311	+64	+26
Space technology	256	273	305	+32	+12

Source: Budget of the United States, Fiscal Year 1993.

In *Japan*, innovation and the diffusion of new technologies are supported by a wide array of activities, and managed mainly by the Agency of Industrial Science and Technology, attached to MITI. A number of new and continuing projects are in operation, financed by a 100 per cent R&D subsidy given by MITI to the main contractor NEDO (New Energy and Industrial Technology Development Organisation). NEDO entrusts R&D to secondary contractors (usually consortia), with the resulting results and intellectual property jointly owned by NEDO and the secondary contractors. Participation is open to foreign firms as one of the secondary contractors or consortia participants. The projects include:

- The Large Scale Project for promoting R&D in areas thought to be of particular national importance. During 1991, nine projects fell under this heading. One new project involves micromachine technology for medical applications, with an R&D budget of 29 million yen in 1991.

- The R&D project on basic technologies for future industries. Under this umbrella heading, a number of programmes (11 in 1991) are in operation aimed at the development of innovative basic technologies for establishing future industries. The programmes cover five fields (superconductivity, new materials, biotechnology, new electronics devices and software). There were three new projects in 1991, with a combined R&D budget of 138 million yen.

- The R&D project on medical technology, aimed at the rapid development and marketing of reasonably priced, high performance apparatus. Of the ten projects in operation in 1991, two new projects received funding of 10 million yen.

In addition to these projects, a program is under way aimed at the improvement and expansion of high-level research facilities (Research Facility Development Program). One half of the initial investment will be financed by capital from NEDO and from private and local government agencies (on a 2/3 to 1/3 basis, with NEDO earmarking 2.4 billion yen). The remaining will be covered by an interest-free loan by the Japan Development Bank and by loan guarantees from other agencies. The feasibility study of the IMS (Intelligent Manufacturing Systems) Programme is also under way, aimed at studying prospects for international collaboration in research of manufacturing technologies (integration and standardisation of existing manufacturing technologies, development of production systems for the 21st century). The feasibility study examines modalities for collaboration, including requirements for participation, technical themes, including criteria for evaluating and approving research projects, as well as contribution and funding arrangements and guidelines for the sharing of information and intellectual property rights. Finally, a number of projects are under way on environment-related industrial technologies in which private firms, national laboratories and universities are cooperating under the management of RITE (Research Institute of Innovative Technology for the Earth); five international cooperation agreements are also in progress in this area.

In *Belgium*, the Wallonia Regional Executive has acted to encourage employers to engage workers with a view to training them for their new jobs. A decree issued in December 1990 provides that industrial firms which have signed an agreement with the Community and Regional Office for Vocational Training and Employment (Forem) may receive financial assistance for hiring staff to be trained by the enterprise. This incentive is also offered to employers who wish to train recruits engaged on indeterminate-duration contracts in the context of the creation, expansion or restructuring of the firm. In addition, Forem is authorised to help defray the training costs of companies which take on new staff to replace persons transferred to work with new production technologies.

At the same time, the Flemish Regional Employment Office was empowered in September 1991 to provide, at the request of an employer, various services designed to assist a worker or a group of workers in finding suitable new employment or in taking advantage of the opportunities for advancement existing within the firm. Further, the Flemish Regional Executive set out in a decree of January 1991 a framework for the provision of training and assistance to independent workers and small and medium-sized enterprises. The measures concerned involve, e.g., apprenticeship, entrepreneurial training, further education and retraining, as well as assistance to independents and SMEs and training in management consultancy.

The same decree establishes a Flemish Institute for the Independent Enterprise, which is responsible for promoting and coordinating training and assistance to firms. Finally, a decree issued in July 1991 by the Executive of the German-speaking Community provides for the establishment of accelerated management courses for heads of enterprises.

In *Denmark*, a Foundation for Industrial Development has been established whose aim is to accelerate the development of new products considered too risky to be carried out without some form of external support. The Foundation has been established with the help of a one-off capital injection of 2 billion Danish kroner, financed mainly by revenues from privatisations. The payment of interest on this capital will be used to co-finance industrial development projects (up to 50 per cent of costs), and capital plus a market rate of interest have to be paid back if the project is successful. In addition, Denmark's Fund for Basic Research was established in 1991, by which it will be possible to increase publicly-funded basic research by 200 million kroner a year. Finally, starting in 1991, enterprises participating in international R&D projects such as the EC R&D programmes or programmes under the Nordic Industry Fund, are allowed to reduce their revenues for tax purposes by 125 per cent of the expenses incurred in their participation in such projects.

With respect to *consultancy services*, a new Act on the Promotion of Industry and Trade has recently come into effect, whose aim is to simplify and coordinate the promotion system. Support for technological services is now given partly as basic support to a number of authorised technological service institutes (including regional technological information centres, and covering on average 10 per cent of their turnover), and partly as project support. As a result of amalgamations and cooperation agreements, the number of authorised technological service institutes has been reduced. Another important element in the new Act on the Promotion of Industry and Trade is the establishment of the Industry and Trade Development Council. In addition to taking over the tasks of other councils and committees now dissolved, it is supposed to play an active role by giving advice to the government on all issues related to industrial policy in the broadest sense of the word.

In terms of *labour-related measures*, the Danish Ministry for Industry published in March 1992 a report on improving conditions for entrepreneurs. The report contains eighteen proposals for improvements in information, consultancy, education, administrative simplifications and financing. In addition, a report on the coordination of vocational adult education and adult training was finalised in May 1992 by a Committee under the Ministry of Labour. The report examines the existing vocational education system and puts forward proposals for its improvement, including suggestions for better coordination between the different ministries and agencies involved.

In *France*, initiatives for the promotion of intangible investment have a high policy priority, and funding for the civil budget for R&D (BCRD) increased by over 7 per cent in 1991 to reach FF 48.7 billion in 1991 [5]. Measures for assisting innovative activities, industrial research or technology development are focused around two axes: support for large national or international innovative projects (through programmes such as EUREKA, or strategic programmes such as JESSI or those for HDTV); and assisting the development of research and the diffusion of technologies in SMEs (through for example the ANVAR agency or the regional innovation and technology transfer centers -- CRITTs).

In *Germany*, the federal government is currently putting emphasis on helping the new *Länder*, in this transition period, to strengthen their research capacities by means of special support measures and to promote efforts by companies to reach the technological level of the industrialised countries in western Europe. These measures focus on support to and promotion of financing of research projects; in-company R&D personnel; co-operation between companies and research institutes from the old and the new *Länder*; joint industrial research; technology-oriented business start-ups; technology parks and business incubators; and with know-how and technology transfer.

In 1992, the federal government is making available DM 180 million for the interim financing of efficient research companies spun off from the former *Kombinats*. In addition, a public research infrastructure is being developed, of which companies are expected to make use. Finally, the federal government is helping to create a network of twenty-two agencies for technology transfer and the promotion of innovation in the new *Länder* which is to be affiliated to appropriate institutions such as the Chamber of Commerce and Industry. Additional transfer agencies will be established for applied technological knowledge.

The federal government is aware that, in the longer run, industry itself must be able to create and maintain market-oriented industrial research capacities. State R&D promotion programmes are subject to regular external and independent evaluation by scientific institutes which contribute to the drafting, implementation and evaluation of the programmes. They also make recommendations on their development.

In terms of measures to promote advisory services to industry, SMEs, in particular in the new *Länder*, are encouraged to make use of industry-related consulting services through the existence of various public grant-related support schemes in the field of consultancy. These entail contributions towards the cost of external consultancies; information and training events; management improvement, further training and information access programmes supported by the Rationalisation Board of German Industry (*Rationalisierungskuratorium der Deutschen Wirtschaft*); and information on framework conditions of a market economy. The involvement of managers and skilled personnel from western Germany in firms in the new *Länder* is also encouraged.

With respect to labour-related measures, the policies pursued by the federal government to assist in the re-integration into working life of unemployed persons and persons faced with imminent unemployment aim to cover a range of needs and situations. A first category concerns General Programmes dealing with training and re-training, Job creation schemes (by communities and non-profit-making organisations), and various wage cost grants to assist in the employment of so-called problem group employees. Such general programmes are supplemented by more targeted schemes dealing with the re-integration of persons such as the long-term unemployed or the young mothers. A third category concerns the employment situation in the new *Länder*, where the difficulties associated with the restructuring and reconstruction period, require especially generous measures of a temporary nature. These measures concern special regulations on short-time work payments (phased out on 31 December 1991, except for structurally weak sectors, where they will remain in place until 31 December 1995), additional promotion of training and re-training (up to 31 December 1992) and a relaxation of the conditions governing granting of support under the job creation schemes (up to 31 December 1992). It should be noted that the companies in the new *Länder* in cases of short-term work since 1 January 1992 have only had to pay 50 per cent of the regular contributions to health and old-age insurance. From 1 July 1992 they will be required to pay 100 per cent of the regular contributions to the health insurance, as in the rest of the country.

In *Italy*, the legal framework for labour mobility was redefined in July 1991. The new measures are intended to adapt the Italian legislation to EC directives concerning collective layoffs due to staff reduction, to conversion or to cessation of activity; to extend the possibility of ordinary application of the Wage Supplementation Fund (*Cassa Integrazione Guadagni*) to clerks and to managers; to remove the dysfunctions associated with the system of long-lasting wage integrations; and to provide for a group of both new and renewed regulations.

In the *Netherlands*, technology policy has in recent years focused on the promotion of collaboration between universities, R&D institutes and industry. For certain scientific disciplines, initiatives have been taken to create centres of excellence. In October 1991, the Innovation Stimulation Scheme (INSTIR) came to an end, while new initiatives on telematics were implemented.

A number of industry-related consulting services are available. Following an assessment study, the programme "quality and logistic management" was prolonged up to 1994. The evaluation concluded that a large number of companies have learned to pay attention to quality-management but that the introduction of integrated quality systems seems to be slow. In the next years, the programme will give special attention to the diffusion of knowledge and in-company environmental control. The programme on "Subcontracting and Outsourcing" has been extended to the end of 1994, also following an evaluation study. Attention will be given to projects in which local subcontractors work for main (international) suppliers, especially on technology and development of new products (see Box 5).

The government has stepped up its efforts towards a more active labour market policy. Following a report of the special Commission on an improved matching between labour supply and demand, an agreement was reached among government and industry concerning the financing of secondary vocational training up to 1994. From the industry side, a commitment was made towards participation in the improvement of such vocational education.

In *Portugal*, the financial incentives provided under PEDIP, the comprehensive set of programmes to improve the competitiveness of the country's industry, have been reformulated so as to place greater emphasis on the quality

---

Box 5. **The subcontracting and outsourcing programme in the Netherlands**

Subcontractors in the Netherlands are facing two major challenges: more stringent requirements from large outsourcing firms and increasing competition. Small and medium scale subcontractors that do not meet these challenges will in time fall by the wayside, and this would considerably weaken the industrial structure.

In 1988, the Netherlands Ministry of Economic Affairs launched the programme "Subcontracting and Outsourcing". This awareness campaign consists of demonstration projects in eight selected product market combinations, such as telecommunication and office equipment, automotive, etc. The programme stimulates subcontractors to improve their operations in the field of just-in-time delivery, logistics and quality-management. The budget for the programme amounts to 35.4 million guilders and covers the period 1988-94.

In 1991, the programme was reviewed. One of the main conclusions was that European outsourcing companies appear to favour long-term relationships with only a selective group of high-quality subcontractors. To achieve such a relationship, two major elements are extremely important: technological innovation -- to keep the company up to date -- and a willingness to co-operate. Nevertheless, forms of co-operation such as joint production are not without problems.

For this reason, the scope of the programme "Subcontracting and Outsourcing" has been modified in order to promote mutual co-operation between main contractors and subcontractors within the subcontracting pyramid. As a result, two categories of projects are part of this demonstration programme:

- mutual co-operation in the field of technology and product development;
- improvement projects in the field of just-in-time delivery, logistics and quality-management.

of the projects supported. More weight is to be given to considerations such as the technological content of the activities concerned, the investment to be carried out in modernisation and innovation, and the prospects for long-term competitiveness. At the same time, the incentives under the National System of Quality Management have been restructured with a view to enhancing producer and consumer awareness of industrial design and quality, to developing a specific management capability in this area, and to creating conditions for mutual recognition as between different systems and institutions involved in certification.

Another scheme geared to improving competitiveness -- the Productivity Missions programme -- has undergone modification. In particular, the programme's activities concerned with co-operation, subcontracting and partnerships have been restructured in order to accelerate the establishment of co-operative networks bringing together firms sharing common goals with respect to marketing and distribution, production, supply, and quality and design. Finally, Science and Technology Parks are being set up in the Porto and Lisbon metropolitan areas.

In *Spain*, an Industrial Technology Action Plan has been drawn up for the period 1991 though 1993 with a view to raising the R&D effort towards the levels prevailing in the country's more advanced EC partners and to improving the technological balance of payments (see Box 6). The plan aims at process and product development and diffusion in priority sectors and regions so as to enhance the international competitiveness of Spanish enterprises. This entails: an increase and a qualitative improvement in the human and technical resources devoted to R&D, particularly in SMEs; the channelling of R&D resources to regions having a priority status because of their economic growth prospects; the involvement of more firms in in-house innovating activity; and an enhancement of the capacity of enterprises to assimilate advanced technologies through an improvement in their R&D potential.

Box 6. Spain: Technological Action Plan

The Spanish government has approved a Technological Action Plan developed by the Ministry of Industry, Trade and Tourism for the period 1991-93. The plan focuses on technological support for industrial enterprises in view of the Single European Market. It follows and co-ordinates industrial activities in advanced technologies (electronics, biotechnology, materials, etc.) and complements them with lines of action applied to the infrastructure, to training of research personnel and to the diffusion of technological advances. Its essential lines of action are as follows:

- Direct support to project development;
- Fostering of technical and human resources;
- Co-ordination of R&D efforts;
- Build up of infrastructure for servicing innovation firms;
- Internationalisation of Spanish technology;
- Institutional support for technological development.

The new Technological Action Plan is implemented by means of the following sub-plans:

- Electronics and information national plan;
- Industrial advanced automation plan;
- Research promotion plan in the pharmaceutical industry;
- Technological development plan in biotechnology, chemical technologies and materials;
- Plan for technological support to basic and manufacturing industrial sectors;
- Technological infrastructure plan;
- Programme for technical and specialised training and firms.

This basic framework is complemented with two other specific programmes: a programme for technological development in environmental activities; and the Industrial Property Office Programme for Support to Business.

The elaboration of this framework follows from the awareness of the need for complementary efforts to participate in the initial phase of the Single Market in a better competitive position, in areas where the technological development efforts have not yet reached a sufficient competitive maturity and strength.

Various specific measures are designed to implement the plan, including assistance provided to firms, coordination of the overall R&D endeavour to avoid duplication of effort, creation of a research infrastructure with respect to R&D services and training, and steps to encourage the internationalisation of the Spanish technological effort.

A number of sectoral sub-plans have been established under the general Industrial Technology Action Plan. These cover such fields as electronics and information technology; advanced automation; pharmaceuticals; biotechnology, chemicals and materials; and basic industries. The budget of the Industrial Technology Action Plan amounts to Ptas 58 000 million in assistance to R&D projects, in the form of subsidies and loans.

In the meantime, a Technological Infrastructure Plan was adopted in 1991 in order to improve the technological infrastructure for R&D, the relevant training activities and the general climate for technological endeavour. In addition, the tax deduction allowed on R&D investments was raised in 1992.

Alongside their efforts to raise the technological level of industry, the Spanish authorities are pursuing a related objective: integration of quality considerations into Spanish industry as a factor of competitiveness, especially in the context of the Single European Market. A National Plan for Industrial Quality, in effect from 1990 through 1993, seeks to achieve this aim by promoting: the utilisation of goods and services of recognised quality, recognition of the quality of Spanish products abroad, improved quality control in enterprises, and the fuller development of the relevant technical infrastructure. The last-mentioned policy thrust involves standardisation, certification, testing laboratories, measurement and control. The government is also endeavouring to strengthen existing provisions for ensuring the safety of industrial products and processes; and it is envisaged that an Industrial Safety Plan, linked to the Quality Plan, will be developed between 1992 and 1995.

In parallel to the efforts described above, the government is also carrying out policies to enhance industrial performance through counselling and training in management know-how and labour skills. A major concern of Spanish policy is the adjustment of industry to the opportunities and challenges presented by the Single European Market, a programme has been set up to assist firms in resorting to outside consultants for help in diagnosing their strategic situation, particularly in the light of the development of the Single Market.

In the area of *training*, a programme has been set up for a three-year period (1991 through 1993) to promote Technical and Industrial Qualification in the Enterprise. This programme, also established largely with a view to the industrial adjustment required by the integrated European market, provides support for training staff responsible for enterprise functions such as management, business strategy, production and technological development.

In the *United Kingdom*, a number of programmes are carried out in implementation of the main R&D policy focus of the Department of Trade and Industry: the encouragement of pre-competitive collaborative research. In this connection, the following can be noted:

- There are at present thirty programmes under LINK, a government-wide initiative for collaborative research associating industry with the science base. The fields dealt with include electronics and communications; food and agriculture; bio-science and medicine; materials and chemicals; measurement and sensing; and engineering. Total funding is some £370 million, including both government and industry financing.

- Seventeen Advanced Technology Programmes (ATPs), which promote longer-term collaborative research so far. They cover areas such as advanced computing, high-temperature superconductivity and advanced robotics. Since 1988 the DTI has approved grants totalling £185 million for this activity.

- A number of activities not covered by the two schemes mentioned above bring together companies, especially small and medium-sized enterprises, within the ambit of the General Industrial Collaborative Projects.

A recent DTI initiative to promote innovation is SPUR (Support for Products under Research), launched in March 1991. SPUR provides a fixed-level grant up to a maximum of £150 000 for single-company new product and process development projects which demonstrate significant technical advance. Over £32 million has been made available for applications received from industry over the next three years.

A number of schemes have been designed specifically to encourage SMEs (see also section C) to embark upon technological innovation. One of these is the MPI (Manufacturing Planning and Implementation Studies Programme), which helps smaller firms pay for external experts to assist them in planning the use of advanced manufacturing technologies. Some £11 million in government funding is being earmarked for this programme up to February 1994. At the same time, SMART (Small Firms Merit Award for Research and Technology) offers, on the basis of an annual competition open to individuals or businesses with fewer than 50 employees, grants to support innovative technological projects. In February 1992, a further three-year programme of competitions was launched with funding of £42 million.

A policy area of key importance in 1992 comprises measures to encourage the exploitation of the UK's strong academic science base for industrial purposes. Government instruments for furthering that objective include not only the LINK collaborative research, mentioned above, but also the Teaching Company Scheme which seeks to improve industrial performance through the effective use of academic knowledge and expertise.

In the same context, two schemes announced in October 1991 to promote the commercial exploitation of the research resources of higher education institutions seek, respectively, to help these institutions conduct audits of the resources available to them for specific research projects as well as of their organisational structure and to strengthen their industrial units or, in a few cases, to create such units where they do not already exist.

Finally, increasing importance is attached to international technological collaboration exemplified inter alia by UK participation in a number of European programmes. Of the 495 currently approved EUREKA projects, for example, UK organisations are taking part in 129, with an estimated total value of £2.7 billion. One should also note UK participation in the new European Community TELEMATICS programme launched at the beginning of 1992 to further information technology penetration in selected sectors, as well as in ESPRIT, which was to begin its third phase in the summer of 1992. In a wider international context, DTI has initiated an Engineers to Japan Scheme to send industrial engineers from the UK to that country in order to broaden their experience by working in Japanese firms.

Assistance with consultancy services continues to be a strong policy area. The Consultancy Help scheme aims to improve the competitiveness of SMEs (see also section C) by offering subsidised consultancy services in order to encourage the use of expert outside advice in key management functions as a regular part of management strategy. The areas covered include business planning, design, quality, manufacturing and services systems, marketing and financial and management information systems. The scheme provides a subsidy of 50 per cent of consultants' fees (two thirds in Assisted and Urban Programme Areas) and is available to individual firms with fewer than 500 employees in most manufacturing and service sectors. The budget allocation for 1991-92 is £59 million.

With respect to the improvement of the human resources available to business and industry, the government published in May 1991 a White Paper on Education and Training for the 21st Century, which announces a range of measures to encourage young people to develop their full potential, whether through work-based training or continuing education or a mix of both. At the same time, work has continued towards attainment of the objectives set out in the 1988 White Paper, Employment for the 1990s. One of the main achievements in this regard has been the completion of the full network of 82 employer-led, locally-based Training and Enterprise Councils (TECs), and the 22 local enterprise companies in Scotland, responsible for the planning and delivery of government training programmes (see also section C).

On the business side, the Confederation of British Industry (CBI), in association with others in the business and training world, has issued national education and training guidelines, geared to qualifications based on the acquisition and assessment of relevant skills in the workplace.

Other recent developments related to training and the development of human resources include the following:

- The Investors in People programme, initiated by the National Training Task Force, in association with the TECs, the CBI and other organisations, has now recognised thirty firms as qualified Investors in People, and over 600 companies have made a commitment to work towards the specified national Standard for action to develop human resources.

- At the end of 1991, some 270 000 young people were enrolled in the Youth Training Programme, launched in 1990 with a view to providing broad vocational education and training, mainly for 16 and 17-year-olds, and to producing better qualified entrants to the labour market.

- The operational phase of eleven pilot projects, covering about 10 per cent of 16 and 17-year-old school leavers under the Training Credits Initiative, began in April 1991. This programme, announced in March 1990, offers an entitlement for young people who have left full-time education to purchase training relevant to their employment aspirations. The next round of credit schemes is to start in April 1992, covering another ten per cent of school leavers.

- More flexible arrangements for the Employment Training scheme, launched in 1988 to provide individually tailored training for the long-term unemployed, were introduced in 1990-91 to allow TECs to respond better to local labour markets. Some 139 000 persons were training under ET at the end of 1991.

- Employment Action is a new initiative begun in October 1991, offering temporary work of community interest to long-term unemployed people who wish to maintain their vocational skills. It provides an alternative to Employment Training for those who do not want or need training towards an occupational qualification.

In *Austria*, in keeping with the shift away from physical investment support towards aid for intangible investments, 77 per cent of all financing accorded in 1991 under the TOP programmes of the Ministry for Economic Affairs was aimed at furthering innovation and technology transfer. Moreover, the financial level of federal assistance has been further reduced, the outlays earmarked for the investment activities concerned amounting to Sch. 1.1 billion annually for the period 1991-94. The Austrian authorities consider that the shift in the focal point of investment support, along with the moderate levels of aid given and the primarily SME character of the beneficiaries, brings the country's programmes into line with EC criteria.

Assistance for industrial R&D, innovation and technology diffusion is granted through a number of special funds. During the year under review, grants by the Research Promotion Fund for the Economy (FFF), totalling some Sch. 1 billion, went to 465 projects, the major part of the aid being allotted to electrical engineering, chemicals, machinery and steel products. The textiles industry, a sector important to Austria but deficient in research, was also given preference in 1991. And for the first time, some of the financing under this Fund was set aside to encourage participation in European R&D projects. This aid, combined with assistance from the Innovation and Technology Fund (ITF), made it possible to subsidise, to the extent of about Sch. 128 million, Austrian participation in 48 international research projects (COST, EUREKA and various EC research and technology programmes).

Some of the key projects financed by the above-mentioned Innovation and Technology Fund (ITF) recently became operational; these deal with laser technology, space technology and flexible, computer-integrated production by SMEs. Previous focal points of ITF-supported R&D such as environment technology and new materials have been maintained.

At the same time, the Research Promotion Council (FFR) which sets technological priorities, has given preference to projects of particular significance to Austrian technological development that are carried out in co-operation between industry and the universities. The Council has so far approved four main R&D subject areas: the reliability of mechanical systems; laser technology for materials-working processes; equipment and methodology for medical diagnosis, therapy and rehabilitation; and computer-aided simulation of highly complex technological processes.

In *Finland*, the growth of national R&D expenditures in real terms has averaged over 10 per cent annually, bringing the ratio of R&D to GDP to 2 per cent. The government's target is to raise this ratio to 2.7 per cent of GDP by 1997. This implies annual real increases of 7 to 9 per cent for public and private R&D expenditures. R&D appropriations in the approved 1992 budget have increased in accordance to this objective. More generally, public measures to improve enterprise capabilities in the development and application of new technologies are encouraging the formation of networks of enterpreneurial services, the diffusion and application of new technology by means of programmes to be implemented in technology centers and the development of risk financing. Government support for the provision of industry-related consulting services operates through grants from the Ministry of Trade and Industry (in operation since 1989), although the amounts involved are modest.

With respect to labour-related measures, and in response to higher unemployment levels, the weight of public support in budgetary terms has moved towards passive labour market measures such as unemployment compensation. Nevertheless, appropriations for the development of manpower services, vocational training and adult education have also increased in recent years.

In *Norway*, the governmental R&D budget in 1991 (totalling 7.3 million Norwegian kroner) was slightly lower than the preceding year, but expected to record a real growth in 1992 of 4 per cent, reflecting the general policy aimed at strengthening the R&D sector. The public technological-industrial research system is undergoing a number of organisational changes that should simplify it and make it more accessible to users. These involve the merging of the existing five research councils into the Norwegian Research Council, the concentration of technological research institutes into regional units and the consolidation of support into fewer and larger R&D programmes, while giving users more influence in the design of research projects. Budgetary allocations for R&D contracts have increased, reaching 112 million Norwegian kroner in 1991, while this type of programme underwent an evaluation in 1991 with positive results. In terms of international co-operation, after partial participation in the EC's second framework programme of research, Norway intends to participate as a full member in the third EC framework programme, provided the negotiations on the European Economic Area come to a successful conclusion.

Government support for consultancy services in Norway is mainly concentrated in SMEs or given as part of regional policy (see relevant sections). Labour market measures, as in the preceding year, have been stepped up in order to meet the increasing rates of unemployment in general, and the rates of long term and youth unemployment in particular. Out of 170 000 unemployed persons in 1991, 49 300 of them were enrolled in different kinds of labour market programmes, mostly in higher education and vocational training. After these rapid increases in enrolment, Norway now allocates more resources to active labour market policies than most other OECD countries.

In *Sweden*, support for industry-related R&D is an explicit objective of the industrial and technology policy of the newly-elected government. Participation in the EC's R&D programmes is being promoted as an important means of acquiring technological know-how, and the funding for participation in these programmes has increased. Concerning labour-related measures, the new government intends to reinforce the active labour market policies that have been implemented in recent years. Active job referral, guidance and training have become important tools to combat the rising unemployment. Training is provided for those unemployed, in order to facilitate a change of occupation or as on-the-job training. The aim of on-the-job training is to overcome occupational bottlenecks and utilise the experience of the existing workforce. In addition, grants are provided for the compensation of job-related moving or costs related to job-seeking.

In the area of support for the provision of industry-related consultative services, a committee of experts, appointed in 1989 in order to investigate why productivity gains were comparatively weak in the 1980s, presented its final report in 1991 (see Box 7). The report casts light over areas where productivity gains have been particularly poor, and points out areas where concrete action could improve future productivity prospects.

In *Switzerland*, the six priority research programmes for which the Federal Council had requested SF357 million for the period 1992-1995 (see the 1991 *Annual Review*) have been approved by Parliament. However, in view of the deterioration in the Confederation's finances and the cuts made in the 1992 budget, the appropriations for this activity in 1992 have been reduced by about half. The possibility of a linear reduction of 10 per cent for the remaining three years has not been ruled out. The budgetary restrictions will limit the extent to which the government is able to contribute to the development of Switzerland's scientific potential by, inter alia, improving the links between fundamental and oriented research and between the economy and the universities and other research bodies.

Box 7. Productivity in Sweden: Restoring the growth potential

Lagging productivity growth in Sweden prompted the government to appoint in 1989 an advisory panel to investigate the background to the slow growth of productivity and to provide policy-makers with the foundations of a policy for promoting growth. The panel's conclusions and recommendations, presented at the end of 1991, are summarised below [1].

Causes of the lagging productivity growth

In attempting to identify the causes of the slowdown in productivity growth, the panel distinguished between factors accounting for the exceptional drop in productivity in the mid-70s and after the mid-80s and longer term structural problems. Short-term factors explaining the depth of stagnation in the 1970s included the heavy dependence on oil and an energy-heavy industrial structure which amplified the impact of the oil crises. During the 1980s, the structure of stabilisation policy was an important reason for the fluctuation in productivity over time. Two big currency devaluations briefly boosted productivity by raising capacity utilisation, but also reduced pressure for structural change.

In addition to cyclical factors, the panel identified a long-term weakening of the forces of productivity: the combined effect of wage formation, taxation and transfer payments and currency policy was to weaken the link between inputs for production and real payments. Motivation for new capital formation weakened, as devaluations rewarded companies with high profits which they had not had to fight for by increasing productivity, and thus put a premium on existing operations. The pace of structural reform slackened; the movement in the Swedish pattern of specialisation towards production with a high level of real and human capital was broken in the 1980s.

Structural problems adversely affected the formation of human and real capital and the efficiency of resource utilisation. Problems with the educational system resulted in skill shortages. Taxation of small businesses may also have had a negative impact on the willingness to invest, while the taxation system on borrowing and saving had powerful distorting effects. Resource allocation was also adversely affected by regulatory provisions in certain sectors, and by the weak competition in the public sector. Finally, the small volume of incoming foreign investment implied less capital and new technology and reduced competitive pressures.

A strategy for higher productivity

The Advisory Council on Productivity made a number of recommendations both to industry and to the State. These were based on the premise that Swedish productivity problems have a number of causes; thus, no single sweeping formula or solution exists. A variety of measures are thus needed so as to increase the forces underpinning increased productivity, improve the quality of factors of production and enhance the efficiency of utilisation of resources.

In its recommendations to industry, the panel emphasised the importance of modern work organisation for bringing about productivity benefits. The importance of shorter chains of command, more teamwork, job rotation, and better personnel education as an integral part of work were stressed, as were instituting a productivity-promoting system of rewards.

> Box 7 *(cont).* **Productivity in Sweden: Restoring the growth potential**
>
> By the nature of its task, however, most of the panel's recommendations were reserved for the State. The task of government is to design the framework and to help create the necessary conditions for long-term growth, by using instruments such as taxes, transfers, legislation, infrastructure, and education. This implies a stable stabilisation policy that does not "accomodate" corporate profitability problems. It also involves a number of measures aimed at motivating the formation of physical and human capital, and technological and organisational renewal.
>
> Central to these measures is the encouragement of internationalisation and the opening up of more sectors to competition. The panel urges gaining access to the EC single market, as well as maintaining a firm, credible exchange rate, as devaluations weaken the incentives for improved productivity. In order to increase competition, it proposes *inter alia* the automatic revision of regulatory provisions every three years, the reduction or abolition of some regulations in agriculture and in the construction industry, the break-up of concentration in the food sector, and deregulation of domestic air services and long-distance bus services.
>
> Strengthening incentives for the build-up of human capital involves the modernisation of work organisation, the reform of wage-setting, rewarding initiative and responsibility, and the expansion and improvement of education. Given its size and role in the economy, the renewal of the public sector is important in this context: its productivity can be stimulated through more efficient work organisation, while keeping pressure on costs.
>
> In order to improve incentives for the formation of physical capital, the panel recommends a number of measures to streamline the capital market and augment savings, to improve the productivity of the existing capital stock, and to modernise and expand the infrastructure. Examples are the revision of the pension system, a reduction of taxation on savings, the amendment of rules on companies takeovers to increase foreign investment, and the expansion and renewal of road and rail networks.
>
> Finally, in terms of technology development, the panel's recommendations put an emphasis on the diffusion of innovations to the business sector, by the elimination of impediments to the mobility of financial capital, skilled labour and managerial competence, and access to an efficient venture capital market. The State should concentrate on the early stage of the technology development process and on projects with a long-term and risky nature.
>
> 1. Advisory Panel on Productivity (1991), "Forces of Productivity and Prosperity", Swedish Ministry for Industry and Commerce.

Parliament has also approved a SF150 million Confederation contribution to the Swiss Microelectronics programme, the total cost of which is estimated at SF245 million for a six-year period. Aimed at improving the qualifications of engineering school graduates and the performance of Swiss industry in the application of microelectronics, the programme provides, in its initial phase, for the establishment of four to six skill centres in which several engineering schools are to be associated. In a second phase, the centres will receive support from the two federal polytechnic schools.

In the meantime, the CIM (computer-integrated manufacturing) programme, approved by Parliament in 1990, became fully operational in 1991 upon the establishment of seven decentralised training centres. This scheme, designed in particular to promote the adoption of CIM technologies in SMEs, brings into play the concerted efforts of the Confederation, all the cantons and a wide range of schools and universities as well as economic organisations. Some 1000 firms have already manifested an interest in the programme and about 100 projects, involving a total cost of SF72 million, are under way.

In the area of technology transfer, sixteen Swiss institutions with close links to the higher technical schools or regional industry assistance bodies have created a videotex facility providing information on services available in this field as well as setting up a technology exchange open to research institution technology suppliers and industrial users. Technology demand emanating from the European TII (Technology, Innovation, Information) network is also disseminated by the Swiss Videotex.

With respect to the human resource requirements of industry, the administration is currently preparing the legal framework for a special vocational diploma to be awarded upon passage of a test to be taken at the same time as the final examination of the basic vocational training course. It is considered that the new diploma will facilitate the access of meritorious students to the higher technical schools.

The programme instituted in 1990 to alleviate skilled manpower shortages through special training and skill upgrading measures is being allotted overall financing of SF162 million for the period 1990-96. The scheme has enabled engineering schools to offer post-graduate programmes in specific fields. It also provides support for the development of new occupational courses, the ex post qualification of persons not having followed the usual occupational training programmes and the training of foreigners and women, in particular women wishing to re-enter the labour market after having withdrawn to devote themselves to family occupations.

A number of social measures taken in response to the deterioration of the labour market situation should also be noted -- e.g., the prolongation of unemployment insurance eligibility rights, the simplification of controls in cantons suffering from particularly high unemployment, the amendment of the unemployment insurance system so as to improve the lot of the unemployed while augmenting their chances of finding work.

In *Australia*, the tax concession for R&D will be indefinitely extended after June 1993 at a level of 125 per cent of R&D expenditure. Deduction of up to 150 per cent had been in place during several years. Although the tax concession is broad-based and available to the majority of companies undertaking R&D in Australia, projects must meet Australian content provisions. The estimated gross cost to revenue of the incentive in 1990-91, in terms of company tax foregone, was A$265 million. An evaluation of the cost effectiveness of the scheme is currently carried out by the Bureau of Industry Economics (BIE). The initial impact study suggests that the tax concession has had a positive effect on R&D budgets and on the amount of reported R&D. The study will be completed at the end of 1992 and will make recommendations about its continued application and eventual changes to improve its effectiveness.

In addition to the tax concession, the Grants for Industry Research and Development (GIRD) Scheme has been prolonged, with a budget for 1991-92 of A$32.2 million, comparable to the allocation in previous years. The Scheme, introduced as a complement to the tax incentive, supports pre-competitive strategic R&D in specific generic technologies. Two types of grants may be provided: discretionary, available to companies unable to derive adequate benefit from the tax concession (e.g because they have no taxable income), or generic, for the development of technologies where commercial returns are difficult to capture. After a review of the Scheme in 1991, support continues to be available for R&D in biotechnology, information technology, and communications technology, while manufacturing and materials technology, and environmental technology have been added to the list of eligible areas.

A number of other programmes are also in operation. The infrastructure supporting innovation and the commercialisation of research have been strengthened by the establishment in 1991 of twenty more centres in the context of the Cooperative Research Centres Programme, established in 1990 (see the 1991 *Annual Review*). The National Procurement Development Programme (NPDP) assists Australian companies research, develop, trial and demonstrate products and services required by government. The programme provides grants for up to 50 per cent of total eligible project costs. Funds allocated for 1991-92 are A$7.4 million. Finally, in terms of international collaboration, the feasibility study for the Multifunction Polis (MFP) project has been completed and the project is under way. The MFP will be an international complex acting as a focus for scientific, technological and cultural activities.

In terms of improving the human capital into production processes, the government embarked on a training reform agenda some years ago, aimed at increasing the quality, flexibility and skills development of the workforce. It is aimed at the establishment of a national framework for competence-based training (which will be implemented from 1993), a new national framework for accreditation and curriculum development and a unified entry-level training system. At the same time the Training Guarantee Scheme (TGS) was introduced, as a targeted measure aimed at improving the efforts of firms which do not invest adequately in training. Under the scheme, employers with a national payroll of US$214 000 or more at 1 July 1991 (indexed annually) are required to spend the equivalent of 1 per cent of their payroll on eligible training activities (1.5 per cent from July 1992). The scheme covers private and public sector employers.

B. Policies directed at industrial sectors

During the 1970s and early 1980s, the sectoral component of industrial policy was generally the most important. Measures to promote industrial activities would in most OECD countries be in general directed either towards industries in decline, or towards promising activities, usually in high technology industries. The recent evolution of industrial policy towards more horizontal measures and towards improving the quality of inputs to industry in general has diminished the importance of sectoral programmes in the overall design of industrial policy.

Despite however this shift in the philosophy and practice of policy, measures directed at industrial sectors are still very much in existence. The primary reason is that difficulties in the adaptation of certain industries to rapid structural changes have led many governments to continue to support certain industrial activities largely for social

Table 6. **Financing pattern of reported sectoral policies**

Financing instrument	Shares (%)				Economic costs subsidised	Shares (%)			
	1986	1987	1988	1989		1986	1987	1988	1989
Grants	59.4	41.3	49.6	65.8	Production	36.6	24.1	27.3	39.9
Loans	0.4	0.4	0.2	0.2	General Investment	44.7	60.4	52.3	35.7
Guarantees	3.9	0.7	1.7	5.3	Specific Investment	2.1	1.5	2.1	2.1
Equity capital	4.6	38.4	23.4	2.1	Export-related	..	..	..	..
Tax concessions	1.2	0.8	0.6	0.6	Non-profit	0.0	0.02	0.02	0.02
Mixed instr.	30.5	18.4	24.5	25.9	R&D	16.6	14.0	18.3	22.3
Total	100.0	100.0	100.0	100.0	Total	100.0	100.0	100.0	100.0

Source: OECD, Industrial Subsidies database, March 1992.

reasons. The second reason is that in the intensified international competition, many governments still perceive gains in supporting certain industries that are considered strategic to industrial development and international competitiveness.

Not all measures directed at industrial sectors have the same economic costs. Some, while focused on particular activities, aim at enhancing the quality of inputs and the infrastructure. Such measures are usually addressed at market failures and do not distort the allocation of resources. In effect, the differential take-up rates of such policy measures of a horizontal character blurs the line between what is a horizontal and what a sectoral approach to industrial policy. At the same time however, there are a number of sectoral policies in existence in OECD Member countries that artificially attempt to shield certain industries from international competition and thus distort the allocation of resources. In the current recessionary environment, there is a resurgence of these defensive-type sectoral policies which can only retard the necessary adaptations in different countries to cope with shifts in comparative advantage.

The recently completed first phase of the OECD Industrial Subsidies database provides a good overview of sector-specific policies of 22 Member countries during the 1986-89 period. During that period, sector-specific policies mainly targeted declining sectors and/or sectors exposed to fierce international competition. Support offered by several governments to high-technology areas was -- for the most part -- centered around specific technologies and not confined to specific industrial sectors; they were therefore not reported as sectoral policies (aid to the aerospace industry being the principal exception to this). However, in spite of the fact that defensive sectoral policies seem to have lost ground in most countries in the 1980s, total reported expenditures for sectoral policies did not tangibly decrease throughout the period: they gravitated around US$5 billion yearly, with an exceptional peak of around US$6 billion in 1987.

Most sectoral programmes target the shipbuilding industry, and a significant number of programmes address the steel, textiles, and automobile sectors. A smaller number of programmes serve the aerospace and electronics industries. If, in a tentative and preliminary assessment, programmes dealing primarily with adjustment difficulties due to international competition are considered separately from programmes encouraging new-technology-based sectors, it can be observed that the former represent the bulk of sectoral expenditures, although the proportion diminishes over time. Such adjustment programmes accounted for 78 per cent of total sectoral expenditures in 1986, 80 per cent in 1987, 75 per cent in 1988 and 68 per cent in 1989. In contrast, aid to new-technology-based sectors (including aerospace) represented around 22 per cent, 20 per cent, 25 per cent and 32 per cent of total reported expenditures for the respective years.

The overall financing pattern of sectoral policies is displayed in Table 6. Sectoral programmes mostly utilise grants, and a significant fraction use *ad hoc* combinations of mixed instruments. They primarily subsidise general investment costs and direct current production costs (for sectors facing intense international competition). Current production subsidies play a much larger role in this policy area than in others. A notable trend during the period 1986-89 has been the net increase in the share of R&D subsidies.

Some recent developments in government policies addressed to industrial sectors are outlined below.

In *Canada*, a private sector panel on the North American automotive industry, established jointly by Canada and the United States in 1989 in accordance with the Free Trade Agreement, was to report to the two governments during the second half of 1991, but has delayed its submission to mid-1992. The panel was assigned to assess the state of the industry and to propose public policy measures and private sector initiatives for improving competitiveness.

With a view to a successful Uruguay Round agreement reintegrating textiles and clothing trade into normal GATT rules within ten years, and the prospective creation of a North American Free Trade Area, the main thrust of federal policy for this sector has been to implement a framework of measures to help the industry compete internationally without special protection. This framework contains initiatives in the trade, industrial and labour areas.

In the *trade* area, the major focus is on improving access to the US market and developing free access to the Mexican market under the FTA and NAFTA respectively. Another focus is on the provision of strategic market intelligence and export marketing advice to help the industry to take optimal advantage of the export opportunities offered by the NAFTA as well as to expand its activity in other international markets following the conversion of the Multilateral Fibre Arrangement. An additional objective is to bring the textiles tariff structure into line with that of Canada's main trading partners in order to improve the competitive cost position of the clothing and other major textile product manufacturers.

In the *industrial* area, the emphasis is on helping the industry develop market strategies through the provision of information, counselling and financial support. Further, the creation of productive partnerships and networks among manufacturers, designers, suppliers and customers is encouraged.

In the *labour* area, the focus is on encouraging industry-led initiatives for human resource development and on promoting more effective linkages between industry, educational and training institutions, and governments.

Within the overall policy context indicated above, the fashion apparel branch was selected for one of a series of sector campaigns aimed at improving competitiveness. A campaign plan for this branch was completed and was under consideration for full implementation in 1992.

The Canadian International Trade Tribunal (CITT) has completed an investigation into the competitive state of the fresh and processed fruit and vegetable industries. This enquiry, the first of its kind to be undertaken by the CITT, was made at the request of the industries concerned, and the findings were expected to be issued in mid-February 1992. In autumn 1991, the CITT also undertook to review Canadian policy concerning the allocation of import quota permits for food products under the Import Control Act. Policy recommendations by the CITT were expected in late 1992.

In addition, an Agricultural Policy Review (APR), undertaken in 1989, was concluded in 1991, and the government was reviewing recommendations emerging from the review and seeking to implement some specific recommendations. An Agri-Food Competitiveness Council, consisting of private sector representatives and government observers, has been set up to continue the progress on competitiveness issues begun in the APR.

On a broader front, sector competitive initiatives (sector campaigns), which attempt to improve the competitive position of selected industries where analysis indicates significant benefits may be expected, are being implemented in some dozen sectors. In addition to those previously announced (see the 1991 *Annual Review*), campaigns have been approved for commercial education and training and for photonics.

In the *European Community*, a number of communications by the European Commission have followed the benchmark communication *Industrial Policy in an Open and Competitive Environment* (COM(90)556), issued in November 1990. The first of these (April 1991 -- SEC(91)565) dealt with the issues at stake and proposals for action regarding the European electronics and information technology industry (see last year's *Annual Review*). Also during April 1991, the Commission issued a communication on *Promoting the Competitive Environment for the Industrial Activities Based on Biotechnology within the Community*. The communication defines a Community framework for industrial activities related to biotechnology, and lists a series of measures deemed necessary to encourage the competitiveness of industries using such new technologies, including proposals in the areas of intellectual property legislation, the legal framework, standards and ethics.

The maritime and textile industries are two other sectors where the European Commission sought to apply the general principles of the EC industrial policy approach. *New Challenges for the Maritime Industries* (COM(91)335) stresses the common industrial, commercial and environmental interests of industries ranging from armaments, shipbuilding, and maritime equipment to maritime services and the exploration of natural resources, notably fisheries. The communication calls for a strengthening of the maritime industry, parts of which are facing structural adjustment problems, and the creation of a discussion forum consisting of all interested parties. *Improving the Competitiveness of the Community's Textile and Clothing Industries* (COM(91)399) considers the current challenges faced by this industry and the actions that the Community could take to encourage further structural adjustment. It emphasises in particular the importance of the acceleration of the diversification process in regions heavily dependent on textiles and clothing. Concerning the international context, much weight is attached to the satisfactory conclusion of multilateral and bilateral negotiations. It should be recalled that the multifibre agreement, managing trade flows in this industry between developed and developing countries, will cease to exist at the end of December 1992.

In *Denmark*, a Network Scheme for Tourism has been in force since 1 June 1991. Its aim is to improve the viability of the Danish tourist trade by establishing vertical and horizontal networks. Vertical networks eligible for support are those promoting the development of tourist destinations, and consisting of different parts of the tourist trade and/or crossing municipality or county borders. Horizontal networks aim to promote the establishment of chains, composed for instance of companies and institutions within the same line of business. Support under the scheme is granted for preliminary or feasibility studies, planning, or for the establishment and operation of projects. The Network Scheme is expected to run until the end of 1993 on a budget of approximately 50 million Danish kroner.

In *Germany*, there are sectoral policy measures in two areas: aerospace and shipbuilding. In the case of the aerospace industry, such a policy has been in existence for some time. In the case of the shipbuilding industry, past federal policies for the shipbuilding industry located in the western part had to be pursued and supplemented in favour of the shipbuilding industry in the new *Länder*. In all other cases, including the car and steel industries, the federal government makes great efforts to enhance the interest of potential foreign and domestic investors in the new *Länder*. Financial support to investment is granted within the framework of the general programmes (including necessary capacity reduction).

The German aerospace industry continues to strengthen its international, especially European, co-operation in both the civil and the military areas and the aircraft and space segments. All of its major programmes are shared with European partners, e.g. Airbus or large-scale space infrastructure projects like Columbus, Hermes, Ariane 5. Additional company alliances have been inherited by the industries, e.g. Eurocopter or the BMW/Rolls Royce joint venture.

The federal government is about to review its policies in at least four areas: (i) civil aircraft: whether to support and to what extent the future regional aircraft (90 to 120 seater), within the framework of existing support schemes and in line with GATT stipulations; (ii) the extent of the co-operation with non-ESA countries in the case of the large-scale space projects (an issue to be considered at the ESA Council of Ministers meeting in Spain); (iii) the extent of federal support to civil developments of the NH 90; and iv) whether to purchase the European Fighter Aircraft for its Armed Forces.

In the shipbuilding industry, the federal government continues to consider that persistent distortions of competition on the international shipbuilding market require it to continue its aid to western firms in the form of the shipyard aid (*Werfthilfe*) i.e. an interest rate subsidy (federal support amounts to DM 950 million for deliveries in 1990-92 and DM 700 million for deliveries in 1993-95); and its competition promotion support (*Wettbewerbshilfe*), whose ceilings were reduced from 14.9 per cent in 1990 to 9.5 per cent in 1991 i.e. below the ceilings authorised by the EC in both years (with joint federal, 2/3, and *Länder*, 1/3, support amounting to DM 1 000 million for contracts concluded between 1 July 1987 and 31 December 1990, and DM 450 million for contracts concluded in 1991 and 1992).

The EC Council has agreed on special measures for eastern German shipyards as an exception to the 7th Shipbuilding Directive which were due to pass through the legislative procedure in July 1992. Central elements of the agreement are grants of up to a maximum of 36 per cent of average turnover linked to a severe (40 per cent) capacity reduction for the eastern German shipyards. The programme ends in 1993.

In *Greece*, the government submitted for approval to the European Commission a 5-year plan for the restructuring and modernisation of the Greek textile and clothing industry. The plan aims at securing the future viability of activities in the industry by achieving the necessary degree of labour and product specialisation for the evolution of the industry towards the manufacture of high quality products in segments where a comparative advantage exists (such as cotton).

The proposed plan covers the following aspects: (i) modernisation, with a number of initiatives for the modernisation of equipment throughout the production chain of textiles and and clothing; (ii) labour-related measures, with funds earmarked for education and training programmes as well as proposed measures for retraining the labour force; (iii) technical assistance, outlining Research and Technology centers and their services to the industry; and (iv) design, distribution and promotion activities. The suggested financing requirements for the plan's implementation are estimated at 1.9 million ECUs. As the government expects that in the process of its implementation, the restructuring plan will entail job losses in the industry, this figure includes the costing out of initiatives aimed at minimising the social costs involved.

In *Italy*, in the context of the steel industry restructuring plan, new rules have been put in place in order to regulate the supply of funds. The target of the plan are small and medium-sized enterprises, which can obtain contributions for 25 per cent of their total investment costs up to the amount of 700 million lire, and for 80 per cent of their services purchases up to 30 million Lire.

In the *Netherlands*, broad support is given to the implementation of High Definition Television (HDTV). An important step towards the introduction of HDTV, to be fully implemented in 1994-95, was the commercial launching of the D2-MAC widescreen standard in 1991. Widescreen television programmes will be broadcast by the public broadcast company, with the support of the programme production company, PTT-Telecom and Philips. The parties involved are organised in the Netherlands Platform HDTV that assisted in the preparation and co-ordination of this initiative.

In *Portugal*, a new programme -- PROMIM -- has been established with a view to strengthening the competitiveness of the wooden furniture industry in the domestic and foreign markets. It seeks to promote new activities, the introduction of products with higher technological content and improved management and marketing.

In *Spain*, the development of sector-specific restructuring plans (*Planes de Reconversión*) for key industries in the early 1980s represented a major thrust in the country's move away from the Franco era policy of national self-sufficiency, involving strict government controls, towards an industrial structure allowing full integration into the European Community. In industries such as steel and shipbuilding, the plans aimed at cushioning the social effects of the large-scale layoffs required by restructuring while improving competitiveness in the capacity remaining; in other sectors, such as textiles, the objective was to maximise international competitiveness while keeping down employment losses.

The treaty on the admission of Spain to the EC in 1986 took account of the fact that restructuring, which had commenced later in that country than in other European nations, would need more time for completion in some sectors. Thus Spain was exempted from certain EC restrictions on state aid until 1990; the government could, e.g., provide support for workforce reduction and balance sheet improvement in steel and shipbuilding, while, in textiles, latitude was given for state assistance to move away from tangible towards intangible factors of competitiveness such as quality, fashion and design.

In the phase of complete integration into the EC, underway since 1990, the emphasis has been placed on preparing industries in which restructuring plans had been extended beyond 1986 for a full opening up to EC competition and for moving towards a full compliance, in those sectors, with EC restrictions on state aid.

In the meantime, the government has decided to divide public sector firms into two main groups, with the National Institute of Industry (INI) maintaining an overall supervisory function with respect to all the enterprises concerned. Starting in 1992, the profitable firms are to be placed within a limited liability company, disjoined from the state budget as from 1993 and operating in accordance with the same criteria as a private holding company; it is envisaged that, in the future, equity participation in the enterprises concerned may be opened to outside capital. On the other hand, structurally unviable firms will be brought together within a state company, which will decide on their sale or liquidation. The remaining state enterprises, which are to be found largely in the mining, steel, shipbuilding and military equipment sectors, are likely to continue to receive government assistance, at a steadily declining rate and linked to restructuring plans.

In *Austria*, the restructuring of Austrian Industries (the state-owned enterprises holding company) has continued; in view of the world-wide recession in steel and chemicals, further extensive restructuring is considered necessary. At the same time, the internationalisation of the public sector firms has intensified. About one-third of Austrian direct investments abroad are accounted for by Austrian Industries; and their share in such investments is increasing. By far the major part of these investments, as well as of Austrian Industries' participation in international joint ventures, has involved enterprises in the EC area.

In *Norway*, a 50 per cent reduction in the electricity tax rate for producers in the ferro alloy industry, already in effect during the first three quarters of 1991, has remained in force during the first half of 1992. This measure has been prompted by the large exports of such cheap metal products from central and eastern Europe and China and their effects on Norwegian industry.

In *Switzerland*, the new telecommunications law, approved by Parliament in June 1991 and expected to take effect on 1 May 1992, aims at removing a number of obstacles to competition in this sector. Under this legislation, only the telecommunications infrastructure and the basic telephone service (voice transmission) will remain a state monopoly. The provision of equipment (telephones, enterprise switchboards, telex, telefax) will be opened to competition but will continue to be subject to official approval. In order to avoid creating a situation in which the government postal, telephone and telegraph service plays the role of both judge and interested party, and to ensure respect for the competitive system, a new Federal Communications Office will carry out the regulatory function. The effects of the liberalisation will be felt mostly in the fields of international communications and data transmission.

In *Australia*, the government has put in place a number of industry-specific programmes that aim at facilitating the restructuring of mature industries or fostering competitive strengths in key industries. Mature industry programmes include the Passenger Motor Vehicle (PMV) plan, the Textile, Clothing and Footwear (TCF) plan as well as the Metals-Based Engineering Program. Other industry programmes cover pharmaceuticals, telecommunications, aerospace, biotechnology, and information industries.

Under the Passenger Motor Vehicle (PMV) Plan, the Australian government has since 1985 attempted to increase the industry's efficiency, so that it could compete with imports at lower levels of government assistance, to provide better quality for consumers at reduced prices while at the same time minimising disruption to production and employment during the transition to a more efficient industry. Under the PMV Plan, trade restrictions have already been reduced considerably. In April 1988, quotas on the import of cars were abolished, while the 85 per cent Local Content Scheme was abolished in January 1989. Between 1985 and 1992, the nominal tariff rate on imported cars and components was lowered from 57.5 per cent to 35 per cent. Under new arrangements that came into effect in March 1991, tariffs on PMVs will continue to decrease by 2.5 per cent per year, to 15 per cent in the year 2000. Tariffs on light commercial and four-wheel drive vehicles and components will be reduced from 15 per cent in 1992 to 5 per cent by July 1996, in accordance with reductions in general tariffs. Minimum volume requirements will be retained in a modified form to the end of 1996.

As part of its review of overall industry assistance measures, the government also recently examined the arrangements for the Textiles, Clothing and Footwear (TCF) industries. It decided to terminate import quotas by March 1993, to reduce tariffs to a maximum of 25 per cent by the year 2000, and to abolish bounties by July 1995. To assist the TCF industries in this adjustment phase, the government provides up to A$120 million in assistance through the Industries Development Strategy.

Other notable industry-specific measures include:

- The Metal-based Engineering Programme, started in 1989 and aimed at increasing the export capability of engineering industries. About 130 companies and consortia have been assisted since its inception.

- A programme for the pulp and paper industry, aimed at both ensuring adequate conservation and encouraging forestry industry restructuring. Draft legislation will be considered during 1992.

- The Pharmaceutical Industry Development Programme covers a range of initiatives designed to encourage the development of the Australian pharmaceutical industry. Initiatives include the extension of patent life and the establishment of a pricing authority which is required to take into consideration the impact of its pricing decisions on the level of manufacturing and R&D activity in the industry.

- The ending of offset requirements in civil aerospace purchases, which hitherto characterised, together with defence purchasing, the development of the Australian aerospace industry. This has been coupled with international agreements ensuring that Australian firms will be allowed to bid for aero-component work internationally.

- The Australian Space Industry Development Strategy, aimed at promoting the development of commercially viable industries based on space technologies. Budgetary allocations (A$6.3 million in 1991) have been made for seed-funding (varying from 50 to 100 per cent) of a limited number of projects that meet certain selection criteria.

- The Construction Industry Reform Strategy, launched in December 1991, and embracing the areas of labour market reform, industry development and building regulation. Under the strategy, contractors will have to meet certain performance criteria in order to be eligible to tender for public works.

- The Major Projects Group of senior officials was formed during 1991 as the initial point of contact and facilitation at the Commonwealth level for proponents of major resource and resource processing projects. The Major Projects Group was set up to, within 45 days, identify and seek to resolve impediments or consider ways in which projects could be facilitated.

Finally, the Information Industries Strategy, equally revised in the framework of the Industry Statement of March 1991, aims at encouraging the IT industry in Australia to take advantage of the rapidly growing domestic and world market for IT goods and services. The focus will increasingly be on the most rapidly growing parts of the industries, namely software and services. Initiatives aim at encouraging exports and improving international integration, supporting industry infrastructure and R&D, while government purchasing policy is also used for developing the industry and encouraging the adoption of new technologies and standards.

C. Measures to support small and medium-sized enterprises

Small and medium-sized enterprises play an increasingly vital and dynamic part in the economies of Member countries. But governments are also concerned with the challenges, opportunities and pressures that SMEs are facing in the context of the rapidly changing technological environment and the globalisation of economic activities. These are stemming mainly from technical innovations, diversification and sophistication of consumer goods, skills and labor shortages, access to information, production and distribution networks.

While it is widely recognised that the creation of an economic climate which favours enterprises is essential, at the same time stimulating the creation and development of SMEs and improving their competitiveness are objectives that are pursued resolutely in many countries. Against this background, the examination of recent measures taken in Member countries shows that certain trends are emerging or are being reinforced, in particular:

- The improvement of access that SMEs have to financing, with in addition some countries finding it necessary to alleviate SMEs financial difficulties caused by the recent economic recession;

- The emphasis put on enabling SMEs to make self-help efforts to respond adequately to the on-going changes and avail themselves of the right factors to be more competitive. In this respect, the promotion of technological and market information, vocational training, and of technical and management assistance through intermediary bodies is widely spread in most countries. But there is a need for a greater coherence and efficiency of the resources administered by these institutions and of the many services provided to SMEs;

- The support for industrial co-operation between large firms and small firms or between small firms, as a basis for Member countries competitiveness. This co-operation which takes various forms of "partnerships", through a variety of networks, tends to be promoted nationally and internationally. This is in particular the case for SMEs in the EC countries which have to prepare for and take advantage of the 1993 Single Market.

A number of recent government measures taken with respect to SMEs are summarised below.

In *Canada*, the fostering of an entrepreneurial culture constitutes an increasingly important objective of industrial development. This concern is reflected in the initiatives implemented under the Entrepreneurship Awareness Program and in the creation of a National Entrepreneurship Development Institute as a non-profit, non-governmental organisation.

Among the specific services offered to the smaller firms, one may note the recent establishment of the Manufacturing Assessment Service (MAS), designed to help growth-oriented SMEs improve their competitive position through identification of key action areas in relation to production, technology, planning and quality. The MAS provides a confidential professional assessment of a company's manufacturing and management process; this involves an innovative approach which uses information collected in a computer-assisted telephone interview as the basis for a subsequent on-site assessment by a consultant.

Finally, it may be noted that the Canadian Federal Business Development Bank, an agency with a long record in the financing of SMEs, co-hosted, in Montreal, the 1992 annual OECD Small Business Conference, the theme of which was "Globalisation and Small Business".

In *Denmark*, measures aimed at SMEs have always been an important part of overall industrial policy. As a result of rising unemployment, however, and because of the potential of SMEs for generating new employment, there has been an increase in initiatives incorporating measures aimed at improving business conditions for small and medium-sized firms in 1991 and early 1992. These include the Foundation for Industrial Development and other similar initiatives supporting the development of the technological infrastructure (see section A(ii) above), the Network Scheme for Tourism (section B above), the Industrial Use of Environmental Technology Programme (section F below) and the Export Networks Programme (section G below).

In *France*, the government has an active policy of assisting small and medium-sized enterprises adapt to the changing international economic environment. Initiatives are aimed at helping them with some of the difficulties they are facing, namely with R&D investments, training, management, the lack of investment in general, or with the high bankruptcy rate. A recent plan for SMEs announced in September 1991 consists of eleven measures of a fiscal nature (such as the reduction of taxes, tax allowances for capital expansion, exemptions from capital gains in some activities, extension of the tax credit for training) and some measures of an administrative nature, such as the simplification of social security declarations.

In *Germany*, the dual policy emphasis on creating the conditions for the development of SMEs in the new *Länder* and on preparing the country's smaller firms to take advantage of the opportunities arising from the single EC market is being continued. Business start-ups in the new *Länder* are supported mainly through the equity support and loan programmes of the ERP, with total equity amounting in 1991 to DM 3.2 billion (48 000 applications) and total loans to DM 4.9 billion (56 600 loans). Investment promotion in the new *Länder* is also supported through ERP investment and environment protection loans.

In addition, support is available for consultancies, training, and to attend fairs in order to strengthen the marketing function of eastern German firms. From 1992 onwards, support will be granted to innovation projects by SMEs in the new *Länder*, while aid to R&D staff, to joint industrial research and to the restructuring of research potentials is being continued. The federal government also continues to contribute to preparing SMEs, including in the eastern part, for the European market through the EURO-FITNESS programmes and related action e.g. EURO telephone, and the EURO-INFO-CENTRES network. Finally, the *Treuhandanstalt* adopted in the Spring 1991 guidelines on a privatisation policy in favour of SMEs.

In *Greece*, the Hellenic Organisation for Small and Medium Size Enterprises (EOMMEH -- the main agency responsible for SMEs), has recently elaborated a 5-year plan (1993-97) for the development of SMEs. The main measures proposed in order to tackle the difficulties associated with the adjustment to the conditions of the EC Internal Market cover financing (mutual guarantees for SMEs, seed and risk capital, interest rate subsidies for loans), integrated technical assistance and consultancy, promotion and development of the craft industry, and assistance with collaborative ventures. The financing requirements for the implementation of the plan are estimated at 114 billion drachmas.

In *Italy*, legislation supporting innovation and development of SMEs, reported in the 1991 *Annual Review* while proceeding through its approval path, was finally enacted in October 1991. This new law, to which about

1 500 million lire have been allocated for the period 1991-93, is aimed at fostering innovation, competition, and competitiveness of SMEs, with particular regard for the development of southern regions. It promotes the diffusion and development of new technologies; the establishment of consortia providing services to SMEs; the enhancement of the financial infrastructure; the establishment and development of small firms in areas affected by industrial restructuring activities, following EC decisions; and investment by small innovative enterprises. Special attention is devoted to matching the overall measure with the process of internationalization carried out by SMEs.

In the *Netherlands*, a management support scheme for small and medium-sized enterprises was wound up in January 1992. Only specific measures to support SMEs remain in place, like special programmes in the field of information, training and financing. A new initiative has been the "Action to stimulate the application of micro-electronics", which aims at the application of micro-electronics within at least 500 SMEs in the next four years.

In *Portugal*, where small and medium-sized enterprises account for 45 per cent of gross added value in industry and 50 per cent of the country's total exports, a strong policy focus is directed to these firms. A recent measure is the establishment of a system of incentives projects aimed at the creation, expansion or modernisation of small-sized manufacturing and extractive enterprises.

In *Spain*, SMEs constitute a particularly important part of the industrial and commercial fabric: over nine-tenths of the workforce in industry and commerce are engaged in establishments of fewer than 500 employees, and nearly half in units of fewer than 50. The broad array of policies for assisting and encouraging these firms has assumed increasing importance in recent years. The measures taken in this field are implemented by the Ministry of Industry, Trade and Tourism acting through the Institute for Small and Medium-Sized Industrial Enterprises (IMPI) and the State Agency for the development of industrial design.

The activities of IMPI may be grouped under five headings:

- *Information*. IMPI deploys various mechanisms for providing SMEs with information of a general nature; information relevant to EC support, regulations and research programmes; and continuously updated information adapted to the needs of individual firms.

- *Financial support*. IMPI utilises a number of financial instruments, such as support for the System of Mutual Guarantees. In addition, direct capital investment is available from the Enterprise Promotion Agency, which can take equity shares in SMEs.

- *Inter-enterprise co-operation*. IMPI provides support for the Collective Action Groups through which SMEs can help overcome the disabilities resulting from small size by pooling their resources and engaging in different forms of joint action. More generally, the Institute encourages co-operation, not only between Spanish firms, but also at the European Community level, with a view to eliminating technical, economic and cultural barriers and promoting technology diffusion.

- *Participation in Community programmes*. SME participation is encouraged in European programmes such as EUROPARTNERSHIP, which aims at furthering co-operation among the smaller firms and remedying regional imbalances; SPRINT, which is designed to promote exchanges in the area of technological innovation; and STRIDE, which seeks to improve research and innovative capacity in less-developed or declining regions.

- *Industrial design*. An Industrial Design Plan, in effect from 1992 through 1995, aims at promoting industrial design as a factor of competitiveness and as a means towards the integration of new products in the development process. Special tax relief has been made available for design-related investment and expenditure.

In the *United Kingdom*, the network of Training and Enterprise Councils (TECs), and of local enterprise companies (LECs) in Scotland, has been fully operational since the summer of 1991 (see also section B). The main activities of the Employment Department's former Business and Enterprise programmes which have been taken over by the TECs and LECs, operating on a performance contract with the Employment Department but enjoying considerable latitude to meet their local areas' needs, are as follows:

- The Enterprise Allowance Scheme which, since it began in 1983, has helped over 560 000 people to set up their own businesses;

- Business Enterprise Training, which has each year assisted more than 100 000 firms of all sizes in improving the effectiveness of their training;

- Business Counselling, information and advice previously provided by the government's Small Firms Service.

The above activities now form part of a more integrated package of support offered by the TEC network, which is viewed as bringing greater coherence to government assistance to small businesses and new start-up firms. A number of initiatives, as noted in the 1991 *Annual Review*, remain under direct government control: the Loan Guarantee Scheme; government support for the Prince's Scottish Youth Business Trust, which helps young people set up or expand their firms; and measures to encourage enterprises in depressed inner city areas under the Action for Cities programme.

In *Austria*, small and medium-sized enterprises occupy an especially important place in the economy. In 1988, the year for which the latest statistical analysis is available, firms with fewer than 500 represented 99 per cent of all industrial enterprises. During the period 1983-88, net job creation was accounted for entirely by SMEs. These firms also experienced much faster growth in gross output and in investment than did the larger enterprises.

In November 1991, new regulations on support for existing SMEs and prospective high-performance new start-ups went into effect. Under these regulations, subsidised projects must be geared to significant competitiveness goals, contribute to the attainment of economic policy objectives, and impact favourably on regional economic structures. Assistance may be given to both physical and intangible investments.

At the same time, efforts begun as early as 1975 to expand subcontracting contacts between Austrian suppliers of accessories and large foreign producers have had considerable success, notably in the automotive sector. The value of such transactions in that industry amounted to Sch. 37 billion between 1975 and 1991, nearly offsetting the value of automobile imports. Similar efforts have been undertaken in the electronics and office machine industries and will be intensified in the future. Finally, counter-trade agreements have been concluded with foreign producers of military equipment; such arrangements have been used, to a considerable extent, for the procurement of new technologies for such Austrian industries as aeronautics and electronics.

In *Finland*, the current recession has led the government to introduce a new financial measure in order to support those small and medium-sized enterprises that have been caught by serious financial difficulties, but which are considered healthy and competitive in the long run. Since banks are unable to take more risks in those firms, the aim of the loan scheme is to avoid bankruptcies resulting from liquidity problems. The loans, amounting to 500 million markka, have been awarded by the Regional Development Fund (KERA) at interest rates that are some percentage points below market rates.

In *Norway*, the majority of enterprises employ less than 100 people, while this group accounts for 60 per cent of employment in the private sector. The Small Business Fund, the Regional Development Fund and the Industrial Fund are important sources of financial support for SMEs within the state bank system. A merger between these institutions and the Norwegian Industrial Bank was approved by the Storting in spring 1992 (see section A above), aimed at a more efficient and co-ordinated use of the resources administered. In order to increase equity capital for SMEs, the requirements for stock exchange listing have been eased. For promoting technology transfer to SMEs, two national foundations exist (the National Institute of Technology and the North Norwegian Institute of Trade and Industry); half the costs of these services are financed by the users. Finally, there were three programmes aimed at improving the technological competence of SMEs in 1991, with a budget allocation of 50 million Norwegian kroner.

In *Sweden*, a government bill on a new policy for SMEs was presented in late 1991. The aim of this policy is to generate a general environment that promotes the creation of new firms and growth, productivity-enhancement and innovativeness among existing small firms. Measures include simplification of employment regulations and rules on the ownership of firms, the promotion of competition, and the creation of a market for private venture capital without state interference. Also, participation in the small-business programmes of the EC is being sought, while business operations in EC-countries are being encouraged. In 1991, the Parliament decided that lending through the Regional Development Funds would have to be reduced. Out of a total fund of 2.8 billion Swedish kroner, 1.6 billion must be repaid to the state. The government considers, however, that some financing from the Funds will be needed in the future as a complement to other credit institutes. As the Regional Investment Funds take higher risks than commercial lenders, many small companies would find themselves without financing in their absence. In order to increase the supply of risk capital for small companies, six venture capital companies were established in 1991. The intention is for private capital to account for the major part of financing needs.

In *Turkey*, where SME promotion is a major axis of industrial policy, an expanded effort is currently under way in the framework of several projects. A total of 64 new Organised Industrial Estates is being developed, with government financial assistance, under the 1992 investment programme for this activity; four of these estates are expected to be completed in 1992. In the meantime, the Small and Medium-sized Industrial Development Organisation (SMIDO) established thirteen new development centres in 1991 (see Box 8).

In *Australia*, the establishment of the Small to Medium Sized Enterprises Development Program, announced as part of the 1991 Industry Statement, seeks to increase the international competitiveness of small and medium-sized enterprises by improving their access to information and to overseas markets. As part of the Program, which consists of nine elements, training and practical assistance will be offered to 250 SMEs to enter export markets. Also, a national business referral service will give easy access to sources of business information, while the operations of the National Industry Extension Service will include the traded services sector. Overall, the government approved funding of A$14 million over three years to the SME Development Program. The programme will be reviewed in late 1993.

> **Box 8. Small and medium enterprises in Turkey**
>
> Small and medium-sized enterprises occupy a very important place in Turkey. According to the 1985 Census of Industry, establishments employing fewer than 50 persons comprised 98.8 per cent of all manufacturing establishments, employed 45.6 per cent of the total number of workers in manufacturing, while producing 19.8 per cent of manufacturing value added. Including in this structural portrait the medium-sized establishments -- i.e. those employing from 50 to 199 workers -- brings the corresponding figures for the whole SME category to 99.6 per cent, 57.4 per cent and 31.7 per cent respectively.
>
> Against this background, the Turkish authorities consider that a key element of its approach to national economic and industrial development is policy action to support and strengthen small and medium-sized firms. To that end, they have devised a wide range of measures including, for example, assistance in the establishment and operation of small-industry co-operatives as well as the promotion of industrial estates where small-scale manufacturing activities may be concentrated in specific sites and benefit from a shared technological and economic infrastructure.
>
> A particularly comprehensive component of SME policy consists of the work carried out by the Small and Medium-sized Industry Development Organisation (SMIDO), which was set up in April 1990 and which, since then, has significantly broadened the scope of its activities.
>
> SMIDO is a public-sector body linked to the Ministry of Industry and Trade. Its operations are governed by a General Assembly, an Executive Committee and a Presidency, and its task is to help improve the efficiency and competitiveness of the smaller enterprises through broad-gauged support packages impacting on their production, management and marketing functions.
>
> Upon its establishment, SMIDO took over all the activities of the Small Industry Development Organisation (SIDO) as well as the training functions of the Industrial Training and Development Centre (ITDC). Eight specialised development centres, located in different parts of the country, were transferred from SIDO and ITDC to SMIDO, and many other units have been set up subsequently.
>
> The SMIDO units include sector-specific centres as well as technological development, quality improvement, consultancy, training, information, marketing and investment guidance centres. They also include testing and analysis laboratories and common facility workshops.
>
> Major importance is accorded to considerations of product quality in the activities of the SMIDO centres. At the quality improvement centres, for instance, modern testing equipment and mobile spectrometers are employed in quality inspections, and mobile testing units are also available for use in the common facility workshops.
>
> With a view to integrating SMIDO activities into the overall fabric of industrial development, the majority of the centres have been established within industrial estates, while three technology development centres have been situated on university campuses in order to stimulate industry-university co-operation. Finally, the international ramifications of SMIDO's activities should be noted -- e.g., participation in a UNDP-UNESCO joint project to establish a scientific and technical information network covering ten countries, initiation of an international programme for assisting Hungarian SMEs, and consultancy services offered to countries such as Kenya and Indonesia.

D. Regulatory reform and competition policy in industry

Regulatory reform and competition policy are two industrial policy areas of increasing importance in OECD Member countries. This is the result of a growing awareness of the distortions created by excessive government regulation and direct intervention in the functioning of markets. In addition, technological developments have transformed market structures and with that the market failures associated with them, thereby necessitating a reform of the competition and regulatory framework which was in place in order to mitigate their negative consequences.

The policy framework that has evolved in this area is a pragmatic combination of two approaches. The first is the "structural" approach which presumes in general that there is a positive relationship between intense competition and increases in social welfare, with the policy implication that competitive market structures should be defended at any cost through a vigorous antitrust policy. The second approach (the "dynamic" approach) is more flexible, and involves a case-by-case study in order to assess whether the benefits of large size or of reduced number of firms (economies of scale, increased competitiveness, dynamic efficiency gains) are outweighed or not by the costs (increased market power, static efficiency losses)[6]. According to this approach, dominant firms can owe their position to superior performance, and concentration is often the natural consequence of a competitive process in which only the most efficient survive, rather than necessarily a symptom of imperfect competition. In this context, and in cases where "contestable markets" exist, the role of policy is to sanction the abuses of market power through "rules or reason", rather than *per se* prescription.

This evolution in policy is related to a number of developments which have complicated the design of regulatory or legal frameworks. The increased globalisation of economic activity and the creation of the EC single market are both processes which have led to a reconsideration of the geographical concept of the relevant "market" to be used as a basis for competition policy. Effective policies of deregulation and competition can no longer be formulated exclusively on domestic grounds. At the same time, these processes have exposed firms to more intense competitive pressures, and have in many cases resulted in firms and governments adopting strategies designed to weaken their competitive impact. In this context, the importance of harmonisation and establishment of internationally accepted rules will grow as an issue.

With respect to *privatisation and the operation of state-owned enterprises*, government policies continue to be marked by two types of action: complete or partial privatisation, and the restructuring of those firms that remain in the public sector in order to fully expose them to the disciplines of the market. In practice, these approaches can be combined in various ways, and their implementation can vary greatly in accordance with the economic and industrial structure of different countries.

Privatisation is well advanced in a number of OECD countries, while still at its beginning and facing some difficulties in others (see Table 7 for a distribution of public enterprises by industry). In those countries where a process of privatisation has been under way for some years, recent initiatives have focused on creating the right regulatory environment in order to ensure that public monopolies are not replaced by private monopolies or duopolies. It has in effect sometimes proven to be more difficult to create competitive conditions than to privatise in the first place, especially in some service sectors such as telecommunications and transportation. The initial approach of assuming that a change in ownership automatically creates the incentives for the emergence of competitive pressures has been replaced with the realisation that a regulatory framework is still necessary in order to avoid the abuse of dominant positions in sectors that were until recently considered to be "natural monopolies".

Policies directed to those state-owned enterprises that are not being privatised have also evolved over the years in response to the need to meet increased capital requirements, to bolster technological, managerial or marketing strength, or in order to assist in the restructuring of public firms in difficulty. In France, for example, minority participation in French public firms by domestic or foreign private firms is now authorised on a case-by-case basis,

Table 7. **Distribution of public enterprises by industry, 1989**[1]

As a percentage of value added in each industry

	Post office	Telecommunications	Electricity	Gas	Oil	Coal	Railways	Air transport	Road transport	Steel	Shipbuilding
United States	90	0	25	0	0	0	25	0	0	0	0
Canada	100	25	100	0	0	0	75	75	0	0	0
Japan	100	33	0	0	..	0	25	0	0	0	0
Belgium	100	100	25	25	..	0	100	100	100	50	0
Germany	100	100	75	50	25	50	100	100	25	0	25
France	100	100	100	100	..	100	100	75	50	75	0
Italy	100	100	75	100	..	..	100	100	25	75	75
Netherlands	100	100	75	75	..	..	100	75	50	25	0
Spain	100	50	40*	75	..	50	100	100	0	50	75
United Kingdom	100	0	100	25	25	100	100	0	0	75	50
Austria	100	100	100	100	100	100	100	100	100	100	..
Sweden	100	100	50	100	..	..	100	50	25	75	75
Switzerland	100	100	100	100	..	..	100	25	0	0	..
Australia	100	100	100	100	0	0	100	75	0	0	..

* National source.
1. Figures should be considered rough approximations.
Source: Oxley, H. *et al.* (1990), "The Public Sector: Issues for the 1990s", OECD Economics Department Working Paper No. 90, December.

provided that such acquisition involves the augmentation of a company's existing equity capital and is based on a "strategic agreement" with the investor. At the same time, policy has evolved in EC countries in response to the increased European Commission powers in the area. A more strict recent interpretation of the relevant article from the Treaty of Rome considers illegal almost any action in which the state as owner acts differently from a private investor. This diminishes the freedom of national governments to manage public companies and is likely to reinforce the trend towards full or partial privatisation.

Finally, the problems facing one major OECD country, Germany, in its effort to privatise and restructure the industry of the former East Germany need to be mentioned, as they provide insights into the difficulties facing the transition of central and eastern European countries to market economies. The approach taken has been innovative and operates through the setting of an agency (the *Treuhandanstalt*) whose aim has been to privatise, close down or split-up a very large number of enterprises, under a mandate where restructuring in order to return enterprises to viability and privatisation are twin objectives. The agency has been remarkably successful so far, but is likely to face increasingly difficult choices in the near future.

Some recent measures of regulatory reform, competition policy, privatisation and some concerning state-owned enterprises in Member countries are indicated below.

In the *United States*, new legislation was enacted to address problems in the commercial banking sector. The Federal Deposit Insurance Corporation Improvement Act, enacted in late 1991, tightened bank regulation and increased the deposit insurance fund's borrowing capacity by US$70 billion. It also linked bank supervision to banks' equity capital levels and other statistical measures and empowered bank regulators to take steps to close troubled banks even before they fail, so as to limit the cost to the Bank Insurance Fund.

The Administration has also presented a banking reform proposal to Congress for 1992. The proposal would permit nationwide banking and branching, allow banks to affiliate with securities and insurance companies and permit commercial companies to affiliate with banks.

The Safe Medical Devices Act was recently enacted to ensure that products of this kind entering the market were safe and effective. The law establishes new requirements to be met by manufacturers, including postmarket surveillance of high risk devices while users are required to report deaths associated with faulty medical devices. The industry is concerned that the law will slow the product approval process; add to manufacturers' regulatory costs; and hamper the industry's ability to compete in domestic and international markets.

Finally, in January 1992 the US President initiated his regulatory reform initiative. The purpose of the 90-day initiative was to evaluate existing regulations and programmes and to identify and accelerate action on initiatives that would eliminate any unnecessary regulatory burden in order to promote economic growth, without threatening health and safety. Two key elements of regulatory reform that agencies have been asked to focus on are ensuring that regulation rely on upon performance standards instead of command-and-control requirements and that regulations rely upon market mechanisms to the maximum extent possible. On 29 April 1992 the moratorium was extended for an additional 120 days and was recently extended again for a year.

In *Canada*, the 1990 annual review of the National Transportation Agency on the operation of the existing regulatory legislation indicated that the industry had been directly affected by the economic recession, fuel price increases due to the Persian Gulf crisis, a rapidly globalising world economy and a rise in the value of the Canadian dollar as against the US dollar. The overall profitability of the industry deteriorated in 1990, partly as a result of economic weaknesses but also because of the pricing strategies adopted. Canadian carriers have pointed to a number of fiscal and regulatory differences between Canada and the Untied States, which they allege create imbalances and affect their ability to compete with US carriers.

Against this background, a series of measures were announced in December 1991 to strengthen the sector. These include refinements to the tax system with respect to air, rail and truck transport, and a temporary programme providing cash-flow benefits now in exchange for reduced income tax deductions in the future. In addition, a comprehensive review of the operation of various transport regulatory acts is being undertaken by an independent panel. The panel is to report to the Minister of Transport by 31 January 1993.

In the past year, government policy has given higher priority to deficit reduction in the transport industry while maintaining the safety of the system. A number of initiatives have been taken to improve operations, reduce costs or increase revenues for facilities and services provided by the government.

With respect to state-owned enterprises, the government reaffirmed, in the February 1991 budget, its commitment to seek improved management and stated that, in the light of this engagement, it would continue to privatise those activities best performed by the private sector. In keeping with the desire to streamline government operations, the functions of the Office of Privatisation and Regulatory Affairs have been redeployed: ongoing and future privatisations will be managed within the Department of Finance, reporting to the Minister of State (Finance and Privatisation). In addition, net proceeds from privatisations will in the future be deposited into a new account for use in debt servicing and reduction.

Privatisation activities continued in 1991, with the issue of treasury shares by Petro-Canada, the state-owned oil company, and Cameco, and the sale of Nordion International Inc., formerly the Radiochemical Company of Atomic Energy of Canada Ltd; this brought the total number of privatisation operations so far to 21. Other privatisation moves are envisaged, including the sale of Telesat Canada, the Royal Assent having been granted to the Telesat Canada Reorganisation and Divestiture Act.

In *Japan*, the government was presented in July 1991 with the first report on administrative and regulatory reform, in accordance with the calendar agreed in December 1988. The report's recommendations aim to decrease public regulations by half during this decade, to abolish regulations that impede entry of new firms into particular industries and to rationalise social regulations in accordance with changes in society brought about by technological innovations. In accepting the report prepared by the Council for Administrative Reform, the government committed itself to promote administrative and financial reforms along the lines of the report's recommendations.

The Japanese government is committed to substantive action and structural reform in several policy areas in the direction of greater market openness, partly as a result of discussions in the context of the Structural Impediments Initiative (SII). A report was released in May 1991, assessing progress made since the June 1990 Joint Report (*First Annual Report of the US-Japan Working Group on the Structural Impediments Initiative*). Among the most important areas are the strengthening of the Anti-Monopoly Act and the deregulation of the retail distribution system. Criticism of the Anti-Monopoly Act has centered on its reliance on warnings, surcharges and administrative orders, rather than on criminal prosecutions, and on the

---

Box 9. Industrial structure in Japan: efficient or exclusionist?

In trade disputes with Japan, attention often centers on whether Japanese industrial structure -- in particular the existence of closely-knit corporate groups known as *keiretsu* -- restricts competition and acts as an impediment to trade and international investment.

Keiretsu are groups of firms characterised by close business relations and long-term commitments among members. Members of a group are interlinked through cross shareholdings, long-standing buyer-supplier arrangements, interchange of personnel, and the sharing of information. They can be classified into three types. The first is a horizontal industrial grouping with a lead bank and a trading company at the centre. The second is a vertical grouping, formed between independent firms, as is found in a number of key industries such as automobiles and electrical or electronics equipment. The third is the case where a manufacturer of goods organises its own distribution network, in which retail and wholesale outlets are tied together, with suggested prices often decided by the producer[1].

These business practices provide the advantages of a stable, forward-looking trading environment and suggest that there is an efficiency rationale behind the existence of *keiretsu*. At the same time, it is thought that in many cases they can act as an impediment to new entrants, both domestic and foreign. Vertical *keiretsu* are alleged to favour intra-group transactions unduly, and to discriminate against non-group members. Foreign firms trying to enter the market criticise the cross-shareholding of horizontal *keiretsu* as one of the barriers to direct investment and market access. Finally, distribution *keiretsu* may inhibit competition at the retail level.

The difficulty with analysing the impact of *keiretsu* on trade and competition starts when attempting to identify them and their role in the Japanese economy. A 1986 survey identified 17 major *keiretsu*, holding 25 per cent of annual sales in Japan in 1985, and with the nine largest Japanese trading companies, all members of *keiretsu*, handling 44 per cent of exports and 68 per cent of imports[2]. The 1989 update of the same survey however found 47 major *keiretsu*, while another source listed 46 *keiretsu* for 1989, but with only 23 of these overlapping with those of the previous survey. Thus, definitions are not consistent either between sources or over time.

Conceptual difficulties notwithstanding, a recent study[3] has identified three contrasting positions in the debate about the appropriate policy response to *keiretsu*. The first is that of *benign neglect*, a policy stance based on the belief that *keiretsu* do not have an important impact on Japanese economic performance. Evidence showing that intragroup transactions are not very large is used to support this view. A 1981 study for example found that within-group transactions account only for 11 per cent of their sales and 12 per cent of their purchases[4]. Other studies however have concluded that in some sectors intra-*keiretsu* transactions can account for over 50 per cent of firms' total trade[5]. Proponents of this position also cite the low rates of return typically earned by large companies which are *keiretsu* members as evidence that competitive pressures are strong[6], as well as studies showing that Japanese trade patterns can be adequately explained by other economic variables, such as factor endowments[7].

fact that the financial, transportation and agriculture sectors escape its full application [7]. In addition, significant price differentials of imported consumer goods between Japan and other countries have come under scrutiny as reflecting impediments to competition and barriers to entry (see Box 9). In order to address these criticisms, the Anti-Monopoly Act and its implementation have been strengthened (by, for example, increasing the surcharge on cartels from 1.5 to 6 per cent of sales for large firms, by increasing the number and amount of surcharge payment orders on cartels, or by reforming the damage payment system so as to alleviate the plaintiff's burden of proof). With respect to the retail distribution system, the Large Scale Retail Law was revised in May 1991 (with effect from 1992), with a view to simplifying and shortening opening procedures, thought to be responsible for large delays and uncertainty for potential investors in the sector.

After its merger law took effect in September 1990, the *European Community* has now at its disposal the legal framework for enforcing an international competition policy whose aim is to contribute to the creation of a more competitive climate in Europe. The merger law allows the EC to veto all mergers and acquisitions involving firms with a combined turnover of more than 5 billion ECUs, providing that at least 250 million ECUs worth of these sales are in the EC. The only exceptions to this rule are mergers involving companies that derive two-thirds of their business from the same EC state. The European Commission has used its authority on several occasions, for instance when rejecting the proposed take-over of the Canadian aircraft manufacturer De Havilland by Aerospatiale and the Italian Alenia company, in October 1991. In January 1992, the European Commission proposed rules designed to accelerate approval of certain co-operative

---

Box 9 *(cont)*. Industrial structure in Japan: efficient or exclusionist?

The second policy stance, *trust busting*, argues instead that *keiretsu* create entry barriers for newcomers and that they engage in anticompetitive practices. This view is based on evidence from studies showing that both horizontal and vertical types of *keiretsu* are associated with Japanese industries with unusually low imports by OECD standards [8]. Such findings have been criticised however, on the argument that they hinge on how *keiretsu* are identified. If *keiretsu* are actually defined by the extent they use local suppliers, the result that they reduce imports could just as well reflect patterns of comparative advantage rather than discriminatory behaviour [9].

The third policy stance is the *dilemma position*. It concedes that *keiretsu* have a negative impact on Japanese imports and on the ability of foreign firms to enter the Japanese market, but argues that they have also been an important reason for the superior performance of the Japanese economy. This view is supported by evidence showing that rather than just reducing imports, vertical *keiretsu* also boost exports, suggesting that both of these effects could be due to increased efficiency rather than exclusionary practices. *Keiretsu* may serve as a more efficient substitute for vertical integration, permitting reliable supply while preserving corporate flexibility [10].

Economic theory suggests that discriminatory relationships do not reduce economic efficiency, provided that they operate in markets that are highly contestable. From this perspective, if current reforms under way achieve their aim to make the Japanese distribution system and final goods markets in Japan become truly competitive, then *keiretsu* relationships should be less of a source of economic distortion and international friction in the future.

1. OECD (1991), *OECD Economic Surveys: Japan*, Paris.
2. Dodwell Market Consultants (1986), *Industrial Groupings in Japan*, Tokyo.
3. Lawrence, R. (1991), "Efficient or Exclusionist? The Import Behaviour of Japanese Corporate Groups", *Brookings Papers on Economic Activity*, 1.
4. Imai K. (1990), "Japanese Business Groups and the Structural Impediments Initiative", in Yamamura, K, (ed)., *Japan's Economic Structure: Should It Change ?*, Seattle: Society for Japanese Studies.
5. Gerlach, M (1989), "Keiretsu Organisation in the Japanese Economy", in Johnson, C. and D' Andrea Tyson, L. (eds)., *Politics and Productivity: The Real Story of Why Japan Works*, Cambridge, Mass.: Balinger.
6. Yoshitomi, M. (1990), "Keiretsu: An Insider's Guide to Japan's Conglomerates", *Economic Insights*, 1.
7. Saxonhouse, G. (1989), "Differentiated Products, Economies of Scale, and Success to the Japanese Market", in Feenstra, R. (ed)., *Trade Policies for International Competitiveness*, Chicago: Chicago University Press.
8. Lawrence, R., *op. cit*. and Petri, P. (1989) "Japanese Trade in Transition: Hypotheses and Recent Evidence" in Krugman, P. (ed)., *The US and Japan: Trade and Investment*, Cambridge, Mass: National Bureau of Economic Research.
9. Saxonhouse, commenting on Lawrence, R., *op.cit*.
10. Lawrence, *op.cit*.; Aoki, M. (1990), "Towards a Model of the Japanese Firm", *Journal of Economic Litterature*, 28.

joint ventures in business areas like research, purchasing, and sales planning.

In September 1991, an agreement was reached between the *European Community* and the *United States* regarding the mutual application of competition laws. One of the aims of the accord is to avoid conflicts of jurisdiction between US and EC antitrust authorities. The agreement provides for direct cooperation between the European Commission and the Anti-Trust Division of the Department of Justice and the Federal Trade Commission of the United States. Specifically, the agreement establishes a procedure under which one party may notify the other of anti-competitive activities carried out on the territory of the other party which are adversely affecting the first party's interests. Such practices can refer to any company, whether from any of the party's territories or from third countries. The party that receives a notification will then have to consider whether or not to initiate new or expand ongoing enforcement activities. The agreement also contains provisions on exchange of information, consultation, notification and a number of other aspects.

In *Belgium*, where the 1960 legislation on protection against abuses of economic power was considered not to have fully met its objectives, a new law on competition was adopted in August 1991. This law prohibits restrictive business practices, but allows for exemptions from the application of the general principle in certain cases. Such exemptions may be granted on an individual basis, and normally after prior notification is given, for practices of which the beneficial effects on competition are deemed to outweigh the negative consequences. Exceptions can also be made for certain categories of business agreements on the basis of a decision taken by the Minister of Economic Affairs with the advice of the Competition Council.

In addition, the 1991 legislation establishes a priori control of business concentration by way of a requirement for prior notification. The law prohibits concentration levels which are likely to jeopardise competition because they create or strengthen dominant market positions. However, such concentration levels may be authorised if they contribute to technological or economic progress. The activities of the state and other authorities (regions, communities) are subject to control to the extent that such control does not hinder the accomplishment of their legal mission.

The provisions of the new law, which is being phased in until it becomes fully applicable on 1 May 1993, are to be implemented by three bodies:

- The Competition Service, existing within the Ministry of Economic Affairs, will investigate restrictive business practices as well as specific cases for which proceedings are to be engaged, and will also ascertain that decisions are effectively carried out.
- A newly created body, the Competition Council, composed of magistrates and competition specialists, is empowered to take decisions in cases subjected to investigation.
- The Competition Commission, a pluripartite body established within the Central Economic Council, is to give its opinion, either on its own initiative or at the request of the King, the Minister of Economic Affairs or the Competition Council, on certain draft texts as well as on general competition policy issues.

In *Denmark*, the government has during the 1980s taken a number of initiatives in order to improve the efficiency of the public sector and to make the production and delivery of services more market-oriented. This approach has led to the privatisation of many state-owned enterprises, to an increase in tendering-out procedures and to a number of experiments with "free-agencies". New regulations for the submission of tenders have been introduced, whereby all ministries are under an obligation to suggest suitable tasks for tendering; selected state agencies and institutions have been given increased managerial scope in return for improvements in efficiency and quality of service.

In terms of competition policy, an amendment to the Competition Act came into force on 1 June 1992. It regulates the publishing of information about on-going investigations, public access to cases and the rules of appeal. Negotiations on possible more fundamental reforms have also started recently, with the participation of representatives from industry, trade unions and state-owned enterprises. The issue at stake is whether there is a need to change the current principles underlying competition regulations in Denmark. These are guided by the principle of public access and control of monopolies and restrictive business practices with transparency as the main instrument to promote competition. The alternative is based on the prohibition of anti-competitive agreements of substantial influence and against the abuse of dominant positions, with the possibility of exceptions for individual companies or certain categories of agreements.

In *France*, competition policy and regulatory reform have become more active in recent years and are now a central plank of the government's strategy for achieving structural adjustment. Many recent initiatives have been geared to conforming to EC legislation with respect to the completion of the single market. Two areas are especially relevant in this regard: the control of cross-border mergers and acquisitions and public procurement [8]. In addition, with respect to state-owned firms, a change in legislation in 1991 allows private firms, national or foreign, to take minority stakes as strategic investors in nationalised companies.

In *Germany*, the Deregulation Commission set up by the federal government submitted its final report in Spring 1991. This report deals with the following fields: insurance, transport, electricity industry, technical inspection and experts reports, markets for legal and economic consultancy, the crafts and the labour market. On the basis of this report, a Working Group consisting of Delegates of the coalition parties has submitted policy proposals which are now in the process of implementation. In addition, the Government Railway Commission has submitted an expert report on the restructuring and the deregulation of rail transport. Also, in 1992 the federal government will take first steps to open the markets for mobile radio communication services.

It is the view of the federal government, that the European Commission and the national authorities must fight the risk of the creation of new oligopolies or cartels at the supra-national level e.g. in the form of so-called strategic alliances. In the R&D field also, it is important to guarantee competition so that major technology-oriented industries can be competitive and efficient. Joint R&D activities, as a vehicle for considerable potential innovation need to be promoted. At the same time, the risks involved in the reduction or elimination of competition in R&D should not be underestimated. The federal government considers that existing legislation provides a sufficiently flexible framework to accommodate both objectives.

Privatisation of formerly nation-owned firms in the new *Länder*, for which the *Treuhandanstalt* is responsible, is making good progress. By the end of May 1992, more than 7 600 of the original 10 800 firms had been sold. More than 1.1 million jobs were saved and investments of DM 138 billion were initiated. While the share of foreign investors was still quite small in early 1991, there was a marked increase towards the second half of the year and in 1992. By the end of May 1992, 390 companies had been sold to foreign investors and 1 350 management buy outs (MBOs) had been authorised. For the new *Länder*, the application of federal anti-trust legislation proved to be effective and has aided the work of the *Treuhandanstalt*.

As regards the old *Länder*, the privatisation programme established in 1985 was essentially completed. In Spring 1992, the federal government was due to submit specific proposals for further privatisations. Of the two special assets owned by the federal government, the splitting-up of the *Deutsche Bundespost* into three separate companies in the medium-term opens the possibility of allowing new shareholders, while the opening of the *Deutsche Bundesbahn* is also due to be discussed.

In *Greece*, the programme of privatisation drawn up by the new government in July 1990 had not by the end of 1991 succeeded in meeting its targets. The proceeds from the sale of public "ailing" enterprises were after 18 months only 2.5 billion drachmas. In order to accelerate the process, a new law was enacted at the end of 1991 whose purpose it is to simplify liquidation procedures and to reinforce competition rules. The law also resulted in some administrative changes, with the reinforcement of the Ministerial Committee for Privatisation (now consisting of the Ministers of National Economy, Finance, and Industry, Energy and Technology), as well as with the setting up of a Secretariat for Privatisations under the Minister for Industry, Energy and Technology.

In early 1992, the Ministerial Committee for Privatisation reviewed the progress to date and decided to proceed by July 1992 with the privatisation of 141 out of 155 companies belonging to public entities under the Ministry of Industry, Energy and Technology. In addition, the Committee set as a target the privatisation of about 330-360 of the 770-780 companies currently in the public sector. Finally, at the end of March 1992 a provisional contract of sale was signed for 69.8 per cent of the capital stock of "Heracles General Cement Company", one of the leaders of the European cement market. The total amount of the sale is 124 billion drachmas, of which 120 billion will be paid in cash to the Hellenic Industrial Reconstruction Organisation upon the signing of the final contract (which is subject to EC Commission approval), with the remaining 4 billion payable at the end of 1994. The consortium of buyers has undertaken to keep the company in "normal operation" for the next seven years.

In *Italy*, the approval of a new antitrust law in January 1991 marks a substantial step towards a legislative framework that is conducive to privatisation activity (see Box 10). The law makes provision for the conversion of public corporations, the elimination of public shareholding, and the sale of parts of public property. The reasons for putting in motion a process of privatisation can be traced to the necessity to enhance the value of productive activities and to the urgent need to reduce the large public debt, especially in the context of Italy's obligations within the European Community.

In addition, two new laws regulating financial markets were adopted. Since January 1991, public disclosure of takeover bids has become mandatory whenever a high risk of discrimination against some shareholders is envisaged. Four types of public takeover bids are introduced in the legislation: preventive (concerning an eventual buyer with the intention of gaining control); subsequent (concerning the purchase of the majority of stocks not through the stock market); residual (concerning the takeover of remaining shares by the shareholder with a controlling majority); or incremental (concerning a takeover bid that involves the increase in the shares of the shareholder in possession of half of the shares necessary for control). In May 1991, following an EC Directive, a variety of unfair business practices related to stock exchanges have been banned, e.g. insider trading, "tipping", and counselling.

In the *Netherlands*, a marked deviation from the tradition of tolerating cartels can be signalled, now that the government is revising its competition policy. This initiative should be seen in light of harmonisation with EC competition policy [9]. In May 1991, a White Paper on competition policy was issued, outlining legislative initiatives to encourage competition. An important step was

> **Box 10. Italy: the new anti-trust law**
>
> Given the extent of public ownership and public shareholding, the weight of state-controlled firms and their use as instruments of industrial policy, a legal framework for limiting restrictive business practices was not felt necessary in Italy until recently. Until the adoption of such a law in 1990, Italy was alone of all major OECD countries without legislation protecting competition. A number of initiatives were taken during the 1950s and 1960s in this direction but none came to fruition, leaving a situation with no coherent framework for mergers, acquisitions, bankruptcies, reallocation of property rights and corporate structure.
>
> The new economic and political setting of the 1980s, marked by the acceleration of European integration, intense processes of industrial restructuring, and the widespread failure of sectoral policies, revealed all the weaknesses associated with a lack of regulations governing competition. Since the mid-1980s a series of surveys on the functioning of markets were made, on which the final drafting of the anti-trust law was based. The new law, which complements the European legislation, regulates firm behaviour possibly resulting in anti-competitive effects with respect to:
>
> - Agreements;
> - Abuses of dominant market position;
> - Concentration.
>
> With respect to horizontal and vertical agreements and to the abuses of dominant market positions, control is mainly obtained by specifying the generic categories of operations that are forbidden, and indicating the situations in which the supervising authority can exceptionally authorize such behaviour. As far as concentrations are concerned, preventive notice of remarkable mergers, acquisitions, and joint-ventures has to be given to the supervising authority, which then authorizes or prohibits the operations.
>
> The anti-trust law applies to private, public or mixed capital enterprises operating within the Italian territory, with the exception of companies managing services of general economic interest or operating in a monopolistic market.
>
> After a period of adjustment which lasted a little more than one year, the anti-trust law is now fully operational. In 1991 and in the first three months of 1992 the supervising authority took 322 decisions, expressed 30 opinions, and made 3 recommendations. Its activity involved companies in both the public and in the private sector. As an illustration, Sip (public telephones) was accused of abusing its legal monopoly position by precluding 3C Communications from introducing into the Italian market a new credit-card payment service; Eni (public energy) was fined 500 million lire for not having informed the supervising authority of its purchase of Enimont shares from Montedison; and a negative opinion was expressed on the take-over by Fininvest (private media) of Manzoni, an advertising dealer.
>
> The supervising authority in this initial period is addressing its activity also to resolving any source of ambiguity. It is making a serious effort to clarify the various rules of the new law expressed in too general terms, in order to prevent firms from incurring heavy penalties. On this matter the authority is urging the government to implement the anti-trust law by determining the criteria on which exceptional authorizations of anti-competitive concentrations have to be based. It is striving to define the boundaries of its jurisdiction vis-à-vis other supervising bodies: the Central Bank, the publishing and radio broadcasting supervisor, the private insurances supervising institute (ISVAP). Based on its acts to date, it appears that the authority is determined to interpret any dispensation to its jurisdiction in a restrictive manner.

the announced ban effective January 1993 on so-called horizontal price arrangements between companies in the same trade, except for price arrangements in franchising. Some other revisions of competition policy are on their way or being considered.

Concerning state-owned enterprises, a few important firms were wholly or partly privatised. The government sold 36.6 per cent of shares in Volvo Car BV, the Dutch car manufacturer, to Mitsubishi. The state remains the owner of 33.3 per cent of the stock. Following the new arrangements in ownership, the name of the company changed into Netherlands Car BV, a company that will assemble Mitsubishi cars next to a range of Volvo cars. The government also sold its stake of 46 per cent in Vredestein NV, a tyre producer, to a private investment company.

In *Portugal*, one development in this area has been the drawing up of a privatisation plan for the oil company

Petrogal, Portugal's largest commercial enterprise. At the same time, a number of state-owned firms have been transformed into public-funded limited liability companies; they include Air Portugal, Electricity of Portugal and the National Steel company, as well as enterprises in, inter alia, the shipbuilding, cement, pulp and paper and banking and finance sectors. The policy with regard to state-owned enterprises which, in given cases, may involve rationalisation, financial restructuring or full or partial privatisation, has continued to be implemented with respect to firms in a broad array of sectors.

In the *United Kingdom*, the Competition and Service (Utilities) Act of 1992 strengthens the powers of the bodies regulating the gas, electricity and water industries and promotes competition in the provision of gas and water services.

Since 1979, the UK government has pursued a very active policy of privatisation. To date, 44 major businesses and some smaller concerns have been sold to the private sector, involving around 900 000 employees [10]. Current privatisation plans include asset sales of £5.5 billion a year until 1992-93, including further sales of water and electricity companies in England and Wales. Future plans include the privatisation of British Coal, British Rail and the government's residual holdings of British Telecom.

In *Austria*, a number of regulatary reform measures have been taken recently. Regulatory controls on unalloyed scrap iron and steel were fully eliminated with the expiry of the scrap control legislation on 30 June 1992. Existing export restrictions on aluminium and copper scrap were to be abolished as from 1st January 1993. In those branches of the food industry where competitive activity has been weak owing to the high degree of regulation and protection, structural changes have been accelerated.

In the meantime, a further liberalisation of administrative price controls was envisaged for the first half of 1992. Price regulation was to be maintained only for medicines and for line-conveyed forms of energy because of the limited competition; and such regulation was to be replaced as soon as possible by competition-oriented measures. Finally, parliament has taken up new government competition legislation, which involves the abolition of obsolete provisions and the adaptation of existing stipulations on unfair competition. In December 1991, a draft amendment to the industrial code, prepared with a view to extensive liberalisation and deregulation, was submitted to general expert opinion.

In *Finland*, a government proposal on deregulation and stricter competition rules has been sent to parliament. Its objective is to strengthen the position of the authorities in the control of market practices and increases the cases where restrictions to competition are forbidden by law. The reform should improve the functioning of markets, and brings Finnish competition legislation close to that applied in EC countries.

Privatisation of state-owned companies is one of the main industry-related policy targets in Finland, aimed at both curbing public expenditures and shrinking the public sector's share of the economy. However, the current economic climate has not been supportive, and the depression of the domestic stock market has effectively hampered the privatisation of state-owned enterprises. Major steps in privatisation were last taken some years ago. So far, the state has not dissipated any majority stakes in leading state-owned companies, and earlier privatisation initiatives (such as that of the oil and chemicals company Neste Oy) have remained in a preparatory stage.

In *Norway*, the state owns interests in companies within the mining, petroleum, and manufacturing sectors. The government has justified subsidies to certain state-owned enterprises on the basis of regional policy considerations, as many of these companies are located in sparsely populated and vulnerable areas. As deficit problems have mounted however, steps have been taken to reduce subsidies and give priority to restructuring, in order to make state-owned enterprises more profitable and self-supporting. In certain local communities where state-owned companies have been the main source of employment, programmes towards the stimulation of alternative employment by private companies are in operation and in some areas are now drawing to a close. The government has no overall privatisation programme for state-owned companies, and plans to review proposals for industrial co-operation, financing for expansion and/or acquisition on a case-by-case basis taking into account the development possibilities of the different companies from a commercial standpoint.

The liberalisation of legislation regarding regulations, especially with respect to setting up businesses and trading, is at the same time being actively pursued through a Committee appointed in 1990 and reporting to the Ministry of Industry on a quarterly basis. Procedures for reporting information to the authorities are also being simplified, in order to reduce the burden to industry and especially to smaller firms.

In *Sweden*, a privatisation programme for state-owned companies was approved by parliament in December 1991. The programme, one of the key elements of the new Swedish industrial policy, sets forth the guiding principles for the privatisation process that will last ten years, starting off in 1992. The privatisation programme includes those firms that used to be owned by the state-owned management company Fortia, such as Procordia, LKAB (mines), ASSI (pulp and paper), SSAB (steel), Vattenfall (electricity), Domanverjet (forests), and Nordbanken. Deregulation and competition issues fall now under the responsibility of the Ministry of Industry, renamed as Ministry of Industry and Commerce. Swedish deregulation and competition policy is undergoing a review since the agreement between the EFTA and the EC will result in a European Economic Area where uniform competition rules will exist next to national regulations.

In *Switzerland*, the Cartels Commission has undertaken a major information campaign aimed at inducing the public authorities to give wider scope to the play of competition in government procurement. The Cartels Commission is also following closely the liberalisation measures in the telecommunications industry.

In *Australia*, the government is pursuing policies aimed at the restructuring of industries and at addressing a number of serious infrastructure problems which inhibit the ability of industries to compete internationally. Following the deregulation of the financial sector, the domestic airlines and telecommunications industries are presently undergoing restructuring and a comprehensive program is being implemented for the reform of shipping, land transport and the waterfront. Discussions are also underway aimed at reforming intergovernmental relations and improving the working of the Australian Federation. Finally, in intellectual property regulation, a new Patents Act, in effect as from April 1991, has replaced the one from 1952. Apart from improving the administration of the patent system, the new act is characterised by tougher requirements for issuing standard patents.

E. Regional development policies

After a number of years in which regional policy underwent an important transformation reflecting the structural adjustment process in the OECD economies, it is now entering a new stage of transformation. The driving forces behind the latest regional policy changes are not an outcome of macro-economic conditions but lie in the necessity for a variety of regions to adjust to a new geopolitical context. Examples of such adaptation are the important place of co-operation with central and eastern European countries, the preparation for the European Single Market and the European Economic Area, and coping with the impacts of the North American Free Trade Agreement. At the beginning of the 1990s, adjustment to geo-political changes has become for a number of OECD Member countries an additional regional policy objective, next to the aim to reduce regional disparities and to contribute to macro-economic structural adjustment. It calls for new and innovative practices in regional policy, and brings to the fore the importance of transfrontier co-operation and international co-ordination.

At the same time, the dynamics of regional economic development are becoming increasingly complex. A distinction between the impacts of structural and of conjunctural factors on regional disparities is necessary, especially since the effects of these different sets of factors might be somewhat contradictory. According to the latest report on recent regional policy developments in OECD countries [11], regional disparities have continued to widen in Japan, Italy, France, Spain, and Portugal, while Greece's relative position within the European Community continued to worsen. At the same time however, in a number of countries whose current economic downturn started relatively early, such as the United Kingdom, the United States and Canada, the recession was in the first place felt by the most developed regions, giving rise to a phenomenon of "negative regional re-balancing". Similar effects can be noticed in Australia, Finland, and Sweden.

Apart from these cyclical trends, a strong undercurrent in the form of structural factors shapes the regional environment as well. One of the most important structural trends is the internationalisation of the OECD economies in general and the globalisation of industrial activities in particular. A recent OECD report on the issue suggests that the effects of globalisation in the form of inward foreign direct investment offers little help in reducing regional disparities [12]. In most of the countries analysed, such investments tend to be directed to prosperous more than to lagging regions. Globalisation also appears to reinforce specialisation of regions. Regions geared towards a particular industry have a high chance of specialising further in that industry, due to inward foreign direct investment. This tendency might be undesirable from a regional policy point of view, since specialisation increases the vulnerability and jeopardises the fragile economic bases of lagging regions.

These cyclical and structural trends are shaping a new environment for regional policy. Rather than relying exclusively on either exogenous or endogenous developments, regional policy in the 1990s is likely to be most effective when seeing regional strengths and weaknesses in light of a changing international environment. When dealing with these new challenges, its impact will be greatest when improving the overall business environment of the firm, rather than when it relies on direct forms of aid. An emphasis on the development of a suitable technological and educational infrastructure belongs to the primary objectives of such a policy.

A number of recent regional policy measures relating to the above themes are outlined below.

In *Japan*, the government promotes the creation of towns combining industrial, academic and residential features. These designated areas, intended to invigorate and promote the independence of the local economy, benefit from tax incentives and low-interest financing for high-tech industries and residential and road construction. In 1991, twenty one local governments revised their Technopolis development programmes in order to move toward the next stage of development. In addition, the coverage of policies aimed at the decentralisation of economic activities was broadened. Two new projects were added to the list of localities that are eligible for government incentives when constructing industrial high-tech facilities (so-called Research Core Policies). Such facilities function as local centers of R&D and aim at enhancing local industrial infrastructures; they are supported by preferential tax treatments, low-interest financing, and loan guarantees. Similarly, three new areas (in Hokkaido, Fukushima, and Gunma prefectures) became eligible for assistance in the promotion for siting designated types of business with a significant growth potential (the "brains of industry") in certain localities.

In the *European Community*, the Commission is stepping up its efforts to support lagging areas in order to help them prepare for European Monetary Union. These proposals, as formulated in the Maastricht Treaty, call on the more developed EC countries to make a greater effort to help the poorer south and periphery of the Community. The proposed Budget for the 1993-97 period reflects this increased commitment to the development of lagging and industrially declining areas. Much support will continue to be channelled through the structural fund, for which resources will be growing progressively up to about 29 billion ECUs in 1997. These funds will especially benefit Greece, Ireland, Portugal, and Spain. A newly created cohesion fund, with an estimated size of 2.5 billion ECUs a year, will be used for an improvement of the environment and infrastructure in the same four countries.

In *Germany*, the existing joint federal government/*Länder* programme "Improving the Regional Economic Structures" was extended in 1991 to be available for all the new *Länder* for a first period of five years, with the possibility to extend additional support exceptionally in view of specific requirements of structural policy and with additional financing for the new *Länder*. To contribute to the financing of such measures, the federal government and the new *Länder* will contribute jointly (50/50) DM 3 billion each year for five years. The maximum support rates for commerce-related investment in plants range from 23 per cent for construction to 20 per cent for expansion and 15 per cent for rationalisation. These rates can be topped-up with non-regional investment support up to a maximum of 12 percentage points bringing the maximum allowed rate to 35 per cent. A part of the joint federal government/*Länder* Programme totalling DM 2.4 billion was adopted for 1991 and 1992 within the framework of the Upswing East Project (*Gemeinschaftswerk Aufschwung Ost*) for areas in the new *Länder* and is aimed at promoting also investment and industry-related measures.

In the *Netherlands*, the northern region continues to suffer from economic problems and is still lagging behind the general economic development. The regional development programme for this region has therefore continued, and so has the Investment Grant Scheme. In terms of investment and employment, the southern and eastern regions of the country have been catching up with the national average. As a consequence, regional development programmes in these regions will be abolished after 1992, with the exception of the programme for the south-eastern part of Limburg which will last until 1994.

In *Portugal*, four recent initiatives have been taken in this policy field: (i) the provision of incentives and the development of infrastructure needed for industrial diversification in the Val do Ave area, hit by the crisis in the textiles industry; (ii) the drawing up of a plan on land use in the Algarve, which will lead to the creation of four zones of industrial concentration; (iii) the establishment of a plan for land use and development in the Douro River region; and (iv) the provision of support structures to encourage small investment projects in Setubal, which has been affected by shipyard restructuring.

In the *United Kingdom*, regional policy support instruments remain Regional Selective Assistance, Regional Enterprise Grants, higher levels of support under the Consultancy Initiatives, and a programme of factory building by English estates, or Scottish and Welsh agencies. Nevertheless, the government has devised special assistance packages to meet particular area problems that have arisen in the past year.

First, in order to cope with the effects of some 2 850 British Steel job losses in 1991, as well as of a large number of direct and indirect job losses expected at Ravenscraig in 1992, the government endorsed the case for an Enterprise Zone in North Lancashire and will hold discussions with the European Commission on proposals for establishing the zone. Secondly, a special programme has been drawn up to help generate new employment in Barrow and West Cumbria, which suffer from a combination of geographic isolation and heavy reliance on two employers who have announced major planned redundancies.

In *Finland*, a reform of regional development policies is now being considered. An expert committee and several working groups have made proposals for the change of both legislation and instrumentation. As in other policy areas, the reform of regional development policies is considered necessary in the light of the approaching integration agreement with the European Community. The most important proposal concerns the shrinkage of the extent of state regional assistance, from a coverage of 50 per cent to 30 per cent of the population. Recommendations have also been made for improving the return on public resources and for restructuring the large number of organisations operating in the field of regional policy. The proposals are expected to be implemented gradually, from 1993 onwards.

In *Norway*, the Regional Development Fund administers grants for entrepreneurs, and has become a considerable source for finance, especially now that its appropriations have more than doubled, from 35 million Norwegian kroner (NOK) in 1991 to 75 million Norwegian kroner in 1992. The grants are allocated by the counties. A quarter of the increase in the sources for the Venture Fund (20 million out of 80 million NOK) will be channelled to venture companies in the North of Norway that transfer risk capital and know-how to companies at their early stage of development. In 1991, total allocations for various regional development schemes amounted to nearly 1.8 billion Norwegian kroner, a level that has been regarded as very high in relation to the Norwegian GDP [13]. Such an extensive instrumentation, however, should also be seen in the light of the sparse population, the particular living conditions, and the vulnerable economic base of extensive parts of Northern Norway.

In *Switzerland*, Parliament approved in October 1991 an increase in the resources available for assisting investment in mountain areas. In the period 1992-2000, SF800 million, to be allotted in annual instalments, will supplement the SF500 million fund which was set up in 1974 and was augmented by SF300 million in 1984. The additional resources will make it possible to continue support for infrastructure investment in keeping with existing legislation. An exceptional measure was also taken in order to reduce the backlog of demands (totalling SF300 million) for investment assistance in mountain areas; the government estimates that this unblocking of funds will bring forward total investment worth SF1.2 billion for these areas.

In *Turkey*, minimum-wage earners in the priority development areas, which cover 33 provinces, are to be exempted from taxation in 1992, under the provisions of the annual regional development programme. This programme also calls for the preparation of special projects with a view to job creation in the eastern and southeastern Anatolian regions as well as land grants to private-sector tourism development activities in the eastern and southeastern Regions. Investments in the tourism projects will be tax-free during a ten-year period, and the basic infrastructure will be provided by the state.

F. Industry-related environmental and energy policies

In the discussion about the appropriate policy response to pressures on the natural environment exerted by economic activities, it has become increasingly clear that two policy approaches must be pursued in parallel and in a complementary way:

- Traditional policies of environmental management directly aimed at reducing the pollution burden; and
- Integration of environmental concerns into sectoral policies, including the various aspects of industrial policy.

Policy integration requires horizontal co-ordination between the respective administrative branches. This may involve trading-off between conflicting goals of environmental protection and industrial development. Often, however, "win-win" situations can be identified that are both conducive to reducing the pollution burden and to increasing allocative efficiency throughout the economy.

Recently, two areas of environmental policies have received particular attention in a number of OECD Member countries. The first is a rising awareness of global environmental problems such as climate change, the depletion of the ozone layer or deforestation which have led to policy proposals and policy actions concerning, *inter alia*, air emissions. As many of these emissions (e.g. carbon dioxide) are directly linked to the use of energy, possible measures to curb emissions have a direct impact on industry in general and its energy-intensive branches in particular. Considerations concerning the cost-effectiveness of various policy instruments to implement emission reductions will therefore be of great importance for the industries concerned.

At the same time, several countries have initiated new policy measures to reduce the amount and the hazardousness of waste generated by industry and private households. The choice of policy instruments to achieve objectives of waste reduction varies widely, and includes voluntary agreements with industry, compulsory use of recycled raw material, fees or deposit-refund systems. The impact on industry as well as the environmental effectiveness will be governed by the choice and the precise formulation of the policy measures. Additional costs may arise for industry but they have to be weighed against business opportunities in eco-industries and environmental services that are developing rapidly.

Environmental and safety concerns continued to influence energy policy developments in 1991 and complement the traditional objective of energy supply security. Government action such as the promotion of energy efficiency improvements and the development and utilisation of alternative energy sources show the complementary role of energy and environmental policies pursued by many OECD governments. In a number of instances, increases in energy taxes have been proposed as a means to internalise environmental costs due to energy use. From an industry viewpoint, this must be assessed with regard to international competitiveness and in view of the fact that the level of energy taxation already varies greatly across OECD Member countries.

The short-lived increase in oil prices in late 1990 had brought about renewed concerns regarding the capacity of OECD economies to absorb oil price increases. While the brief 1990 experience could provide no conclusive answers, this capacity seems to have increased over the years as a result of reduced energy intensity of production, greater diversification of energy sources and structural reforms, including efforts of deregulation of the energy industry and more rapidly adjusting capital and labour markets.

Some recent industry-related environment and energy policy initiatives are noted below.

In the *United States*, follow-up actions under the Clean Air Act included a pledge by the President to halt production of chloroflourocarbons (CFCs) by the end of 1995. This commits the United States to a faster phaseout schedule of CFCs than the Clean Air Act (which adopted the deadline under the Montreal Protocol) of the year 2000. Progress in implementing the Act was also made, notably, in rule-making (particularly in regard to tradeable SO_2 emissions) and in establishing the National Acid Precipitation Assessment Program.

In *Canada*, the Green Plan published by the government in December 1990 (see *Annual Review* 1991) set forth the target of stabilising emissions of CO_2 and other greenhouse gases at 1990 levels by the year 2000. In this context, federal and provincial Energy and Environment Ministers have worked together to develop a draft National Action Strategy on Global Warming, which proposes a phased and progressive approach to the stabilisation of greenhouse gas emissions. And the government has now approved an Efficiency and Alternative Energy Programme as a first step in implementing Canada's commitment to stabilisation. The programme involves a number of initiatives for achieving -- through information, regulation, R&D and persuasion -- greater energy efficiency and the utilisation of alternative energy sources in all end-use sectors.

In *Japan*, the two oil shocks prompted a response from industry and government that led to one of the highest levels of energy efficiency in the OECD area. Increasing concern with global environmental issues such as global warming, depletion of the ozone layer and acid rain have prompted the elaboration of a long term action programme (so-called "New Earth 21"), identifying a number of broad areas for policy action: the promotion of energy and resource conservation; the encouragement of introduction of clean energy sources (safer nuclear plants, new and renewable energy sources); the development of innovative environment-friendly technologies (re-utilisation technologies, third-generation CFC substitutes); and the development of future energy sources (nuclear fusion, solar power generation). In terms of recent policy measures for the prevention of industrial pollution, a new law promoting the utilisation of recycled resources came into force in October 1991, after its adoption by the Diet. The Law aims to reduce waste generation at the production, circulation and consumption stages. More specifically, it contains acts on the promotion of the use of recycled resources and by-products in manufacturing. It also contains measures that promote the production and facilitate the collection of recyclable products.

Concerning energy-related measures, an additional special petroleum tax at half the conventional rate was levied starting in April 1991 as an exceptional measure for a period of one year in order to cover part of the Japanese contribution to the peace-keeping activities in the Persian Gulf area. The Coal Mining Council submitted a report to the government in June 1991, stating that in view of the last phase of structural adjustment in the industry, a stepwise reduction of domestic coal production would be required, as well as diversification by mining enterprises. In addition, the report recommends the development of a new "Coal Policy" as part of overall energy policy, consisting of the stabilisation of imports of coal, and the development and diffusion of clean coal technologies.

In *Belgium*, where regional authorities now have responsibility for environment policy, the Brussels-Capital region has empowered its executive to give a high priority to the prevention or reduction of waste and to action for limiting its harmful effects. The executive is authorised to take a series of detailed measures to attain that objective, including the labelling of harmful products accompanied by indications on ways of eliminating or recycling them. One area which has received particular attention is the elimination of waste containing polychlorinated biphenyls (PCBs). The executive has also set out the conditions for obtaining the augmented tax deduction made available for environment-related R&D.

At the same time, a five-year plan on waste management is to be drawn up by the Brussels Institute for Waste Management in association with the Regional Cleanliness Agency; the plan is to be subjected to public enquiry and officially promulgated by the Brussels executive.

In the Flemish region, an "ecological authorisation" is now mandatory before an industrial or commercial establishment can be put into operation or be transformed. In certain cases, a security report is required - notably, where it is intended that the establishment will be using dangerous materials or is to serve as a depository for such substances.

In the Wallonia region, an important development is the decree of July 1991 concerning taxes on waste materials, which are imposed on both household and non-household wastes. The revenues accruing from these taxes will be assigned in full to a special fund to provide financing for a series of measures related to waste elimination, reduction and treatment, as well as to pollution prevention and the rehabilitation of polluted sites.

In *Denmark*, the new environmental Act which took effect on 1 January 1992 has as one of its fundamental principles the aim of promoting the use of cleaner technology. The Act also incorporates a variety of new policy instruments such as environmental agreements with industry, eco-audit, environmental labelling schemes, and gives wider access to the application of economic instruments. At the same time, a number of programmes promoting research concerning industry and the environment are being run by the Ministries of Industry, the Environment and of Education. Examples are the Industrial Use of Environmental Technology Programme, run for the period 1991-94 by the Ministry of Industry with a budget of Danisj kroner 130 million, the two action programmes for cleaner technology and for recycling run by the Ministry of the Environment with a total budget of Danish kroner 470 million for the 1990-92 period, and the Strategic Environment Research Programme, run by the Ministry of Education for the 1992-96 period and with a total budget of Danish kroner 300 million. The Ministries of Industry and of the Environment have also established close co-operation on issues of common interest, and published a joint report on "Industry and the Environment" in April 1992. A general conclusion of the report is that increasing environmental requirements should not be seen as a threat to industry.

In addition, the Danish parliament approved in early 1992 a bill fixing an environmental tax on carbon dioxide (CO_2) emissions from certain products used for the production of energy, at a rate of Danish kroner 50 per ton of CO_2 emissions. At the same time, and in order not to harm the international competitiveness of highly energy-consuming Danish firms, the parliament also approved a bill authorizing the government to partially compensate these firms for the CO_2 tax through subsidies.

In *Germany*, a large number of measures have been taken to protect the environment which have a significant impact on industry. These relate, in particular, to waste disposal (in addition to those already referred to in the 1991 *Annual Review*): e.g. more stringent rules for underground waste storage; the introduction of volume-related and pollutant-related economic incentives to avoid waste; to immission control: e.g. limiting the use of highly volatile halogenated hydrocarbons, prohibiting the use of CFCs and halon for a number of larger scale uses, or prohibiting the use of Scavanger (a dioxide-producing additive); to emission control, either directly or through the promotion of alternative technologies and energies; to environmental damage and its registration; and to the prevention of water pollution focusing on reducing nitrogen and phosphorus and avoiding or limiting dangerous substances. The Act on Detergents and Cleansing agents (*Wasch- und Reinigungsmittelgesetz*) was extended to the new *Länder*.

The federal government has also recently presented the framework conditions it intends to create for its energy policy in view of the new economic, ecological and international challenges. The concept thus takes account of the fundamental change in the factors which have an impact on energy policy resulting from the unification of Germany, the risks of the greenhouse effect, the progress made on European integration and the fundamental changes in central and eastern Europe and in the ex-Soviet Union. It underlines the market orientation of the energy policy of united Germany.

In *Italy*, the government recognises that environmental and industrial policy are increasingly interlinked and has taken initiatives to reduce the harmful impact of production activities on the environment. Legislative activity in 1991 mainly focused on the formal introduction of EC directives. Intervention has centered on the problems arising from pollution by industrial waste; air pollution by auto-vehicle emissions; from the market introduction of dangerous products; and from noise pollution by machine devices.

With respect to energy, two laws were approved in the beginning of 1991 in the context of the national plan aimed at a more efficient use of energy, and the development of alternative energy sources. The first outlines a variety of norms concerning the realization of new private buildings and all public works, the management of the installation of heating systems, and the creation of energy-manager posts within industrial and civil units with high consumption rates. The second law provides for a broad deregulation in order to bring the Italian norms closer to those of the European legislative system. An important step in this direction is represented by the final liberalization of oil prices. It is now widely accepted that the energy market in Italy must involve a number of public and private agents, operating in a open and competitive environment.

In the *Netherlands*, in accordance with the National Environment Policy Plan (see the 1990 *Annual Review*) the Minister of Economic Affairs and the Minister of the Environment presented a White Paper to parliament on environmental technology. The paper, emphasising the role of innovation in helping achieve a more sustainable growth, contains measures to stimulate technology transfer between universities and industry; to promote diffusion of knowledge of environmental technology; and to encourage development of environmental technology. An important element of government policy in this area is the reaching of voluntary agreements between government and industry, aimed at agreed environmental targets. The attraction of these agreements for industry lies with the assurance of government not to come up with new measures without adequate consultation.

In *Spain*, an Industrial and Technological Environment Programme, which has been established for the period 1990-94, seeks to strengthen the environment-related capital goods and engineering services sectors as well as to promote the efficient adjustment of Spanish industry to the requirements of environmental protection. In 1991, a total of 680 projects in this area received financial assistance, priority being given to technological development and pilot schemes.

At the same time, a National Energy Plan has been launched for the decade 1991-2000, having as objectives: improvement in energy efficiency; a shift in the structure of primary energy demand, reflecting a greater reliance on natural gas and renewable energy sources and reduced dependence on nuclear energy, oil and coal; intensified exploitation of indigenous energy resources; security of foreign supply through increased diversification in the consumption of hydrocarbons (more weight given to gas and less to oil); achievement of a better balance between considerations of cost, diversification, self-sufficiency in energy supply, and environmental protection. The plan assigns a significant role to R&D in making possible the adjustments needed for the attainment of the national energy objectives.

In the *United Kingdom*, an Advisory Committee on Business and the Environment was established jointly by the Departments for the Environment and for Trade and Industry in May 1991. Its aim is to provide a strategic-level dialogue between government and business on both immediate and longer-term environmental issues, and its members include business leaders from a wide range of companies across Britain.

A major government focus in this area is on the encouragement of recycling and the minimisation of waste. A White Paper, This Common Inheritance, has set, as a target to be met by the year 2000, the recycling of half of the household waste which it is possible to recycle, and measures are being put in place designed to meet that goal. More recently, the government began to develop, in association with local authorities and industry, new targets for energy recovery from incineration and from landfill gas.

Among various other moves aimed at recycling and waste reduction, the following can be noted:

- The government issued, in July 1991, guidance to local authorities for recycling plans they are required to produce under the Environmental Protection Act.

- After discussions with the government, the tyre industry has set up a voluntary "green levy" to help finance the recycling or safe disposal of used tyres, and the newspaper publishers have agreed to aim, in co-operation with the newsprint producers, at increasing the proportion of recycled fibre used in newsprint to at least 40 per cent by the year 2000.

In addition, the government supports a number of environment-related research activities and promotes the adoption by industry of environmentally benign technologies. It has also been developing a voluntary "eco-labelling" scheme for identifying the more environmentally benign consumer products, and the UK has played an active role in the discussions leading up to the agreement, in December 1991, on an EC scheme in this area.

In *Austria*, the promulgation of a decree on the recycling of beverage containers and packaging has led to the establishment of a collection and recovery system for beverage and food packaging by a private association representing a wide range of industrial and commercial interests involved. This activity is aimed, inter alia, at reducing waste upstream of the consumer's end, i.e. at the production stage.

At the same time, in 1991, 210 000 tonnes of used paper -- 18 per cent more than in the previous year -- were collected in households. The paper industry has undertaken to take over at current international prices, the entire amount of used paper collected in Austria for recycling. Other collection activities under way include, for instance, used glass, batteries, and old plastic pipes as well as credit, membership and similar plastic cards.

Three environment-related decrees directed to business and industrial establishments were issued in 1991. They concern: the handling and storage of inflammable liquids; the fitting out of industrial plants with gas displacement lines for stationary fuel containers; the identification of plants representing a source of danger and the responsibilities of the owner in the event of an accident.

In *Finland*, the government is expected in the course of 1992 to set out a strategy for an energy policy in the 1990s and beyond. The most important choice it faces is a decision over whether the increased future demand for energy should be satisfied by nuclear or by fossil energy. The high energy intensity of Finland's industry also implies that environmental considerations that are taken into account in energy production have a significant impact on the industry. Thus the reduction of emissions required by international agreements or the requirement to use recycled paper in paper production is expected to lead to a restructuring of the paper industry.

In *Norway*, the government continues to give a high priority to environmental policy. The main principle guiding this policy -- the polluter pays -- has led the government to issue environmental taxes that reflect the environmental costs of using resources, while at the same time giving incentives to producers for limiting pollution. The recent special carbon dioxide-emission tax has been slightly increased for gasoline (while favouring the use of unleaded fuel), and from 1 July 1992 extended to coal and coke that is used for heating purposes. The reconsideration of the industry's emission permits which started in 1988 continued in 1991. Several plants have new and stricter requirements, especially within the pulp and paper industry. It is estimated that, as a result of these requirements, industry will have to invest approximately 3 billion Norwegian kroner by 1995 to reduce its emissions. Nevertheless, the government considers that in a medium-term perspective, higher environmental standards may form a comparative advantage.

The deregulation of the energy sector, opening up the market and giving new opportunities to Norwegian industry, has been pursued. Under the new Energy Act, that entered into force on January 1st 1992, industrial users are free to buy power from the supplier with the best offer, while transfer of this power to the plant will be guaranteed by the grid operator. Transfer prices will be regulated to ensure that "common carriage" is established in the grid. In concordance with these measures, the state-owned power producer Statkraft will be split up into a grid-owner and a power-producing company.

In *Sweden*, the recognition of the concept of sustainable growth has instigated the formulation of an environmental policy that is a constituent part of economic policy. In this view, rather than only bringing about additional costs, environmental claims are also driving forces behind innovation and the creation of markets. As a consequence, the environment industry has become one of the fastest growing sectors. In the field of environmental and energy policies, several tax measures were taken. Parliament adopted a proposal to introduce a revenue-neutral but differentiated automobile tax, based on the environmental impact of each category of cars. A modification in energy taxation aims at increasing the competitiveness of combined heat and power plants.

Energy policy is based on an inter-party agreement among the Social Democratic, the Liberal, and the Centre Party. According to the agreement, the phase-out schedule of nuclear power plants and the rate at which it can proceed will depend on the success of electricity conservation measures, the supply of environmentally acceptable power generation, and the feasibility of maintaining internationally competitive electricity prices. The guidelines for energy policy set forth a programme for energy conservation and detail several measures for promoting energy production with renewable sources of energy, such as biomass, wind power and solar heat.

In *Switzerland*, the first report on the state of the environment was published in 1991; follow-up reports are to be issued at three-year intervals. A federal campaign has been launched with a view to heightening public and business awareness of the need to reduce the production of waste materials. The four-year campaign, which is receiving an allotment of SF9 million, provides inter alia for advisory facilities aimed in particular at SMEs.

In *Turkey*, a solid-waste control directive, which went into effect in March 1991, is currently being implemented with respect to packaging materials made primarily of plastics and metals. Enterprises which market products packaged with these materials are required by the directive to recover and recycle the empty bottles and containers.

G. Measures related to international investment and trade

The growth of foreign investment and trade slowed in 1991, although both continued to expand faster than output as they have over many years. The slowed growth is generally attributed to the recession in North America and lower economic expansion in western Europe. The deceleration of trade, and possibly foreign investment, may have bottomed-out in the second half of 1991 and a modest recovery may be underway [14].

The surge in foreign direct investment in the second half of the 1980s was accompanied by commensurate growth in cross-border trade within international enterprises. In 1990, nearly 40 per cent of world merchandise trade took place within the largest 350 enterprises [15]. More than a third of US trade in 1990 was between US companies and their affiliates abroad, while about a fourth of the imports of Japanese companies were from their affiliates in east Asia. These examples illustrate how foreign investment is reshaping international trade and leading to the global integration of manufacturing.

The attitudes and policies of many countries appear to be appreciably more open and favourable toward foreign investment than trade. In particular, inward investment is actively sought by all OECD countries whereas barriers to imports are extensive and were significantly reduced by only a few countries over the last decade.

Countries in all parts of the world have recently liberalised conditions for foreign investment and ownership. Many have gone further and developed costly packages of incentives aimed at attracting foreign firms. Indeed, the competition between countries (and regions within them) for such investment often produces international frictions and calls for multilateral disciplines in order to reduce its incidence.

This positive stance towards foreign investment and associated multinational enterprises (MNEs) represents a significant shift in view on the part of several countries which in the past often regarded MNEs as a mixed blessing for the local economy. Now, in contrast, the presence of MNEs tends to be seen as providing beneficial investment, stimulating competition, transferring useful technologies and skills as well as enhancing the competitiveness of the host economy and creating jobs.

Present attitudes toward trade appear to be more ambivalent, if not negative in some instances. Whereas governments generally profess strong support for open, unfettered trade, many of them at the same time resort to various kinds of protectionism and discrimination. The latter seem to arise mainly from concerns such as possible job losses and trade imbalances as well as from efforts to protect and aid specific industries which are regarded as having strong growth prospects or as having a key role in national economies.

Whatever the reasons, numerous OECD countries have adopted policies which undermine the principle of equal treatment of trading partners. They have often applied administrative measures, such as anti-dumping, against individual firms, and placed a large and growing part of trade under "voluntary" export restraint agreements. As a result, distortions to the functioning of product markets have become even more widespread in the OECD areas [16]. Ironically, these developments are growing at the same time as an increasing number of countries in Latin America, Africa and central and eastern Europe are moving unilaterally towards greater trade liberalisation.

Anti-dumping and countervailing duty actions are again on the rise and spreading beyond the OECD. Although the GATT rules allow the use of such measures, it is their misuse that draws concern. The number of anti-dumping investigations initiated in 1991 nearly doubled over the preceding year, growing from 96 to 175. These numbers, however, greatly understate the impact of such administrative actions, in that the mere threat of an investigation can induce foreign firms to alter prices, lower imports or possibly to enter into a "voluntary" arrangement. Furthermore, an increasing number of non-OECD countries have recently passed, or are in the process of developing, anti-dumping legislation. These developments, collectively, may signal a sharp growth in anti-dumping actions if the latter are misused as tools of retaliation.

The voluntary restraint arrangements, made outside the GATT rules, have become a prominent feature of trade. Nearly 300 such arrangements were identified by GATT in 1990. These "grey areas" measures, which for all practical purposes are akin to managed trade, cover various products (e.g. automobiles, electronics, steel, and textiles) and regulations (e.g. government procurement and intellectual property). They deviate from the requirements of a liberal trading system in three main ways: they involve quantitative limitations; they are discriminatory; and they are handled outside the framework of established rules. The proliferation of such arrangements raises the question of whether the present situation -- in which the multilateral system and managed trade are "co-existing" -- is sustainable" [17].

Finally, the widespread emergence of regional trading arrangements arouses considerable concern. Four new arrangements were announced in 1991 and several more in early 1992. Such arrangements generally adhere, so far, to the principles of liberal trade. It is not clear, however, whether the arrangements will ultimately be "building blocks" or "stumbling blocks" toward a global system that is liberally oriented with respect to trade and foreign investment.

Furthermore, it has been argued that intra-regional trade is less effective than its inter-regional counterpart in maintaining vigorous competition and eroding monopoly profits. Freer trade within regions brings undoubted benefits but it cannot fully compensate for barriers to open, multilateral trade. In addition, discriminatory restrictions on inter-regional trade almost always give rise to distortions in intra-regional trading arrangements, as different countries within the region seek to appropriate a greater share of the rents the restrictions create [18].

A number of recent measures relating to international investment and trade are noted below.

In the *United States*, the Enterprise for the Americas Initiative (EAI) was launched in mid-1990 with the aim of strengthening Latin American and Caribbean economies through expanded trade and investment, and reducing their official debt to the United States. By the beginning of 1992, 31 countries had signed 16 agreements covering trade and investment. The EAI and the Uruguay Round are regarded as mutually complementary by the United States. Successful completion of the Uruguay Round would set international baseline standards for services trade, intellectual property protection, investment performance requirements, and other areas that would make negotiation of free trade in the hemisphere easier.

The US President announced on 12 August 1992 that the United States, Canada and Mexico had completed negotiation of a North American Free Trade Agreement (NAFTA). The NAFTA will phase out barriers to trade in goods and services in North America, eliminate barriers to investment, and strengthen the protection of intellectual property rights. As tariffs and other trade barriers are eliminated, the NAFTA will create a massive open market -- over 360 million people and over US$6 trillion in annual output.

The Japan-US Structural Impediments Initiative (SII) was continued and the first annual report was issued in May 1991 (*First Annual Report of the US-Japan Working Group of the Structural Impediments Initiative*). The aim of the initiative is to address systemic barriers to competition and trade in both economies, including those structural barriers that deter balance of payments adjustment and limit access to each other's market. The principal areas considered include savings and investment, land use, the Japanese distribution system, exclusionary business practices, *keiretsu* practices, and pricing. The Japanese government, in particular, is committed to allowing increased investment in public sector infrastructure, more vigorous enforcement of Japan's antimonopoly law, and the liberalisation of the Large Scale Retail Store Law. The two governments agreed, in early 1992, to reinvigorate the SII through strengthening policy initiatives including new commitments to address the aspects of the business environment of both countries that might impede structural reform including market access, foreign investments and competitiveness.

A new US-Japan Semiconductor Trade Arrangement became effective in August 1991, replacing the 1986 accord. The 1991 Arrangement addresses market access problems confronting foreign firms in Japan as well as the dumping of semiconductors by Japanese suppliers in the US market. In evaluating progress, the arrangement accords particular attention to foreign market share, and also considers increases in design-ins and other long term business relationships between US and Japanese firms. The arrangement reflects the expectation that foreign market share can attain more than 20 per cent by the end of 1992 through continuous efforts by foreign suppliers and Japanese users. The Government of Japan believes this level can be attained and welcomes its realisation.

The US Trade Representative will seek to negotiate a limited extension of the voluntary restraint agreements (VRAs) on machine tools with Japan and Taiwan. The extended VRAs (originally negotiated in 1986 for national security reasons) will attempt to remove import restrictions progressively over a two-year period on several types of machine tools.

The Omnibus Trade and Competitiveness Act of 1988, Special 301, requires the US Trade Representative to identify whether there are countries (so-called "priority countries") that deny adequate and effective protection of intellectual property rights (IPR). In 1991, India, China and Thailand were designated as priority countries. The Special 301 investigation into the IPR practices of China was resolved successfully in January 1992; the investigation into India's practices was terminated in February 1992, and resulted in an "unreasonableness" finding. No immediate trade action was taken, but an interagency group is developing options for trade action should negotiations with India prove unsuccessful.

A number of actions were taken under provisions of Regular Section 301 of the Act in 1991. These included the initiation of investigations of the patent practices of Thailand; the EC Third Country Meat Directive; and access barriers to the Chinese market. In other actions, the United States is monitoring an agreement with Japan on "major projects"; commitments by Thailand concerning copyright practices and enforcement; and a renewed agreement with the EC on import restrictions (corn and sorghum) stemming from EC enlargement.

In *Canada*, the authorities reported on the progress made in 1991 in the implementation of the Canada-US Free Trade Agreement (FTA). The promulgation of regulations and the various rounds of tariff reductions and eliminations took place on schedule. Among the other ongoing activities under way in 1991 were binational consultations on rules of origin, work on harmonising technical standards, and efforts to resolve a number of agricultural trade issues. In addition, seven binational panel reviews of trade remedy actions were requested with respect to Canadian and US. anti-dumping and countervailing duty decisions; four of the requests were Canadian. Four panel decisions, of which three involved review of US agency determinations, were rendered during the year.

In *Japan*, measures to promote inward foreign investment such as providing investment-related information through the Japan external Trade Organisation (JETRO) and low-interest loans to foreign affiliates through the Japan Development Bank have been in place since 1984. A large discrepancy however remains between the Japanese share of total foreign investment (nearly 10 per cent in stock terms) and the proportion of such investment taking place in Japan (under 1 per cent). Moreover, in flow terms, foreign direct investment in Japan totalled only US$2.8 billion in FY 1990, compared with US$56.9 billion of Japanese direct investment abroad [19]. This disparity has raised questions about reciprocal access of foreign investors to the Japanese economy and prompted an extension of measures aimed at promoting inward direct investment. From FY 1992, the government will allocate an increased budget (470 million yen) to JETRO so that it can extend its information gathering and disseminating activities, and will establish a government-financed business supporting company (with a capital of 500 million yen) in order to offer consulting and other management services to foreign affiliates operating in Japan. Preferential tax treatment to foreign affiliates which meet certain criteria will also be introduced from FY 1992, such as extension of carry-over periods of losses, accelerated depreciation of assets and exemption from special land-holding taxes (local taxes). In addition, the Japan Development Bank has extended its policy of low-interest loans to foreign affiliates establishing manufacturing and R&D facilities in Japan in high technology areas and in projects that are expected to contribute to import expansion.

With respect to trade, the government has adopted a number of measures for the expansion of imports in an effort to correct the trade imbalance. The budget allocation for import promotion programmes has increased significantly since FY 1990: 7 billion yen were allocated in 1991 and 10.1 billion yen are budgeted for 1992 (see Graph 2). These programmes include the dispatch of trade experts in foreign countries, the activities of the Japan External Trade Organisation (JETRO) which is helping foreign firms' access to Japan, and promotional campaigns such as "Import Promotion Month". Since April 1990, tax incentives have been introduced for those firms increasing their

Graph 2. **Japan's import promotion budget**
Billion yen

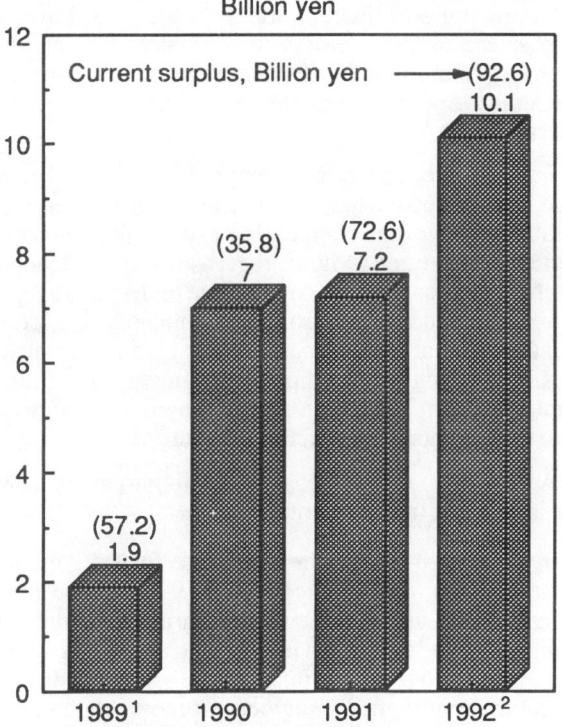

Year	Budget (Billion yen)	Current surplus (Billion yen)
1989 [1]	1.9	(57.2)
1990	7	(35.8)
1991	7.2	(72.6)
1992 [2]	10.1	(92.6)

1. Additional Yen 7.5b in supplementary budget.
2. Planned expenditures.
Source: MITI, Japan.

manufactured imports by more than 10 per cent in any given year. In 1991, imports of manufactured products covered by this scheme registered an 18 per cent increase over the previous year (with imports of products not covered by the tax incentives increasing by 8 per cent). Low-interest loans for import promotion are also available through financial institutions such as the Japan Development Bank (26.5 billion yen in 1990) or the Export-Import Bank of Japan (130 billion yen in 1990). Finally, in an effort to ensure that an adequate infrastructure is in place to facilitate imports, the government is planning the establishment of "Foreign Access Zones" at international airports and ports. These will group together facilities for import procedures, for storage, handling and distribution of imports, and for exhibitions and general import information.

In the *European Community*, an agreement was signed in August 1991 concerning the imports of Japanese automobiles. The agreement, which has been accepted by the Japanese government and almost all European automobile producers, foresees the complete opening up of the EC market for automobiles from 1 January 2000. Until that time, there will be a transition period in which Japanese firms will respect a voluntary limit of 1.23 million imported automobiles per year. There are a number of interpretations of detailed points in the agreement, principally with regard to how future market growth would be distributed between European and Japanese car producers. Nevertheless, by most accounts it appears that the Commission's intention is for European producers to benefit from one third of the market growth from its 1990 level, implying an overall import penetration ratio during the transition period not exceeding 16 per cent. The agreement puts no limits on Japanese investment in the EC, thus leaving room for Japanese automobile companies to increase production within the borders of the Community through transplants. The EC-wide import penetration level for automobiles attains currently around 11 per cent.

In *Belgium*, a law adopted in June 1981 brings major modifications in the basic legislation governing the activities of the *Office National du Ducroire* (OND), the official export credit agency. The law distinguishes between activities described as competitive and those which are carried out on behalf of the state.

With respect to competitive activities, the OND's scope of action has been broadened. The Office is now authorised to take all measures appropriate to guarantee the risks incurred in foreign trade and, as a subsidiary mode of operation, to participate in the financing of foreign trade transactions, where it may act in co-operation with other export credit bodies, including foreign agencies. In the case of special missions involving risks exceeding the OND's normal capacities, recourse may be had to the state budget with respect to the necessary supplementary credits; the Ministers of Economic Affairs and of Finance have a supervisory role in relation to the implementation of such missions.

The law prescribes separate accounting with regard, on the one hand, to operations of the types noted above and, on the other, to those carried out for the state, or on the OND's own account with the backing of a state guarantee. Special financial measures are provided for in the new legislation to enable the office to cope with the disequilibria resulting from the decrease in revenues accompanied by an increase in payments and indemnities. Finally, the law makes available a state guarantee on OND loans from credit establishments as well as on the purchase of securities issued by the office to finance its activities.

In *Denmark*, a new Act On Export Credits replaced on 1 May 1992 the Act On Danish Trade Fund, which contained the former rules on export credit. The new act on export credits contains the basic legislation for a separation of the export credit arrangement in Denmark into a commercial part, run by a joint-stock company on strictly commercial terms, and a continuing public part, itself separated into an advisory capacity and a decision-making authority, and with the latter placed with a newly established Export Credit Committee. The main purpose of the insurance joint-stock company is to act on the commercial market for export credit guarantees in open competition with other credit insurance companies. The market thus covered will mainly be political and commercial short-term risks to OECD countries as well as commercial short-term risks to certain third countries. The public part will cover extraordinary risks (non-marketable risks) i.e primarily political and commercial risks on medium and long-term credits as well as certain commercial risks on short-term credits in connection with exports to under-developed countries and countries in central and eastern Europe.

In addition, the Ministry of Industry has set up the Export Network Programme to help Danish enterprises with their export activities. Under the programme, partial funding is available to companies establishing long-term collaboration on common export activities. It is mainly intended to benefit small and medium-sized firms exporting goods and services; only activities which are beyond the scope of individual companies or which can only become profitable through collaboration are eligible. Funding can be granted prior to or at the introduction of new activities to promote exports and can cover up to 50 per cent of approved expenditure on the new activities undertaken by a network. The grant is repayable where the export network is a success, in the form of a fixed percentage of the exports achieved by the individual companies through the network within a 5-year period.

In *Portugal*, finance mechanisms have been put in place to make available special credit lines in support of the internationalisation of the economy, the development of new export markets and improved competitiveness in the automotive components industry. The financial instruments created by this measure will be directed primarily to the promotion of Portuguese equity partici-

> **Box 11. Foreign direct investment in Portugal**
>
> One of the most striking phenomena that occurred at the time of Portugal's accession to the European Community in 1986 was the "takeoff", and subsequent surge, of foreign direct investment. Total FDI flows, which had only occasionally reached significant levels in previous years, rose sharply after 1986 and were over US$ 2 billion in 1990. They amounted to considerably more in 1991, largely as a result of a Ford-Volkswagen automobile investment, the largest foreign investment in the country's history.
>
> While the major part of overall FDI has been directed to banking and financial institutions, consultancy and other services, a number of substantial investments have been made in manufacturing industry, particularly in the automotive and automotive components, chemicals, paper and electronics sectors. Among the many recent investors are to be found General Motors, Ford, Bosch, Texas Instruments and Saint Gobain. In the aggregate, the EC countries account for the lion's share of FDI in Portugal, with the United Kingdom, France, Spain and Germany playing the leading roles.
>
> The political stability prevailing in Portugal and the availability of a skilled, low-cost labour force represent one facet of the multiple attractions the country presents to foreign investors. Another comprises the liberal regulatory regime and the package of incentives offered, such as grants and temporary exemptions from taxes and social security contributions as well as provisions for accelerated depreciation. Moreover, for non-Community investors, Portugal's membership in the EC offers direct access to the large Community market. It should be added that the privatisations carried out have enlarged the scope of investment possibilities.
>
> For Portugal, the inflow of investment from abroad provides not only a general stimulus to industrial and economic activity but, more specifically, impacts on some of the country's structural needs. In particular, investments in the more upmarket manufacturing activities help to diversify Portuguese industry and to liberate it from excessive dependence on traditional branches where it encounters increasingly sharp competition, notably from developing or newly industrialised countries. This contribution to the structural adjustment of Portuguese industry can have a major regional dimension, as in the case of the foreign investment flows to the ailing Setubal shipbuilding area. In the tertiary sector, as well, FDI offers substantial benefits to the Portuguese economy: consultancy and financial services in particular represent an element of infrastructure indispensable to balanced development.

pation in foreign firms and the provisions of venture capital for projects abroad. More generally, the Portuguese government has a number of incentives in place to attract foreign investment, whose flows have increased significantly in the last few years (see Box 11).

In *Spain*, a support scheme has been created with a view to encouraging international industrial co-operation, thus helping to counteract the excessive fragmentation of the country's production structure and to adapt firms to the increasing globalisation of markets. Assistance will be offered to enterprises concluding co-operation agreements with Spanish or foreign partners as well as to private or public agencies that provide support for inter-firm co-operation.

The government is also striving to improve the inadequate performance of Spanish enterprises in investing abroad by strengthening and coordinating various commercial, financial, fiscal and training measures as well as by reinforcing information in this field.

At the same time, Spain places considerable emphasis on sector-specific export promotion through the activities of the Spanish Institute for Foreign Trade (ICEX). Recently, ICEX has focused on some 30 products in specific markets. The Institute provides financial aid to sectors or individual firms; it has also developed an innovate policy instrument consisting of equity participation in the overseas distribution networks of Spanish enterprises.

In *Austria*, various policy thrusts move in the direction of promoting foreign direct investment, which is seen as an essential contributory factor to enhanced national industrial efficiency. The Information Service for Investors, set up in the Economic Affairs Ministry, has for some time endeavoured to encourage such investment. More recently, the complete liberalisation of foreign currency movements, put into effect by the Austrian National Bank in September 1991, is expected to increase the attractiveness of Austria as a location for industrial investors.

In *Finland*, the consequences of the collapse of the former Soviet Union are amongst the most severe in the OECD area. In 1991, a decline in exports to the former Soviet Union of over 70 per cent can be held responsible for roughly half of the fall in Finnish GDP. Finnish exports also suffered from the slowdown in a number of economies that represent its main markets, notably Sweden, Norway, and the UK. The Finnish government reacted by devaluing the markka by 14 per cent in November 1991, as a short-term response aimed at improving the price competitiveness of Finnish industry. More fundamentally, the government has given a high priority to European integration, as demonstrated by Finland's recent application for EC membership. However, negotiations on full EC membership will not start before 1993, and admittance will at the earliest be possible in 1995. The recent agreement between the EFTA and the EC on the creation of a European Economic Area is therefore the fastest pathway to European integration.

In the context of European integration, the Finnish government is proposing changes in the legislation regarding inward foreign investment. The current law restricts the right of foreigners to invest in Finnish shares and real estate, and requires foreign investors to obtain a permission from the Ministry of Trade and Industry. The practice of the Ministry has been liberal for a number of years, and applications by foreigners for establishing a company in Finland or for acquiring shares in Finnish companies have been approved as a rule. Nevertheless, the current law is now considered obsolete, given that in a more integrated international economic environment factors affecting capital movements cannot differ substantially between countries. The new proposal, coming into force as law in the beginning of 1993 when approved by parliament, will allow foreigners free acquisition of shares and access to property.

Norway, together with the other EFTA countries, has been negotiating with the EC in order to establish a European Economic Area and enable the Norwegian industry to take advantage of the possibilities created by the realisation of the internal market. Free trade agreements with Hungary, Poland and the Czech and Slovak Federal Republic are also being negotiated, and co-operation has started with the Baltic states with the aim of liberalising trade. In terms of foreign investment, the so-called Concession Law which makes foreign ownership of more than 33.5 per cent of a Norwegian company conditional on governmental approval [20] is still in existence. The Norwegian government emphasises the fact that the rules governing concessions have traditionally been liberally applied and thus cannot be considered as a serious obstacle to foreign establishment and investment in the country. The authorities are currently considering the introduction of an obligatory report to the government for all stock purchasers on the acquisition of substantial parts of stock capital in Norwegian companies. The duty to submit such reports is likely to be limited to the acquisition of shares in larger companies only.

In *Sweden*, a more rapid integration in the international economy has become an important economic policy objective, as exemplified by efforts that are made towards the creation of an economic environment that is favourable to foreign investors. In this context, the government abolished the control of foreign ownership in Swedish companies in 1991, thus conforming to international agreements and developments in EC legislation. Some restricted access to voting shares will however continue to be allowed.

In *Switzerland*, the authorities attribute great importance to the need for fuller integration into the international, and especially the European, economy. Participation in the current negotiations on the creation of a European Economic Area represents a first step in that direction. In this context also, the Swiss agency for commercial development -- *L'Office suisse d'expansion commerciale* (OSEC) -- has to respond to an increased demand for information regarding directives and regulations of the European Community. This agency has the status of a private institution and receives SF10 million a year as financial support from the Confederation (representing 45 per cent of its total expenditures). After a difficult period in 1989 and 1990, the agency has recovered its financial health and is now more ready to respond to the increased demand for its services.

In *Turkey*, a Free Trade Agreement signed with EFTA countries in 1991 came into force on 1st April 1992. Under this agreement, trade between the two sides is to be governed by provisions very similar to those laid down in a Protocol between Turkey and the European Community.

In pursuance of the import liberalisation process, Turkey has been applying, as of 1 January 1991, additional postponed customs duty reductions agreed to in the Protocol with the EC. Meanwhile, the phasing-down of direct support to exports has further progressed with the gradual reduction, and the complete elimination at the end of January 1992, of the cash grants given to exporters on an exported unit basis.

In *Australia*, the phased reduction in tariffs that began in the 1980s was extended to 1996 (and to the year 2000 for textiles, clothing and footwear and for the motor vehicle industry). The protection reform programme abolishes the last quotas in textiles, clothing and footwear by 1993, phases out most bounties by 1996, reduces general tariffs to 5 per cent by 1996, reduces tariffs on passenger cars to a maximum of 15 per cent by the year 2000, and that on textiles, clothing and footwear to 25 per cent by 2000. These measures will reduce the effective rate of assistance to Australian manufacturing to 5 per cent by the year 2000, compared to 19 per cent in 1987-88 and around 12 per cent at the end of 1992.

H. International co-operation with central and eastern European countries (CEECs)

Many of the policy initiatives dealt with in the previous sections are relevant to international co-operation in industry. This is particulary true of initiatives to promote intangible investment activities, and especially R&D and technology development. Since 1990 however, the year in which the political and economic transformations in central and eastern Europe started taking place, most initiatives of international co-operation in the OECD area have concerned these countries.

International co-operation initiatives of OECD countries towards the countries of central and eastern Europe and the Commonwealth of Independent States mainly cover technical and financial assistance, through a number of programmes that allow these countries access to western technology and know-how. Such programmes cover management training, assistance to business development, to small and medium-sized enterprises, as well as credit guarantees. Bilateral trade liberalisation measures such as the removal of tariffs or of quantitative restrictions are also in evidence, reflecting the belief that giving access to western markets is the most efficient way of assisting the transition of these countries to market economies and the transformation of the production and trade structure. A number of programmes also deal with industry-related environmental and energy problems.

In addition to direct government initiatives, many programmes are of an intermediary nature, helping firms in the former Soviet bloc develop direct contacts with western enterprises, attract foreign investment or set up joint ventures. Such initiatives join a growing number of similar international co-operation arrangements between firms in OECD countries, as industry is attempting to derive the maximum benefit from the process of globalisation. In the case of the central and eastern European countries however, the success of such programmes is critical, given the uncertainties that foreign investors are facing with respect to the economic situation and the legal and administrative frameworks.

Some recent measures concerned with international co-operation with the countries of central and eastern Europe are indicated below.

The *United States* is expanding its trade and business relations with countries of central and eastern Europe (CEECs), most notably Poland, Hungary and the Czech and Slovak Federal Republic. The United States now has MFN (most favoured nation) trading relations with Poland, Hungary, the Czech and Slovak Federal Republic, Bulgaria and Yugoslavia. Most of the central and eastern European countries (with the current exceptions of Yugoslavia, Romania and Albania) are eligible for duty-free import benefits under the Generalised System of Preferences (GSP) program, as are Lithuania, Latvia and Estonia from early 1992. The US provides additional aid to CEECs through the Seed Act of 1989, and the Freedom Support Act, which will provide aid to the former Soviet Union, as well as remove restrictive provisions of law remaining from the Cold War era.

The United States has entered into trade agreements with Poland, Bulgaria, the Czech and Slovak Federal Republic and Hungary. Last year a new trade agreement with Romania was initialled although it has not been sent to Congress for approval. Investment protection treaties have been signed with Poland and the Czech and Slovak Federal Republic and initialled with Bulgaria; a treaty is currently being negotiated with Hungary. The United States has entered into taxation treaties with Hungary, Poland and Romania and treaties are pending with Bulgaria and the Czech and Slovak Federal Republic.

In addition, the few quantitative restrictions maintained have been relaxed. Textile quotas were effectively tripled, restraints on steel are set to expire in March 1992, and the CEECs obtained access for cheese under the annual country-of-origin adjustment process. As a result of additions to the GSP list and zero tariff items in the MFN tariff schedule some 50 per cent of CEEC exports enter the US duty free.

Several new programmes of technical assistance were recently launched. During Fiscal year 1990 and 1991, the US provided US$1 billion in loans and other types of assistance to countries of central and eastern Europe. The Administration has requested an additional US$470 million in FY92 and US$520 million for 1993. Most funds are for technical assistance to support democratic institutions and free market reforms and provide capital for the Enterprise Funds in Poland, the Czech and Slovak Federal Republic, Hungary and Bulgaria.

In this context, the Enterprise Fund was established to help expand private sector business activities with particular emphasis on small and medium-sized businesses. The Overseas Private Investment Corporation and the US. Trade and Development Program are also operating in central and eastern European countries. The Eastern Europe Business Information Center (EEBIC) serves as a central USG clearinghouse for information on market opportunities and business climates in central and eastern Europe. EEBIC has also recently undertaken a new "Eastern Europe Business Development Program" which can match US company interests with specific trade and investment proposals made by central and eastern European firms.

Under a joint Department of Commerce/Agency for International Development program, the American Business and Private Sector Development Initiative (ABI) was established. ABI is designed to increase involvement of US firms in eastern Europe and the flow of US private capital and commercial expertise to eastern Europe. ABI emphasises business development in five key sectors: agriculture and agribusiness, energy, environment, telecommunications and housing. Programs include the Consortia of American Businesses in eastern Europe which provides grants to trade associations and cooperatives to open offices in eastern Europe through which promotion of products and services of the member companies can take place. ABI programs also include the establishment in early March 1992 of a pilot American Business Center in Warsaw to provide US companies with temporary office space and other business services (e.g. secretarial, telephone, fax and translation).

With respect to relationships with the former Soviet Union, the US/USSR Trade Agreement signed by Presidents Bush and Gorbachev was approved by the Congress and was awaiting approval by the Supreme Soviet at the time of the collapse of the Soviet Union. The agreement, if adopted by the newly independent states, will reciprocally confer MFN (Most Favoured Nation) tariff treatment between the United States and Independent States. The United States and the Soviet Union had also initialled a Bilateral Tax Treaty and held negotiations on a Bilateral Investment Treaty.

The United States hosted a multinational conference in Washington in January, 1992, to discuss immediate humanitarian assistance and future technical and economic assistance. At the conference, President Bush announced a US$645 million package of assistance which included emergency aid of food and medical supplies.

In addition, current US programs to assist the newly independent states include: US$3.75 billion in food credit guarantees, offers of US$165 million in grants of food aid and US$45 million in Defense Department funds for transportation of assistance; US$5 million in funding for a private sector program which has delivered over US$21 million in donated medical supplies and US$400 million to assist in eliminating nuclear and chemical weapons. During 1991, the United States provided over 18 million tons of food.

The United States is also expanding its Special American Business Internship Program to provide at least 150 mid- and senior-level business managers in the former Soviet Union firsthand experience working in a market economy through management internships in private US companies.

In *Canada*, sector-specific co-operation activities vis-à-vis the central and eastern European countries are being set in motion on the basis of the competitive strengths of Canadian industry. Other initiatives have been taken to assist in the development of an effective small business sector and to establish a policy framework for stimulating entrepreneurship in the region.

In *Japan*, the Ministry of International Trade and Industry has developed an extensive technical co-operation programme with the Russian federation and other members of the CIS, in order to facilitate their transition to a market economy. The programme provides management training in the fields of productivity improvement, international business training, and quality control, and advises policy makers and business people in key areas of industrial reform. Making use of Japan's own post-war experience, the programme assists in the framing of a strategy for the conversion of the military industry, and for the development of small and medium-sized enterprises. Along the same lines, assistance is provided for developing a distribution policy (focusing on the development of the retail and wholesale sectors) as well as an industrial policy based on the Japanese experience. Another area of technical co-operation relates to the energy field, including the maintenance and safety of nuclear power plants. Finally, a Japanese Trade and Industrial Exhibition (organised by the JETRO) will provide information on Japanese technologies, mainly to the Russian government.

Japanese cooperation programmes with the central and eastern European countries have continued, centered around assistance with managerial know-how, production management and environmental protection. A number of experts have been dispatched on missions of technical assistance, while trainees from central and eastern European countries have followed seminars in Japan.

In *Denmark*, the government presented in September 1989 an action plan in support of the reform process in central and eastern Europe. The action plan has a number of elements: the creation of an Investment Fund for Central and Eastern Europe, a self-governing institution acting as a shareholder in joint ventures between Danish and local investors or extending loans to such enterprises (with an allocation of US$23.4 million in 1992); the setting up of an Investment Insurance Scheme, whereby the Ministry of Foreign Affairs may, on an insurance basis and within a limit of Danish kroner 1 billion, guarantee investments in CEECs against political risks; the establishment of a Project Fund granting technical assistance in areas such as agriculture, fisheries, energy, or environmental protection (with an allocation of US$15.6 million in 1992); the creation of a Democracy Fund, supporting activities strengthening democracy in CEECs (with an allocation of US$4.8 million in 1992); the establishment of an Industrial and Commercial Trainee Programme, enabling middle management and technical staff from CEECs to receive training in Denmark (with an allocation of US$2.5 million in 1992); the establishment in April 1991 of the Environmental Support Scheme, operating with a budget of US$81 million over 5 years; and the setting up of a Special Export Credit Facility, providing for guarantees of up to 5 million Danish kroner for the period 1991-95.

Germany has concluded bilateral investment treaties with Albania, Bulgaria, the CSFR, Hungary, Lithuania, Poland, Romania, and the CIS. These treaties form the basis for investment insurance provided by the federal government against non-commercial risks and already are used to a large extent by German investors in these countries. The federal government also gives assistance with low interest loans for investment in central and eastern

European countries for which SMEs may apply. Some Länder have funds available for investment purposes in these countries.

The federal government also supports consultancy services for companies in CEECs, aimed at restructuring firms on a market economy basis and boosting their export capability. In addition, measures such as a more favourable Hermes coverage have been taken in order to assist firms in the new *Länder* to gradually adapt their relations with firms in the ex-Soviet Union that are moving towards a market economy. A number of co-operation projects already exist between firms in eastern Germany and the Republics of the Commonwealth of Independent States (CIS) in fields such as mechanical engineering, plant engineering and construction, building materials, food processing and the motor vehicle industry.

Greece continued to participate in 1991 in European Community initiatives such as PHARE for the central and eastern European countries in transition. In the context of the PHARE programme, 128 million drachmas were allocated for training programmes in the fields of agriculture, market research, and in the organisation and management of SMEs.

In the *Netherlands*, the provision of technical and financial assistance towards eastern Europe was further extended, in continuation of a programme first established in 1990. Project assistance was given to a variety of areas including management support, transfer of administrative and technological know-how, transport, education and culture.

In the *United Kingdom*, beneficiaries of bilateral assistance under the Know How Fund, established in 1989, are Poland, Hungary, the Czech and Slovak Federal Republic, Bulgaria and Romania; a separate Fund exists for the Commonwealth of Independent States. Advice and expertise tailored to individual country needs are provided under this activity, the priority areas including the financial services sector and management training. In addition, two schemes exist to encourage British investment in the region.

Double taxation agreements have been signed with Poland, Hungary, the Czech and Slovak Federal Republic, Bulgaria, Romania, Yugoslavia and the Commonwealth of Independent States. The UK has also concluded investment promotion and protection agreements with all the foregoing except Bulgaria and Yugoslavia, with which negotiations are under way.

In *Austria*, the facilities developed by the *Bürges Förderungsbank* for helping in the creation of financial promotion systems for SMEs have attracted the interest of the Czech and Slovak Federal Republic, Slovenia, Poland and the Hungarian Foundation for Enterprise Promotion, which in some cases have already made use of the assistance offered. Support has also been given to various training activities -- e.g., the training of central and eastern European executives in market economy management methods and a "train the trainer" programme for the Czech and Slovak Federal Republic conducted on the theme, "Organisation and Management of Entrepreneurial Training Institutes."

Finally, Austria, along with other EFTA countries, is negotiating free trade agreements with Hungary, the Czech and Slovak Federal Republic and Poland. The original aim of having these accords enter into force simultaneously with the EC association agreements with the central and eastern European countries did not prove to be attainable.

In *Finland*, co-operation with the central and eastern European economies in transition has concentrated in the areas near Finnish borders. Industrial activity has so far consisted of subcontracting-type operations while direct investments have been of less significance. Government assistance is mainly directed to energy conservation and environmental co-operation, industrial feasibility studies and business training.

In *Norway*, in addition to several multilateral support programmes, bilateral links are being developed between Norwegian firms and firms in central and eastern Europe. In the Northern region, contacts and co-operation between Norwegian firms and industry in bordering North-West Russia are developed on a broad scale, while a special advisory service will be set up as well.

In *Sweden*, bilateral co-operation with the central and eastern European countries in general and with the Baltic states in particular has intensified. In the last two years, 6 million SEK were transferred through the Governments Billion Programme from the Ministry of Industry to central and eastern Europe. About 50 per cent of these funds were earmarked for the Baltic states, and the main emphasis in the co-operation programmes has been on the development of small companies.

NOTES AND REFERENCES

1. See OECD (1992), *Technology and the Economy: The Key Relationships*, Chapter 5, Paris.

2. Vickery, G. And Wurzburg, G. (1992), "Intangible investment: Missing pieces in the productivity puzzle", *OECD Observer*, No.178, Paris.

3. OECD (1991), *Industrial Policy in the OECD Countries: Annual Review*, Paris.

4. OECD (1992), *OECD Economic Surveys: Austria*, Paris.

5. OECD (1992), *Science and Technology Policy: Review and Outlook 1991*, Paris.

6. See Schreyer, P. (1992), "Competition Policy and Industrial Adjustment", *STI Review* No.10, OECD, April; and George, K. and Jacquemin, A. (1992), "Dominant Firms and Mergers", *Economic Journal*, 102.

7. OECD (1991), *OECD Economic Surveys: Japan*, Paris.

8. OECD (1991), *OECD Economic Surveys: France*, Paris.

9. OECD (1991), *OECD Economic Surveys : the Netherlands*, Paris.

10. OECD (1991), *OECD Economic Surveys: United Kingdom*, Paris.

11. OECD (1992), "Regional Policy Developments in OECD Countries", document, Paris.

12. OECD (1992), "Globalisation and Local and Regional Competitiveness", document, Paris.

13. OECD (1992), *OECD Economic Surveys: Norway*, Paris.

14. GATT (1992), *Council Overview of Developments in International Trade and the Trading System*, C/RM/OV/3, 17 March.

15. World Bank (1992), *Global Economic Prospects and the Developing Countries*.

16. OECD (1992), *Progress in Structural Reform*, Paris.

17. OECD (1992), *Progress in Structural Reform*, op.cit.

18. OECD (1992), *Progress in Structural Reform*, op.cit.

19. OECD (1991), *OECD Economic Surveys: Japan*, op.cit.

20. OECD (1992), *OECD Economic Surveys: Norway*, op.cit.

Part 3

TRENDS IN INDUSTRY

Data in this part of the report reflect the status of OECD databases in June 1992. Historical data and projections for Germany refer to western Germany only, except where indicated otherwise.

Chapter I

THE MACROECONOMIC ENVIRONMENT AND TRENDS IN PRODUCTION

A. The macroeconomic background

Broad lines of the current economic situation

The expected recovery in the OECD zone in the second half of 1991 did not materialise [1]. Despite the relaxation of economic policies in those countries where activity had been most sharply reined back, growth in the OECD area did not pick up and business and consumer confidence remained relatively depressed in many countries. GDP growth in the OECD area was 1 per cent for the whole of 1991 with practically every OECD country experiencing a slower growth rate or an outright decline in GDP. GDP declined in 1991 in the *United States, Canada,* the *United Kingdom, Finland, Sweden, Switzerland, Australia and New Zealand* (see Table 8 and Graph 3). In some of these countries however, growth resumed during the second half of 1991, in particular in the United States and Canada, while in others (such as the United Kingdom) the recession continued but eased somewhat. In countries such as *France* and *Italy*, which experienced a substantial slowdown or near standstill in 1991 as a whole, activity picked up in the second half of the year (in early 1992 for Italy). *Japan* and *Germany*, which in 1990 and in the first half of 1991 continued to have relatively strong growth, entered a period of much slower growth in the second half of 1991.

Graph 3. Real GNP/GDP
Percentage changes from preceding year [1]

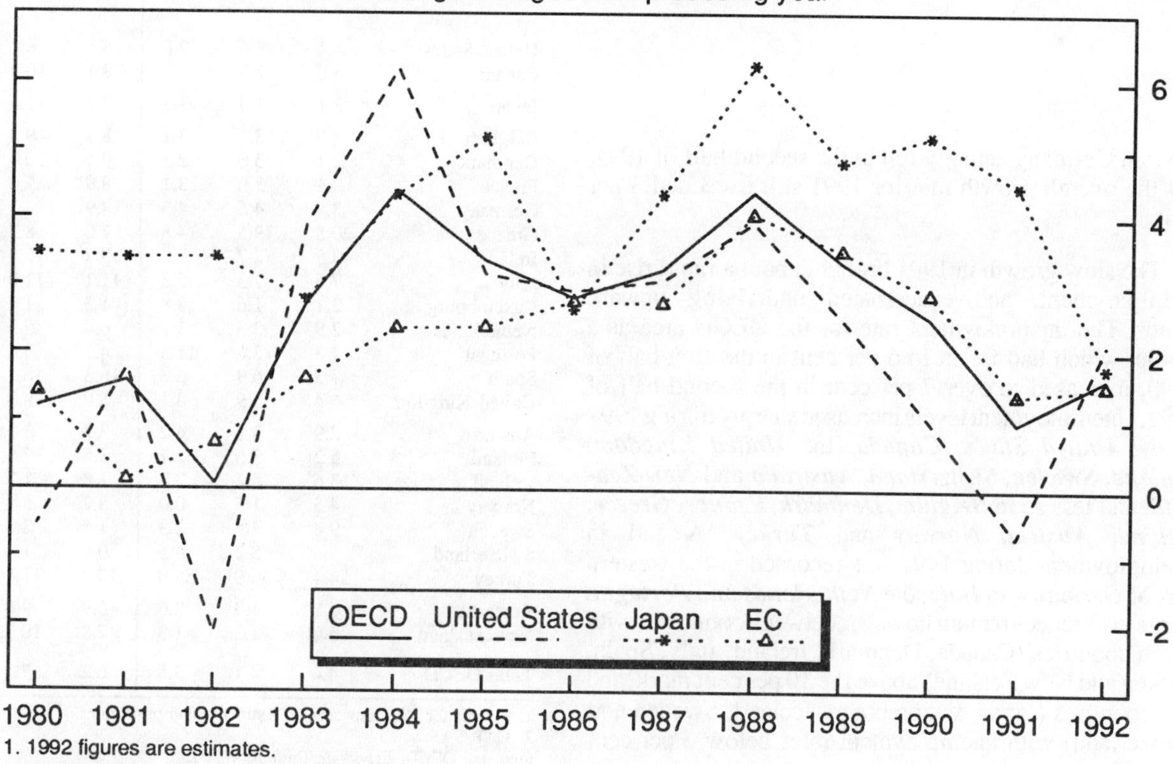

1. 1992 figures are estimates.
Source: OECD, *Economic Outlook No.51.*

Table 8. **Growth of real GNP/GDP and of domestic demand**[1]

Percentage changes from previous year

	Real GNP/GDP			Domestic demand		
	1990	1991	1992	1990	1991	1992
United States	1.0	−0.7	2.1	0.5	−1.3	2.1
Canada	0.5	−1.5	2.3	−0.2	−0.5	2.2
Japan[2]	5.2	4.5	1.8	5.4	3.0	1.6
Belgium	3.7	1.5	1.6	3.4	1.4	1.5
Denmark	1.7	1.0	2.1	−0.8	−0.1	1.6
France	2.2	1.3	2.0	2.6	1.0	1.5
Germany[2]	4.5	3.1	1.3	4.5	3.0	1.3
Greece	−0.1	1.5	1.4	1.0	1.5	1.3
Ireland[2]	8.3	2.3	2.4	5.0	−0.5	0.4
Italy	2.2	1.4	1.5	2.4	2.3	2.0
Luxembourg	2.3	3.1	3.2	3.4	4.8	3.8
Netherlands	3.9	2.0	1.2	3.7	1.7	0.4
Portugal	4.2	2.2	2.8	5.7	4.3	3.8
Spain	3.7	2.4	2.6	4.7	3.0	3.1
United Kingdom	1.0	−2.2	0.4	−0.1	−3.1	0.9
Austria	4.6	3.0	2.1	4.7	3.2	2.2
Finland	0.4	−6.1	−1.3	−0.7	−8.5	−4.5
Iceland	0.1	0.9	−2.6	1.3	4.3	−4.1
Norway	1.8	1.9	2.0	−0.5	−0.7	1.1
Sweden	0.5	−1.2	−0.3	0.2	−2.8	−0.6
Switzerland	2.2	−0.5	0.9	2.2	−0.8	0.5
Turkey	9.2	1.5	5.1	16.4	−1.4	5.5
Australia	1.7	−1.9	2.6	−0.7	−2.2	2.6
New Zealand	0.5	−2.1	2.0	0.0	−6.6	0.6
Total OECD	2.5	1.0	1.8	2.3	0.4	1.7

1. Figures for 1991 onwards are estimates and projections.
2. GNP.
Source: OECD, Economic Outlook No. 51.

Inflation eased in almost all OECD countries, helped by the weakness of domestic demand and the consequent moderation of wage costs and of commodity and energy prices (Tables 8 and 9), but remained above 4 per cent. Underlying inflation, measured by consumer prices excluding food and energy, also declined, while producer prices were stable or falling in many countries. Nonetheless, inflation is proving more intractable in some countries, notably *Germany*, where consumer prices accelerated sharply in 1991 and especially in the second half of the year under the combined effect of higher wage costs, indirect taxes and administered prices[2]. In other countries, and especially in many EC Member countries such as *Italy*, the *United Kingdom, Greece, Portugal* and *Spain*, while inflation is in most cases at lower rates than in previous years, it is still rising faster than the rates dictated by longer-term objectives such as the establishment of European economic and monetary union.

The slowdown of world trade continued in 1991, with a 3 per cent growth rate in volume terms that was the slowest since 1983. A moderate pickup in the second part of 1991 was mainly due to the expansion of intra-OECD GNP in Germany actually fell in the second half of 1991, but the overall growth rate for 1991 still exceeded 3 per cent.

The slow growth in 1991 brought about a rapid rise in unemployment, and exacerbated underlying upward trends. The unemployment rate for the OECD area as a whole, which had fallen to 6 per cent in the first half of 1990, increased to over 7 per cent in the second half of 1991. Unemployment levels increased sharply during 1991 in the *United States, Canada*, the *United Kingdom, Finland, Sweden, Switzerland, Australia* and *New Zealand*, and less so in *Belgium, Denmark, France, Greece, Ireland, Austria, Norway* and *Turkey*. A fall in unemployment during 1991 was recorded in the western part of *Germany*, in *Italy*, the *Netherlands* and *Portugal*. Large differences remain however between countries, with seven countries (Canada, Denmark, Ireland, Italy, Spain, Turkey and New Zealand) above the 10 per cent mark, and five countries (Japan, Luxembourg, Iceland, Sweden and Switzerland) with unemployment rates below 3 per cent (Table 9).

Table 9. **Inflation and unemployment**[1]

	GNP/GDP deflator			Unemployment rate		
	Percentage change from preceding year			Percentages		
	1990	1991	1992	1990	1991	1992
United States	4.1	3.6	2.8	5.5	6.7	7.1
Canada	3.0	2.7	1.9	8.1	10.3	10.4
Japan	2.1	1.9	1.7	2.1	2.1	2.2
Belgium	3.0	3.1	3.1	8.7	9.3	9.7
Denmark	2.1	3.0	2.3	9.5	10.4	10.7
France	3.1	3.0	3.1	8.9	9.4	9.8
Germany	3.4	4.6	4.5	4.9	4.3	4.7
Greece	20.5	19.5	14.8	7.0	8.2	9.4
Ireland[2]	−0.5	2.7	3.5	13.7	15.8	16.9
Italy	7.6	7.3	5.3	11.1	11.0	11.2
Luxembourg	2.1	1.6	3.8	1.3	1.4	1.4
Netherlands	2.9	3.3	3.1	6.4	5.9	6.5
Portugal	14.3	13.6	11.3	4.7	4.1	5.0
Spain	7.3	6.9	6.0	16.3	16.3	16.1
United Kingdom	6.4	6.9	5.1	5.9	8.3	9.8
Austria	2.9	3.8	4.2	3.3	3.7	4.0
Finland	5.2	3.5	2.7	3.5	7.6	11.3
Iceland	13.6	8.2	3.7	1.8	1.7	2.6
Norway	4.5	1.5	0.0	5.2	5.5	5.8
Sweden	9.4	7.5	2.3	1.5	2.7	4.5
Switzerland	5.3	5.2	4.5	0.6	1.3	2.5
Turkey	54.4	56.0	59.0	10.0	11.5	11.8
Australia	4.2	1.3	2.6	6.9	9.6	10.4
New Zealand	5.0	1.3	1.8	7.8	10.3	11.8
Total OECD	4.4	4.1	3.5	6.2	7.1	7.5

1. Figures for 1991 onwards are estimates and projections.
2. GNP.
Source: OECD, Economic Outlook No. 51.

trade. The current account in the **United States** moved to a deficit in the second half of 1991, ending with a deficit that was around 0.2 per cent of GDP for the whole year, while the trade balance improved significantly (Tables 10 and 11). **Japan**'s surplus continued to grow and exceeded 2 per cent of GDP or US$72 billion in 1991, with a trade surplus exceeding US$103 billion. **Germany** moved from a current account surplus to a deficit in 1991, but its deficit declined significantly in the second half of 1991, mainly owing to a fall in import volumes. Current deficits in **France** and the **United Kingdom** declined substantially, while increasing slightly in **Italy** and **Canada**. Of the smaller OECD countries, **Finland, Australia** and **Greece** reduced their current account deficits; **Austria**'s current surplus as a percentage of GDP turned into a deficit, while surpluses increased in **Belgium, Denmark, Ireland**, the **Netherlands** and **Norway**.

Prospects

On the basis of recent trends and in light of the policies in place and the forces at work in OECD economies, growth is expected to gradually accelerate in the second half of 1992 and beyond. OECD GDP is projected to expand at around 1.8 per cent at an annual rate [3]. This growth rate will depend to a large extent on the sustainability of the current recovery in the **United States**, and on the extent of the economic slowdown in **Japan**.

Table 11. **Trade and current balances**[1]
Billion dollars

	Trade balances			Current balances		
	1990	1991	1992	1990	1991	1992
United States	–108.1	–73.6	–74.1	–92.1	–8.6	–41.1
Canada	9.9	7.5	5.5	–18.9	–23.4	–26.6
Japan	63.5	103.3	124.9	35.8	72.6	92.6
Belgium/Luxembourg	0.8	0.1	1.8	3.7	4.0	5.5
Denmark	4.9	4.8	5.5	1.3	2.2	3.1
France	–12.9	–9.3	–0.7	–14.9	–6.3	–1.7
Germany[2]	73.1	24.3	32.8	47.1	–19.8	–15.6
Greece	–10.2	–10.4	–10.9	–3.6	–1.5	–1.7
Ireland	4.0	3.2	4.0	0.9	1.9	2.3
Italy	0.5	–0.2	1.7	–14.4	–20.5	–23.6
Netherlands	10.3	12.2	14.4	10.5	11.7	13.3
Portugal	–6.8	–7.8	–8.2	–0.2	–0.7	–0.7
Spain	–29.5	–30.5	–33.8	–16.9	–15.4	–16.1
United Kingdom	–33.1	–17.9	–19.7	–27.4	–7.8	–14.8
Austria	–6.9	–9.3	–12.2	1.2	–0.2	–0.7
Finland	0.7	2.2	4.7	–6.9	–5.8	–3.8
Iceland	0.1	0.0	0.0	–0.2	–0.3	–0.3
Norway	7.5	9.0	9.0	3.6	5.3	4.7
Sweden	2.5	5.7	7.0	–6.4	–2.2	–1.6
Switzerland	–3.2	–2.2	–1.0	8.6	9.1	9.2
Turkey	–9.6	–7.4	–7.4	–2.6	0.4	0.6
Australia	–0.1	3.4	2.8	–14.3	–10.3	–9.6
New Zealand	0.8	1.5	1.7	–1.4	–0.5	–0.2

1. Figures for 1991 onwards are estimates and projections.
2. Figures for 1991 onwards are for unified Germany.
Source: OECD, *Economic Outlook No. 51*.

Table 10. **Internal and external balances**[1]
Surplus (+) or deficit (–) as a percentage of GNP/GDP

	General government financial balances			Current balances		
	1990	1991	1992	1990	1991	1992
United States	–2.5	–3.0	–3.8	–1.7	–0.2	–0.7
Canada	–3.8	–5.5	–4.6	–3.3	–3.9	–4.5
Japan[3]	+3.1	+2.4	+1.9	+1.2	+2.1	+2.6
Belgium[2]	–5.3	–6.0	–5.5	+1.9	+2.0	+2.6
Denmark	–1.4	–2.0	–2.1	+1.0	+1.7	+2.3
France	–1.4	–2.1	–2.3	–1.3	–0.5	–0.1
Germany[3,4]	–1.8	–2.9	–3.4	+2.9	–1.2	–0.8
Greece	–18.6	–17.1	–14.5	–5.3	–2.2	–2.2
Ireland[3]	–2.0	–1.9	–1.9	+2.4	+4.8	+5.5
Italy	–10.9	–10.2	–11.3	–1.3	–1.8	–1.9
Netherlands	–5.3	–2.7	–3.4	+3.7	+4.1	+4.4
Spain	–4.0	–4.4	–4.9	–3.4	–2.9	–2.8
United Kingdom	–0.7	–1.7	–4.6	–2.9	–0.8	–1.4
Austria	–2.1	–2.3	–2.0	+0.7	–0.1	–0.4
Finland	+1.4	–5.0	–7.7	–5.1	–4.6	–3.2
Norway	+2.6	–0.5	–2.9	+3.4	+5.0	+4.3
Sweden	+4.1	–1.5	–4.1	–2.8	–0.9	–0.7
Australia	+1.4	–2.2	–4.0	–4.8	–3.5	–3.2

1. Figures for 1991 onwards are estimates and projections.
2. Belgium/Luxembourg for current balances.
3. Percentages of GNP.
4. Figures for 1991 onwards are for unified Germany.
Source: OECD, *Economic Outlook No. 51*.

In the **United States**, the revival of residential construction and private consumption should be confirmed during the first half of 1992, and be followed by a pick-up of business investment during the second half, resulting in an acceleration of domestic demand. Also, stronger competitiveness should continue to boost exports and help expand GDP. In **Japan**, the easing of monetary and fiscal conditions, the strong growth of real wages and the potential strong growth of export markets could enable a pick up of growth rates in the second half of 1992 and in 1993. In **Germany** and in Europe more generally, while the tighter monetary conditions will continue to weigh on demand, the sounder financial situation of households and firms could encourage a gradual acceleration of private consumption, followed by one of business investment. The pick-up in world trade will also give a certain stimulus to European economies.

At the same time, there are certain risks and uncertainties in the current outlook that are related to a number of factors. These include the relative sluggishness of the recovery so far, the persistently high unemployment rates, and the fact that lower interest rates and the fall in inflation had a much less rapid and weaker impact on demand and expectations than originally thought. The factors combine with the uncertainty about the extent of the slowdown in

Japan and the imbalances that have resulted from German unification to lend a note of caution to the outlook of an early recovery.

B. Trends in industrial production

Recent trends

Industrial production (covering mining, manufacturing and utilities) declined in the OECD area in 1991. The half a percentage point drop in the index of industrial production followed a 1.7 per cent growth in 1990. The OECD-wide decline was driven by the steep fall in *United States* industrial production (down 2 per cent in 1991, after a 1 per cent increase in 1990). Production growth slowed down in *Japan* from 4.8 per cent in 1990 to 2.2 per cent in 1991. It declined from the third quarter of 1991 and in the first quarter of 1992. In *Germany*, the 2.9 per cent increase in industrial production in 1991 (down from 5.1 per cent in 1990) in the western part of the country contrasts with serious production declines in the eastern part. In the *European Community* as a whole, industrial production stagnated in 1991 (a 0.1 per cent fall), following a 1.9 per cent increase in the preceding year.

The decline in industrial production in general during 1991 was even more pronounced in the manufacturing sector of OECD economies. The index of manufacturing production in the OECD area as a whole declined by 1.1 per cent, following a growth rate of 1.8 per cent in the preceding year (see Table 12). The decline followed a period of strong growth, averaging 2.9 per cent during the 1980s. The countries that experienced the steepest declines were *Finland, Sweden, Canada,* the *United Kingdom* and *Australia*.

In the *United States*, the 2.3 per cent decline in the index of manufacturing production in 1991 can be mainly traced to the fall in real total domestic demand (a 1.3 per cent decline), since the export growth of manufactured goods was of the order of 8 per cent in volume terms. This manufacturing production decline followed a 1 per cent growth rate in 1990 and an average annual growth rate of 3.4 per cent in the 1980-90 period. *Canada* was one of the

Table 12. **Manufacturing production**
Volume

	Percentage change from preceding year				Index (1985 = 100)				
	1989	1990	1991	1980-90[1]	91/Q1	91/Q2	91/Q3	91/Q4	92/Q1
United States	2.9	1.0	-2.3	3.4	114	117	121	118	116
Canada	0.3	-5.3	-6.7	1.8	96	104	98	97	96
Japan	6.2	4.6	2.1	4.4	127	128	128	130	121
Belgium[2]	2.6	6.0	-4.2	2.4	121	123	105	118	115**
Denmark	2.0	0.6	2.3	2.8	107	113	107	114	111
France	4.4	1.9	-1.0	0.9	117	118	103	116	117**
Germany	5.6	5.2	2.9	2.2	122	124	119	127	123
Greece	2.3	-2.5	-1.2	0.3	96	99	105	103	94
Ireland	11.7	4.8	3.3	7.0	154	157	142	165	159
Italy	3.9	-0.9	-2.5	1.3	121	123	96	118	121
Luxembourg	8.0	-0.9	-0.4	3.7	117	126	110	118	117
Netherlands	4.1	3.9	0.9	2.6	117	124	110	123	117
Portugal[3]	2.7	5.7	0.2**	4.1	129	132	115	134**	132**
Spain	4.3	0.0	-1.4	1.8	117	122	103	122	120
United Kingdom[4]	4.1	-0.5	-5.3	2.1	115	112	108	113	114
Austria	6.6	8.6	1.6	2.9	122	131	118	134	123**
Finland	3.6	-0.9	-10.2	2.8	107	109	90	104	105
Norway	0.2	0.1	-1.6	1.0	101	104	91	102	104
Sweden	3.8	-2.7	-8.3	1.6	101	105	81	100	93
Switzerland	2.6	2.7	0.5	2.1	120	122	113	127	120
Turkey	2.1	9.5	1.9**	7.5*	125	132	150	159**	139**
Australia	5.9	-1.4	-5.4	1.8	105	109	112	113	104
New Zealand	1.9	-4.3	-5.0	0.9	86	83	84	92	86**
OECD total	4.1	1.8	-1.1**	2.9	117	120	116	120**	117**

* 1981-90.
** Estimates.
1. Average annual growth rates between indicated years.
2. Excluding ISIC 342, 3853 and 39.
3. Excluding ISIC 322, 332 and 342.
4. Excluding ISIC 353, 354 and parts of 351; including 230 and 290.
Source: OECD, *Indicators of Industrial Activity;* Industry Division.

hardest hit economies, with a decline in manufacturing production for the second consecutive year (6.7 per cent in 1991, preceded by a 5.3 per cent decline in 1990). The decline was more pronounced in durable manufactures (8.7 per cent) than in non-durables (4.6 per cent). The output of service industries, on the other hand, was more resilient to the economic downturn, registering a slight increase in 1991.

Japan was one of the OECD countries whose manufacturing sector slowed down the least in 1991. Its 2.1 per cent growth rate is less than half that attained in 1990 or during the 1980-90 period, but remains one of the strongest performances in the OECD. It can be traced to strong growth in both domestic demand and export volumes for manufactured goods, even though growth rates were slower than in preceding years. Production was particularly strong in the electrical machinery industries, while it declined in motor vehicles.

In the *European Community*, *Germany* was the only of the large countries where manufacturing production increased in 1991, albeit at a slower rate than in previous years. This increase in production in the western part of the country is in contrast to manufacturing production declines in many industries of the new *Länder*, and is driven primarily by domestic demand, since export volumes of manufactures declined by 4 per cent in 1991. The index of manufacturing production decreased in the *United Kingdom* and *Italy* for the second consecutive year. The steep decline in the UK can be traced mainly to the falling domestic demand; in contrast, export volumes of manufactures increased by 2.5 per cent. In *France*, production declined by 1 per cent in 1991, following an increase of 1.9 in 1990 and a moderate annual growth rate of 0.9 per cent between 1980 and 1990. Of the smaller EC countries, manufacturing production declined sharply in *Belgium*, and less so in *Greece*, *Spain* and *Luxembourg*. It increased slightly in the *Netherlands* and *Portugal*, and more so in *Denmark* and *Ireland*. The 3.3 per cent growth rate of manufacturing production in Ireland, while the highest in the OECD area for 1991, represents a decline from the growth rates in previous years. Nevertheless, by the end of 1991, manufacturing production in Ireland was 60 per cent higher in real terms than in 1985.

Among the other European countries, the manufacturing production declines in *Sweden* and *Finland* are exceptional. The rate of decline in Finland is symptomatic of the deep economic recession under way, with a collapse of domestic demand (a 7.6 per cent fall in 1991) and of export volumes for manufactured goods (a decline of over 8 per cent). In both Finland and Sweden, the third quarter of 1991 was the lowest point, with manufacturing production at 90 and 81 per cent of the levels in 1985. The decline in *Norway* was moderate in comparison (1.6 per cent), while manufacturing production was stagnant in *Switzerland* (up by 0.5 per cent) and increased in *Austria*, partly as a result of the strong volume growth for its manufactured exports. Finally, outside Europe, the index of manufacturing production in *Australia* and *New Zealand* declined for the second consecutive year, following a drop in domestic demand and despite very strong volume growth for manufactured exports.

Sectoral patterns

The sectoral incidence of the decline in OECD manufacturing production in 1991 was uneven. While production declined in most industries, positive growth rates were still in evidence in a number of sectors, notably in electrical machinery, petroleum refining, chemicals and chemical products, paper an paper products, and in the food, beverages and tobacco industries. Production fell sharply in wood and wood products, textiles, non-metallic mineral products, iron and steel, transport equipment, non-electrical machinery, basic metals, fabricated metal products, and motor vehicles (see Table 13 and Graph 4).

Textiles. 1991 was a difficult year for the textile and apparel industry. Production declined by 3.2 per cent (2.4 per cent in textiles), a steeper decline than in 1990. Uncertainty prevailed over costs due to large variations in raw material prices. The emerging textile producers from Asia continued to erode OECD countries' market shares while the restructuring in the central and eastern European countries (CEECs) holds both the promise of an emerging new market and a threat to OECD producers from the increased competitiveness of firms in those countries. Textile production declined in most OECD countries and particularly in *Finland* (by about 15 per cent), *Sweden*, *Turkey* (reversing a healthy progression in 1990), *Belgium, Canada, Greece*, the *United Kingdom*, *Spain* and *France*.

Paper and paper products. Production in the paper and paper industry stagnated in 1991, with a growth rate of 0.4 per cent, following an expansion of 2.6 per cent in 1990. These growth rates are much below the expansion during the 1980s, which averaged 3.4 per cent annually. The slowdown was more pronounced in the pulp segment of the industry. Production declined significantly in *Turkey, Finland, Australia, Canada, Sweden*, the *United Kingdom* and *Belgium*, and less so in *Switzerland, Denmark, Norway* and *Greece. Luxembourg, Ireland, Germany,* and *Spain* experienced strong production growth at levels above those of the preceding year.

Iron and steel. Steel production declined by 3.3 per cent in 1991, reflecting the weakness in most of the steel consuming sectors, including construction, vehicles, engineering and machinery. The production decline was particularly steep in the third quarter of 1991; a slight recovery in the fourth quarter was followed by further decline in the first quarter of 1992. In most OECD countries the steel industry has reported substantial reduction in income, or losses, this year, due to the weakening of

Table 13. **Manufacturing production by industry**[1]
OECD total

ISIC		Percentage change		
		1989-90	1990-91	1980-90[2]
3	Total manufacturing	1.8	−1.1	2.9
31	Food, beverages, tobacco	2.6	1.5	1.7
311/312[3]	Food	2.3	1.8	1.7
313[3]	Beverages	2.9	0.2	1.7
314[4]	Tobacco	2.6	3.6	−0.2
32	Textile, wearing apparel and leather	−2.7	−3.2	−0.5
321	Textiles	−1.7	−2.4	0.1
33	Wood and wood products	−0.5	−4.2	0.9
34[5]	Paper and paper products	2.6	0.4	3.4
35	Chemicals	2.1	0.6	3.0
351/352[6]	Chemical products	2.1	0.7	2.7
353[7]	Petroleum refineries	3.2	1.7	−0.5
36	Non-metallic mineral products	0.9	−4.2	1.0
37	Basic metal industry	−0.5	−2.8	0.7
371[8]	Iron and steel	−0.8	−3.3	−0.1
372[8]	Non-ferrous metals	0.6	−1.5	1.9
38	Fabricated metal products, machinery and equipment	2.9	−1.0	4.4
381	Fabricated metal products	1.6	−2.0	1.4
382	Non-electrical machinery	4.1	−2.8	5.0
383[4]	Electrical machinery	4.0	2.3	6.8
384	Transport equipment	2.6	−2.7	3.1
3841[9]	Shipbuilding and repairing	7.7	−0.7	−1.2
3843[9]	Motor vehicles	0.7	−2.0	3.2

1. Totals calculated on the basis of 1987 weights using current exchange rates. Switzerland, Iceland and New Zealand are not included (except for ISIC 3).
2. Annual percentage change between indicated years.
3. For ISIC 311/312 and 313, OECD total excludes Spain, Austria and Australia.
4. For ISIC 314 and 383, OECD total excludes Australia.
5. For ISIC 34, OECD total excludes Portugal.
6. For ISIC 351/352, OECD total excludes Austria and Australia.
7. For ISIC 353, OECD total excludes Sweden and Australia.
8. For ISIC 371 and 372, OECD total excludes Denmark, Ireland, Netherlands, Australia.
9. For ISIC 3841 and 3843, OECD total excludes Canada, Ireland, Netherlands, Austria, Finland, Norway, Turkey, Australia (also Denmark and Sweden for ISIC 3843).
Source: OECD, *Indicators of Industrial Activity*; Industry Division.

demand and a continuing decline in steel prices. Restructuring efforts in the industry have continued, as firms attempt to face the depressed demand and price volatility through plant closures, labour shedding, joint ventures to lower costs or mergers to reduce capacity. The weak outlook in OECD countries is compounded by the mounting difficulties facing producers in the CEEC countries which suffered sharp falls in production last year[4].

Production declined by over 10 per cent during 1991 in the *United States*, as a result of the weak demand of all steel consuming sectors. Steel shipments to the car industry declined by over 15 per cent, and those to construction by over 11 per cent. Steel exports remained higher than expected, reflecting stronger demand in some export markets as well as the improvement in the international competitiveness of the US steel industry. In *Canada*, production declined by about 2 per cent, reflecting a much sharper drop in domestic consumption of steel.

Steel production in *Japan* was resilient during the first half of 1991, Production declined however from the third quarter on, and fell by nearly 10 per cent in the first quarter of 1992. This downward trend can be to a large extent traced to declines in the construction, automotive and industrial machinery sectors. In the countries of the *European Community,* which taken together remain the largest producer of steel in the OECD area, production declined sharply in the *United Kingdom* (by over 10 per cent) and *Portugal*, and less so in *France, Italy* and *Germany*. For the EC as a whole, production declined by over 2 per cent, although a slight recovery was apparent from the fourth quarter of 1991. Among the other European countries, there was a steep production decline in *Turkey, Sweden* and *Austria*, and a more moderate one in *Norway*.

Chemicals. The downturn experienced by the OECD chemical industry in 1990 worsened in 1991. Production in chemicals and chemical products stagnated (0.6 per cent growth, following a 2.1 per cent growth in 1990), while

Graph 4. **Manufacturing production in selected industries**
Percentage changes

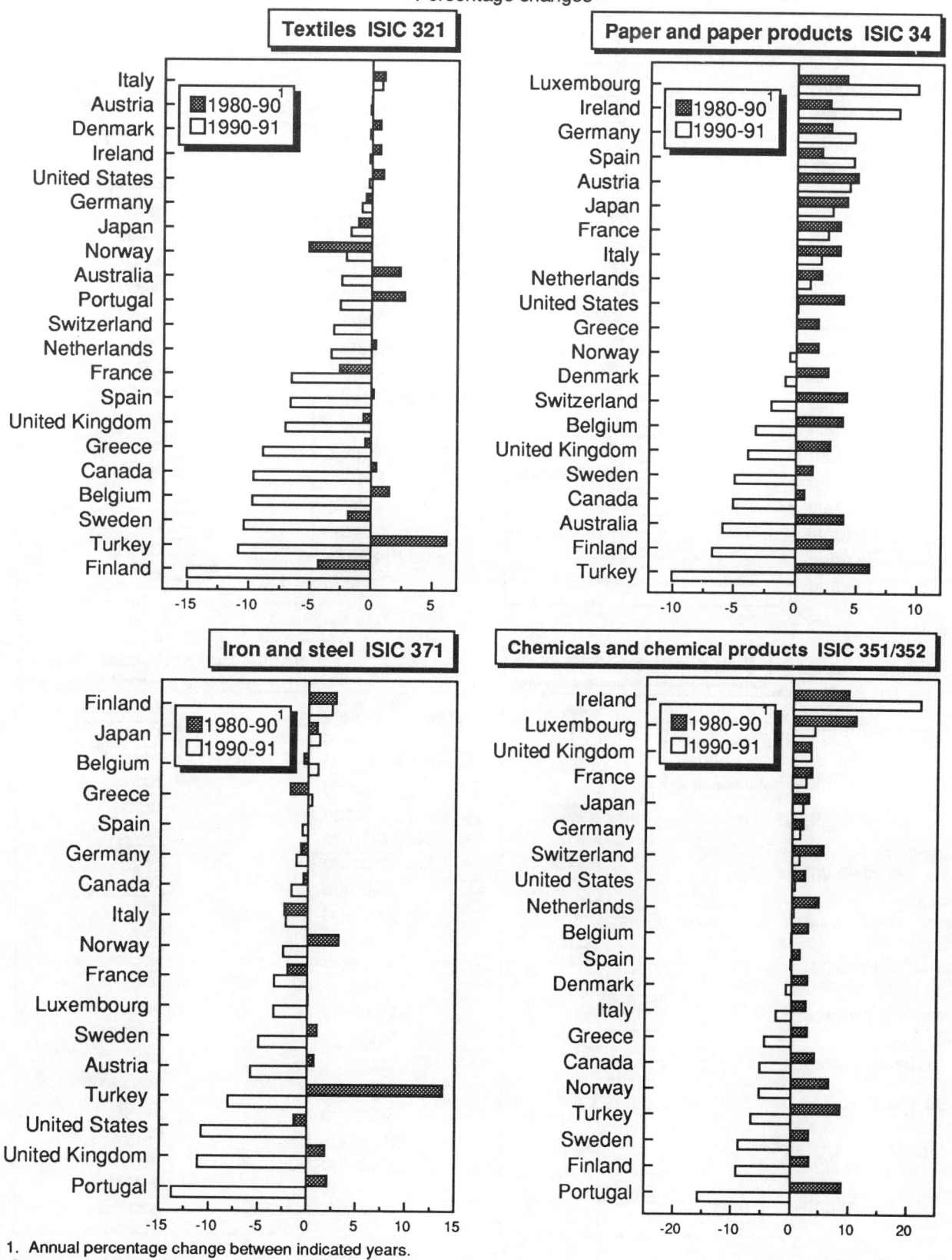

1. Annual percentage change between indicated years.
Source: OECD, *Indicators of Industrial Activity.*

Graph 4 (cont). **Manufacturing production in selected industries**
Percentage changes

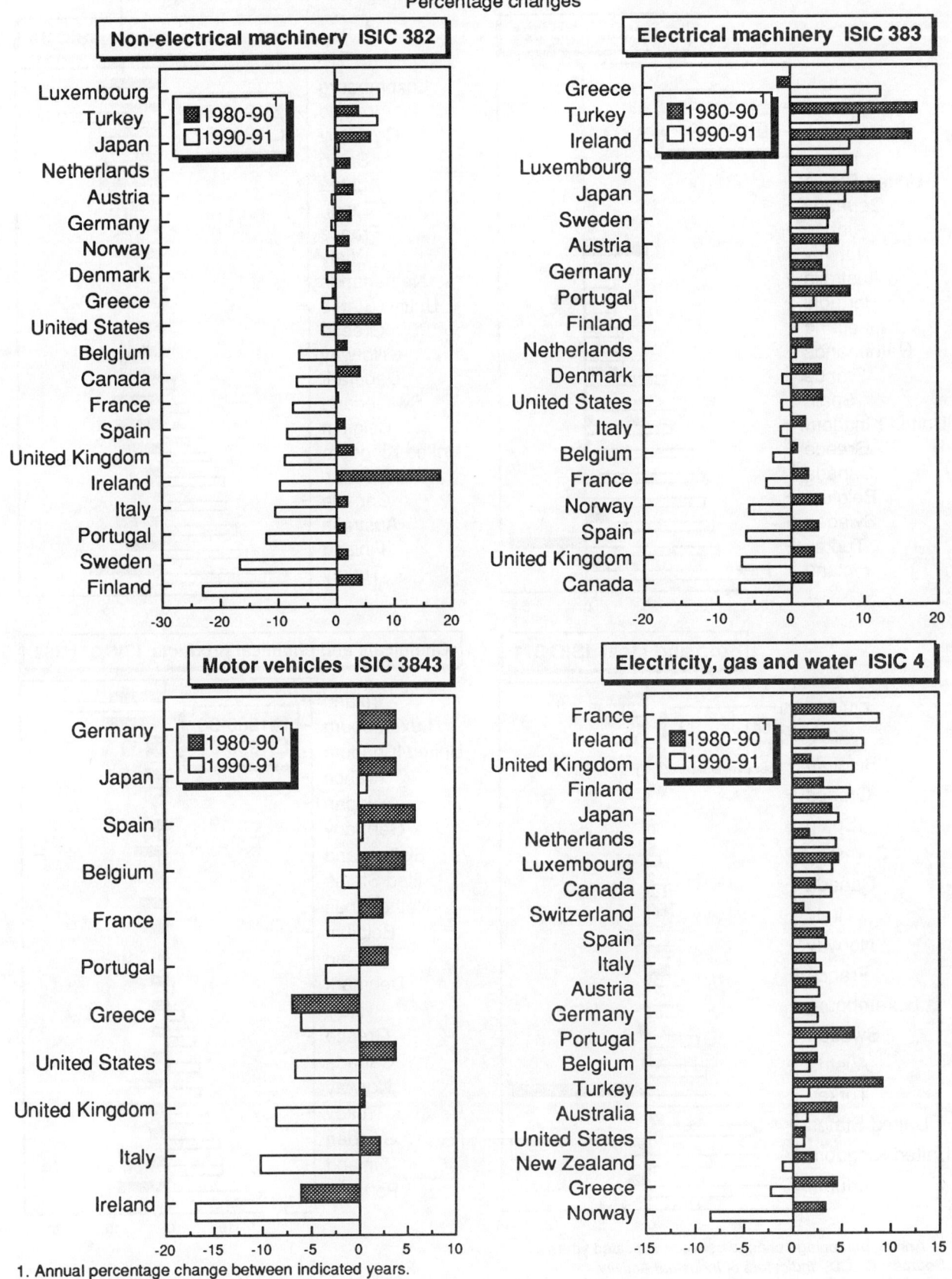

1. Annual percentage change between indicated years.
Source: OECD, *Indicators of Industrial Activity.*

that of petroleum refining fared better with a growth rate of 1.7 per cent. The economic recession and the Gulf crisis reduced demand for *basic chemicals* while capacity expansion which was planned for in the boom of the 1980s has continued to come on stream, increasing competition further. At the same time, the increased capital costs required by tougher environmental legislation put a further squeeze on profit margins. Bulk chemical companies thus face an increasingly uncertain outlook, shaped by falling prices, sagging demand and soaring environmental costs. In sharp contrast, and despite their common scientific base with bulk chemicals (including refineries), developments in *pharmaceuticals* are quite distinct from those in other segments of chemicals industries. Helped by ageing populations and increasingly expensive and sophisticated drugs, the pharmaceutical industry has been growing over the last decade without much cyclical dependence. Nevertheless, increasing concerns about escalating health costs are leading to attempts by governments to limit public expenditures and control prices on drugs which could reduce future growth even in this apparently recession-immune segment of the industry.

In the *United States*, there was a drop in 1991 in the constant price growth rate of shipments of chemicals and chemical products, reflecting diminished requirements in the chemical processing industries, such as automotive products, construction materials, or electronic goods. The US pharmaceutical industry, on the other hand, recorded a 9.4 per cent increase in shipments in 1991 (about 4 per cent in real terms) to reach about $59 billion [5]. The structure of the US industry is changing in response to increasing R&D costs, growing sales of generic drugs, and government regulations. In the *European Community*, the chemical sector represents about 10 per cent of total EC manufacturing value added and nearly 30 per cent of world production. In 1991, production of chemicals increased by just below 2 per cent and is projected to grow at rates exceeding 3 per cent in 1992 and 1993 [6]. Of the EC member states that are large producers, constant value shipments of chemicals increased in *Germany, France* and the *United Kingdom,* while stagnating in *Spain* and falling in *Italy* and *Portugal*. Outside the EC, *Sweden* and *Finland* experienced sharp drops in production, while production in *Switzerland* and *Japan* continued to grow but at slower rates.

Motor vehicles. Production in the motor vehicles industry declined by 2 per cent in 1991, following a 0.7 per cent growth in 1990 and a 3.2 average annual percentage growth during the 1980-90 period. This downturn affected manufacturers in most large producer countries. In the *United States,* shipments in volume terms declined by over 7 per cent, leaving production at just over 90 per cent of its 1985 level. The record losses and substantial cut-backs by the world's largest vehicle manufacturer, General Motors, are an indication of the competitiveness challenges facing North American car producers. Production in *Japan* increased slightly in 1991, following 5 per cent growth the year before, while Japanese vehicle manufacturers recorded disappointing profits for the first time. In Europe, the diverging performance in different

Graph 5. **Motor vehicle production**
1989, Percentages

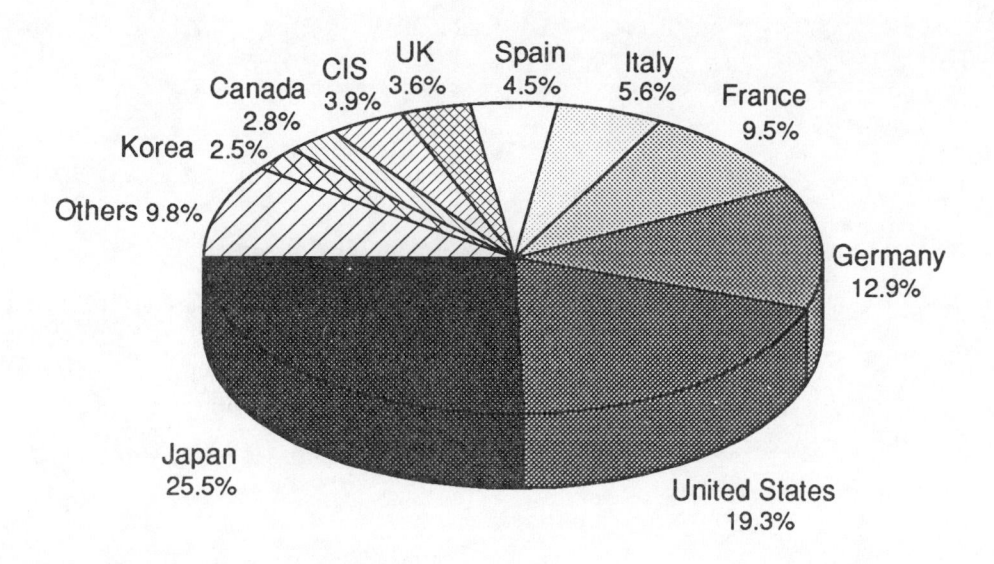

- Canada 2.8%
- CIS 3.9%
- UK 3.6%
- Spain 4.5%
- Italy 5.6%
- France 9.5%
- Korea 2.5%
- Others 9.8%
- Germany 12.9%
- United States 19.3%
- Japan 25.5%

Source: CEC, *Panorama of EC Industry 1991-92.*

markets which had started in 1990 continued in 1991. Of the large car manufacturers (see Graph 5), production increased only in (western) *Germany*, although at a slower rate than in 1990, as there was an ebbing in the surge in domestic demand from the eastern part of the country, and in *Spain*. *France,* the *United Kingdom,* and *Italy* all experienced production declines, of the order of 3 to 10 per cent. Of the smaller European countries, production in *Portugal* increased by over 5 per cent, while it declined sharply in *Ireland* and *Greece* (by over 15 per cent).

Electrical machinery. After reasonably strong growth in 1990 (4 per cent), production in electrical machinery industries (including communications equipment and semiconductors) slowed down to 2.3 per cent in 1991, a rate of expansion much below the almost 7 per cent average annual growth rate between 1980 and 1990. *Spain, Canada,* the *United Kingdom* and *Norway* experienced production declines in 1991 exceeding 5 per cent. In *semiconductors*, worldwide revenues increased by about 8 per cent, a better performance than in 1990 when sales were flat. However, this good overall picture masks a mixed performance of different product categories, as sales of microprocessors and of microcontrollers continued to boom, while the market of commodity memory chips experienced severe oversupply and rapidly falling prices. In the *United States,* shipments increased by 7 per cent in constant price terms, and are estimated to increase by 8 per cent in 1992 [7]. With *Japan* and the *United States* accounting for about 45 and 40 per cent respectively of the world market, production and trade in this industry is heavily influenced by the series of semiconductor agreements between the United States and Japan and between the *European Community* and Japan (see Part 2 of the report, section G).

Table 14. **United States computer industry**

	Million current dollars			Percentage change from preceding period	
	1990[1]	1991[2]	1992[2]	1991	1992
Shipments	59 750	58 500	61 000	–2.1	4.3
+ Imports	23 321	25 841	29 320	10.8	13.5
– Exports	24 111	25 872	27 800	7.3	7.5
US demand	58 968	58 469	62 520	–0.8	6.9

1. Estimated, except imports and exports.
2. Forecast.
Source: US Department of Commerce, *1992 US Industrial Outlook;* OECD, Industry Division.

Non-electrical machinery. In the non-electrical machinery industry (including computers and office machinery), the index of production declined by 2.8 per cent in 1991, a dramatic change from the 4.1 per cent growth rate of the preceding year. Most OECD countries experienced production declines, with the sharpest falls in *Finland* (over 20 per cent), *Sweden, Portugal* and *Italy*. In *computers*, almost all major hardware manufacturers are in difficulties, reporting declining sales and losses in 1991. In the *United States,* shipments by the computer industry decreased by 2 per cent in 1991, but are expected to grow by over 4 per cent in 1992 (see Table 14). Production in *Japan* slowed down, while in the European Community, producers faced a difficult year in 1991 with a number of producers posting profits and initiating recovery plans, often through collaborative agreements.

Chapter II

TRENDS IN FACTOR INPUTS

A. Employment

Recent trends

The decline in manufacturing employment, a tendency that already set in during 1990, gathered momentum in 1991 and resulted in an OECD-wide decrease of 2.8 per cent (Table 15). Although the effects differ to a great extent from one country to another, the evolution in manufacturing employment was for every OECD Member state less favourable in 1990-91 than in the preceding period. Throughout 1991, manufacturing employment diminished in the majority of countries, with a slight recovery in the fourth quarter in a small number of OECD Member states.

Reflecting their relatively strong industrial performances during a global economic downturn, *Japan,* (western) *Germany,* the *Netherlands, Italy,* as well as *Ireland* were the only countries where manufacturing employment continued to grow, although at a slower rate than during the preceding year. Several European countries

Table 15. **Manufacturing employment**[1]

	Percentage change from preceding year				Index 1985 = 100				
	1989	1990	1991	1980-90[2]	91/Q1	91/Q2	91/Q3	91/Q4	92/Q1
United States[3]	0.4	-2.2	-4.0	-1.0	94	94	95	95	..
Canada	0.5	-8.8	-13.7	0.1	89	91	91	87	84
Japan	1.4	2.8	2.3	1.2	108	111	110	110	109
Denmark	-0.3	0.1	-3.0	-0.3	92	93	94	92	..
France	0.8	0.6	-1.5	-1.7	95	95	94	93	92
Germany	-0.1	4.3	1.1	-0.8	106	106	107	105	..
Greece[4,7]	0.2	-1.6	-6.2	-0.2	92	92	95	91	..
Ireland	2.5	3.0	0.7*	-1.6	103	103	105	105*	..
Italy[5,6,7]	-0.6	1.8	0.5	-1.4	100	100	100	99	97
Luxembourg	-0.1	-1.2	-0.9	-1.4	94	93	95	95	..
Netherlands	1.3	2.0	0.5	-1.0	107	107	106	106	..
Portugal	-1.4	-1.9	-3.8*	-2.0	89	88	87	87*	..
Spain[7]	3.9	3.5	-3.4	-0.6	111	111	110	111	..
United Kingdom	-0.2	0.0	-5.5	-2.8	93	91	90	88	..
Austria	0.9	1.7	-1.4	-1.3	95	97	98	96	..
Finland	2.2	-0.5	-10.5	-1.1	87	88	85	78	76
Norway	-5.8	-2.4	-5.0	-2.2	86	85	85	82	82
Sweden	1.4	-3.3	-11.0	-1.2	92	90	88	84	82
Switzerland	0.9	1.4	-2.3	-0.4	101	100	100	98	96
Turkey	0.1	1.2	-8.7*	1.4	97	97	97	97*	..
Australia[7]	3.3	-2.6	-6.1	-0.4	102	99	98	99	98
New Zealand	-8.8	-4.0	-6.9	-2.1	79	77	70	72	..
OECD	0.4	0.0	-2.8*	-0.7	97	97	97	96*	..

* Estimates.
1. Figures do not, in general, cover total employment but only employees. Furthermore, for a number of countries, the sample refers to all firms exceeding a minimum size threshold.
2. Annual percentage growth rates between indicated years.
3. Excluding 385.
4. Enterprises employing at least 10 persons.
5. Sample survey taken in the first week without public holidays in each quarter.
6. Including construction.
7. *Main Economic Indicators.*
Source: OECD, *Indicators of Industrial Activity; Main Economic Indicators;* Industry Division.

(*France, Spain, Austria, Switzerland, Denmark,* and *Turkey*) with positive growth rates in manufacturing employment up until 1990 recorded a decline in 1991. The situation deteriorated further in the *United States*, the *United Kingdom*, *Australia*, and *New Zealand*, countries that were already facing declines in manufacturing employment in 1990 or before. Developments were particularly negative in *Sweden*, *Finland*, and *Canada*, where employment in manufacturing plunged by over 10 per cent in one year.

Structural issues

Taking into account the developments of the last few years, it becomes apparent that manufacturing employment has drastically diminished in several OECD Member countries, following declines during a number of consecutive years. In *New Zealand*, after a constant drop in employment in manufacturing, hardly three of the four manufacturing workers that were employed in 1985 were still employed at the end of 1991. Since 1985, manufacturing employment diminished by roughly 20 per cent in *Finland*, *Norway*, and *Sweden*. In contrast, between 1985 and the end of 1991, the number of employees in manufacturing has grown in *Japan,* (western) *Germany, Ireland,* the *Netherlands* and *Spain*. At the same time, in an environment of intensified international competition, a number of large firms in globalised industries in some countries are shedding jobs under increasing competitive pressures. Recent developments thus indicate that beyond their cyclical component, employment losses raise some issues of a structural character, emanating from the sectoral, occupational, and regional dimensions of employment fall-out.

Sectoral patterns of employment fall-out. The overall decline in manufacturing employment in the majority of OECD Member countries cannot be attributed to a few industries facing structural adjustment problems (see Graph 6). Although industry-specific dynamics do play their role, they appear to be overshadowed by economy-wide cyclical forces. For example, countries such as the *United States* or *Canada* with substantial losses in manufacturing employment have hardly any or no industries with employment gains, while countries with a growth in manufacturing employment, notably *Japan*, recorded employment gains in almost every sector.

This being said, traditional industries like textiles, clothing, leather, and footwear, appear to have recorded the largest employment losses in virtually all countries analysed. In *Canada* and the Nordic countries, employment decreased in these industries by often as much as 20 or 30 per cent. In *Germany*, the employment losses in leather, footwear, and clothing could well be related to the fact that these traditional industries are found to a great extent in the eastern part that is facing massive adjustment problems. But employment in more advanced and technology-intensive industries such as chemicals, electrical machinery, and transport equipment, has not been saved either. The pulp and paper, and the wood products industry appear to have fared relatively well.

The seriousness of the fall-out in manufacturing employment has been accompanied by downward tendencies of employment in other sectors of the economy as well. The shedding of labour in manufacturing has not been cushioned by a growth in service industries, with a rapid rise in overall unemployment as a consequence. This has also been the case in countries such as *Sweden* and *Finland* for which labour market discrepancies to the current extent are a virtually new phenomenon. Although the downward tendencies in service employment are certainly not as serious as in manufacturing, the service sector appears to have been more affected than during previous recessions [8]. Finance, insurance, real estate and business services have been affected in particular, but wholesale and retail trade, and transportation and communication industries have also been touched.

Occupational patterns of employment fall-out. In times of recession, blue-collar workers are usually hit by unemployment to a much greater extent than white-collar workers. Although this pattern seems to hold up in the current recession as well, there is some evidence that white-collar workers have been affected more than during previous recessions. White-collar jobs have not only been suppressed in the service sector, but in many manufacturing industries as well. After an extended period of restructuring, rationalisation and production automation, manufacturing firms might not have much room anymore to enhance productivity levels on the shopfloor. In light of increasing competition, they may now also be looking for efficiency improvement among white-collar support staffs, usually at headquarters. Moreover, one can assume that a certain number of white-collar jobs, created in large numbers during the 1980s, has proven to be unsustainable in the current downturn.

Regional patterns of employment fall-out. The regional implications of the recent economic downturn are markedly different from those of earlier recessions. On the basis of recent regional unemployment data from a few countries where the recession set in early, it can be concluded that the unemployment rates in core areas have risen sharply, more so than in lagging areas. In the *United States,* the *United Kingdom*, and *Canada* core areas with many white collar jobs have recently seen rapid increases in unemployment. Starting from a comfortable position until as late as 1989, after years of vigorous growth, these areas are now facing unemployment rates that are around or above their national averages (see Table 16). Massachusetts, New York, and California used to be states with low unemployment rates in 1989. Two years later, Massachusetts had the highest US rate of unemployment after the state of Mississippi, while New York and California had above-average unemployment rates as well. The Canadian core province of Ontario has also seen a rapid

Graph 6. **Manufacturing employment**
Percentage changes

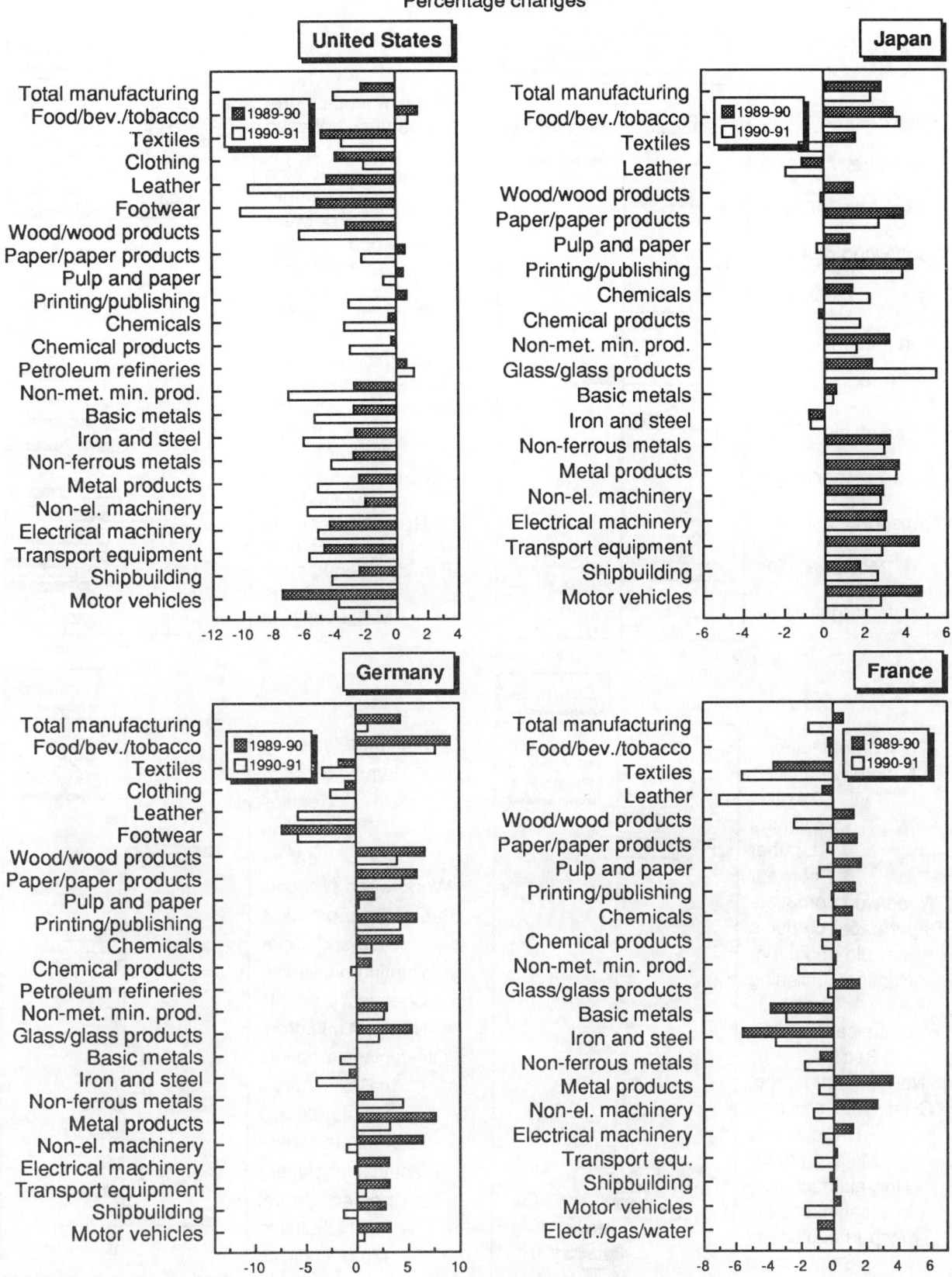

Source: OECD, *Indicators of Industrial Activity.*

Graph 6 (cont). **Manufacturing employment**
Percentage changes

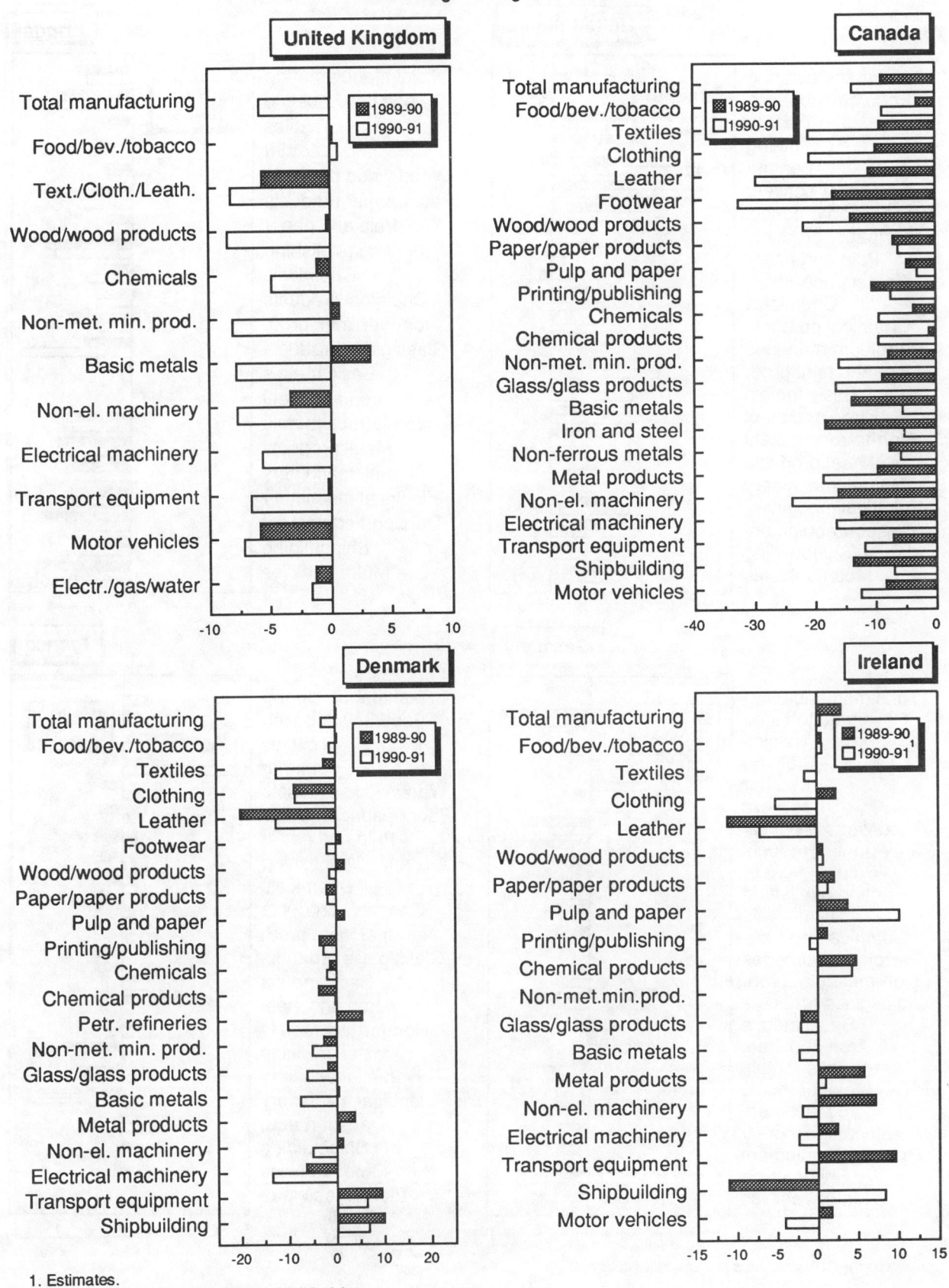

Source: OECD, *Indicators of Industrial Activity*.

1. Estimates.

Graph 6 (cont). **Manufacturing employment**
Percentage changes

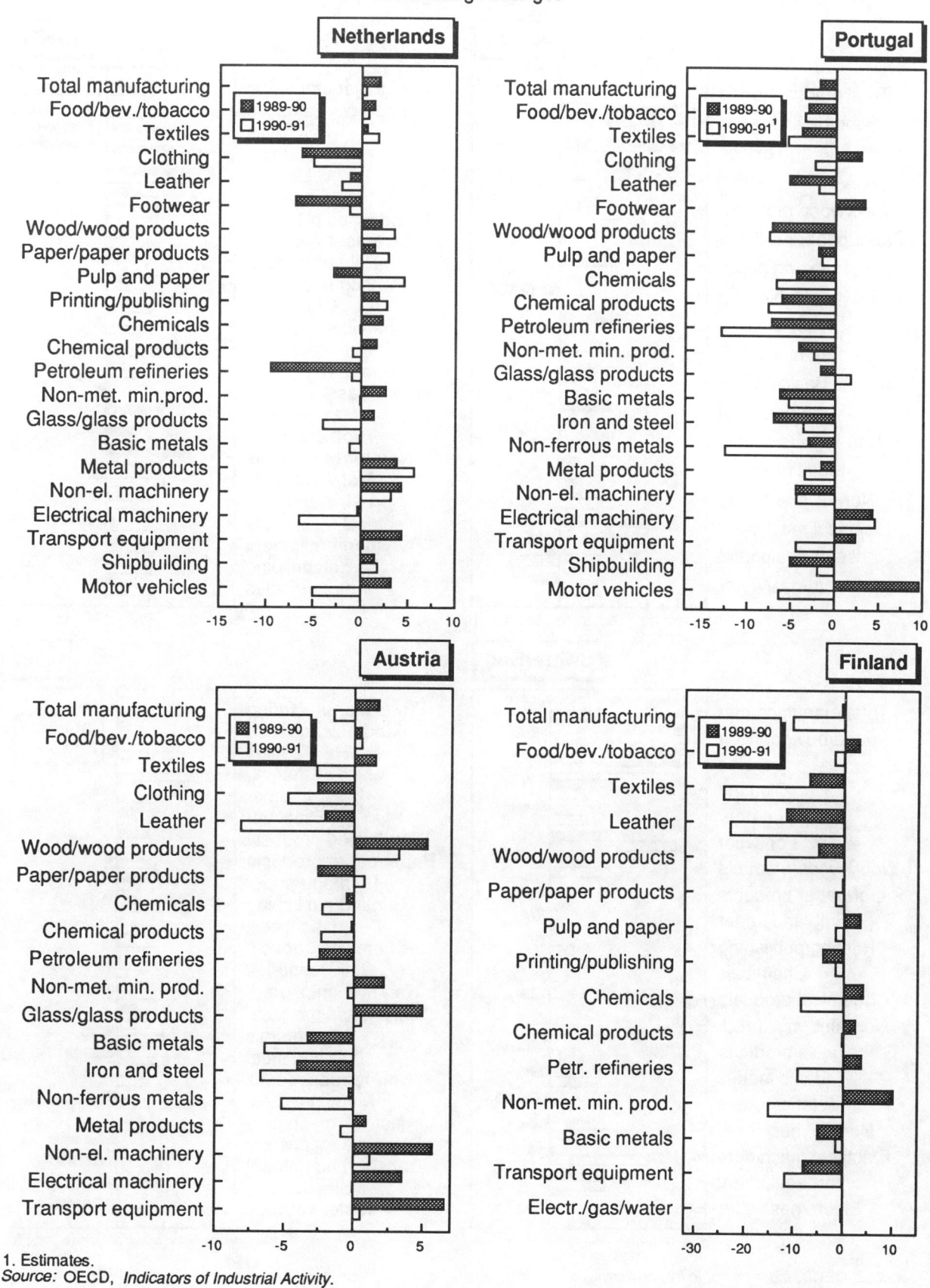

1. Estimates.
Source: OECD, *Indicators of Industrial Activity*.

Graph 6 (cont). Manufacturing employment
Percentage changes

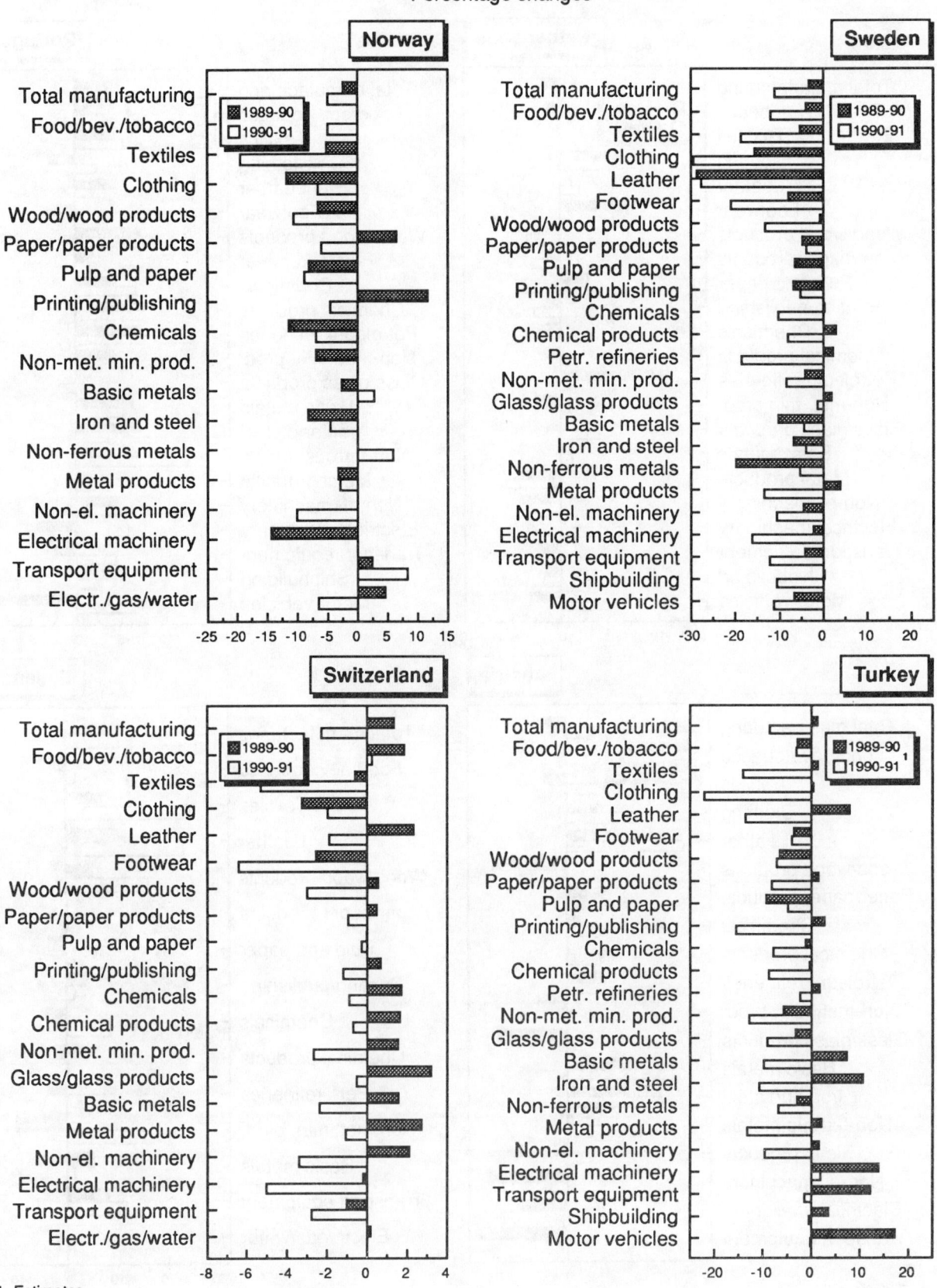

Figure: Bar charts showing percentage changes in manufacturing employment for Norway, Sweden, Switzerland, and Turkey, comparing 1989-90 and 1990-91 across manufacturing sub-sectors.

1. Estimates.
Source: OECD, *Indicators of Industrial Activity.*

unemployment rise, leading to levels that are now almost equal to the national average. In the United Kingdom, the recession started unlike previously in the relatively prosperous South East of England. As a consequence, there has been considerable narrowing of divergence in regional employment rates. Although there is some doubt whether the contraction of this spread of unemployment will continue, tentative figures on the beginning of 1992 do not yet show any break with the above trend.

Table 16. **Unemployment rates in some "white collar" regions**

	Unemployment rate			Percentage of national rates		
	1989	1990	1991	1989	1990	1991
United States[1]						
Massachusetts	3.9	5.8	9.5	72	107	138
New York	4.7	4.7	7.2	87	87	104
California	5.5	5.0	8.0	102	93	116
Canada						
Ontario	4.4	6.3	9.8	65	83	97
United Kingdom[2]						
South East	3.9	3.8	6.9	62	67	85
Greater London	5.1	4.8	7.9	81	84	98

1. Refers to the months of June/July.
2. Seasonally adjusted.
Sources: US Department of Labor, *Monthly Labor Review*, various issues; UK Department of Employment, *Employment Gazette*, various issues; Statistics Canada, *The Labour Force*, various issues.

This atypical regional pattern of employment fall-out might be partly explained by the fact that large cities in core areas have become important platforms for international activities. These platforms are likely to be disproportionally affected by the downturn in the global economy, more so than lagging regions. An alternative explanation suggests that these unconventional regional dynamics are a consequence of equally unconventional sectoral and occupational patterns of employment fall-out. Whereas both agriculture and manufacturing are commonly over-represented in lagging and often peripheral regions, the service sector is found to a much greater extent in large urban centres in more prosperous core regions. Core areas also tend to have many more white-collar jobs, not only within services but within the manufacturing industry as well. It is in these core areas that most headquarters of manufacturing firms and fast-growing business services such as finance, insurance, computing, advertising and real estate tend to be located. Consequently, these core areas are also likely to be the first to benefit from a pick-up in economic activity, so that regional disparities might increase once again [9].

B. Investment

Recent trends

Business investment in the OECD area grew at a brisk rate from 1984 to 1989, before slowing in 1990 and falling in most countries in 1991. Gross private non-residential fixed capital formation for the total of OECD countries increased by 4.2 per cent during 1990 and declined by 1.8 per cent in 1991. It is projected to decline further in 1992, but at a more moderate rate (Table 17) and to pick up again in 1993, as the recovery of output induces an increase in capacity utilisation and business profitability.

Table 17. **Growth of gross private non-residential fixed capital formation**[1]

Percentage changes from previous period seasonally adjusted at annual rates

	1989	1990	1991	1992
United States	2.2	1.2	−6.7	0.1
Canada	6.0	−3.2	−1.9	2.2
Japan	16.6	12.4	6.1	−1.7
Belgium	17.3	9.3	3.4	1.5
Denmark	3.1	3.2	0.1	−1.0
France[2]	7.8	4.3	−1.9	−1.3
Germany[2]	8.5	10.5	8.6	0.5
Greece	13.6	6.2	−0.3	3.8
Ireland	16.4	14.8	−6.1	0.5
Italy	4.8	1.5	0.1	3.5
Luxembourg	−6.5	9.4	6.5	5.4
Netherlands	6.7	8.4	1.8	−1.5
Portugal	5.6	7.3	3.3	4.0
Spain	15.6	4.0	1.2	1.7
United Kingdom[2]	8.1	−1.1	−11.9	−3.8
Austria	7.9	8.6	5.4	3.8
Finland	15.5	−7.1	−20.0	−10.0
Iceland	−17.0	9.1	0.0	−9.5
Norway	−2.5	−34.2	3.6	−5.0
Sweden	13.8	−3.3	−12.8	−6.7
Switzerland	5.9	2.8	−3.2	−1.4
Turkey	3.3	19.2	−3.1	4.2
Australia	13.8	−5.6	−14.3	0.3
New Zealand	17.3	−1.9	−11.0	1.0
Total OECD	7.7	4.2	−1.8	−0.3

1. Figures from 1991 onwards are estimates and projections.
2. Data not comparable with those of Graphs 7 and 8.
Source: OECD, *Economic Outlook No. 51*.

In the *United States,* gross fixed capital formation in 1991 registered a steep decline (6.7 per cent), following the slowdown in the previous two years. It is projected to recover somewhat in 1992. Business investment declined also as a percentage of value added, falling below 13 per cent in 1991, in contrast to an average exceeding 14 per cent during the 1980-88 period (Table 18). The moderate 0.6 per cent decline in the value of plant and equipment expenditures in total industry during 1991 (1 per cent decline in 1987 US$) reflected the relative resilience of investment in the non-manufacturing sector during the economic downturn. Investment in manufacturing declined by almost 5 per cent, reversing the 5 per cent growth rate of 1990, and more so in durable goods industries than in nondurables (Graph 7). Particularly steep declines occurred in the pulp and paper industry (a 30 per cent fall), in iron and steel (15 per cent), in stone and glass (12 per cent), as well as in textiles (10 per cent decline), motor vehicles (9 per cent) and fabricated metals (8 per cent). The food and beverages and the chemical industries were the two exceptions, registering strong investment growth in 1991. In non-manufacturing industry, investment continued to expand, as a result of strong investment activity in transportation (especially in the air transport segment), and despite a decline in investment in utilities.

According to the US Department of Commerce, business plans a 4.6 per cent increase in spending for new plant and equipment from 1991 to 1992, a downward revision from an earlier estimate of a 5.4 increase [10]. This would put the new level of planned spending at US$554 billion, of which US$182 in manufacturing (accounting for 33 per cent of total investment in industry in 1992, down from 36 per cent in 1990). The planned investment levels in manufacturing represent a 0.4 per cent decrease in spending since 1991. This can be traced to the 1 per cent planned decrease in investment in non-durable goods industries (and especially in petroleum), despite some strong planned increases in the food, textiles, chemicals and rubber sectors. In contrast, planned investment in durable goods industries in 1992 is slightly below 1991 levels, with contrasting underlying detail: steep investment decreases are planned in non-ferrous metals and non-electrical machinery, with a recovery of investment rates in electrical machinery, and in stone, clay and glass. Finally, firms in the non-manufacturing sector plan to increase investment by over 7 per cent in 1992, with large increases planned in electric utilities, commercial services and rail transportation.

Business investment continued to increase in *Japan* during 1991, but half as fast as in 1990 (a 6.1 per cent growth rate in 1991, as opposed to 12.4 per cent the preceding year). Japan's economic downturn occurred much later than that of other OECD countries, so that fixed capital formation is expected to decline in 1992 (by 1.7 per cent), just as investment is picking up elsewhere. The slowdown in investment during 1991 was not as pronounced as that of the growth of GDP, so that investment rates (the volume of gross fixed capital formation as a percentage of real value added in the business sector) increased in 1991 to reach 25 per cent, and are now well above the 17 per cent average rate during the 1980-88 period.

After strong growth in the first half of 1991, plant and equipment expenditures in Japan declined slightly during the second half of the year and are projected to decline by over 3 per cent in 1992 (Graph 7). Investment in manufacturing has been more vulnerable to the downturn: investment rates in 1991 were at 4 per cent half of those for industry as a whole, and are projected for an 8 per cent decline in 1992. Strong investment increases were registered during 1991 in petroleum refining (31 per cent), non-ferrous metals (27 per cent) and in iron and steel (19 per cent). The pulp and paper industry was severely hit, registering a record 40 per cent decline in plant and equipment expenditures. In 1992, steep declines are expected in industrial machinery, non-ferrous metals, processed metals, pulp and paper, and chemicals. Petroleum refining, shipbuilding and food are the only industrial sectors expected to increase their investment expenditures. In contrast to manufacturing industries, non-manufacturing plant and equipment expenditures increased strongly in 1991 (by over 10 per cent), and are expected to remain unchanged in 1992, despite significant projected declines in investment expenditures in the services sectors, and especially in the wholesale, retail and electricity industries.

Business investment performance varied widely in *European Community* countries during 1991. While the growth of gross fixed capital formation was lower than in 1990 in every EC country, the level declined only in the

Table 18. **Investment as a percentage of business sector value added**

Volume

	Average 1980-88	1989	1990	1991	1992
United States	14.1	13.7	13.7	12.9	12.7
Canada	17.0	18.4	17.8	17.9	17.8
Japan	17.1	23.3	24.8	25.1	24.3
Belgium/Luxembourg	13.4	17.3	18.2	18.5	18.4
Denmark	15.5	18.4	18.5	18.2	17.6
France	16.8	17.2	17.5	17.0	16.4
Germany	15.4	16.4	17.3	18.2	18.0
Greece	15.3	12.7	13.4	13.2	13.5
Ireland	22.2	16.4	17.4	16.0	15.6
Italy	17.5	15.1	14.9	14.7	15.0
Netherlands	15.1	18.0	18.7	18.5	18.0
Spain	16.8	19.6	19.7	19.5	19.4
United Kingdom	12.4	18.5	18.0	16.3	15.7
Austria	21.1	22.3	23.0	23.4	23.8
Finland	19.2	23.3	21.7	18.7	17.1
Norway	29.4	40.8	27.1	29.7	28.5
Sweden	16.6	20.8	20.1	17.8	16.7
Switzerland	15.3	21.5	21.6	21.0	20.5
Australia	19.4	22.8	21.1	18.5	18.0
New Zealand	14.0	20.7	20.2	18.4	18.1

Source: OECD *Economic Outlook No. 51;* Industry Division.

Graph 7. **Investment by industry**
Plant and equipment expenditures
Percentage change in value from preceding period

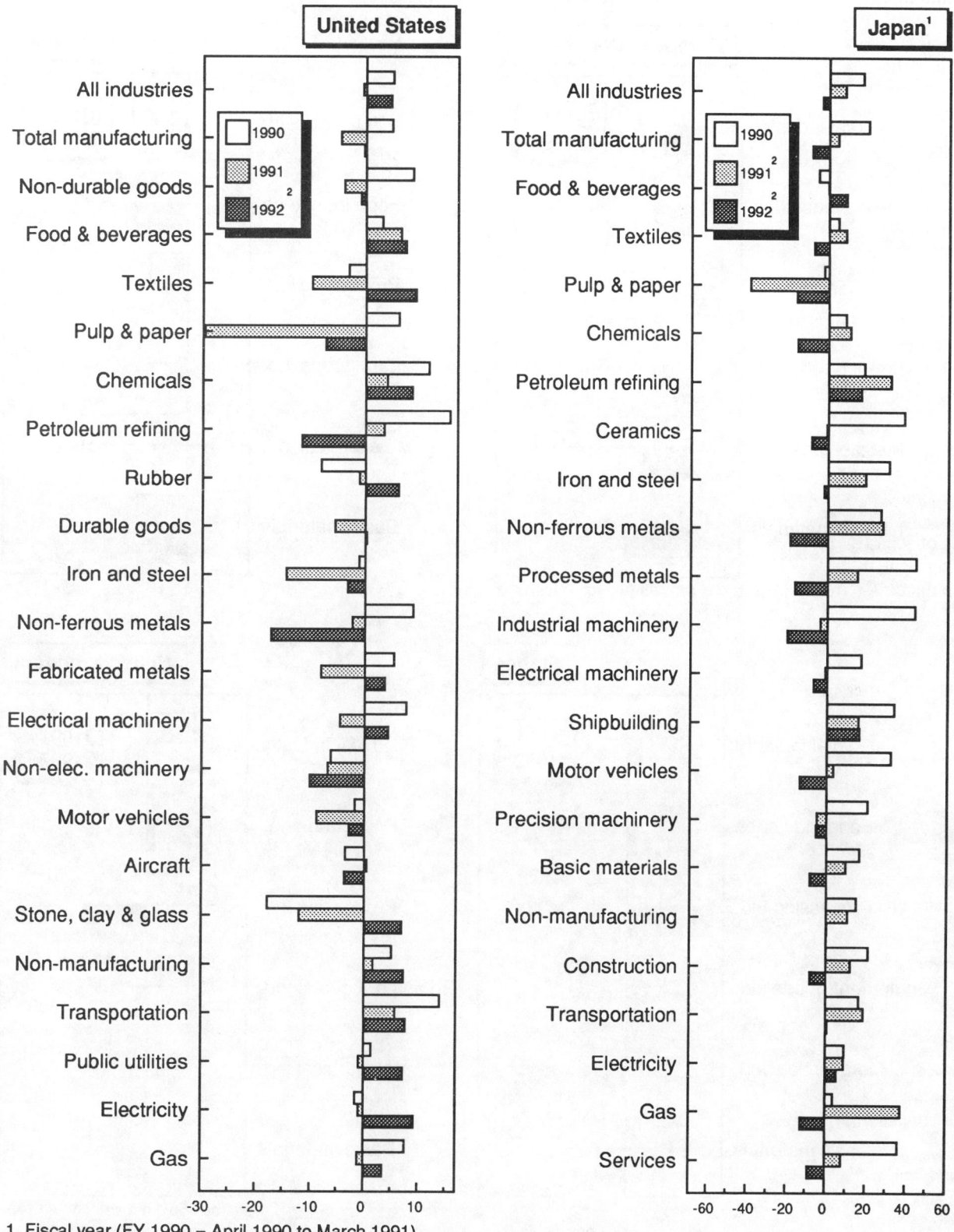

United States

- All industries
- Total manufacturing
- Non-durable goods
- Food & beverages
- Textiles
- Pulp & paper
- Chemicals
- Petroleum refining
- Rubber
- Durable goods
- Iron and steel
- Non-ferrous metals
- Fabricated metals
- Electrical machinery
- Non-elec. machinery
- Motor vehicles
- Aircraft
- Stone, clay & glass
- Non-manufacturing
- Transportation
- Public utilities
- Electricity
- Gas

Legend: 1990, 1991[2], 1992[2]

Japan[1]

- All industries
- Total manufacturing
- Food & beverages
- Textiles
- Pulp & paper
- Chemicals
- Petroleum refining
- Ceramics
- Iron and steel
- Non-ferrous metals
- Processed metals
- Industrial machinery
- Electrical machinery
- Shipbuilding
- Motor vehicles
- Precision machinery
- Basic materials
- Non-manufacturing
- Construction
- Transportation
- Electricity
- Gas
- Services

Legend: 1990, 1991[2], 1992[2]

1. Fiscal year (FY 1990 = April 1990 to March 1991).
2. Estimates based on planned capital expenditures reported by business.

Source: US Department of Commerce, Bureau of the Census; Tankan, Bank of Japan.

Graph 7 (cont). **Investment by industry**
Gross fixed capital formation
Percentage change in value from preceding period [1]

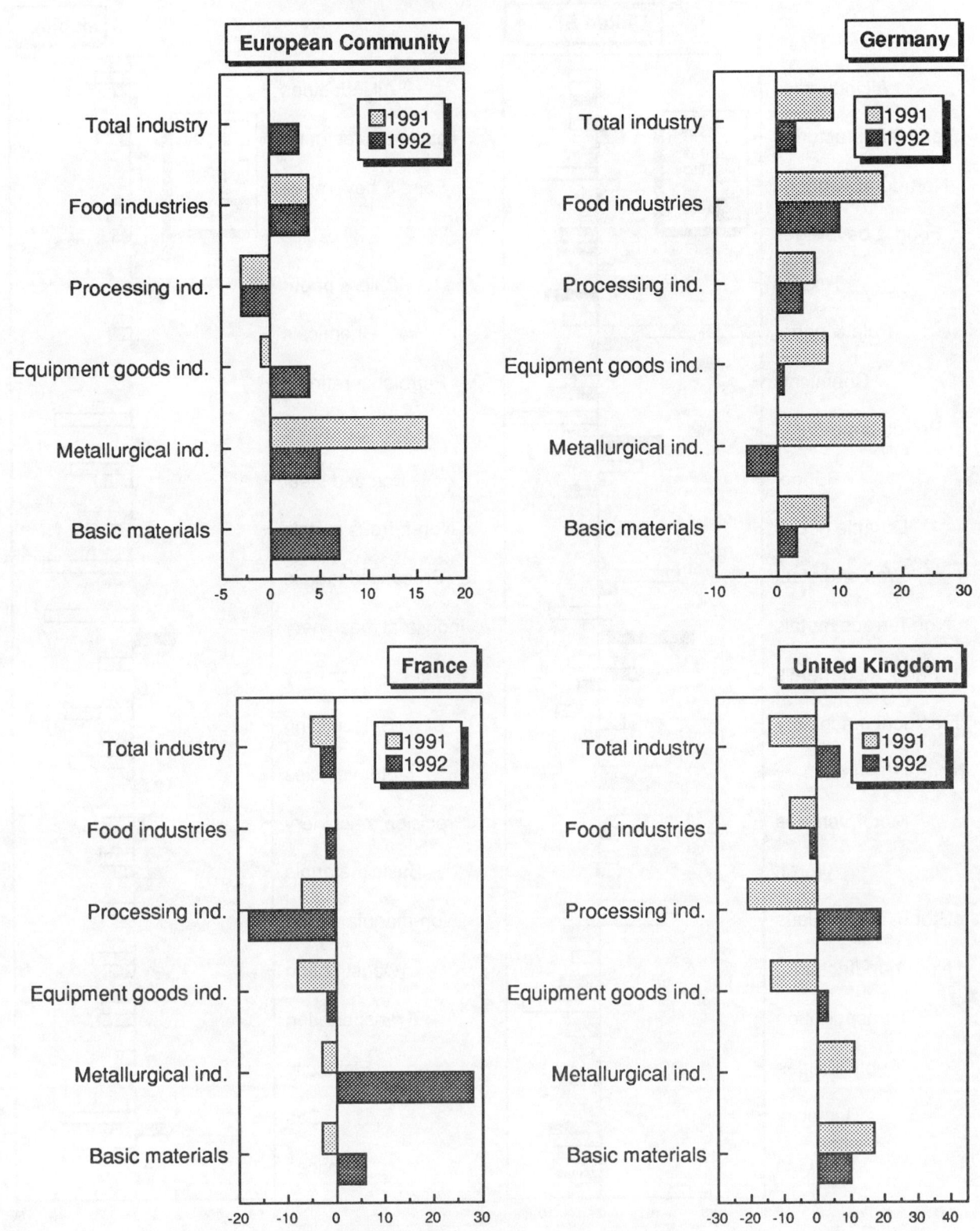

1. From the EC Investment Survey; 1992 data are planned GFCF expenditures.
Source: European Economy, Supplement B, January 1992.

United Kingdom, Ireland, France and *Greece*. In *Germany*, gross fixed capital formation barely slowed from its 1990 growth rate, but is expected to stagnate in 1992, and to decline slightly in manufacturing (Graphs 7 and 8). Firms in metallurgical and in food industries increased their investment expenditures significantly during 1991, while in 1992 the metallurgical group is the only industry group expected to reduce its gross fixed capital formation expenditures. In *France*, investment in industry as a whole declined by 1.9 per cent in 1991, following strong growth in 1990, and is projected for a moderate decline in 1992. The value of investment expenditures in all industry groups decreased in 1991, while in 1992 firms in the metallurgical group of industries plan a substantial increase in their investment expenditures (of the order of 28 per cent).

In the *United Kingdom*, the sharp drop in investment during 1991 (by 11.9 per cent), following stagnant levels in 1990, is expected to recover somewhat in 1992, due partly to planned increases in the investment expenditures of the basic materials and metallurgical industries. Investment in *Italy* has been more resilient, slowing from its 1990 level to a 0.1 per cent growth rate in 1991. It is expected to pick up in 1992 for industry as a whole, and to decline in manufacturing, because of large planned investment declines in metallurgical and processing industries. Of the smaller EC countries, the declines in total industry gross fixed capital formation expenditures during 1991 in *Ireland* and *Greece* are noteworthy, following the high investment rates of 1990. In Ireland however, investment in manufacturing continued to grow (it was in 1990 two and a half times the level of 1985 in volume terms), while it is projected to increase during 1992 in both countries.

Among the other European countries, investment declined particularly sharply in *Finland* and *Sweden*, and less so in *Switzerland* and *Turkey*. In Finland, gross fixed capital formation expenditures decreased by 20 per cent, following a 7 per cent decline the previous year. The volume of gross fixed capital formation in manufacturing also decreased, for the third consecutive year (Graph 8), and in particular in the forest industry, and in the textiles, leather and clothing sectors (declines ranging from 20 to 30 per cent). Sharp investment declines were also registered in service industries, and especially in wholesale and retail trade [11]. In both countries, investment is projected to decrease in 1992 as well, but at a lower rate. In *Norway*, investment recovered from a 30 per cent decline during the period 1987-90; it registered a moderate increase in 1991 but is expected to decline again in 1992. In *Austria*, gross fixed capital formation expenditures slowed, but continued to grow at a relatively high 5.4 per cent.

Outside Europe, gross fixed capital formation declined in *Canada* for the second consecutive year, but is projected to recover in 1992. The decline in investment was in real terms at about the same rate as the decline in GDP, with the result that as a percentage of value added, investment remained unchanged at nearly 18 per cent. The investment declines in 1991 in *Australia* and *New Zealand* were more serious (14.3 per cent and 11 per cent respectively), and large enough to decrease investment rates by 2 percentage points (Table 18). Gross fixed capital investment expenditures are projected for a moderate pick-up in both these countries in 1992.

Structural issues

The recent slowdown in investment activity, following the widespread recovery of business investment expenditures during the second half of the 1980s raises several questions relating to the factors underlying the strength and the decline of investment activities and the role of policy measures aimed at raising investment.

The broad developments in aggregate business fixed investment expenditures during the 1980s can be traced to a number of factors. Among these, the most important are the recovery in output growth after the 1981-82 recession which raised the demand for capital and hence for investment, the recovery of rates of return to pre-recession levels, the improvement in the cash flow and leveraged positions of firms, and the decline in the cost of equity financed as stock markets boomed. To these should be added the reduced volatility of the economic climate during the extended boom of the 1980s, as well as the introduction of new innovations, particularly in computer technology, which raised the marginal productivity of capital [12]. At the same time, significantly higher interest rates, wage moderation in OECD countries and the winding down of investment incentives may have reduced the demand for capital, with firms shifting to somewhat less capital-intensive production techniques.

These factors together provide a broad explanation for investment behaviour. At the same time however, and despite decades of research in the area, significant disagreement remains about the relative importance for investment demand of interest rates, investment incentives or even output. Investment incentives are motivated by the beneficial effects of buoyant investment activity: growth is stimulated and output and consumption possibilities are increased. Other possible effects could come from embodiment: to the extent that new technology is embodied in physical capital, investment could spur productivity growth. However, there are a number of reasons why incentives to invest may not increase welfare as much as claimed. First, to the extent that savings remain constant, incentives to raise the demand for investment goods (for example, by introducing investment tax reliefs) will tend to raise real interest rates or the price of investment goods, thereby offsetting the effect of the tax changes on the cost of capital. Second, based on intensive examination of the US experience with the introduction and withdrawal of such incentives in the 1980s, there is considerable doubt that such incentives do in fact raise investment demand [13].

Graph 8. **Gross fixed capital formation**
Manufacturing
Volumes, Index 1985=100

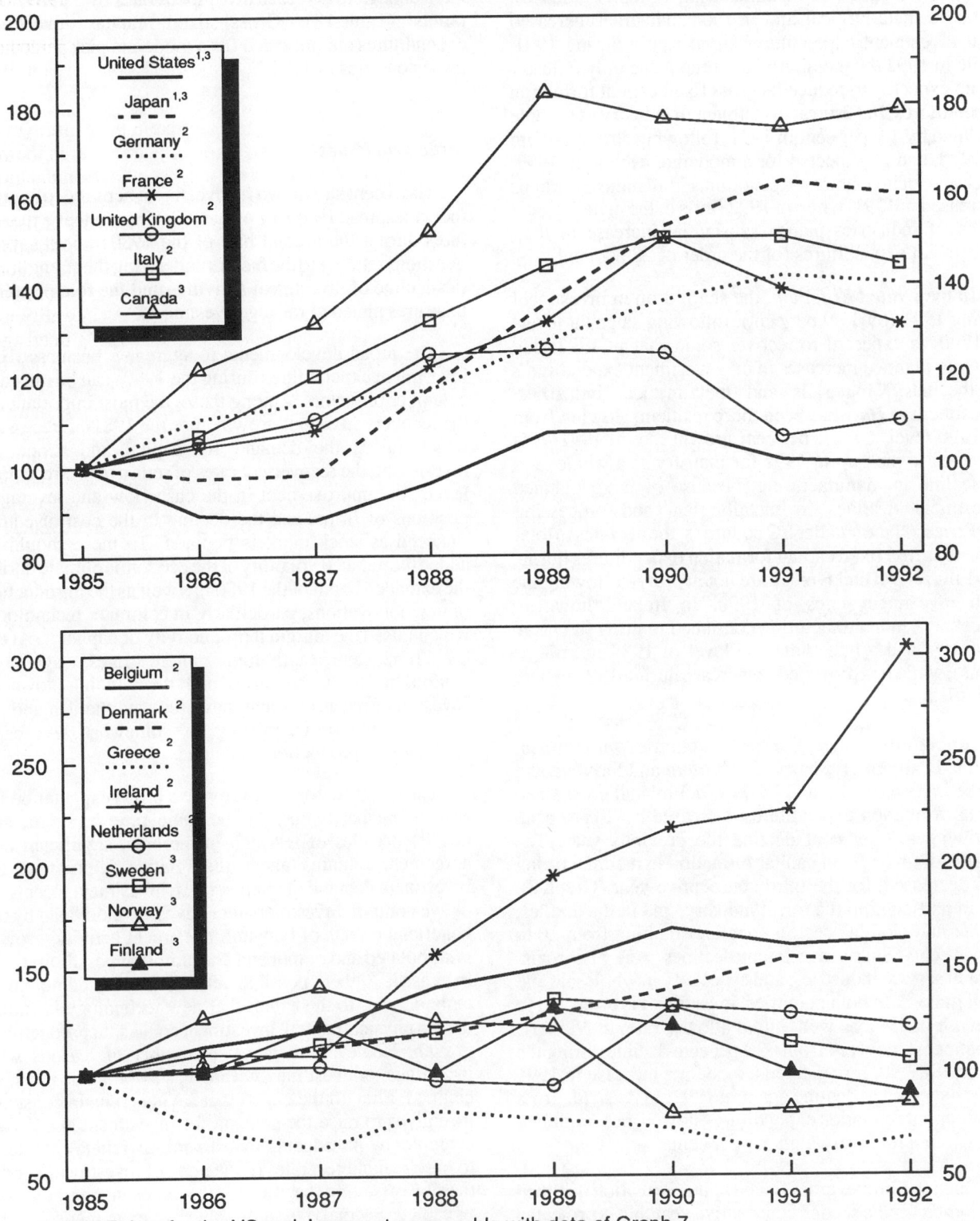

1. GFCF data for the US and Japan not comparable with data of Graph 7.
2. Data from the EC investment survey; 1992 figures are investment plans.
3. Data from 1990 onwards are estimates and projections.
Source: OECD/ISDB database; *European Economy,* Jan. 1992; Industry Division.

Finally, even if government incentives raise physical investment and the capital stock, they may be causing capital to be misallocated in use. All these reasons suggest that policy measures such as accelerated depreciation and investment tax credits should be viewed with caution, and underlie the ongoing reforms of tax systems and investment incentives in most OECD countries (see also Part 2, section A).

C. Capacity utilisation

The rate of capacity utilisation is an important indicator of the level of industrial activity. As such, this indicator confirms that 1991 has been a year in which the economy slowed down throughout the OECD area. Recent quarterly movements show no clear-cut departure from this downward trend (Table 19). In virtually every OECD Member state, capacity utilisation rates decreased, with the exception of *Spain* where the percentage of firms operating at full capacity continued to increase. The decline in capacity utilisation in 1991 in *Germany*, that of the index of operating rate in *Japan* and of the percentage of firms operating at full capacity in *Austria* and *Norway* all came after increases for three successive years. *Ireland*, the *Netherlands*, and especially *Switzerland* showed a decline in capacity utilisation after stable rates until recently. The majority of Member states, including the *United States, France* and *Italy,* continued their downward trend in capacity utilisation rates which started in 1989. The downswing was particularly sharp in *Canada*, the *United Kingdom, Sweden* and *Finland*. In Finland, the percentage of firms operating at full capacity plunged from 61 in 1989 to only 14 in 1991.

In the *United States*, the decline in the capacity utilisation rate in 1991 was more pronounced than in the year before, falling from 82.3 to 78.1 per cent for manufacturing as a whole (Table 20). Interrupting a hesitant recovery that had set in during the summer of 1991, capacity utilisation dropped again in the first quarter of 1992. The slowdown of activity has been more pronounced in durable goods than in non-durables, especially in iron and steel, motor vehicles and in the aerospace industry. Capacity utilisation rates in iron and steel seemed to be on a rising trend again in the second part of 1991, after a performance that had been particularly poor in the first half of the year. 1991 was unusually unfavourable for the US motor vehicle industry. The low capacity utilisation rates in this industry, 67 per cent against 73 per cent in 1990, support the argument about the chronic excess production capacity of the three large US car manufacturers. The downturn of the aerospace industry is likely to be more structural than cyclical in

Table 19. **Capacity utilisation in manufacturing**

Percentages

	1988	1989	1990	1991	91/Q1	91/Q2	91/Q3	91/Q4	92/Q1
United States[1]	83.6	83.9	82.3	78.2	78.0	77.9	78.7	78.2	77.3
Canada[1]	86.3	83.8	78.0	72.7	71.6	72.9	73.7	72.6	72.4
Japan[1,2]	101.0	103.3	105.7	104.2	105.4	104.8	104.3	102.2	99.1
Belgium	79.3	81.0	80.9	78.6	79.4	79.8	78.8	76.3	..
Denmark	80.0	81.8	81.0	80.3	81.0	81.0	80.0	79.0	..
France	86.2	88.0	86.8	84.0	84.5	84.0	84.3	83.1	..
Germany	86.4	88.7	89.5	87.3	88.3	88.2	87.0	85.8	..
Greece	76.2	77.7	77.4	77.2	75.8	77.2	77.6	78.3	..
Ireland	74.7	77.2	77.0	76.1	74.4	75.5	78.1	76.3	..
Italy	78.6	80.4	79.6	77.0	77.2	77.4	76.7	76.7	..
Luxembourg	83.8	85.5	83.5	81.3	82.0	81.0	83.0	79.0	..
Netherlands	84.4	85.8	85.6	84.2	85.3	84.9	83.7	83.0	..
Portugal	80.5	81.3	81.0	78.4	79.0	77.7	79.0	78.0	..
Spain	65.0	65.3	67.7	69.3	62.0	77.4	61.0	76.8	60.0
United Kingdom	93.7	89.3	84.7	77.7	78.4	77.2	78.0	77.2	..
Austria[4]	35.5	47.0	49.0	35.0	38.3	39.2	34.2	28.4	..
Finland[4]	53.0	60.8	42.8	14.3	22.0	12.0	13.0	10.0	18.0
Norway[4]	26.3	27.0	29.3	24.0	28.0	25.0	21.0	22.0	16.0
Sweden[4]	61.8	55.8	40.3	22.3	25.0	23.0	22.0	19.0	18.0
Switzerland	87.8	89.2	89.1	83.5	84.8	83.2	83.3	82.8	..
Australia[1,3]	45.0	22.0	5.8	4.0	4.0	5.0	4.0	3.0	7.0
New Zealand[1,3]	4.5	5.5	4.0	3.5	4.0	4.0	1.0	5.0	5.0

1. OECD, *Main Economic Indicators*.
2. Index of operating rate, 1985 = 100.
3. Firms operating at above normal capacity.
4. Relative share of full capacity utilisation.
Source: OECD, *Main Economic Indicators, Indicators of Industrial Activity*; national sources.

Table 20. **Capacity utilisation in the United States**
Per cent of capacity, seasonally adjusted

	1989	1990	1991	91/Q1	91/Q2	91/Q3	91/Q4	92/Q1
Total manufacturing	83.9	82.3	78.1	78.0	77.9	78.7	78.3	77.0
Durables	82.8	81.1	75.8	75.8	75.7	76.2	75.4	74.1
Primary metals	86.6	84.9	77.4	76.4	74.6	79.1	79.2	78.0
Iron and steel	83.7	82.9	73.4	72.4	69.5	74.8	76.7	76.0
Non-ferrous	90.9	87.8	83.5	82.6	82.6	85.8	83.1	81.0
Non-electrical machinery	82.2	82.2	77.0	78.8	77.4	76.6	75.4	74.2
Electrical machinery	81.6	80.0	76.1	75.8	76.8	76.5	75.3	74.8
Motor vehicles	79.2	73.0	67.5	60.5	66.7	71.1	71.5	67.3
Aerospace	83.5	84.0	76.7	80.2	77.2	75.9	73.7	71.3
Non-durables	85.5	83.9	81.5	81.0	80.9	82.1	82.0	81.0
Textiles	88.9	86.5	85.3	80.6	84.5	88.2	88.3	86.6
Paper	91.8	91.8	89.4	88.2	87.7	91.2	90.5	87.8
Chemicals	83.3	81.5	79.0	78.8	78.2	79.5	79.6	78.8
Petroleum	87.9	89.3	88.6	88.4	88.6	89.0	88.4	88.0

Source: *Federal Reserve Statistical Release.*

nature, due to the reduced Department of Defence spending. Capacity utilisation rates in this industry declined steadily from 80 per cent in the first quarter of 1991 to 71 per cent in the same quarter of 1992.

The decrease of capacity utilisation in *Japan* marked a break with an overall increase up to 1990, signaling that this country is now also affected by the global economic downturn. The trend in the index of operating rate (Table 21) shows that the decrease in capacity utilisation remained marginal until the third quarter of 1991, before declining steeply in the fourth quarter. When compared to 1990, several industries still managed to increase their 1991 index of operating rate, notably ceramics, petroleum and coal products, and pulp and paper. However, industries such as fabricated metals, machinery and equipment, chemicals, and rubber products established in 1991 capacity utilisation indices that were clearly below those of 1990.

Trends in capacity utilisation throughout the *European Community* are similar to those in most other OECD countries. The decrease in capacity utilisation throughout 1991 resulted in an overall rate of 82 per cent, compared to 85 per cent during the preceding year (Table 22). Rates continued to decline in the first quarter of 1992. As in the United States and Japan, the slowdown affected investment and intermediate goods more so than consumer goods. The downturn was especially sharp in metals, shipbuilding, and mechanical engineering, including machine tools and office and data processing equipment. The shipbuilding industry recorded the lowest capacity utilisation rates of all industries up until the first quarter of 1992.

Table 21. **Capacity utilisation in Japan**
Index of operating rate (seasonally adjusted)[1], 1985 = 100

	1989	1990	1991	91/Q1	91/Q2	91/Q3	91/Q4
Total manufacturing	103.3	105.7	104.2	105.4	104.8	104.3	102.2
Iron and steel	110.4	114.2	114.3	119.1	117.4	115.0	106.0
Non-ferrous metals	111.6	114.3	114.3	116.5	114.8	114.2	111.7
Fabricated metals	119.5	121.8	120.3	117.7	121.6	119.1	123.3
Machinery and equipment	96.3	98.8	96.2	97.4	96.3	97.1	94.3
Ceramics	106.0	111.7	113.5	115.4	118.3	112.3	108.5
Chemicals	111.0	111.8	109.4	111.9	110.0	107.9	108.0
Petroleum and coal	110.6	120.1	125.2	122.8	126.2	125.9	125.9
Pulp and paper	124.3	127.0	127.5	128.5	130.0	125.8	125.6
Textiles	100.0	99.7	99.0	99.0	99.2	98.9	98.8
Rubber products	106.7	103.5	101.2	103.6	98.6	100.6	101.8

1. Index of operating rate = index of production/index of capacity.
Source: Bank of Japan (1992), *Economics Statistics Annual 1991.*

Table 22. **Capacity utilisation in the European Community**
Percentages, seasonally adjusted

	1990	1991	91/Q1	91/Q2	91/Q3	91/Q4	92/Q1
Total industry	85.0	82.1	83.4	82.2	81.4	81.4	80.5
Consumer goods	85.8	83.3	84.3	83.6	82.6	82.7	81.9
Investment goods	85.9	81.7	83.9	82.0	80.6	80.1	79.2
Intermediate goods	84.6	81.5	83.3	80.8	80.8	80.9	80.9
Textile industry	82.5	80.1	82.1	80.8	78.5	79.9	80.6
Footwear and clothing	86.8	85.1	85.7	85.6	84.5	84.6	84.2
Timber/wooden furniture	83.5	81.7	82.8	81.5	81.5	80.5	80.8
Paper/printing	86.3	83.8	86.1	84.1	83.1	81.5	81.6
Leather	82.7	79.5	82.9	80.1	78.1	76.9	78.4
Plastics	83.5	81.5	84.7	80.5	80.2	80.7	80.7
Mineral-oil refining	90.7	87.6	89.2	87.2	86.8	88.3	88.5
Metals	84.3	80.7	81.7	80.3	78.5	82.4	80.7
Non-metallic minerals	83.2	81.5	82.4	81.3	80.6	80.9	81.2
Metal articles	83.4	80.3	81.8	80.3	80.0	79.1	78.0
Mechanical engineering	86.0	80.8	83.0	81.6	80.2	78.4	78.2
Machine tools	89.1	83.1	86.7	83.8	81.3	79.9	77.6
Office and data processing	85.1	81.6	85.3	84.8	77.8	78.4	81.1
Electrical engineering	84.3	81.7	83.0	83.4	80.3	79.3	79.5
Shipbulding	83.8	77.1	76.4	72.7	75.6	83.5	73.8
Rubber products	83.4	81.1	80.0	80.7	81.5	82.1	85.3
Instrument engineering	84.8	82.9	84.8	82.9	82.7	81.2	83.0

Source: *European Economy* (1992), Supplement B, No. 2, February.

D. Costs and prices

Growth in manufacturing producer prices in the OECD area continued to slow down in 1991 for the second consecutive year, reflecting the generally slack demand and the lower capacity utilisation rates (Tables 23 and 24). With manufacturing unit labour costs rising strongly, this implied lower mark-ups and is consistent with evidence of lower profitability rates. Movements in import unit values, another cost component influencing factory-gate prices, varied widely both by country and by type of product: import unit values of manufactures increased in most countries, while that of raw materials decreased for raw materials and energy, partly due to the lower world oil price following the end of the Gulf War (Table 25). Energy-intensive sectors (such as iron and steel, non-ferrous metals, and pulp and paper) showed a significant drop in producer prices, although lower capacity utilisation rates and the economic slowdown are likely to play a role in this context as well. Following wage increases in many countries, manufacturing unit labour costs rose strongly (see Table 48 below).

In the *United States*, producer prices in manufacturing were in 1991 just 0.6 per cent above the 1990 level, while prices actually declined between the first and the second quarter. Import unit values of manufactures and above all of energy fell considerably, while those of raw materials declined marginally. Export unit values increased in manufactures and services, but fell in raw materials and energy (Table 26). In manufactures, both import and export unit values are expected to increase in 1992, whereas for raw materials and energy they are expected to decline. Apart from petroleum refining, the fall in producer prices was strongest in non-ferrous metals, leather, and basic metals. Increases in producer prices were strong in tobacco and fairly strong in transport equipment. In *Canada*, an overall decline of one per cent in producer prices is the result of sharp reductions in the prices for the important basic metals and paper industries, an equally sharp increase in tobacco, and more moderate price movements in all other industries. A large share of the decline in producer prices can be contributed to significantly lower import unit values, which are in their turn related to the relatively strong position of the Canadian dollar. At the same time unit labour costs grew strongly, reflecting the fact that labour-shedding proceeded more slowly than the fall in output.

Manufacturing producer prices in *Japan* increased in 1991 by 1.7 per cent, a change similar to that in the year before. During 1991, a slight downward movement of production prices is discernible from the first quarter on. Manufacturing labour costs increased, but import unit values dropped sharply, by 11.5 per cent in raw materials and by 8 per cent and 10 per cent in manufactures and in

Table 23. **Producer prices in manufacturing**

	Percentage change from preceding period				Index 1985 = 100				
	1989	1990	1991	1980-90[1]	91/Q1	91/Q2	91/Q3	91/Q4	92/Q1
United States	5.0	3.8	0.6	2.8	113	112	112	112	112
Canada	2.0	0.3	-1.1	3.8	112	110	109	109	109
Japan	2.1	1.6	1.7	-0.5	98	97	97	97	97
Belgium	6.7	0.0	-1.0	3.1	94	94	94	95	94
Denmark	6.2	1.8	1.1	4.8	110	111	111	111	109
France[2,3]	5.4	-1.2	-1.3	5.1	108	106	105	104	104
Germany	3.4	1.4	2.1	2.0	105	105	106	107	107
Greece	12.2	18.4	17.7	16.9	214	223	232	237	244
Ireland	4.8	-1.6	0.9	5.4	107	109	109	109	110
Italy[2]	5.9	4.1	3.3	6.5*	121	121	122	122	123
Luxembourg	7.6	-2.1	-2.5	4.0	96	97	97	95	94
Netherlands	4.8	-0.6	0.6	0.0*	93	92	93	93	92
Spain	4.2	2.2	1.3	7.1*	112	112	112	112	..
United Kingdom	5.5	6.6	5.2	5.7	126	128	129	129	130
Austria[2,4]	1.7	2.9	0.9	1.5	99	99	97	97	98
Finland	6.6	1.8	-0.3	4.8	113	112	112	113	114
Norway	5.2	2.5	2.4	5.3	124	124	125	125	125
Sweden	8.0	4.3	1.9	7.0	129	128	128	128	127
Switzerland	4.3	1.5	0.4	1.6	102	102	103	102	..
Turkey	61.6	46.9	55.3	45.8**	971	1 097	1 223	1 350	..
Australia	6.7	6.0	1.5	7.0	140	139	140	140	140
New Zealand	6.6	4.2	0.6	7.9**	129	130	129	130	131
OECD total[2]	5.4	3.9	2.6	3.1	116	117	117	117	118
OECD excl. Turkey[2]	4.6	3.3	1.9	2.5**	113	113	113	113	113

* 1981-90.
** 1982-90.
1. Annual percentage growth between indicated years.
2. OECD, *Main Economic Indicators*.
3. Producer prices: intermediate goods.
4. General wholesale price goods.
Source: OECD, *Indicators of Industrial Activity*; *Main Economic Indicators*; Industry Division.

energy. They are expected to continue to decline in 1992, albeit at a slower pace. Apart from the reduction in world oil prices, these drops are likely to have been caused by the position of the Japanese yen that became particularly strong in 1991. The sectoral evolution of producer prices is broadly in line with OECD-wide tendencies, except for the food industry that faced a relatively strong increase in producer prices. The steepest decline was in non-ferrous metals, with producers prices falling by nearly 9 per cent (Table 24).

In the majority of countries within the *European Community*, producer price inflation slowed down or prices dropped outright. Growth in producer prices slowed in *Denmark, Italy, Spain*, and the *United Kingdom*, while producer prices fell in *Belgium* and *France*. This movement occurred despite strong increases in labour costs per manufacturing unit. The reduced producer price inflation in these and other EC countries is above all due to the sharp fall of prices in the basic metal industry. As part of its inflationary tendency, producer prices increased in *Germany* more so than in the year before, largely as a consequence of higher labour costs. Prices rose especially in petroleum refineries and in non-metallic mineral products, and less so in transport equipment and non-electrical machinery, while they decreased in non-ferrous metals, basic metals and in pulp and paper. Producer price inflation remained at a very high level in *Greece*.

The growth in manufacturing producer prices declined considerably in all other OECD countries, with the exception of *Turkey* that faced a 55 per cent increase in 1991, even higher than the 47 per cent rate in 1990. Most other countries, such as *Finland, Sweden, Switzerland* and *Austria* (general wholesale price goods), showed producer price changes in the 0 to 2 per cent range (a 0.3 per cent decline in Finland), which is lower than the respective increases in unit labour costs. This absorption was facilitated by a decrease in import unit values, especially in raw materials. The fall in producer price inflation in

Table 24. **Producer prices in main manufacturing industries**
Percentage change from preceding year, national currencies

Sector	ISIC code	United States			Japan			Germany			France			United Kingdom			Italy			Canada		
		1989	1990	1991	1989	1990	1991	1989	1990	1991	1989	1990	1991	1989	1990	1991	1989	1990	1991	1989	1990	1991
Total manufacturing	3	5.0	3.8	0.6	2.1	1.6	1.7	3.4	1.4	2.1	5.4	-1.2	-1.3	5.5	6.6	5.2	5.9	4.1	3.3	2.0	0.3	-1.1
Food/beverages/tobacco	31	4.9	2.8	-1.8	1.1	2.4	4.2	2.5	0.3	1.6	5.1	0.8	0.7	4.6	5.5	6.7	5.2	2.7	7.8	2.7	2.1	1.2
Food	311	4.5	3.5	0.0	2.7	3.2	4.4	..	..	3.8	4.5	-0.7	0.3	5.0	4.3	4.5	5.1	2.1	4.0	2.2	1.6	0.4
Beverages	313	3.6	2.0	2.8	-0.4	1.1	2.9	1.9	2.0	0.8	9.3	9.1	2.2	3.9	7.7	10.7	4.5	6.1	7.7	5.9	2.9	3.3
Tobacco	314	13.4	13.7	12.6	-0.3	-0.1	0.0	4.2	4.1	1.4	5.3	2.4	5.8	2.6	7.2	12.4	7.9	6.8	0.6	5.0	8.0	10.7
Textiles/clothing/leather	32	2.9	2.3	1.1	3.0	-0.2	2.1	1.9	1.7	0.9	2.3	0.2	-0.4	4.8	4.8	4.7	4.1	1.7	1.8	2.5	2.0	0.9
Textiles	321	..	..	..	..	..	..	1.9	1.3	0.9	1.9	-2.0	-1.4	4.6	4.8	3.9	4.3	1.7	-1.9	2.1	1.1	0.2
Clothing (excl. shoes)	322	2.5	2.6	1.8	2.6	2.2	2.3	2.0	2.4	2.1	3.8	3.1	2.8	4.3	4.4	5.0	5.1	2.2	4.8	2.7	2.4	1.2
Leather	323	1.7	4.2	-5.2	..	..	..	0.8	1.5	1.0	..	..	..	4.4	6.4	-1.2	2.1	0.9	0.5	2.1	2.8	-0.4
Shoes	324	4.9	4.0	2.4	..	..	..	2.1	2.1	2.0	..	..	..	4.1	4.6	5.3	1.6	1.5	4.5	4.4	4.2	3.7
Wood/wood products	33	6.6	2.3	1.8	6.5	4.6	-1.4	4.0	4.9	2.0	3.4	4.4	3.7	4.9	7.6	3.4	3.8	3.8	3.3	3.8	-0.6	-1.7
Paper/paper products	34	5.7	2.5	1.2	2.5	0.5	3.1	3.8	1.9	1.7	..	..	..	5.5	6.2	4.8	7.3	2.7	4.5	3.7	-0.3	-5.8
Pulp/paper/paperboard	3411	6.0	0.4	-2.3	2.8	-0.8	-1.4	5.6	-0.6	-4.1	8.3	-2.4	-7.1	6.0	2.4	-1.9	5.6	1.0	-0.4	3.1	-2.3	-12.0
Printing/publishing	342	..	..	..	..	..	..	3.0	2.4	3.0	..	..	..	3.7	5.5	4.9	7.8	3.2	10.9	5.1	3.1	3.3
Chemicals	35	..	..	..	2.7	4.7	3.5	6.2	1.1	2.9	6.8	3.0	-0.1	6.7	9.1	2.9	..	..	..	1.9	5.1	-1.4
Chemical products[1]	351/352	7.1	-1.0	-1.2	1.7	1.1	3.7	3.0	-1.5	-0.5	4.7	-2.1	-3.7	3.3	2.2	-2.5	3.8	-1.3	10.1	1.9	-2.1	0.8
Petroleum refineries	353	13.6	22.2	-10.2	5.6	14.6	2.3	17.8	6.1	8.6	9.2	5.3	0.2	6.9	13.2	5.1	10.7	20.1	8.7	1.4	12.8	-3.2
Non-met. mineral products	36	1.3	1.8	1.8	1.7	2.3	3.8	1.6	3.0	4.4	2.7	2.7	3.2	6.5	6.6	4.7	4.3	5.8	9.7	1.7	1.2	-0.7
Glass/glass products	362	0.0	-2.0	-1.4	1.5	-0.4	1.9	1.8	3.4	2.5	2.0	3.2	2.4	3.9	4.4	3.6	2.4	2.5	4.7	0.8	-0.3	-0.8
Basic metals	37	4.3	-3.2	-4.9	5.2	0.6	-1.5	6.8	-4.6	-4.4	10.9	-8.4	-8.7	7.4	0.9	0.1	12.2	-4.9	-6.1	-1.1	-9.6	-8.5
Iron and steel	371	2.9	-1.6	-2.8	3.8	1.5	1.6	4.6	0.1	-2.4	9.4	-2.5	-8.3	4.0	2.1	0.5	11.1	-3.6	-5.6	2.3	-1.8	-2.9
Non-ferrous metals	372	6.2	-5.5	-8.1	8.5	-1.3	-8.9	11.3	-13.8	-9.0	13.4	-17.7	-9.4	11.9	-6.2	-8.0	18.2	-11.7	-6.9	-4.5	-17.3	-15.4
Metal prod./machinery/equ.	38	..	..	..	0.4	0.0	0.4	2.3	2.6	3.0	..	..	..	5.5	6.3	5.3	5.9	3.8	2.2	2.0	0.8	0.9
Metal products	381	5.2	1.3	0.5	3.8	2.2	2.2	3.1	2.9	2.8	..	..	..	6.7	5.3	5.7	6.8	3.7	2.0	2.9	0.8	0.1
Non-electrical machinery	382	2.6	..	..	2.6	2.0	2.1	2.7	3.3	3.6	..	..	..	6.8	8.3	5.9	6.2	5.1	7.5	4.6	2.6	1.8
Electrical machinery	383	2.6	1.5	1.3	-1.9	-2.6	-2.1	1.2	1.4	1.9	..	..	..	3.6	5.1	5.2	4.2	1.7	1.2	3.6	-0.2	-0.6
Transport equipment	384	3.0	3.2	4.1	-2.1	-1.1	-0.1	2.3	2.8	3.5	..	..	..	7.3	7.0	6.3	..	..	..	-0.3	0.6	2.0
Shipbuilding/Ship repair	3841	..	..	..	..	..	..	..	..	..	..	..	..	..	..	..	..	..	..	3.2	3.6	-0.6
Motor vehicles	3843	2.7	1.8	3.3	-2.3	-1.3	-0.3	2.3	2.8	3.5	..	..	..	7.3	7.0	6.3	5.5	3.8	6.4	-1.2	0.5	2.6
Electricity/Gas/Water	4	..	..	..	..	..	..	1.0	-1.1	-0.4	0.6	2.4	2.9	..	..	..	..	..	..	..	..	..

1. United States and Canada, excluding ISIC 352.
Source: OECD, *Indicators of Industrial Activity*.

Table 25. **Import unit values in local currency**
Percentage change from preceding year

	Manufactures			Raw materials			Energy			Services		
	1990	1991	1992	1990	1991	1992	1990	1991	1992	1990	1991	1992
United States	0.6	–0.4	0.5	–0.3	–0.2	–2.7	22.1	–12.7	–10.4	3.8	4.7	..
Canada	0.0	–1.8	2.7	–4.8	–4.6	2.9	23.5	–13.2	–4.6	2.5	..	..
Japan	6.1	–7.8	–2.3	1.6	–11.5	–3.1	30.2	–9.9	–17.2	3.7	..	..
Belgium/Lux.	–0.9	–1.6	1.5	–9.2	–5.8	–1.7	5.8	–0.7	–15.2	3.4	3.4	..
Denmark	–2.9	0.6	0.8	–10.0	–2.9	–1.4	1.8	4.3	–10.0	–0.1	4.0	4.0
France	–2.8	–1.0	–1.2	–20.3	–8.9	–5.6	8.1	–2.4	–13.8	3.1	..	..
Germany	–3.5	1.6	1.7	–8.6	–5.9	–3.8	10.1	–0.7	–13.3	2.9	..	..
Greece	10.5	13.7	12.8	8.0	5.0	5.3	7.0	18.9	–7.0	17.1	..	..
Ireland	–5.9	2.7	3.5	–2.3	–4.4	–2.6	–0.4	6.8	–6.3	3.4	..	..
Italy	–0.9	0.9	2.1	–7.5	–3.6	2.3	7.6	–1.1	–14.1	3.7	..	..
Netherlands	1.8	0.3	1.3	–37.5	–8.0	2.2	5.4	–6.1	–5.5	2.6	..	..
Portugal	4.3	1.7	1.5	2.8	–2.0	–4.4	14.7	–0.5	–9.0	6.2	..	..
Spain	–2.0	–1.8	1.4	–18.7	–8.8	–5.3	6.0	–4.5	–11.1	3.3	..	..
United Kingdom	1.2	–1.9	1.4	–4.5	–16.8	–6.6	14.6	–5.6	–13.5	3.3	..	..
Austria	–3.1	4.0	3.6	–8.0	–13.1	–5.5	11.8	–5.4	–23.2	3.4	3.1	..
Finland	1.1	3.2	7.9	–8.2	–2.7	6.9	10.3	5.5	–0.5	2.2	..	..
Iceland	12.3	8.5	6.4	2.4	–4.5	–4.7	13.6	–11.8	–14.7	17.7	..	..
Norway	1.5	2.3	1.4	–10.2	–9.8	–4.9	14.2	–3.6	–11.1	4.3	4.0	4.0
Sweden	–1.0	–0.6	0.6	–7.2	–0.7	–4.1	12.4	–9.3	–13.5	4.5	4.0	..
Switzerland	0.2	0.9	6.4	–3.1	–1.1	1.3	10.6	–0.5	–10.1	3.0	..	..
Turkey	26.2	58.9	78.5	27.5	56.5	7.1	31.1	22.6	5.2	57.8	..	..
Australia	–0.8	–0.7	4.6	–1.6	–3.0	3.2	32.3	–1.1	–13.7	5.2	4.9	..
New Zealand	–1.3	2.6	6.8	5.3	–2.7	4.3	24.8	3.2	–0.4	2.2	..	..

Source: OECD, *Economic Outlook No. 51.*

Table 26. **Export unit values in local currency**
Percentage change from preceding year

	Manufactures			Raw materials			Energy			Services		
	1990	1991	1992	1990	1991	1992	1990	1991	1992	1990	1991	1992
United States	0.4	0.4	0.7	5.2	–0.5	–6.6	7.7	–4.0	–0.1	4.8	4.8	..
Canada	–1.9	–2.4	0.0	–5.8	–9.1	5.4	12.9	–9.1	3.0	4.2	..	..
Japan	3.9	–0.3	0.3	5.0	0.5	–9.8	29.0	–11.0	–10.1	2.6	..	..
Belgium/Lux.	–2.5	–2.3	1.6	–8.5	–6.4	–0.5	4.8	5.4	–2.5	2.4	2.4	..
Denmark	–0.6	0.4	1.0	–10.0	0.3	1.9	7.9	–6.0	–10.0	2.1	–1.6	2.8
France	–2.0	–0.6	–1.1	–10.6	–4.1	0.1	6.4	11.2	–8.2	2.7	..	..
Germany	–0.7	0.1	2.2	–10.3	–9.8	–3.6	4.3	2.0	–18.3	2.8	..	..
Greece	12.1	12.8	8.8	13.7	6.9	6.8	19.9	28.5	–25.3	16.5	..	..
Ireland	–9.0	–0.4	2.2	–14.9	–13.8	1.4	0.7	2.1	–14.2	3.6	..	..
Italy	2.9	2.4	2.6	–8.3	6.4	–2.7	7.0	–1.7	13.7	4.8	..	..
Netherlands	–2.2	–0.9	1.5	–6.2	–4.3	0.3	13.7	1.4	–0.8	3.6	..	..
Portugal	3.4	0.8	3.5	–1.8	–2.2	–5.6	11.1	–10.2	0.0	5.9	..	..
Spain	–1.9	0.8	2.2	–7.1	–8.7	–5.6	1.3	–3.1	–12.3	4.2	..	..
United Kingdom	2.4	–0.3	1.8	–2.3	–7.1	0.4	19.7	–7.2	–6.1	3.8	..	..
Austria	–0.9	–0.3	0.9	–2.2	–9.1	–7.4	–42.4	13.8	11.4	3.1	2.6	..
Finland	–1.4	–1.9	5.9	–4.1	13.6	4.9	20.2	–15.4	–2.1	2.7	..	..
Iceland	13.9	4.1	2.1	4.4	3.8	5.7	0.0	0.0	0.0	15.7	..	..
Norway	–8.5	2.7	4.8	–3.5	–5.6	1.9	17.7	–4.9	13.4	4.0	3.2	3.2
Sweden	1.2	0.8	–0.4	1.2	0.2	–4.4	11.6	–8.8	10.9	6.0	5.0	..
Switzerland	2.2	3.7	6.0	–0.4	–0.3	1.1	11.4	–1.0	–15.9	3.2	..	..
Turkey	38.4	56.9	77.7	32.9	48.1	–2.7	65.8	36.2	9.1	59.0	..	..
Australia	–3.9	–6.4	1.4	–5.2	–13.6	–2.6	7.2	2.6	–9.2	3.2	4.7	..
New Zealand	–0.6	1.3	6.2	–6.3	–19.0	–0.1	28.8	–7.2	–10.6	..	..	..

Source: OECD, *Economic Outlook No. 51.*

manufacturing was particularly sharp in *Australia* and *New Zealand*, reflecting the slowdown of these economies, but also helping them to regain price competitiveness in the years to come.

E. Industrial research and development

General trends

Industrial R&D is defined as R&D activities carried out in the business enterprise sector, regardless of the origin of funding. While the government and the higher education sectors also carry out R&D activities, it is industrial R&D that remains most closely tied with the creation of new products and production techniques. The recent evolution of R&D expenditures in the business enterprise sector (BERD) for the OECD area shows that the growth (at fixed prices) of industrial R&D has slowed substantially since 1985. As shown in Graph 9, after many years of expansion, during which R&D expenditure in the business enterprise sector grew much faster than GDP, progress has been relatively slow since 1985. From 1987-88 onwards industrial R&D expenditure in the OECD area has been growing at about the same rate as GDP.

Of the five OECD countries which are the leaders in industrial R&D performance in the OECD area (*United States, Japan, Germany, France, United Kingdom* -- together accounting for 87 per cent of total OECD BERD in 1990), Japan was by far the country which most increased its industrial R&D potential during the 1985-90 period (Table 27). Despite the marked slow-down in the growth of industrial R&D in the OECD area as a whole, the Japanese BERD growth rate increased during that period eight times more rapidly than in the United States and approximately twice as rapidly as the growth rate of BERD in the European Community as a whole. During 1990, it increased by more than 10 per cent in real terms, in sharp contrast to the 2 per cent increase in Germany and the real decline of 1.5 per cent and 1.1 per cent in the United States and the United Kingdom. Of the five largest OECD countries, only France had (with 7.5 per cent) in 1990 a growth rate of industrial R&D that was comparable to that of Japan.

The evolution of BERD in these countries has brought about an important change in the geographic distribution of industrial R&D (Table 28). The rapid expansion of BERD in *Japan* brought the share of Japanese BERD in the OECD area up from 16.4 per cent in 1985 to 20.4 per cent in 1990. In contrast, the very slow growth of BERD in the *United States* since 1985 caused a decline in the share of that country in total OECD BERD during the period 1985-90 (from 50.5 per cent to 44.9 per cent). While therefore the United States remains by far the most

Graph 9. **Industrial research (BERD) and GDP in the OECD area**
Annual growth rates
1985 prices

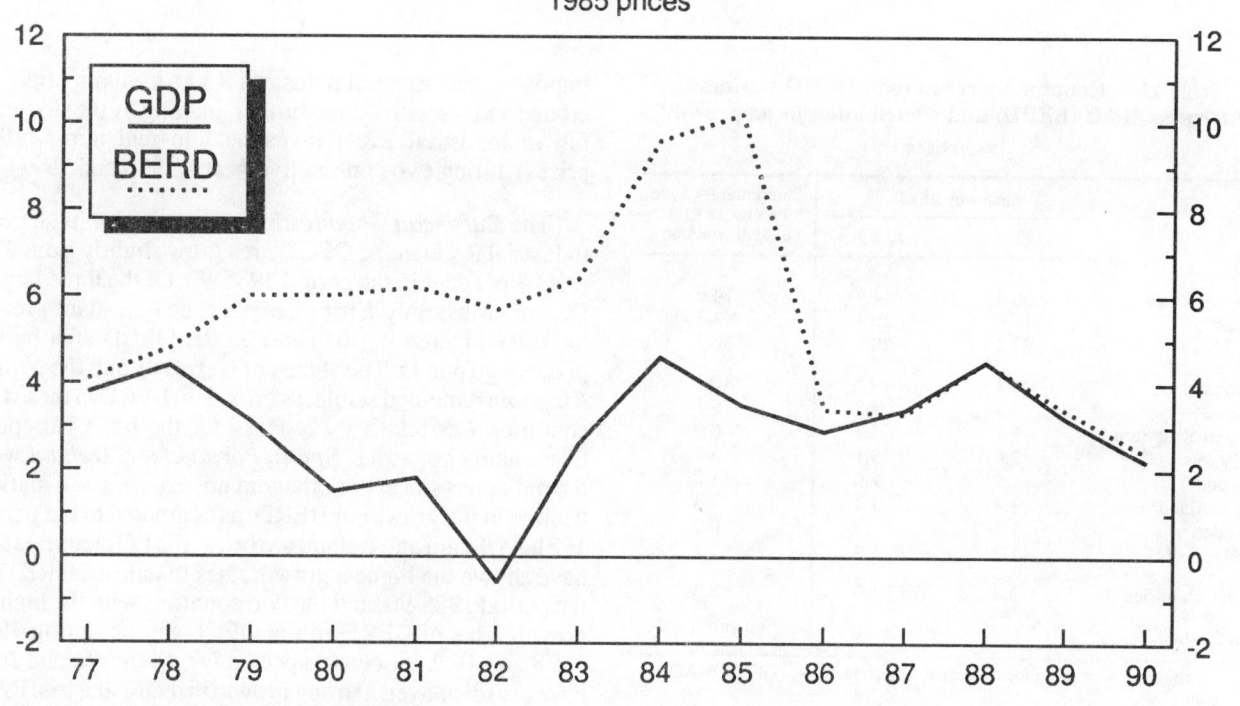

Source: OECD, STAN/ANBERD database.

Table 27. **R&D expenditures in the business enterprise sector**
Percentage change from the preceding year (1985 prices)

	Average annual growth rate			1986	1987	1988	1989	1990	1991
	1975-81	1981-85	1985-90						
United States	5.2	8.6	1.0	2.1	1.8	2.8	0.0	-1.5	-0.8
Canada	10.6	8.9	2.4	6.8	1.9	2.9	-1.9	2.6	2.3
Japan	8.2	11.2	8.0	1.2	6.1	10.7	12.0	10.4	..
Belgium	5.4	5.6	3.6	2.4	3.2	3.5	5.0	3.7	..
Denmark	5.4	9.9	6.7	10.0	8.0	4.9	4.3	6.4*	..
France	4.4	4.9	5.2	1.5	4.3	5.2	7.8	7.5	..
Germany	6.1	5.2	3.4	3.4*	4.8*	3.4	3.5	2.0	..
Greece[1]	25.6	21.5	3.1	0.9	8.7	3.3	4.4	-1.4	..
Ireland	9.0	10.3	9.9	11.1	6.1	3.9	12.5	16.2	..
Italy	4.9	8.5	6.9	6.0	6.1	7.6	6.8	7.9	3.9
Netherlands	0.8	5.6	3.0	13.0	6.9	0.7	-1.7	-3.1*	..
Portugal[1]	15.2	3.9	4.0	1.1	8.3	4.9	3.6	2.3	..
Spain	1.8	14.1	14.2	15.8	8.6	22.0	9.3	15.8	12.3
United Kingdom	4.1	1.9	3.6	5.6*	1.4	2.6	3.4	-1.1	..
EC total[1]	4.8	5.0	4.5	5.9	4.3	4.3	4.6	3.4	
Finland	8.7	12.7	8.6	9.0	8.2	9.6	9.7	6.5	..
Iceland	24.1	17.8	12.5	..	11.5	..	27.2	1.0	0.9
Norway[1]	4.9	15.3	2.6	13.9	3.6	-2.8	-4.6	3.9	5.1
Sweden[1]	5.1	10.1	0.0	3.0	4.0	-1.6	-3.1	-2.1	..
Switzerland	-1.1	9.8	4.4	10.5	3.9	3.8	1.5	2.6	..
Australia	0.0	15.2	10.8	24.7	4.2	11.3	3.5	11.2*	..

* Secretariat estimates.
1. Data for these countries and for the EC total are partly estimates.
Source: OECD, STAN/ANBERD database.

Table 28. **Country shares in total OECD business enterprise R&D (BERD) and contribution to its growth**[1]
1985 prices

	Shares of BERD		Contribution (%) to total OECD BERD growth, 1985-90
	1985	1990	
United States	50.5	44.9	14.6
Japan	16.4	20.4	42.2
EC	27.2	28.7	36.7
Germany	10.1	10.1	10.1
France	5.8	6.3	9.1
United Kingdom	5.7	5.7	6.0
Italy	2.6	3.1	5.6
Canada	1.7	1.6	1.2
Switzerland	1.4	1.4	1.8
Sweden	1.3	1.3	0.0
Netherlands	1.2	1.2	1.1
Other countries	3.3	4.0	8.3
Total OECD	100.0	100.0	100.0

1. Only countries accounting for more than 1 per cent of total OECD BERD are reported.
Source: OECD, STAN/ANBERD database.

important performer of industrial R&D, its domination has eroded and is set to decline further, judging by the first-ever fall in industrial R&D investment in real terms (1985 prices) during two consecutive years (1990 and 1991).

The *European Community* as a whole saw its share of industrial R&D in the OECD area grow slightly from 27.2 to 28.7 per cent in the period 1985-90. Of the three largest EC countries, only *France* experienced constant growth in BERD, increasing its share in the OECD area by 0.5 percentage points. The shares of *Germany* and the *United Kingdom* remained stable, as growth in BERD in these two countries was relatively modest. Of the other European Community countries, *Spain, Portugal* and *Ireland* were the only ones since 1985 that did not experience a marked decline in the growth of BERD, as compared to the period 1981-85. Spain and Ireland are by far the EC countries that have shown the highest growth rates in industrial R&D in the period 1985-90, and the two countries with the highest growth rates of BERD in the OECD region during 1990 (15.8 and 16.2 per cent respectively). *Denmark* and *Italy* have also displayed a strong growth in their industrial R&D since 1985, even though it has progressed at a lower pace than between 1981 and 1985. The remaining OECD countries all experienced a substantial drop in the growth rate of industrial R&D since 1985 relative to the period 1981-85. This is most evident in *Canada, Norway* and *Sweden,* with growth in industrial R&D in these countries being very weak since 1988.

Industrial R&D is funded from many sources, and these have contributed in different ways to the recent changes. Table 29 gives a breakdown of the sources of funds for industrial R&D for the biggest R&D performers in the OECD, and shows that growth in industrial R&D in the period 1985-90 was largely financed by the enterprises themselves. The extreme case is *Japan*, where growth in industrial R&D was almost entirely due to the financing of enterprises, and where the contribution of other sources of funds has been negligible. In contrast, in *France* and the *United Kingdom*, while enterprises provided the bulk of the financing, foreign funds also played an important role. Table 29 also shows that national Governments have widely withdrawn funding for industrial R&D in almost all countries. From 1985 to 1990, the real value of the government sector funds for industrial R&D has declined in the *United States, Germany,* the United Kingdom and the EC as a whole, while it increased marginally in *France*.

Table 29. **Contribution of different sources of funds to growth in industrial R&D**
1985-90

	Business funds	+ Government funds	+ Foreign funds	+ Other domestic sources[1]	= Total BERD growth
United States[2]	6.1	–0.8	..	..	5.3
Japan	47.0	0.0*	0.1	–0.1	47.0
Germany	18.9	–2.5	1.8	0.0*	18.4
France	20.3	0.5	8.2	0.0*	29.0
United Kingdom	14.9	–3.0	7.5	0.0*	19.4
EC total	21.0	–0.6	4.2	0.0*	24.6

* Negligible.
1. Funds from higher education and private non-profit institutes.
2. For the US, business funds for BERD include foreign funds and all other national sources of funds for BERD.
Source: OECD, STAN/ANBERD database.

Sectoral aspects

Underlying these broad trends at the aggregate level, significant changes have occurred in R&D expenditures at the level of individual industrial sectors and sub-groups between 1985 and 1990. Table 30 illustrates the geographical distribution of the R&D in the OECD by industry groups for 1985 and 1990. It shows that since 1985 the share of OECD industrial R&D held by the *United States* has decreased substantially in all but one industry group (other transportation equipment). The decrease has been considerable in services, machinery, chemical-linked industries and the other manufacturing industries group. Nevertheless, despite these significant declines in the OECD shares accounted for by the United States in almost every industry group, the US remains in 1990 the leading R&D performer in six out of nine industry groups. Its domination remains considerable in aerospace (over 75 per cent), in machinery, other transportation equipment and services.

In contrast, *Japan*'s share of R&D in the OECD zone has increased in all industry groups between 1985 and 1990. The increase has been important in machinery, in the chemical-linked industries, in metals and in the other manufacturing industries group. These increases have meant that by 1990, the Japan's share of industrial R&D in the chemical-related industries exceeded that of both the US and the EC, while that held in machinery exceeded the share of the EC. Japan also consolidated from 1985 to 1990 its position as the largest R&D performer in the metals group, accounting in 1990 for over 40 per cent of the total R&D performed in the OECD zone.

Relative to the evolutions in the shares held by the United States and Japan, the R&D shares held by the *EC* countries as a whole have stayed stable in most industry groups since 1985. The EC significantly increased its share of R&D in only two industry groups, aerospace and services. Taken as a whole, the EC was in 1990 the leading OECD performer in the R&D carried out in chemicals. Finally, the other eleven OECD countries account in most industry groups for a small fraction of the total R&D performed; only in services did they account in 1985 and 1990 for over 10 per cent of total industrial R&D.

The changes that have occurred since 1985 in the distribution of the R&D in most industry groups between the *United States*, *Japan* and the *EC* can be examining more closely by looking at the sectoral composition of industrial R&D within each of these three regions. Using the same industrial classification as in Table 30, Graph 10 presents the shares of total industrial R&D in 1985 and 1990 by each of the nine industry groups in the United States, Japan and the EC. The graph shows significant differences in the sectoral composition of BERD in 1985 and 1990. The most important difference is with respect to the share of BERD held by the aerospace sector, which accounts by far for the highest proportion (close to 25 per cent in 1990) of BERD in the United States, almost twice the proportion in the EC, while accounting for less than one per cent of Japan's BERD in 1990. Between 1985 and 1990 however, the aerospace share of BERD in the United States decreased by two percentage points, thus explaining the reduction of the US share of total OECD BERD performed in this industry during that period.

Graph 10. **Sectoral composition of business R&D**
Billions of $PPPs

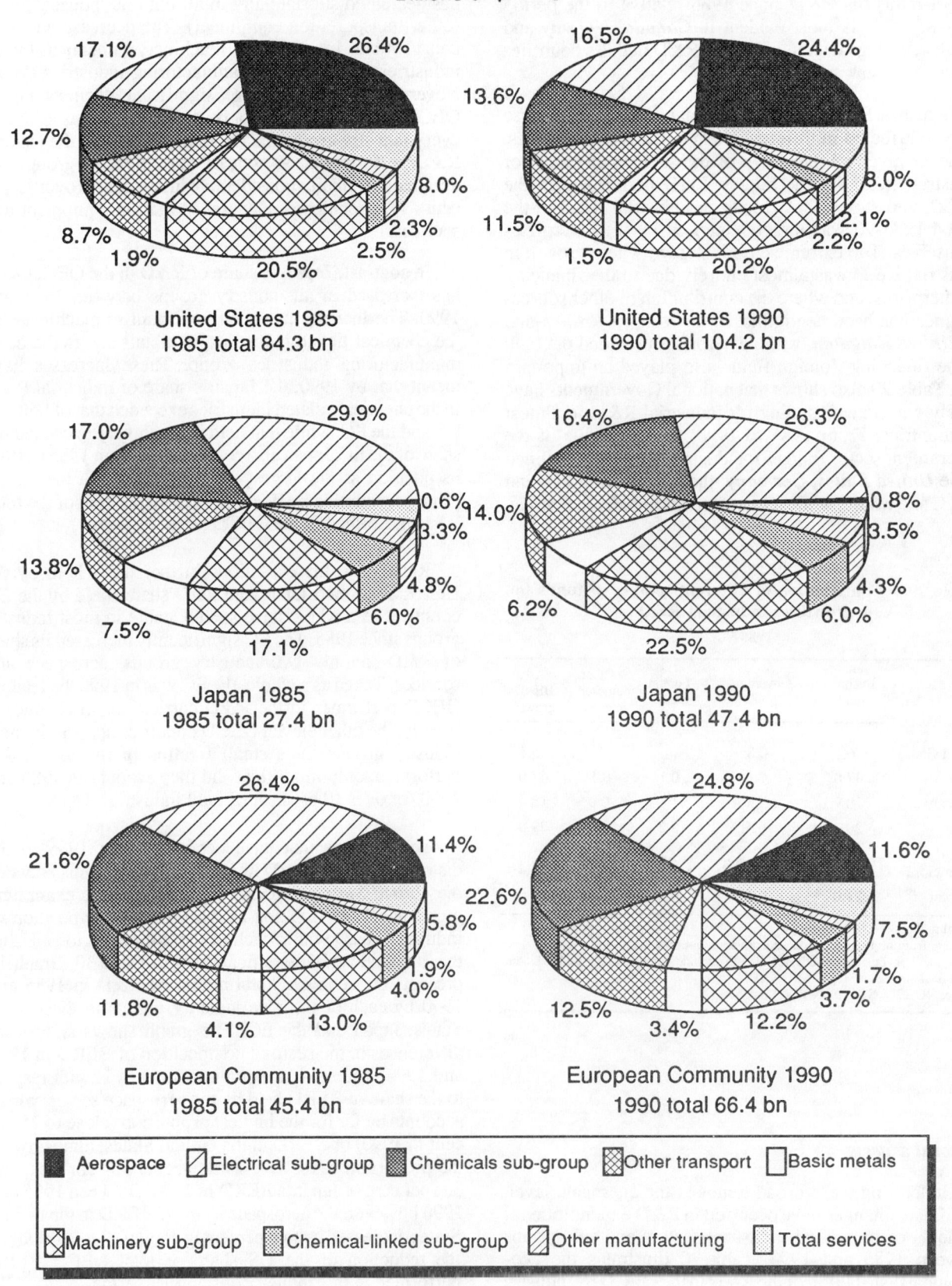

United States 1985
1985 total 84.3 bn
- 26.4%
- 17.1%
- 12.7%
- 8.7%
- 1.9%
- 20.5%
- 2.5%
- 2.3%
- 8.0%

United States 1990
1990 total 104.2 bn
- 24.4%
- 16.5%
- 13.6%
- 11.5%
- 1.5%
- 20.2%
- 2.2%
- 2.1%
- 8.0%

Japan 1985
1985 total 27.4 bn
- 29.9%
- 17.0%
- 13.8%
- 7.5%
- 17.1%
- 6.0%
- 4.8%
- 3.3%
- 0.6%
- 14.0%

Japan 1990
1990 total 47.4 bn
- 26.3%
- 16.4%
- 6.2%
- 22.5%
- 6.0%
- 4.3%
- 3.5%
- 0.8%

European Community 1985
1985 total 45.4 bn
- 26.4%
- 21.6%
- 11.8%
- 4.1%
- 13.0%
- 4.0%
- 1.9%
- 5.8%
- 11.4%

European Community 1990
1990 total 66.4 bn
- 24.8%
- 11.6%
- 7.5%
- 1.7%
- 3.7%
- 12.2%
- 3.4%
- 12.5%
- 22.6%

Legend:
- Aerospace
- Electrical sub-group
- Chemicals sub-group
- Other transport
- Basic metals
- Machinery sub-group
- Chemical-linked sub-group
- Other manufacturing
- Total services

Source: OECD, STAN/ANBERD database.

Table 30. **Shares of OECD industrial R&D (BERD) by industry group**[1]

Percentages
OECD total = 100 for each industry group

	United States		Japan		EC		Other countries	
	1985	1990	1985	1990	1985	1990	1985	1990
Aerospace	79.7	75.1	0.6	1.1	18.1	22.4	1.6	1.4
Electrical/electronics	39.9	35.6	22.6	25.8	32.4	33.8	5.1	4.8
Machinery	59.5	50.6	16.2	25.5	20.0	19.2	4.3	4.7
Other transport	43.1	43.1	22.0	23.9	30.8	29.7	4.1	3.3
Metals	27.0	21.6	34.7	40.1	30.8	30.7	7.5	7.6
Chemicals	40.7	36.9	17.7	20.1	36.7	38.5	4.9	4.5
Chemical-related	36.0	29.0	28.0	35.4	30.3	30.1	5.7	5.5
Other manufacturing	43.6	37.5	29.7	34.7	19.0	18.9	7.7	8.9
Services	58.4	48.9	7.7	9.7	22.5	29.0	11.4	12.3
Total BERD	50.5	44.9	16.4	20.4	27.2	28.7	5.9	6.0

1. Calculations based on data expressed in current dollars and PPPs.
Source: OECD, STAN/ANBERD database.

Another important difference is the much lower share of BERD held by the electronics/electrical group in the *United States* compared to the share of BERD held by that sector in the *EC* and *Japan*. This is despite the fact that the share represented by the electronics/electrical group has decreased noticeably in Japan and the EC during the period 1985-1990. The share of BERD held by the machinery group (including computers) is also quite different between the three regions analysed, with the proportion of BERD represented by this group much higher in the United States and Japan than in the EC. Another industry group with a high variance in the share of BERD between the three regions is the chemicals group (including pharmaceuticals), where the proportion of BERD is much higher in the EC than in the United States and Japan. The importance of the chemicals group within the EC explains why the EC as a whole held the highest share in the OECD zone of R&D carried out in this group (Table 30).

The share in total BERD of the four other manufacturing groups (other transport equipment, metals, chemical-related industries and other manufacturing industries) is highest in *Japan*. This is particularly so for the metals and chemical-linked groups. Finally, the fraction of total BERD expenditures accounted for by services is much lower in Japan than in the *United States* and the *EC*, a reflection possibly of services R&D conducted in Japan by conglomerates classified in manufacturing. In the case of the EC, an increase of 1.7 percentage points from 1985 to 1990 of the share of BERD held by services allowed this industry group to reach in 1990 a proportion of BERD comparable to the share held by services in the United States.

A more detailed breakdown of the sectoral composition of industrial R&D in eight OECD countries is given in Table 31, which presents a list of the ten manufacturing industries that held the highest share of BERD in each of these countries in 1990. The table illustrates the fact that there are significant similarities in the sectoral composition of the BERD of the eight countries, together with some marked differences. The domination of the *electronics* sector is common to all countries, holding the highest share of BERD in all but two countries, the *United States* and *Italy*. The *motor vehicles* industry represents a significant proportion of BERD (more than 11.0 per cent) in every country, except in the *United Kingdom* and *Canada*, and is the leading industry in Italy in terms of per cent of total BERD. Another common feature is the strong position of the *chemicals* industry (top five positions) in every country except Italy and *Sweden*. The biggest differences are in *aerospace*, which accounts by far for the highest share of BERD in the United States, holds an important share of BERD in *France* and the United Kingdom, but is not in the top ten list for *Japan*. *Pharmaceuticals* is important in Italy, Sweden and the United Kingdom, while being much lower in the list for other countries. The *computers* industry accounts for similar proportions of industrial R&D in the United States (11.7 per cent) and in Japan (11.1 per cent), but represents a much smaller share of BERD in all of the other countries.

The table in general shows that industrial R&D is concentrated in the industries which are considered to be the most R&D intensive per unit of output: aerospace, computers, electronics, pharmaceuticals, motor vehicles and chemicals. At the same time however, some industries that are not considered as being R&D intensive have made the list in a few countries, by virtue of the importance they hold in their production or exports. It is the case of the *paper and printing* industry in *Canada* and *Sweden*, the *food, drink & beverages* industry in *Japan* and the *United*

Table 31. Ten biggest R&D performers in eight OECD countries
Percentage in total business enterprise R&D in 1990

	United States		Japan		Germany		France	
1	Aerospace	24.4	Electronics	15.5	Electronics	18.0	Electronics	22.7
2	Electronics	15.2	Motor vehicles	13.7	Motor vehicles	16.4	Aerospace	18.4
3	Computers	11.7	Computers	11.1	Chemicals	15.7	Motor vehicles	12.0
4	Motor vehicles	11.0	Electrical machinery	10.7	Machinery nec.	10.8	Chemicals	9.1
5	Chemicals	6.3	Chemicals	9.7	Aerospace	8.5	Pharmaceuticals	7.4
6	Instruments	5.8	Machinery nec.	7.7	Electrical machinery	7.9	Computers	3.4
7	Chemicals	5.3	Pharmaceuticals	5.3	Pharmaceuticals	5.6	Electrical machinery	3.2
8	Machinery nec.	2.7	Instruments	3.6	Computers	3.5	Machinery nec.	3.1
9	Petroleum refining	2.0	Ferrous metals	3.3	Fabricated metals	2.4	Rubber/plastics	2.9
10	Electrical machinery	1.3	Food/drink/tobacco	2.5	Instruments	1.6	Petroleum refining	2.0
	Other industries	14.0	Other industries	16.7	Other industries	9.6	Other industries	15.8
	Total BERD	100.0	Total BERD	100.0	Total BERD	100.0	Total BERD	100.0
	United Kingdom		Italy		Canada		Sweden (1989)	
1	Electronics	19.4	Motor vehicles	16.2	Electronics	22.4	Electronics	17.4
2	Aerospace	15.0	Pharmaceuticals	13.7	Aerospace	9.3	Motor vehicles	15.7
3	Pharmaceuticals	13.8	Electronics	12.1	Computers	6.9	Pharmaceuticals	12.1
4	Chemicals	10.0	Aerospace	10.8	Pharmaceuticals	4.8	Machinery nec.	11.4
5	Computers	7.4	Electrical machinery	6.9	Chemicals	4.2	Aerospace	5.5
6	Motor vehicles	6.2	Computers	6.5	Petroleum refining	2.8	Paper/printing	5.0
7	Electrical machinery	3.8	Machinery nec.	5.9	Non-ferrous metals	2.7	Computers	3.7
8	Machinery nec.	2.8	Chemicals	5.7	Paper/printing	2.5	Chemicals	3.6
9	Food/drink/tobacco	2.2	Fabricated metals	2.3	Motor vehicles	1.9	Fabricated metals	3.4
10	Petroleum refining	1.2	Rubber/plastics	2.1	Machinery nec.	1.8	Other transport	3.1
	Other industries	18.2	Other industries	17.8	Other industries	40.7	Other industries	19.1
	Total BERD	100.0	Total BERD	100.0	Total BERD	100.0	Total BERD	100.0

nec = non elsewhere classified.
Source: OECD, STAN/ANBERD database, 1992.

Kingdom and the *fabricated metals* industry in **Germany** and **Italy**.

The intensity of R&D expenditures

While the amounts devoted to R&D activities are an important indicator of innovative activity, a more accurate indicator of R&D effort is obtained when R&D expenditures are expressed relative to output or value added. Graph 11 presents the R&D intensity of OECD countries expressed as the ratio of BERD to the domestic product of industry (DPI -- equal to GDP net of the value-added associated with government production which is not classified as being an enterprise activity). Among the large economies, the intensity of industrial R&D in *Japan* has been increasing rapidly since 1985, growing from 2.1 to 2.4 per cent. In contrast, the intensity of industrial R&D in the *United States* has been in decline since 1985, with the BERD/DPI ratio falling to 2.2 per cent in 1990. *Germany*, despite a slight decrease in its ratio, still had in 1990 the highest intensity of industrial R&D of the major economies. R&D intensity increased in *France* and to a lesser extent in *Italy*, while declining slightly in the *United Kingdom* and *Canada*.

Among the medium-sized economies, two countries, *Sweden* and *Switzerland*, have had during the period 1985-90 the highest intensities of industrial R&D of all the OECD countries. After the steep decline in Swedish R&D intensity, which may be due in part to the relocation of some Swedish firms abroad and the moving of their R&D facilities, the highest value for the OECD in 1990 was in Switzerland. Albeit at much lower levels, upward trends

Graph 11. **R&D intensities**
Business enterprise R&D expenditures/Domestic product of industry
Percentages

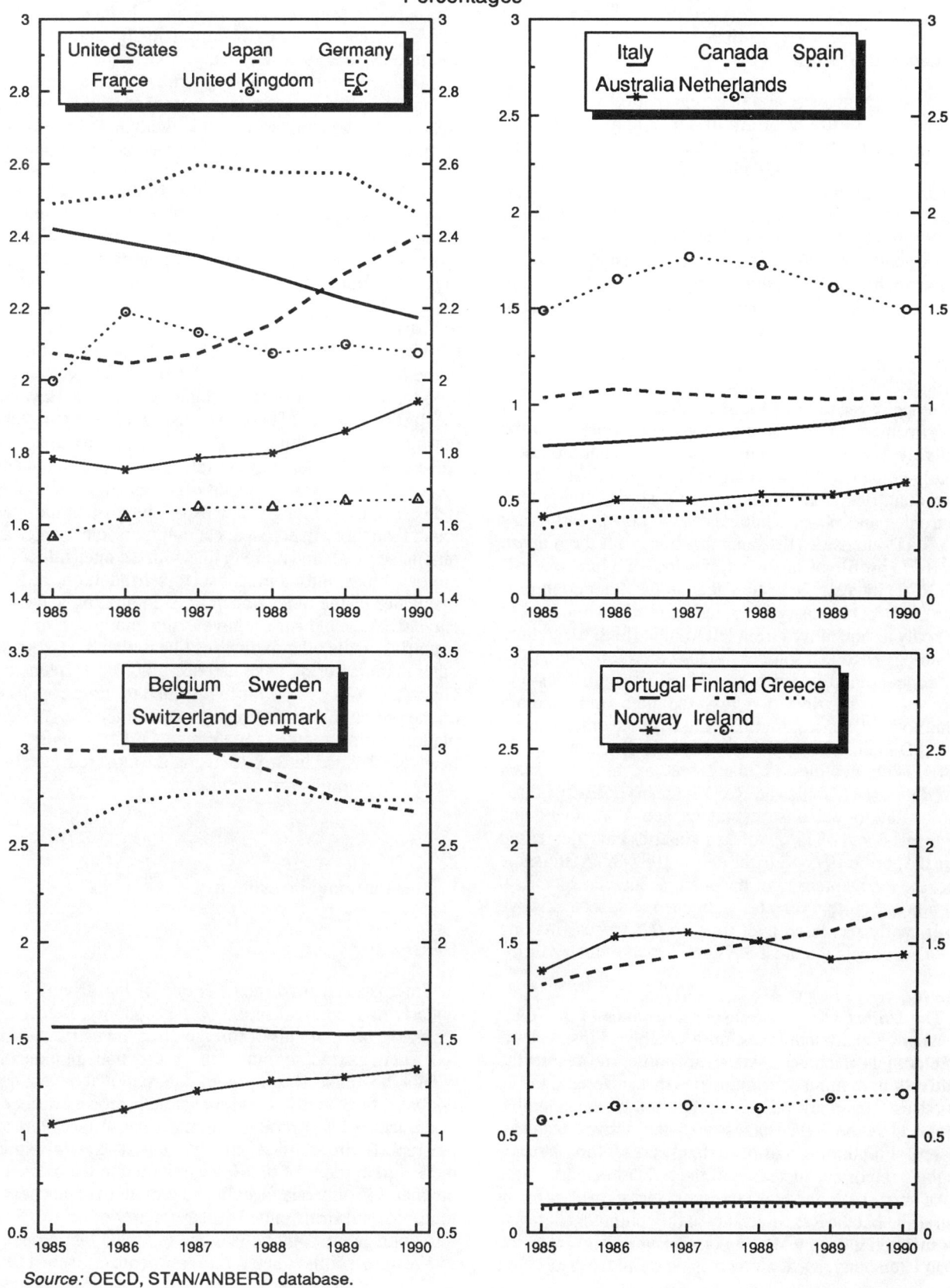

Source: OECD, STAN/ANBERD database.

are discernable in *Spain* and *Australia*, while a significant decline has occurred in the *Netherlands* since 1987. In the smaller economies, R&D intensity is high and rising in *Denmark* and *Finland;* it is lower but increasing in *Ireland*; and very low (less than 0.5 per cent) and flat in *Portugal* and *Greece*.

The R&D intensity at an aggregate level is driven by the intensity of R&D effort in some high technology industries that at the same time account for a large part of industrial production. Graph 12 shows the individual industry detail for the United States, Japan, Germany, France, the United Kingdom and Italy. The individual country graphs represent R&D intensity profiles for two periods, calculated as the ratio of R&D expenditures to production for every manufacturing sector, and listed from left to right according to the standard OECD definition, ranging from high to low technology industries.

A striking general feature of the graphs is that the profiles do not fall uniformly from left to right. There are differences over time within individual countries as well as between countries. The most apparent difference is the relatively low R&D intensity in *Japan* of what are traditionally considered to be high technology industries. In other countries, four industries (aerospace, computers, electronics and pharmaceuticals) have consistently very high R&D intensities that unambiguously set them apart. The R&D profile of Japan exhibits less of a bias towards high R&D intensity industries than in the other countries, since the R&D intensity of the industries does not drop so markedly as one moves from left to right (high to medium technology). R&D resources in Japan therefore seem to be less concentrated in the high technology industries and more evenly distributed across the high and medium technology industries. Another feature of the graphs is that the R&D intensities have not always increased during the 1980s, with declines in many sectors. In the *United Kingdom* for example the R&D intensity ratios of three high technology industries (aerospace, computers and electronics) and of 13 out of 22 industries have decreased from the period 1979-81 to the period 1987-89. At the same time, the R&D intensity of the pharmaceuticals, electrical machinery, motor vehicles and chemical sectors have significantly increased over time, in the process making pharmaceuticals the most R&D-intensive industry in the country.

The *United States* also displays declines in the R&D intensity of many industries, most notably in instruments and electrical machinery. At the same time, and despite the relatively high number of industries that suffered a fall in their R&D intensity ratios, the US shows considerable increases in the R&D intensity of the aerospace, electronics, shipbuilding and other transport sectors. *France* displays important increases in the R&D intensity ratios of the aerospace, and other transport sectors. However, it is striking that the R&D intensity of the computers industry has suffered a decline. In *Japan, Germany* and *Italy,* the R&D intensities reveal an increasing trend from 1979-81 to 1987-89. Every industrial sector in Japan has shown an increase in its R&D intensity ratio, while the R&D intensity ratios of only two sectors in Germany (non-ferrous metal and paper & printing) and three in Italy have decreased. The strongest increases occurred in the aerospace and electronics sectors in Germany, and in the instruments, computers, chemicals and pharmaceuticals sectors in Japan. The pharmaceuticals industry has become the most R&D-intensive industry in Japan, with an R&D intensity surpassing in 1987-89 the ratio of the aerospace industry.

These graphs raise the question of the adequacy of the standard OECD definitions of high, medium and low technology. Overall, it is clear that four industries (aerospace, computers, electronics and pharmaceuticals) have high R&D intensities and unquestionably belong to the high technology group. It is also evident that some industries have consistently low R&D intensities and definitely belong in the low technology group. It is the case of the ferrous metals, fabricated metals, paper & printing, wood & furniture and textiles & clothing sectors. However, the R&D intensities of certain industries have not increased during the 1980s, while that of other sectors have increased substantially. Under present definitions, instruments and electrical machinery are classified as high technology industries, even though their R&D intensities are much lower than those in aerospace, computers, electronics and pharmaceuticals and more in line with the intensities of the motor vehicles and chemicals sectors. In addition, the R&D intensities of the other transport, shipbuilding and stone, clay & glass industries have risen markedly in some countries, while other industries like rubber & plastics and other manufacturing have had declining R&D intensities. Given the policy importance attached to indicators based on the present classification, the R&D intensities of every manufacturing sectors for thirteen OECD countries has been recalculated in Box 12, using the most recent data on R&D expenditures and production.

F. International investment

General trends

International investment is one of the driving forces underlying the globalisation of the economy. Before analysing the broad trends of foreign direct investment during the recent period, it should be noted that globalisation cannot be reduced simply to international investment. Globalisation is a multidimensional process affecting trade, technology, production and finance (see Part 5 of the report). In addition, direct international investment measured in terms of the flows recorded in the balance of payments is only one facet of the growth of assets held by multinational firms outside their country of origin. Firms also pursue the globalisation of their activities by reinvesting profits (such reinvestments are sometimes

Graph 12. **R&D intensity profiles**

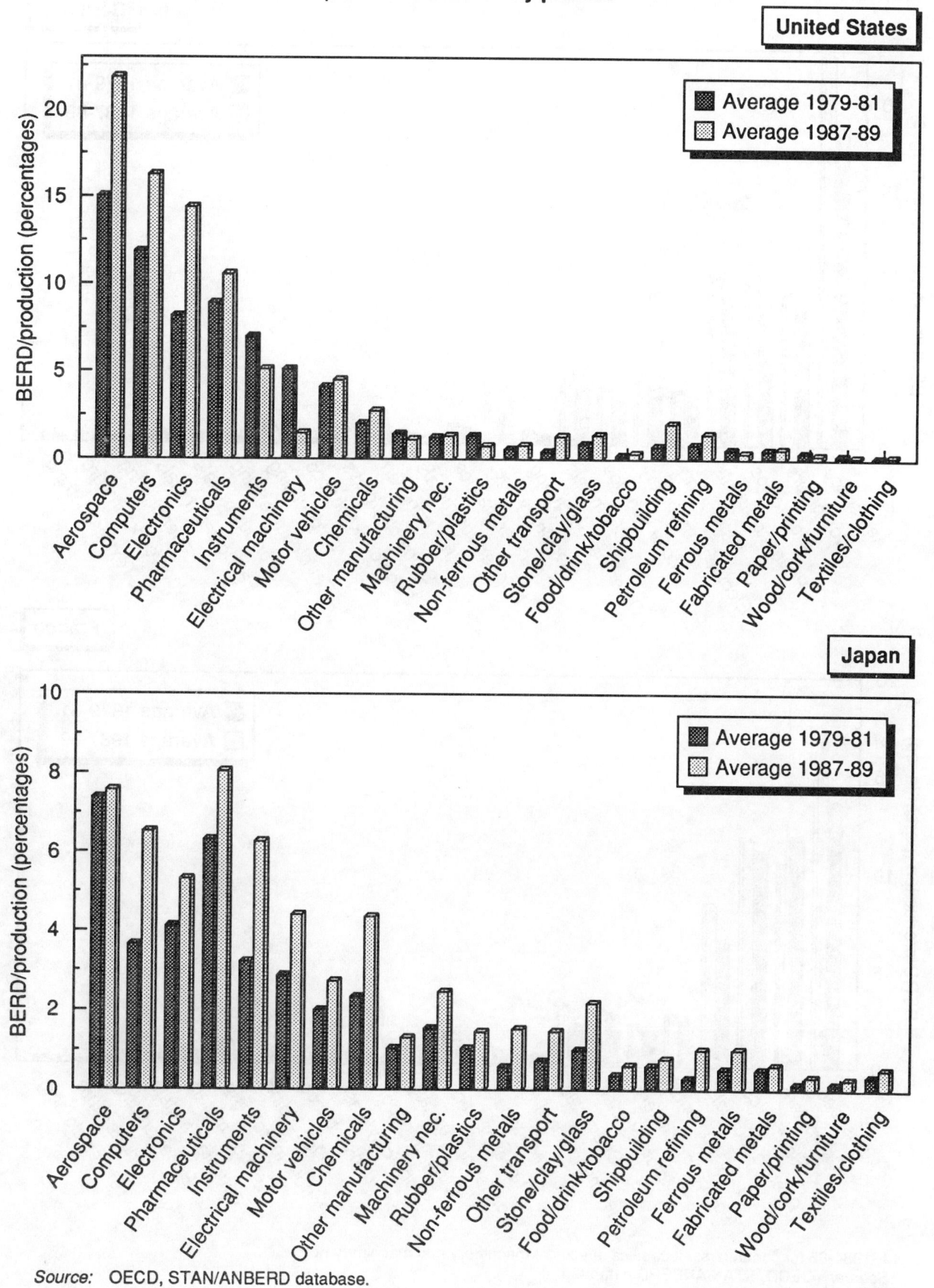

United States

- Average 1979-81
- Average 1987-89

BERD/production (percentages)

Categories (left to right): Aerospace, Computers, Electronics, Pharmaceuticals, Instruments, Electrical machinery, Motor vehicles, Chemicals, Other manufacturing, Machinery nec., Rubber/plastics, Non-ferrous metals, Other transport, Stone/clay/glass, Food/drink/tobacco, Shipbuilding, Petroleum refining, Ferrous metals, Fabricated metals, Paper/printing, Wood/cork/furniture, Textiles/clothing

Japan

- Average 1979-81
- Average 1987-89

BERD/production (percentages)

Categories (left to right): Aerospace, Computers, Electronics, Pharmaceuticals, Instruments, Electrical machinery, Motor vehicles, Chemicals, Other manufacturing, Machinery nec., Rubber/plastics, Non-ferrous metals, Other transport, Stone/clay/glass, Food/drink/tobacco, Shipbuilding, Petroleum refining, Ferrous metals, Fabricated metals, Paper/printing, Wood/cork/furniture, Textiles/clothing

Source: OECD, STAN/ANBERD database.

Graph 12 (cont). R&D intensity profiles

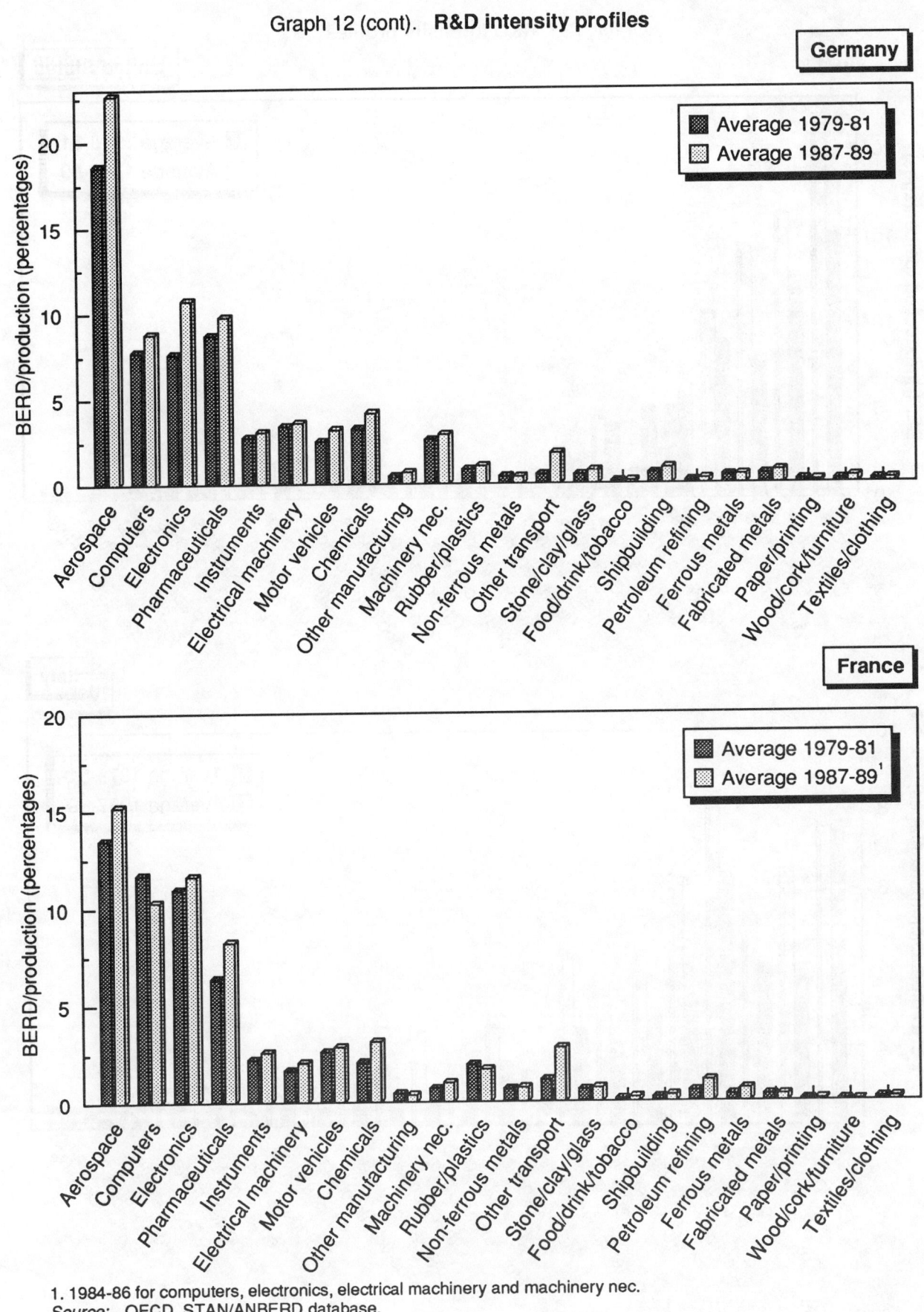

1. 1984-86 for computers, electronics, electrical machinery and machinery nec.
Source: OECD, STAN/ANBERD database.

Graph 12 (cont). **R&D intensity profiles**

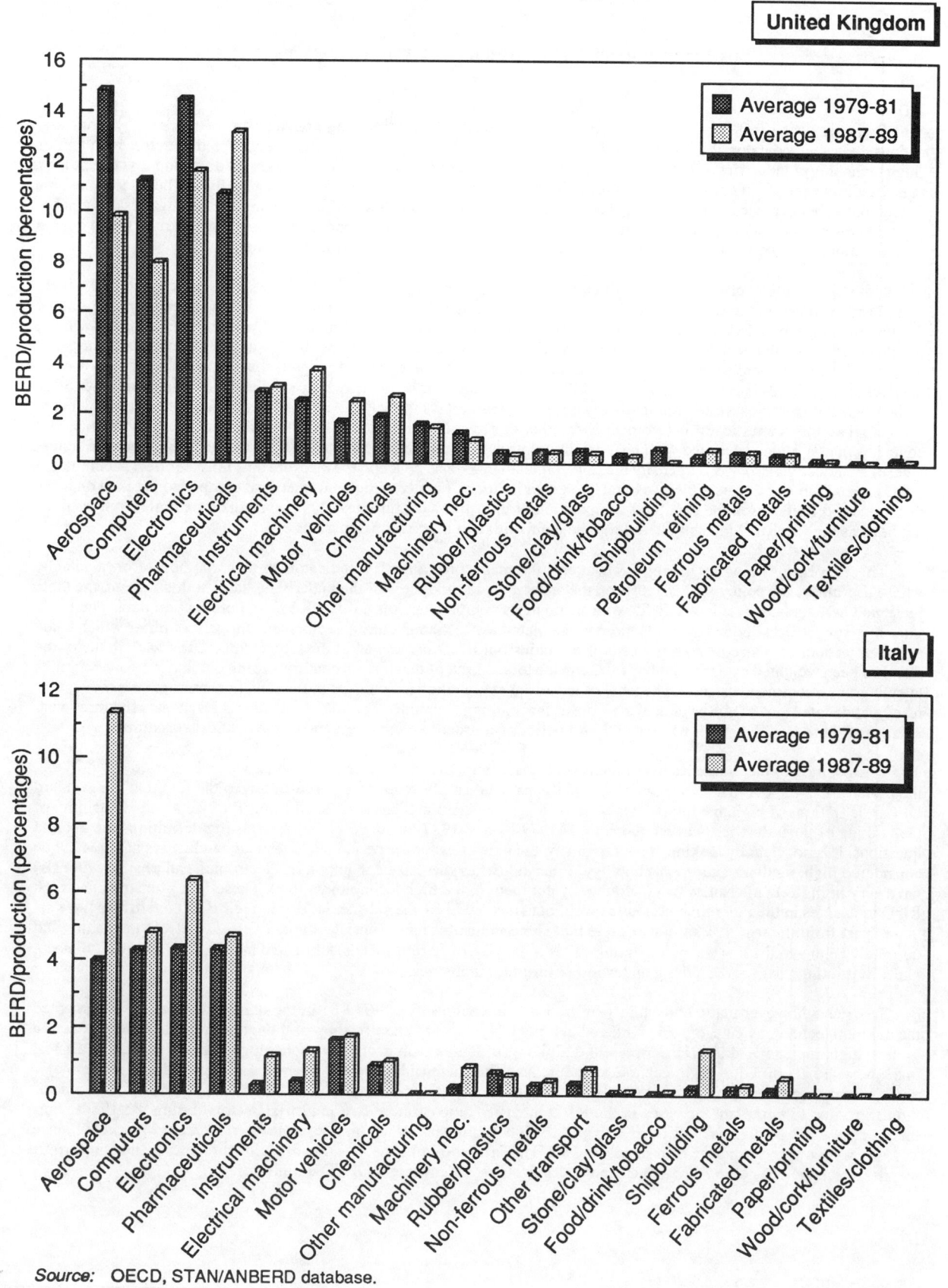

Box 12. Identifying high, medium and low technology industries

Technological effort is regarded as a critical determinant of the continuing competition for markets by firms and nations and as an indicator of their effort to be competitive. As a result, policy is often preoccupied with the evolution of "high technology" industries, often at the exclusion of other considerations. Identifying high, medium and low technology industries however involves many difficulties. In particular, a number of characteristics are usually attributed to industries considered as being in the high-technology category: the need for a strong R&D effort; the presence of high-risks and large capital investments; very rapid product and process obsolescence; strategic importance for governments; or a high degree of international co-operation and competition in R&D, production and world-wide marketing.

Industries could, in principle, be classified using all the above criteria. OECD work so far has been based exclusively on the first of these and used the concept of "technology intensity", usually interpreted as R&D expenditure per unit of production or value-added, as a measure of the technological sophistication of industry. Despite its broad use however, the concept is generally ill-defined and often does not have a clear correspondance with what it typically aims to to measure: the level of technological sophistication of an industry. One of its main shortcomings is that by focusing exclusively on the R&D expenditures in a particular sector, R&D intensity indicators do not take into account the fact that industries often do little R&D themselves while simultansously purchasing as inputs highly R&D-intensive intermediate and capital inputs from other sectors domestically and from abroad. Other shortcomings include a substantial volatility over time and accross countries that is often associated with changes in output which may have little to do with the underlying technological level of an industry. Also, R&D intensity is a flow, rather than a stock, concept: the measure thus fails to reflect accumulated R&D expenditures or the technology capital in a given industry. Finally, simple international comparisons based on it are distorted by differences in the structural composition of industry: a country heavily dependent on natural resources need not have as high an R&D intensity in order to be competitive in international markets.

These problems notwithstanding, R&D intensity remains one of the few indicators of technological effort available, whose usefulness for policy analysis rests on the accuracy and timeliness of the underlying data. In this respect, the table presented here updates previous OECD work using more complete and up-to-date R&D and production data. The R&D intensity ratio (BERD divided by production) is calculated for 22 manufacturing sectors and thirteen countries which taken together account for more than 95 per cent of the industrial R&D performed in the OECD zone [1]. For each industry the ratio has been weighted by each country's share in the total output of the thirteen countries using purchasing power parities to convert to a common currency. The level of industrial aggregation is that used in the OECD's international surveys on resources devoted to R&D [2]. The rank of the industries according to their R&D/production ratios is given based on three-year averages for the 1972-74, 1979-81, and 1987-89 periods (in order to eliminate some of the cyclical variation).

The position of the industries over time reveals that no important changes occurred between the period 1972-74 and the period 1979-81, but that some significants shifts have taken place during the 1980s. Given the fact that the standard OECD definitions of high, medium and low technology industries was last calculated using 1980 data [3], the instability of the ranking of the industries between the periods 1979-81 and 1987-89 suggests that the existing definitions are open to questions. It is not clear by looking at the ranking of the industries for the period 1987-89 which industries should now be considered high, medium and low technology. Four industries (aerospace, computers, electronics and pharmaceuticals) have very high R&D intensities that undoubtedly put them in the high technology group. These four industries had high R&D intensities in the other time periods as well, but since 1979-81 the substantial rise in their R&D intensities have set them apart from the rest. It also indisputable that some industries have consistently had very low R&D intensities and definitely belong to the low technology group. This is the case of ferrous metals, fabricated metals, food, drink & tobacco, paper & printing, textiles & clothing and wood & furniture industries.

It appears however that the instability of the R&D intensities since 1979-81 in the other industries has fragmented the medium technology category and rendered deficient the standard classification of the industries into three distinctive groups: high, medium and low. Under present definitions of high, medium and low technology, instruments and electrical machinery are classified as high technology industries. Their intensities are however now closer to those of the motor vehicles and chemicals industries. In fact, electrical machinery is now positioned behind the motor vehicles and chemicals industries, due to important increases in the R&D intensity ratio of these two industrial sectors during the 1980s. Furthermore, the R&D intensities of other transport, shipbuilding and stone, clay & class have increased markedly since 1979-81, allowing these industries to surpass the R&D intensities of rubber & plastics, other manufacturing and non-ferrous metals, which are considered medium technology industries under present OECD definitions.

Box 12 *(cont)*. **Identifying high, medium and low technology industries**

Based on these shifts between industries due to different patterns of R&D intensities since 1979-81, four, rather than three categories could now be distinguished. The analysis of the R&D ratios for the period 1987-89 renders much more pertinent the division of the medium technology group into two groups: medium-high technology and medium-low technology. The borderline value between these two new groups can be considered to be twice the value of the median of the ratios of the 22 manufacturing sectors. The medium-high group would then consist of instruments and electrical machinery, together with motor vehicles and chemicals, while seven industries ranging from machinery not elsewhere classified (nec) to rubber & plastics would constitute the medium-low technology group.

Intensity of R&D expenditures in the OECD
R&D expenditures/production (percentages)

	1972-74			1979-81			1987-89	
	High			**High**			**High**	
1	Aerospace	19.6	1	Aerospace	14.2	1	Aerospace	20.2
2	Computers	10.4	2	Computers	9.0	2	Computers	12.4
3	Electronics	7.1	3	Pharmaceuticals	7.5	3	Electronics	10.8
4	Pharmaceuticals	6.1	4	Electronics	7.4	4	Pharmaceuticals	10.3
5	Instruments	3.9	5	Instruments	4.9			
6	El. Machinery	3.3	6	El. Machinery	3.2		**Medium-high**	
						5	Instruments	4.8
	Medium			**Medium**		6	Motor vehicles	3.5
7	Motor vehicles	2.4	7	Motor vehicles	2.7	7	Chemicals	3.4
8	Chemicals	2.2	8	Chemicals	2.1	8	El. Machinery	3.2
9	Rubber & plastics	1.2	9	Machinery nec.	1.4			
10	Machinery nec.	1.1	10	Rubber & plastics	1.1		**Medium-low**	
11	Other manufacturing	0.9	11	Other manufacturing	1.0	9	Machinery nec.	2.1
12	Petroleum refining	0.8				10	Other transport	1.9
						11	Shipbuilding	1.4
	Low			**Low**		12	Petroleum refining	1.1
13	Shipbuilding	0.6	12	Other transport	0.7	13	Stone, clay & glass	1.1
14	Stone, clay & glass	0.6	13	Stone, clay & glass	0.6	14	Other manufacturing	1.0
15	Non-ferrous metals	0.5	14	Petroleum refining	0.6	15	Rubber & plastics	1.0
16	Other transport	0.5	15	Shipbuilding	0.6	16	Non-ferrous metals	0.9
17	Ferrous metals	0.4	16	Non-ferrous metals	0.6			
18	Fabricated metals	0.3	17	Ferrous metals	0.5		**Low**	
19	Paper & printing	0.2	18	Fabricated metals	0.5	17	Ferrous metals	0.7
20	Food, drink, tobacco	0.2	19	Paper & printing	0.2	18	Fabricated metals	0.6
21	Textiles & clothing	0.1	20	Food, drink, tobacco	0.2	19	Food, drink, tobacco	0.3
22	Wood & furniture	0.1	21	Textiles & clothing	0.1	20	Paper & printing	0.2
			22	Wood and furniture	0.1	21	Textiles & clothing	0.2
						22	Wood and furniture	0.1

Source: OECD, STAN/ANBERD database.

1. The countries are Australia, Canada, Denmark, Finland, France, Germany, Italy, Japan, Netherlands, Norway, Sweden, the United Kingdom and the United States.
2. OECD (1981), *"Frascati Manual 1980", The Measurement of Scientific and Technical Activities*, Paris.
3. OECD (1986), *OECD Science and Technology Indicators, No. 2*, Paris.

included in the balance of payments) and by debt and equity financing on local or international markets. In other words, foreign direct investment flows are only a partial measure of the globalisation of corporate activities.

After a decade of very rapid growth (nearly 20 per cent annually, i.e. more than four times the rate of export growth during the period 1980-89), outward direct investment by OECD countries slowed in 1990 (with an overall rate of growth of 6 per cent between 1989 and 1990). Outward direct investment by the *United Kingdom* and *Canada* actually fell in 1990. In 1991 the decline was confirmed for all OECD countries for which data are available (Table 32). The most striking decrease was in direct investment by *Japan* which fell by a third; there was also a marked fall in investment by *France* (by 29 per cent), the *United States* (12 per cent), and a slightly less pronounced fall in outward direct investment by *Germany* (7 per cent). In 1991, foreign direct investment by these four countries and the UK, which together account for 72 per cent of total outward direct investment from OECD countries, was on average 22 per cent below its 1990 value.

The slowdown and even the decline in direct investment originating in OECD countries has been accompanied since 1990 by a sharp fall in incoming investment to these countries (see Table 33 and Graph 13). From 1981 to 1990, inflows averaged more than three-quarters of outflows. As a proportion of outflows, they rose sharply to 80 per cent in 1989 and then fell to 69 per cent in 1990. This may indicate the beginning of a shift in the direction of international investment to countries outside the OECD area (developing countries, particularly in Latin America, the Dynamic Asian Economies and the central and eastern European economies in transition). If this trend is confirmed, 1990 might well have been a turning point.

The salient features of international investment during the 1981-90 decade were as follows:

- Investment inflows to the *United States* were twice the amount of outflows (with a positive net balance of US$178 billion). The US was the only one of the major investor countries to be in this position;

- Japan had a slightly larger negative net balance (US$182.5 billion) [14];

- Three countries -- the *United Kingdom*, *Japan* and the *United States* -- were the leading investors, with almost equal shares of total investment from 1981 to 1990 (18.8 per cent, 18.5 per cent and 17.6 per cent respectively).

Table 32. **Outward direct investment flows from OECD countries**[1]

Billion current dollars

	Cumulative flows		Direct investment flows					
	1973-80	1981-90	1986	1987	1988	1989	1990	1991
United States	110.0	176.5	18.7	31.0	17.9	33.4	33.4	29.5
Canada	10.7	36.7	4.1	7.1	5.6	4.5	1.2	3.2
Japan	17.0	185.8	14.5	19.5	34.2	44.1	48.0	31.2
Belgium/Lux.	2.9	21.5	1.6	2.7	3.6	6.1	6.6	..
Denmark	0.9	6.3	0.6	0.6	0.7	2.0	1.5	..
France	13.0	85.7	5.2	8.7	12.8	18.1	27.1	19.3
Germany	22.3	85.2	9.6	9.1	11.4	14.1	22.3	20.8
Italy	3.0	27.9	2.7	2.3	5.4	2.0	7.1	..
Netherlands	18.0	51.5	3.1	7.1	4.0	11.4	12.1	..
Portugal	..	0.4	0.0	0.0	0.1	0.1	0.1	..
Spain	1.2	8.2	0.4	0.7	1.2	1.5	2.8	..
United Kingdom	51.4	188.5	17.6	31.4	37.1	35.2	20.8	17.3
Austria	0.5	4.1	0.3	0.3	0.3	0.9	1.6	1.3
Finland	0.5	12.2	0.8	1.1	2.6	3.1	3.3	2.1
Norway	0.9	8.8	1.6	0.9	1.0	1.3	1.3	..
Sweden	4.2	46.1	3.7	4.5	7.2	9.7	14.1	..
Switzerland	..	31.9[2]	1.5	1.3	8.7	7.9	6.4	..
Australia	2.2	24.6	3.0	5.7	5.7	3.8	1.3	0.1
EC	112.6	475.1	40.9	62.7	76.4	90.5	100.5	..
OECD	267.6	1 001.7	89.0	134.2	159.6	199.1	211.2	(132.0)

1. Includes reinvested earnings.
2. 1983-90.
Source: OECD, Balance of Payments data.

Table 33. **Inward direct investment flows to OECD countries**[1]
Billion current dollars

	Cumulative flows		Flows of direct investment					
	1973-80	1981-90	1986	1987	1988	1989	1990	1991
United States	55.0	354.7	34.1	58.1	59.4	70.6	37.2	22.2
Canada	4.0	12.2	1.0	3.5	3.6	3.5	5.7	5.1
Japan	1.0	3.3	0.2	1.2	−0.5	−1.0	1.7	1.4
Belgium/Lux.	8.4	28.2	0.6	2.3	5.0	6.7	8.2	..
Denmark	1.3	3.5	0.2	0.1	0.5	1.1	1.2	..
France	15.7	43.2	2.7	4.6	7.2	9.6	9.1	10.8
Germany	10.9	16.5	1.2	1.9	1.1	6.7	1.5	2.2
Ireland	1.6	1.2	0.0	0.1	0.1	0.1	1.0	..
Italy	4.5	25.0	0.0	4.1	6.8	2.5	6.3	..
Netherlands	7.4	27.6	1.9	2.3	4.0	6.8	8.3	..
Portugal	0.5[2]	6.4	0.2	0.5	0.9	1.7	2.1	..
Spain	6.6	46.0	3.4	4.5	7.0	8.4	13.7	..
United Kingdom	38.2	122.2	7.3	13.9	18.2	28.0	33.7	21.1
Austria	1.2	3.3	0.2	0.4	0.4	0.6	0.7	0.3
Finland	0.3	2.8	0.3	0.3	0.5	0.5	0.8	0.0
Norway	2.6	4.6	1.0	0.2	0.3	1.5	0.8	..
Sweden	0.7	8.3	0.9	0.6	1.5	1.5	2.3	..
Switzerland	..	12.4[3]	1.8	2.0	0.0	2.2	4.4	..
Australia	9.1	38.1	3.3	3.7	7.2	7.3	6.5	4.4
EC	97.3	326.0	18.0	35.0	51.8	72.4	85.2	..
OECD	172.0	768.1	61.0	105.0	124.6	159.8	146.1	(87.9)

1. Includes reinvested earnings; negative figures indicate net disinvestment in a given year.
2. 1975-80.
3. 1983-90.
Source: OECD, Balance of Payments data.

Trends by geographical area

United States

The most striking development in the *United States* is the fall in both inward and outward foreign direct investment in 1991. After growing very rapidly up to 1989, inward investment fell from over US$70 billion in 1989 to US$37.2 billion in 1990 and to US$22.2 billion in 1991. Whereas in the second half of the 1980s, the United States had attracted virtually half of all investment to the OECD area, in 1990 it accounted for only a quarter, and about the same share in 1991. The explanation for this decline lies in the slowdown of economic activity in the US and in the poor performance of the US subsidiaries of foreign companies, as well as in the attraction of European markets (the EC and possibly the economies in transition). Another factor is that many firms that had made major acquisitions in previous years have now embarked upon a phase of consolidation. Direct investment by Japanese firms has also fallen. Whereas flows from Japan averaged about US$17 billion annually over the previous three years, they fell dramatically in 1991.

In terms of stocks, the largest three investors in the US in 1990 were the *United Kingdom* (26.8 per cent of the total), *Japan* (20.7 per cent) and the *Netherlands* (15.9 per cent). Japan and the *EC* together account for more than three fourths (Table 34). While in terms of flows Europe's share fell up to 1990 and that of Japan rose, the trend seems to have been reversed in 1991: during the first quarter of 1991, Europe accounted for 70 per cent (or US$1.4 billion) of the total flows to the United States.

Finally, it should be mentioned that in 1990, as in previous years, investments by foreign firms in the United States more often involved acquisitions of existing plants than the setting-up of new ones. Acquisitions, most of which were large, accounted for 90 per cent of the total investment expenditure by foreign firms (taking into account all sources of financing, i.e. inward investment and financing by local subsidiaries). Thus, in 1990 eleven

Graph 13. **Outward and inward foreign direct investment flows**
$US million

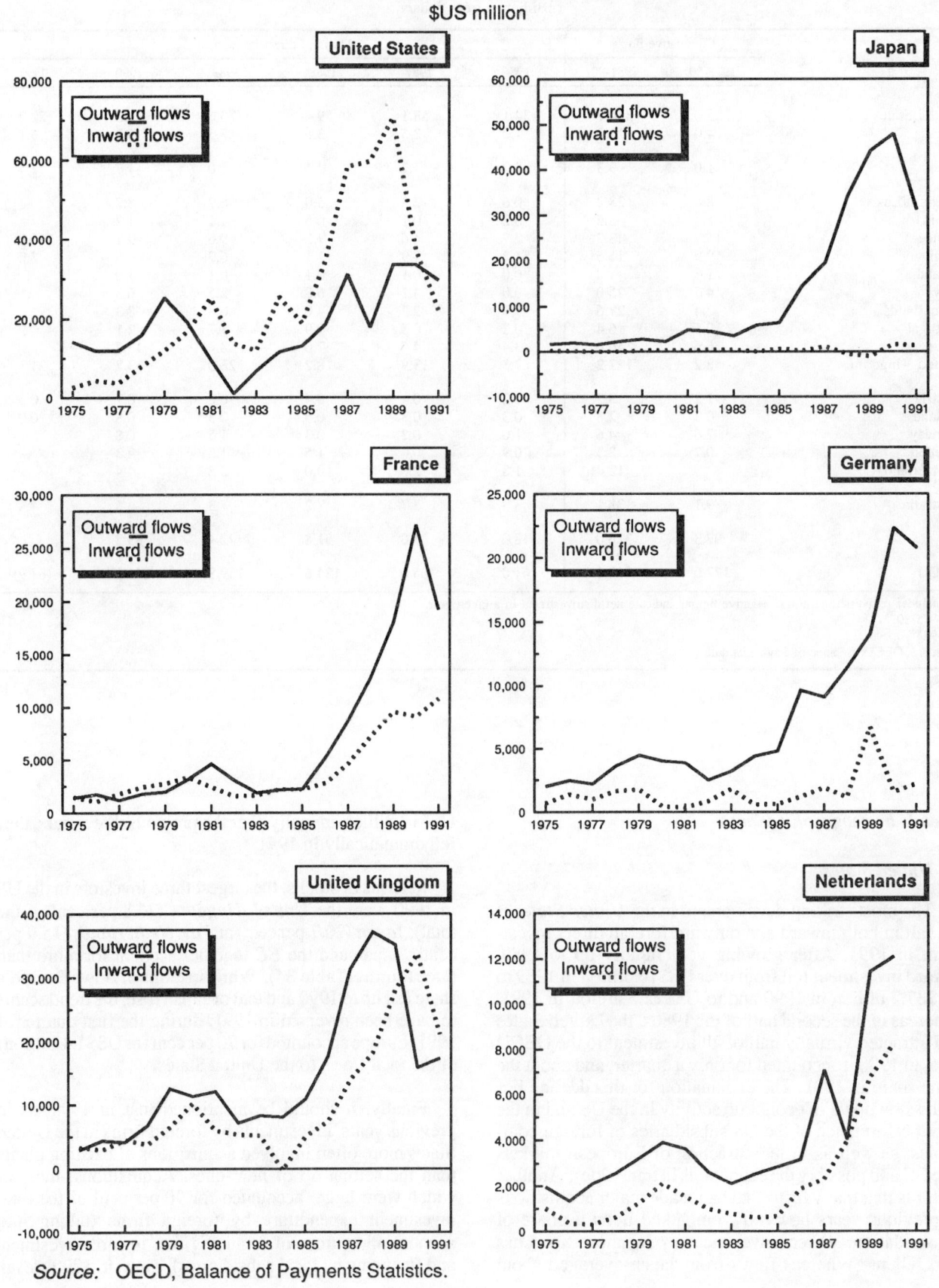

Source: OECD, Balance of Payments Statistics.

transactions of US$1 billion or over accounted for 41 per cent of all transactions, and 86 transactions of US$100 million or over represented 72 per cent. Among the largest transactions, acquisitions by a major French glass manufacturer, by a French tyre manufacturer which became world leader as a result of the transaction, a Swiss pharmaceutical group, a French state-owned chemical company, and a Japanese chemical company are noteworthy. In the non-manufacturing sectors, Japanese groups made important purchases of multimedia companies [15].

Despite the recession, US firms continued to invest abroad. Although investment outflows in 1991 were lower than they were in 1990 (US$29.5 billion compared with US$33.4 billion, or a decline of 11.7 per cent), their decline was less than that of inflows. The *United States* thus became a net outward investor again for the first time since 1980.

Table 34. **Breakdown of US inward direct investments by geographical origin**

Stocks and flows (in percentages)

	Stocks			Flows		
	1988	1989	1990	1988	1989	1990
Canada	8.4	7.7	6.9	2.0	4.6	..
Europe	66.4	65.0	63.5	55.0	61.3	43.8
United Kingdom	30.4	28.2	26.8	35.3	26.7	9.9
Netherlands	15.3	15.1	15.9	9.7	10.4	19.0
Germany	8.0	7.8	6.9	4.0	5.4	2.5
France	4.2	4.5	4.8	5.1	5.1	11.7
EC	59.8	57.8	56.9	54.1	51.7	42.5
Japan	16.2	18.0	20.7	29.1	24.7	46.6
EC + Japan	76.0	75.8	77.6	83.1	76.4	89.1

Source: US Department of Commerce, *Survey of Current Business,* Aug. 1991.

The salient feature of 1991 was massive US investment in Europe. The prospects opened up by the Single European Market, German reunification and the opening-up of the central and eastern European economies in transition, explain why Europe received 70 per cent of US direct investment as compared with 43 per cent in 1990. Preferred investment locations were the *United Kingdom*, with 50 per cent of investment, and *Germany*, with 20 per cent. Many US firms began operations in eastern Germany in order to meet local demand and prepare to export to eastern Europe.

The breakdown of the stock of US investment in the European Community at the end of 1990 shows the

Table 35. **Breakdown of US outward direct investments by geographical destination**

Billion current dollars and percentages

	Stocks 1990		Flows 1990	
	Total	Percentage	Total	Percentage
Developed countries	312.2	74.1	21.2	63.4
Canada	68.4	16.2	2.3	6.8
Europe	204.2	48.4	14.5	43.3
EC	172.9	41.0	9.1	27.2
United Kingdom	65.0	15.4	0.5	1.6
Germany	27.7	6.6	0.8	2.4
France	17.1	4.1	1.5	4.6
Spain	7.5	1.8	0.5	1.5
Ireland	6.8	1.6	1.1	3.4
Italy	13.0	3.1	1.3	3.8
Netherlands	22.8	5.4	2.6	7.7
Other Europe	31.3	7.4	5.4	16.2
Japan	21.0	5.0	1.4	4.3
Developing countries	105.7	25.1	12.2	36.4
International	3.6	0.9	0.1	0.2
Total	421.5	100.0	33.4	100.0

Source: US Department of Commerce, *Survey of Current Business,* Aug. 1991.

Table 36. **Sectoral breakdown of US investments in the EC**

Stocks 1988, 1989 et 1990 in percentages

Sectors	1988	1989	1990
Petroleum	12.0	9.9	10.8
Manufacturing industries	51.7	47.4	47.0
Trade	8.9	9.1	9.3
Banking	5.0	4.6	4.3
Finance	17.6	24.6	23.5
Services	2.6	2.6	3.2
Others	1.9	1.8	2.2
Manufacturing industries	100.0	100.0	100.0
Food production	11.1	9.5	9.9
Chemicals	21.6	23.8	23.5
Metals	4.7	4.2	3.4
Machinery	24.3	22.0	22.0
Electrical/electronic	5.1	5.8	5.6
Transport equipment	11.2	12.8	10.7
Others	23.2	22.0	23.6

Source: US Department of Commerce, *Survey of Current Business,* Aug. 1991.

predominance of the *United Kingdom*, followed by *Germany* and the *Netherlands*, as well as the preponderant share of manufacturing investment (nearly half of the total stock of direct investment) (Tables 35 and 36). The trends for 1991 indicate that this predominance will probably become more marked. In any case, they show that US firms have continued to invest directly and to expand the activities of industrial subsidiaries in order to consolidate their established position in European markets.

Japan

One of the striking features of 1991 was the reduction of Japanese outward direct investment flows by a third. From 1987 to 1990, purchases of overseas assets (direct investment, investment in shares and bonds) amounted to about US$100 billion a year. The decline in direct investment in 1991 was accompanied by a fall in net purchases of shares, down from US$17.9 billion in 1989 to US$6.2 billion in 1990 and to US$3.6 billion in 1991. In 1991, for the first time in eleven years, the net balance on capital movements showed a deficit of US$36.6 billion.

Despite this turnaround -- in terms of direct investment proper -- in its capital balance, Japan is still a net investor, with an annual balance of about US$30 billion. The overall situation, characterised by a large disparity between the size of the stock of foreign investment in Japan (cumulative flows of which are estimated at US$18.4 billion between 1950 and 1990, see Table 37), and the size of the stock of outward investment (estimated at US$310.8 billion at end-1990, see Table 38), seems unlikely to change in the near future [16].

Direct investment inflows to Japan are characterised by a strong presence of US firms (46.5 per cent of cumulative flows in 1990), followed by European firms (27.1 per cent of cumulative flows, of which 7.9 per cent by firms from *the Netherlands*). In 1990, the pattern of investment inflows was reversed, with Europe accounting for nearly 50 per cent and the *United States* for nearly 24 per cent. Firms from the Netherlands were particularly heavy investors. Inward investment in Japan is directed essentially to three sectors of activity: machinery (33.5 per cent of cumulative flows in 1990), chemicals (17.1 per cent) and the distribution sector (16 per cent).

Japanese outward investment also shows the predominance of the *United States* as an investment destination, with 45.9 per cent of outward flows in 1990 and 42 per cent of cumulative flows up to 1990. However, a very sharp fall in Japanese investment in the US in 1991 may be noted. The marked fall in investment in the United States from fiscal 1990 was offset by the brisk growth of investment in Europe, particularly in the *United Kingdom*. Europe thus became the second main area, after the United States and ahead of Asia, in which Japanese firms are stepping up their investment. They are investing in the electronics sector in the broad sense. According to JETRO, of the 592 subsidiaries set up in Europe in 1990, 94 were electronics companies, 48 industrial capital goods companies and 42 computer and office automation companies. Most of these companies (131 out of a total of 184) together with 22 companies in the automobile sector (out of a total of 39 in Europe) are concentrated in the United Kingdom, *France* and *Germany*.

Table 37. **Foreign direct investment in Japan by geographical origin**[1]

Million dollars and percentages

	1988 fiscal year		1989 fiscal year		1990 fiscal year		Cumulated flows 1950-90	
	Total	Percentage	Total	Percentage	Total	Percentage	Total	Percentage
United States	1 774	54.7	1 642	57.4	664	23.9	8 574	46.5
Canada	22	0.7	35	1.2	142	5.1	329	1.8
North America	1 796	55.4	1 677	58.6	806	29.0	8 903	48.3
United Kingdom	112	3.5	81	2.8	54	1.9	653	3.5
Germany	195	6.0	144	5.0	259	9.3	949	5.1
France	27	0.8	25	0.9	74	2.6	301	1.6
Switzerland	273	8.4	87	3.1	142	5.1	1 157	6.3
Netherlands	157	4.8	248	8.7	734	26.4	1 464	7.9
Others	52	1.6	40	1.4	98	3.5	175	0.9
Total Europe	817	25.2	625	21.9	1 361	48.9	4 999	27.1
Hong Kong	44	1.4	63	2.2	62	2.2	515	2.8
Others	586	18.0	495	17.3	548	19.7	4 014	21.8
Total	3 243	100.0	2 860	100.0	2 778	100.0	18 432	100.0

1. Figures not comparable with those of Table 33.
Source: Ministry of Finance, Japan.

Table 38. **Japanese foreign direct investment by geographical destination**[1]
Million dollars and percentages

	1988 fiscal year		1989 fiscal year		1990 fiscal year		Cumulated flows 1951-90	
	Total	Percentage	Total	Percentage	Total	Percentage	Total	Percentage
United States	21 701	46.2	32 540	48.2	26 128	45.9	130 528	42.0
Canada	626	1.3	1 361	2.0	1 063	1.9	5 656	1.8
North America	22 328	47.5	33 902	50.2	27 192	47.8	136 185	43.8
United Kingdom	3 956	8.4	5 238	7.8	6 805	12.0	22 598	7.3
Germany	408	0.9	1 083	1.6	1 241	2.2	4 689	1.5
Netherlands	2 358	5.0	4 547	6.7	2 743	4.8	12 815	4.1
France	463	1.0	1 135	1.7	1 257	2.2	4 156	1.3
Europe	9 116	19.4	14 808	21.9	14 294	25.1	59 265	19.1
Central and South America	6 428	13.7	5 238	7.8	3 628	6.4	40 483	13.0
Asia	5 569	11.8	8 238	12.2	7 054	12.4	47 519	15.3
Australia	2 413	5.1	4 256	6.3	3 669	6.4	16 062	5.2
Total	47 022	100.0	67 540	100.0	56 911	100.0	310 808	100.0

1. Figures not comparable with those of table 32.
Source: Ministry of Finance, Japan.

European Community

The European Community accounts for nearly half of the outward direct investment by the OECD countries. Its share of outward investment, which had been fairly stable, increased at the end of the period (see Table 32). However, the fall in investment by the *United Kingdom*, which began in 1990 and continued in 1991, as well as a fall in that by *Germany* and *France* in 1991, could reverse this trend.

The European Community's share in inward direct investment in OECD countries has been growing for several years. In view of the trends of outward direct investment by the *United States* and *Japan* that have already been examined, this growth could be confirmed for 1991.

Overall, the European Community is a net exporter of direct investment (a total of US$149 billion of outflows from 1981 to 1990, compared with outflows of US$182.5 billion for *Japan* and inflows of US$178.2 billion for the *United States*). Particularly large net investors in the 1981-90 period are *Germany* (US$68.7 billion net outflows), the *United Kingdom* except in 1990 and 1991 (US$66.3 billion net outflows) and *France* (US$42.5 billion). These three countries together with the *Netherlands* together accounted for 80 per cent of EC outward investment in 1990.

The breakdown by country of destination in the EC of US and Japanese investment (Table 39) shows that the preferred locations are the *United Kingdom* (31.8 per cent of the stock of US investment in Europe in 1990 and 38.1 per cent of the cumulative flows of investment from Japan to Europe), the *Netherlands* (11.2 and 21.6 per cent respectively), *Germany* (13.6 and 7.9 per cent respectively) and *France* (8.4 and 7 per cent).

Table 39. **Shares of EC countries and of Europe in foreign direct investments originating in the US and in Japan**

1990, Stocks and flows in percentages

	Investments from the US		Investments from Japan	
	Stocks 1990	Flows 1990	Stocks 1990	Flows 1990
Share of Europe in total	48.4	43.4	19.1	25.1
Breakdown:				
Europe	100.0	100.0	100.0	100.0
EC total	84.7	62.8		
of which:				
United Kingdom	31.8	3.6	38.1	47.6
Germany	13.6	5.6	7.9	8.7
Netherlands	11.2	17.8	21.6	19.2
France	8.4	10.5	7.0	8.8
Other European countries	15.3	37.2	..	..

Source: US Department of Commerce, *Survey of Current Business*, Aug. 1991; Ministry of Finance, Japan.

The pattern of investment between *Europe* and the *United States* seems to have attained a certain equilibrium, since the ratio of stocks of European assets in the United States to stocks of US assets in Europe was 1.26 in 1990; for flows the ratio was 1.12 [17]. In contrast, the situation with regard to *Europe* and *Japan* is very different, since European assets in Japan in 1990 represented only one tenth (8.4 per cent) of Japanese assets in Europe, and the ratio of European flows to Japanese flows was only 9.5 per cent [18].

A large proportion of European direct investment, particularly EC investment, consists of intra-European flows. For example, in 1990 the share of total investment in *France* originating in other EC countries was 54.5 per cent, compared with 13 per cent for US investment, 12 per cent for Japanese investment and 20.5 per cent for the rest of the world. Similarly, according to a survey by the French Ministry of Finance in 1990, nearly half (47.7 per cent) of the employees of French subsidiaries were in EC countries (compared with 21.5 per cent for the rest of the OECD, of which 13.4 per cent in the *United States*). Less recent data for other countries confirm the relative growth of intra-EC flows (from 50 to over 60 per cent for both outflows and inflows), with the exception of the *United Kingdom* -- the country that is the most "open" to overseas investment and where other EC countries account for only a quarter of outward and inward direct investment flows.

In 1991 French firms remained very active in the merger and acquisitions market. This market also slowed to a certain extent during the first half of the year; the total amount of mergers and acquisitions declined by 64 per cent compared to the first half of 1990 (855 acquisitions of a total amount of US$23.3 billion, as opposed to 1 431 acquisitions of a total amount of US$64.4 billion in 1990). Against this background of an overall decline in mergers and acquisitions, French firms led the field, with 119 acquisitions totalling US$5.14 billion, followed by US firms (113 acquisitions totalling US$3.19 billion), UK firms (123 acquisitions totalling US$1.7 billion compared with US$11.4 billion in 1990) and Japanese firms (US$2.66 billion).

Central and eastern Europe

The needs for foreign direct investment in the central and east European countries are multiple: for the restructuring of industry, the transfer of technology and know-how, and the purchase of firms that are being privatised. Despite these needs, foreign direct investment flows have been relatively modest.

Total foreign direct investment, which in 1991 amounted to US$2.7 billion in central and eastern Europe, increased by US$1.4 billion in *Hungary* alone [19]. The number of joint ventures increased rapidly between December 1990 and end-September 1991 (Table 40). Hungary has the largest number of projects -- 10 600, of which nearly 5 000 new ones -- followed by *Poland*, and then the *CSFR* and the *CIS*. In terms of the amount of capital invested as recorded in September 1991, the order of ranking is slightly different since the CIS was set to receive 62 per cent of the cumulative amount, ahead of Hungary with 25 per cent.

It thus seems that the rate at which new projects are being started did not slow in 1991. However, the proportion of projects that actually get off the ground is on average about 50 per cent. Because of the time that it takes to implement them, and the administrative difficulties involved, firms regard such projects as protracted and hazardous undertakings. The size of projects and the western participation in them is not very large either. Some estimates put the average foreign stake at US$0.8 million per project in *Hungary* (January 1990) to US$1.6 million in the CIS and US$0.1 million in *Poland* [20]. Furthermore,

Table 40. **Joint venture projects in central and eastern Europe and in the CIS**

	Number of projects			Registered western capital (million dollars)			
	Dec. 1989	Dec. 1990	Sept. 1991	Oct. 1989	Dec. 1990	Sept. 1991	(%)
Hungary	4 600	5 693	10 600	360	1 000	2 300	25.2
Poland	918	2 799	5 000	80	353	670	7.3
Czech and Slovak Federal Republic	50	1 600	4 000	85	..	500	5.5
CIS	1 274	2 905	3 900	1 700	3 400	5 650	62.0
Total	6 842	12 997	23 500	2 225	4 753	9 120	100.0
Bulgaria	35	140	800[1]	..	..	210[2]	..
Romania	5	1 501	4 196[1]	40	40	260[2]	..

1. On 1st July 1991.
2. On 1st August 1991.
Source: UN/EC.

the case of the former Soviet Union, it fell from an average of US$3.9 million per project in 1987 to US$1.2 million in 1990, and similar trends are evident in Hungary, where investment has increasingly gone into trade and retail services.

Nearly 60 per cent of foreign investment in **Hungary**, the **CIS** and **Poland** comes from western Europe. **Germany** is the leading investor with more than 11 per cent of the total amount invested. Among non-European investors, the **United States** has the same major role.

Despite the recent announcement of projects involving western firms (e.g. in automobiles, food-processing and chemicals) the present economic situation does not give firms a strong incentive to invest in eastern Europe. The recession in 1991 was deeper than forecast (with output down by 12 per cent on average), and it is particularly the uncertain future of central and eastern European economies that causes private investors to hesitate. Even Hungary, which is an attractive investment location, saw

that have been undertaken in eastern Europe are taking time to bear fruit, the social consensus is still fragile, and the legal and commercial framework and practice for investment are still being developed. Lastly, it seems very difficult to establish with any certainty the components of demand and the factors that would permit supply to pick up, if only because of the lack of data on the private sector and on small and new enterprises.

Newly Industrialised Economies of Asia (NIEs)

Following the pattern at world level, since 1985 direct investment flows in NIEs have increased more rapidly than trade (see Tables 41 and 42) [21]. Outward foreign direct investment by Korea, Taiwan and probably Hong Kong, have recently exceeded foreign investment inflows, reflecting the internationalisation of the Asian NIEs.

Incoming foreign direct investment flows to **Korea** increased considerably in 1991 (US$1.3 billion, compared

Table 41. **Inward foreign direct investment to the Asian NIEs by origin**
Million US dollars

	1986	1987	1988	1989	1990	1991
In Korea						
From:						
United States	72	252	295	328	317	296
Japan	198	504	667	461	236	226
Europe	65	189	282	220	236	823
Others	25	105	38	81	14	250
Total	360	1 050	1 282	1 090	803	1 395
In Hong Kong[1]						
From:						
United States	..	676	155	40	75	..
Japan	..	622	174	190	130	..
Europe	..	414	111	100	50	..
Others	..	468	204	130	47	..
Total	..	2 180	644	460	302	..
In Singapore[2]						
From:						
United States	203	257	292	265	582	561
Japan	228	285	340	276	391	415
Europe	100	136	175	280	240	398
Others	133	9	5	10	11	56
Total	665	686	812	829	1 225	1 430
In Taiwan						
From:						
United States	138	414	134	381	540	612
Japan	253	399	431	667	827	618
Europe	187	224	205	531	348	221
Others	190	380	399	839	586	329
Total	768	1 417	1 169	2 418	2 301	1 780

1. Measured by the evolution of stocks.
2. Manufacturing (excluding petroleum refining).
Source: National sources.

Table 42. **Outward foreign direct investments by Asian NIEs**
Million US dollars

	1988	1989	1990	1991
Taiwan				
Official funds	218	930	1 552	1 778
Korea				
Approved funds	479	943	1 625	1 606
Realised funds	224	564	959	1 125

Source: National sources; Korea: Ministry of Finance; Taiwan: Investment Development Commission.

with US$800 million in 1990); there was a particularly marked increase in investment in the manufacturing sector (from US$500 million to 1 billion). The largest increases were in the chemical and petrochemical sectors, which accounted for nearly half of total inflows. The growth of investment from European countries was particularly steep, while US and Japanese investment fell slightly.

Outward Korean investment (approved funds, rather than realised projects) exceeded inward direct investment in 1990 and 1991. Outward flows, while rising rapidly since 1988, stagnated in 1991; nevertheless, the number of projects rose rapidly in 1991, amounting to US$1.1 billion (realised projects). Slightly less than half of this investment was directed to the United States and Canada, but the number of projects carried out in Europe has increased in recent years. Rising wages and labour shortages have prompted an increasing number of Korean firms to move their production to South-East Asia (particularly Indonesia and Malaysia), which have attracted slightly more than one-third (in terms of stocks) of Korean outward investment.

The slowdown of foreign direct investment in *Hong Kong* was confirmed in 1990 for the second year running. Measured in terms of flows, foreign direct investment declined by 66 per cent on 1989. In terms of cumulative investment, Japan was the largest investor (32 per cent), followed by the United States (31 per cent), the United Kingdom (11 per cent) and China (7 per cent). The electronics industry accounts for 30 per cent of the stock of foreign investment, followed by electrical engineering (11 per cent) and textiles and clothing (11 per cent). In terms of outward flows, Hong Kong has become a major investor in Asia. According to Chinese statistics, Hong Kong firms account for 65 per cent of foreign investment in China. They are the second largest foreign investors in Indonesia (Japan being the largest), third in Korea, Taiwan and Thailand, and fourth in Malaysia and the Philippines.

The growth of foreign investment in *Singapore* continued in 1991 (US$1.4 billion compared with US$1.2 billion in 1990). Foreign investment accounted for the bulk of manufacturing investment (domestic investment was only US$275 million in 1991). The largest increase was in investment from Europe which almost tripled. The United States is still the largest investor, followed by Japan. The electronics industry attracts the bulk of investment (42.4 per cent in 1991), followed by the engineering sector (12.8 per cent) and chemicals (11 per cent).

Outward direct investment flows from Singapore attained a record level in 1991 -- US$580 million. The Economic Development Board has estimated the stock of private Singaporean outward investment at US$2.4 billion, more than half of which (55 per cent) in the Pacific Asian countries, 25 per cent in Europe and 20 per cent in the United States. These estimates do not however take account of investments and acquisitions by State enterprises. In 1991, two government agencies acquired large stakes (US$819 million) in a holding group active in the hotel sector in New Zealand.

In *Taiwan*, the decline in inward foreign direct investment that had already begun in 1990 became more marked in 1991. Investment by Japan and Europe fell, while that by the United States increased. The decline hit the services sector in particular (down by 50 per cent), while investment in industry was hardly affected (down by 2 per cent). In industry the pattern varied from one industry to the next: investment flows to the electronics and engineering industries increased sharply, but those to the intermediate goods industries (petrochemicals, iron and steel and non-ferrous metals) fell.

Official sources indicate an increase in Taiwanese outward investment flows in 1991, but they do not reflect actual trends as shown in the statistics published by the host countries, which indicate cumulative investment of US$12 billion between 1987 and 1991 inclusive. Estimates of the Taiwanese presence in China are conflicting: the Taiwanese authorities estimate that 2 500 firms have invested a total amount of US$0.7 billion, whereas the Chinese authorities estimate that 3 000 Taiwanese firms have invested US$2 billion. A survey carried out by the government showed that the profit ratio of the Chinese operations of Taiwanese firms was higher than the profit ratio of their operations in Taiwan, and that most firms were planning to increase the scale of their Chinese subsidiaries, which import over half of their inputs from Taiwan and export their output to third countries.

Chapter III

TRENDS IN PERFORMANCE

A. Productivity

Labour productivity in manufacturing industries increased in most OECD countries during 1991. When measured as the change in the volume of production over employment, the rate of growth of labour productivity in manufacturing was 1.7 per cent for the OECD area as a whole, down from 1.8 per cent the year before (Table 43), and represented the slowest growth in labour productivity in a period of over ten years. This rate of growth reflects the fact that labour shedding in manufacturing occurred at a faster rate than the fall in manufacturing production which OECD countries experienced during 1991.

Table 43. **Apparent labour productivity in manufacturing**
Production/employment[1]
Percentage change from preceding year

	1985	1986	1987	1988	1989	1990	1991
United States[3]	4.0	4.7	5.3	4.8	2.5	3.2	1.8
Canada	3.6	–0.9	–4.9	4.5	–0.3	3.8	8.1
Japan	2.7	–1.2	5.0	5.8	4.8	1.7	–0.2
Denmark	–2.6	4.9	–0.3	5.0	2.3	0.5	5.5
France	2.4	2.8	4.2	6.6	3.6	1.3	0.5
Germany	3.9	0.7	1.2	4.7	5.7	0.9	1.7
Greece[4, 5]	3.8	–0.8	–0.7	3.9	2.1	–1.0	5.3
Ireland[2]	9.5	4.5	11.3	12.2	9.0	1.8	2.6
Italy[4, 6, 10]	3.7	5.8	3.8	6.1	4.5	–2.7	–3.0
Luxembourg	7.0	0.5	0.9	12.1	8.1	0.3	1.3
Netherlands	2.4	1.1	–0.3	5.1	2.8	1.9	0.4
Portugal[2, 7, 9]	4.3	11.3	8.0	3.4	4.2	7.7	4.2
Spain[4]	5.1	1.7	3.3	1.2	0.4	–3.4	2.0
United Kingdom[8]	3.4	3.7	6.7	6.3	4.3	–0.5	0.5
Austria	3.1	3.0	1.4	8.0	5.7	6.7	3.1
Finland	5.0	2.7	7.7	7.6	1.4	–0.3	0.3
Norway	1.5	–1.3	3.6	3.2	6.6	3.4	3.1
Sweden	3.3	1.0	1.3	0.6	2.4	0.6	3.1
Switzerland	3.7	3.1	1.3	9.4	1.7	1.3	2.9
Turkey[2, 9]	5.7	11.9	7.5	–1.8	2.0	8.2	11.6
Australia[4]	5.8	–0.4	3.0	2.6	2.5	1.3	0.7
New Zealand	–4.6	1.5	–2.9	3.0	11.8	–0.3	2.0
Total OECD[2, 9]	3.5	2.8	4.3	5.7	3.7	1.8	1.7

1. Figures do not, in general, cover total employment but only employees. Furthermore, for a number of countries the sample refers to firms exceeding a minimum size threshold.
2. 1991 figures for the underlying employment indices are based on the first three quarters only.
3. The underlying employment indices exclude ISIC 385.
4. Employment indices from *Main Economic Indicators*.
5. Employment indices based on enterprises employing at least 10 persons.
6. The underlying employment indices include construction.
7. The underlying production indices exclude ISIC 322, 332 and 342.
8. Underlying production indices exclude ISIC 353, 354 and parts of 351; they include ISIC 230 and 290.
9. 1991 figures for the underlying production indices are based on the first three quarters only.
10. Employment indices from a sample survey taken in the first week without public holidays in each quarter.
Source: OECD, *Indicators of Industrial Activity; Main Economic Indicators;* Industry Division.

Table 44. **Productivity in the business sector**
Percentage changes at annual rate

	Total factor productivity[1]			Labour productivity[2]			Capital productivity		
	1960-73	1973-79	1979-90	1960-73	1973-79	1979-90	1960-73	1973-79	1979-90
United States	1.6	−0.4	0.2	2.2	0.0	0.5	0.2	−1.3	−0.7
Canada	2.0	0.8	0.0	2.8	1.5	1.2	0.6	−0.5	−2.1
Japan	5.9	1.4	2.0	8.6	2.9	3.0	−2.5	−3.4	−1.3
Belgium	3.9	1.4	1.5	5.2	2.8	2.4	0.6	−1.8	−0.7
Denmark	2.8	1.1	1.4	4.3	2.6	2.3	−1.0	−2.4	−0.7
France	4.0	1.7	1.8	5.4	3.0	2.7	0.9	−1.0	−0.2
Germany	2.6	1.8	0.8	4.5	3.1	1.6	−1.4	−1.0	−0.7
Greece	5.7	1.5	−0.2	8.8	3.3	0.7	−1.2	−2.8	−2.3
Italy	4.4	2.1	1.4	6.3	3.0	2.0	0.4	0.4	0.0
Netherlands	3.1	1.5	0.9	4.8	2.8	1.5	−0.4	−1.0	−0.5
Spain	3.3	1.0	2.0	6.0	3.3	3.0	−3.6	−5.1	−0.9
United Kingdom	2.3	0.6	1.6	3.6	1.6	2.1	−0.6	−1.5	0.4
Austria	3.3	1.2	0.9	5.8	3.2	1.9	−2.0	−3.1	−1.5
Finland	3.2	1.5	2.5	4.9	3.2	3.6	0.0	−1.8	0.3
Sweden	2.7	0.3	0.7	4.1	1.5	1.5	−0.8	−2.3	−1.1
Switzerland	2.0	−0.4	0.5	3.2	0.8	1.1	−1.4	−3.7	−1.1
Australia	1.6	0.8	0.4	2.7	2.2	0.9	−0.4	−1.7	−0.7
New Zealand	0.9	−1.8	0.4	1.6	−1.2	1.4	−0.7	−3.2	−1.4
OECD Europe	3.2	1.4	1.3	5.0	2.7	2.1	−0.6	−1.4	−0.4
OECD	2.8	0.5	0.8	4.1	1.4	1.5	−0.5	−1.6	−0.7

1. TFP growth is equal to a weighted average of the growth in labour and capital productivity. The sample-period averages for capital and labour shares are used as weights.
2. Output per employed person.
Source: OECD, *Economic Outlook No. 51*.

In the **United States**, manufacturing labour productivity increased by 1.8 per cent in 1991, continuing a trend that started in 1987. This rate of growth resulted from a 2.3 per cent decline in the index of manufacturing production and a 4 per cent drop in manufacturing employment. The 8.1 per cent productivity growth rate in **Canada** was the second highest in the OECD and significantly higher than any of the productivity growth rates experienced in that country since 1985. It reflects a very sharp drop in manufacturing employment (of the order of 14 per cent), more than double the decline in production. **Japan** is one of the few OECD countries that registered a modest productivity decline in 1991, a reflection of manufacturing production growing at a (marginally) slower rate than employment (2.1 per cent as against 2.3 per cent). It was the first year since 1986 that a drop in labour productivity was registered, a period during which, in contrast to the declines in production in most OECD countries, manufacturing production has systematically grown faster than employment.

Labour productivity grew in all **European Community** countries during 1991, with the exception of **Italy**. Rates of growth were particularly strong in **Denmark, Greece** and **Portugal**, and less so in **Spain, Ireland** and **Luxembourg**. The underlying reasons varied: employment declined in all these countries except Ireland, while production declined only in Greece, Luxembourg and Spain, but at a slower rate than employment. Productivity in **Germany** rose as a result of production increases outstripping employment gains, while the rise in productivity in the **United Kingdom** and in **France** reflected manufacturing employment losses that were more important than the declines in production. All the European countries that are not members of the EC registered productivity gains, with the highest rates of growth in **Turkey** and the lowest in **Finland**, whose decline in manufacturing production of over 10 per cent was more than matched by manufacturing employment losses. Finally, labour productivity increased in **Australia** and **New Zealand**. In both of these countries, manufacturing employment declined by between 6 and 7 per cent, while the index of manufacturing production fell by between 5 and 6 per cent.

In order to put these recent trends in manufacturing labour productivity in context, Table 44 shows longer term trends in labour, capital and total factor productivity for

Box 13. Productivity: Can we trust the numbers?

Productivity is the economic return obtained on input resources. Its development is the foundation of material prosperity. Its continuing growth has allowed reduction in working hours, multiplication in real wages, higher living standards, improved public health and public education. The long-term sustainability of environmental improvements also depend on continued productivity improvements. Given the importance of productivity gains in realising the fruits of economic growth and development, productivity figures are one of the most closely watched economic indicators. Nevertheless, their derivation is plagued with a host of methodological problems, with the implication that productivity measures should be interpreted with caution.

Attention has recently focused on the measurement of productivity in connection with the resolution of the so-called "Solow Paradox". Named after the Nobel-prize winner economist R.Solow, the paradox involves two apparently contradictory phenomena: that of the recent productivity slowdown, with productivity growth rates failing to recover to their postwar levels, and the belief that technological advance has recently accelerated. The paradox, if true, raises a basic question about the ability of industrial economies to translate an improved technological capacity into measurable increases in productivity and economic growth. The consensus around the resolution to the paradox seems to be that productivity mismeasurement accounts for only a small part of the explanation. The productivity slowdown can be interpreted in part by cyclical factors, and in part by re-interpreting the statement about technological change as one pertaining to the potential of recent technical advance which, if managed correctly, foreshadows future growth in productivity [1]. The debate did nevertheless bring to the fore some serious measurement problems associated with productivity, together with evidence that these have grown worse in recent years. In particular, and since productivity is the return on input resources, discussion has centered on whether either inputs (labour, capital, technology) or output are being measured correctly, and whether as a result there is an increasing tendency for changes in productivity to elude the statistics.

In terms of the *measurement of inputs*, labour productivity figures are sensitive to different conventions in the measurement of labour. Issues such as different skill levels, the use of persons employed vs. hours worked, adjustments for full-time equivalence and for unpaid family workers can all influence the calculation of labour productivity and bias international comparisons. The most serious problems however lie with the measurement of capital inputs and of the impact of technology in the context of calculations of capital productivity and total factor productivity. The measurement of capital stock in most OECD countries reflects the use of quite different and arbitrary average service lives and survival functions for machinery and equipment. To the extent that these are wrong, there is a systematic measurement error. Furthermore, conventional capital stock measures may seriously underestimate the nature and magnitude of both physical and intangible capital (built up through investments in R&D, training, or work organisation) utilised by firms in many sectors in the economy. This problem is likely to be more serious to the extent that cost-reducing and productivity-enhancing inter-industry "spillover" effects from R&D are widespread but not accounted for in traditional productivity measurement. Finally, the definition and measurement of capital stock may underestimate the effect of technical change on output and productivity growth, when the "true" growth rate of technological change that is embodied in new equipemnt has been increasing. Keeping track of different vintages of capital embodying different levels of knowledge, by explicitly considering the link between the rate of technological progress and capital scrapping rates, would be necessary for measuring accurately the effect of technological change on productivity growth.

In terms of the *measurement of output*, much of the source of the measurement problem concerns capturing quality changes brought about by innovative activity when calculating constant price output series. Quality improvements are becoming more important as factors of competition. This makes it difficult to separate the part of price increases due to inflation with that due to improved quality, a problem particularly serious in the service sectors and likely to grow as production is growing more and more differentiated and service-oriented. The conventional price index approach to calculating deflators for output fails to capture quality changes, thus understating the output and productivity growth rate of industries experiencing rapid technological progress (such as computers or telecommunications), as well as the output and productivity growth of industries heavily adopting these technological advances (such as financial services, medical and health services). While the introduction of quality-adjusted price deflators for certain industries such as computers in a few OECD countries addresses part of the problem, at the same time it presents new problems associated with inconsistencies in the construction of various broadly-based price indices and with reduced international comparability. Finally, a related problem concerns the measurement of public-sector productivity. In many countries, productivity growth in non-market government activities is set to zero in official statistics; alternatively, output is measured by the cost of inputs, thus rendering productivity calculations meaningless.

---

1. For an extensive discussion of the "Solow paradox" and of measurement issues in productivity, see OECD (1991), *Technology and Productivity: The Challenge for Economic Policy*, Paris.

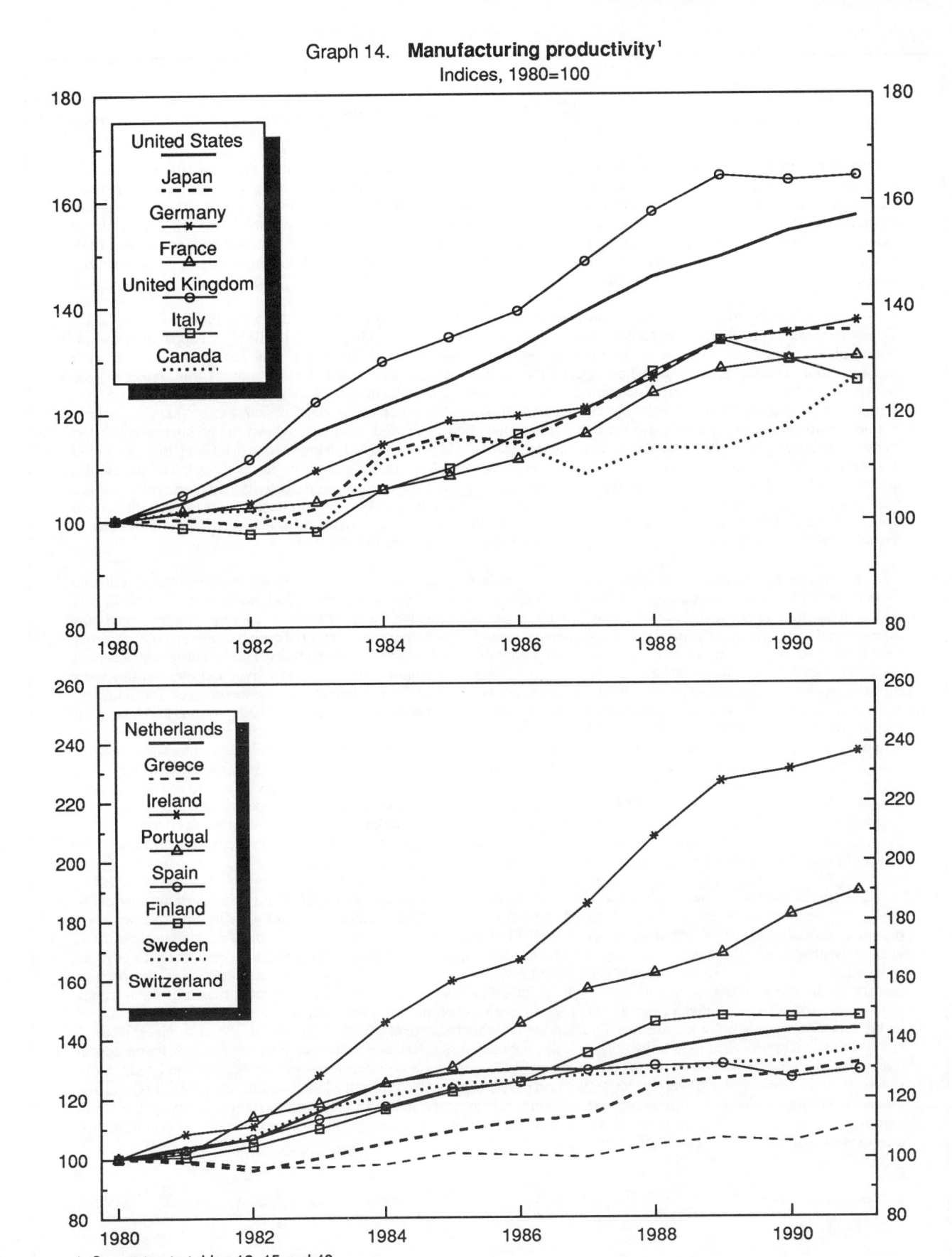

Graph 14. **Manufacturing productivity**[1]
Indices, 1980=100

- United States
- Japan
- Germany
- France
- United Kingdom
- Italy
- Canada

- Netherlands
- Greece
- Ireland
- Portugal
- Spain
- Finland
- Sweden
- Switzerland

1. See notes to tables 12, 15 and 43.
Source: OECD, *Indicators of Industrial Activity, Main Economic Indicators;* Industry Division.

the business sector as a whole (covering manufacturing, energy and service industries). The table shows that for every OECD country, average annual growth rates in labour and in total factor productivity (a weighted average of labour and capital productivity, with labour and capital income shares used as weights) were highest in the 1960-73 period, before declining significantly in the 1973-79 period. The same pattern is true of capital productivity, although the negative growth rates in the early period in most countries reflect the high investment rates and the building-up of the capital stock. Productivity staged a modest recovery in most countries during the 1979-90 period, with the OECD-wide annual growth of total factor productivity increasing from half a percentage point to nearly 1 per cent per annum. Productivity gains however remained more limited in the 1980s than during the 1960s and early 1970s. This slowdown in productivity at a time of rapid technical advances has long puzzled analysts and is known as the "Solow Paradox". The resolution to the paradox has called upon an number of factors, including measurement issues in productivity calculations (see Box 13).

Within manufacturing, the longer term growth of productivity has varied greatly amongst OECD countries. Graph 14 shows the evolution of productivity indices in manufacturing from 1980 to 1991. In the G7 group of economies, manufacturing productivity rose fastest in the *United Kingdom* and in the *United States*, and was in 1991 about 65 per cent and 55 per cent respectively higher than in 1980. The other four countries of the G7 group all had similar manufacturing productivity increases, ending in 1991 with productivity levels that were 25 per cent to 40 per cent higher than in 1980. It is also noteworthy that of all seven countries, *Canada* has exhibited the most fluctuation in productivity growth during the period in question, while Canada, *Italy* and *Japan* all experienced a decline in productivity in the early 1980s.

Outside the G7 group, *Ireland* has experienced strong productivity growth in manufacturing during the 1980s, more than doubling its productivity index between 1980 and in 1991. As a result of its only slightly less rapid productivity increase, *Portugal's* manufacturing producivity level in 1991 was 90 per cent higher than in 1980. In these two countries, a clear catching-up process can be observed, as they started in 1970 with productivity levels much below of the OECD average and have moved much closer to it. Productivity increased strongly also on *Finland* and in the *Netherlands*, although in both these countries it stagnated after 1988 and even declined somewhat in the early 1990s. Slightly slower productivity growth rates in *Switzerland, Sweden and Spain* led to productivity levels in 1990 that were about 30 per cent higher than in 1980. Manufacturing productivity in *Greece* declined through most of the 1980s and was in 1991 barely higher than the 1980 level.

B. Profitability

Whether measured as the share of capital income in value added, or as the rate of return to capital, profitability in the business sector declined in 1991 (see Table 45). Capital income shares fell by an estimated 1.2 per cent in the OECD area as a whole. The decline was particularly pronounced in *Canada, Finland, Switzerland, Australia* and *New Zealand* (more than 5 per cent), and less so in *Italy*, the *Netherlands*, the *United Kingdom*, and *Austria*. The *United States* and *Germany* experienced declines at about the OECD average, while capital income shares fell marginally in *Japan* and *Belgium*. They held steady in *France,* increased slightly in *Spain,* and registered a strong increase in *Denmark, Sweden* and especially *Greece*.

Changes in capital income shares reflect changes in the share of income going to labour. As the latter depends on the combined effect of the evolution in compensation to employees, employment and production in the business sector, the factors underlying the shifts in capital income shares can differ from country to country. In *Canada*, for example, the sharp decline in capital income shares in 1991 occurred despite a drop in employment exceeding that of production and was due to the resilience of wages. In contrast, in *Finland* the 10.5 per cent decline in capital income shares was due to the sharp decline in industrial production. In the countries that had an exceptional increase in capital income shares, the 13.8 per cent increase in *Greece* and the 5 per cent increase in *Sweden* were both due to declines in the wage bill that outpaced changes in industrial production.

Rates of return to capital also declined during 1991 in the OECD area. The relatively modest overall decline (1.3 per cent) masks important differences betwen countries, with *Finland, Sweden, Switzerland, Australia* and *New Zealand* experiencing rates of return that were at least 10 per cent below their 1990 levels, and a number of other countries (*Canada,* the *United Kingdom, Austria, Belgium, Italy* and the *Netherlands*) registering also significant declines. Rates of return increased only in *Denmark, Spain* and especially strongly in *Greece*.

Capital income shares and rates of return are by their construction influenced in part by the same variables. Both are calculated as ratios, where the numerator is gross operating surplus, obtained as the difference between value added and the compensation of employees. While however capital income shares are derived by dividing gross operating surplus by GDP at factor cost, rates of return are calculated as the ratio of gross operating surplus to the capital stock. Changes in the latter due to growth in investment or due to higher replacement or scrapping rates may outweigh the effect of movements in gross operating surplus. Furthermore, both capital income shares and business rates of return are indicators that need to be treated and interpreted with caution. Differing country practices

Table 45. **Profitability in the business sector**[1]

	Capital income shares[2]							Rates of return[2]						
	Av. ann. growth 1970-90	Average for 1980-90	1990	1991	1992	Change 1990-91	Change 1991-92	Av. ann. growth 1970-90	Average for 1980-90	1990	1991	1992	Change 1990-91	Change 1991-92
United States	0.5	32.5	33.3	32.9	33.2	-1.2	0.9	0.3	15.3	16.6	16.4	17.2	-1.6	4.9
Canada	0.1	36.0	33.9	32.0	31.6	-5.6	-1.3	1.2	16.9	16.7	16.0	15.7	-4.3	-1.4
Japan	-1.3	31.9	32.9	32.8	32.1	-0.4	-2.0	-2.6	15.2	15.9	15.7	14.9	-0.9	-5.1
Belgium/Lux.	-0.3	32.6	36.7	36.3	36.4	-0.9	0.2	-0.1	12.7	14.5	14.0	13.9	-3.1	-1.2
Denmark	0.9	33.0	37.5	38.6	39.5	3.1	2.3	-0.4	9.3	10.4	10.7	10.9	2.1	2.1
France	0.5	32.3	36.6	36.6	37.1	0.0	1.5	0.0	12.3	14.2	14.2	14.4	-0.1	1.5
Germany	0.2	34.5	37.4	36.8	36.5	-1.4	-0.8	-0.3	13.4	14.6	14.2	13.9	-2.1	-2.5
Greece	-1.8	32.1	30.4	34.6	37.3	13.8	7.6	-4.6	11.5	9.3	10.8	11.7	15.9	8.8
Italy	0.8	36.7	37.3	36.4	36.9	-2.4	1.5	0.0	13.1	13.3	13.1	13.3	-1.6	1.6
Netherlands	1.2	35.4	40.9	40.0	40.2	-2.3	0.6	0.9	15.2	17.8	17.4	17.5	-2.2	0.3
Spain	0.6	36.5	41.4	42.0	42.0	1.5	-0.1	-0.9	17.9	20.2	20.6	20.2	1.9	-1.6
United Kingdom	0.0	29.1	28.4	27.4	28.9	-3.7	5.4	-0.3	9.0	9.6	9.2	9.9	-3.6	7.6
Austria	0.4	33.8	36.3	39.5	39.3	-2.4	-0.4	-1.1	11.2	11.5	11.1	10.9	-3.4	-1.9
Finland	-0.9	30.6	28.7	25.7	29.4	-10.5	14.4	-1.8	8.9	8.3	6.9	7.6	-17.9	10.7
Sweden	0.4	29.3	29.7	31.1	33.7	5.0	8.4	-0.4	9.2	9.2	10.3	11.5	-12.2	11.3
Switzerland	-1.9	20.7	21.3	19.3	19.3	-9.6	0.1	-2.5	7.5	7.6	6.8	6.7	-11.4	-1.0
Australia	0.1	36.4	37.2	34.7	35.8	-6.9	3.2	-0.6	12.1	12.7	11.1	11.4	-12.7	3.0
New Zealand	0.6	34.3	42.1	39.9	41.2	-5.3	3.3	0.4	12.8	17.1	14.8	14.9	-13.4	0.8
Total of above OECD countries	..	..	34.0	33.6	33.7	-1.2	0.3	..	..	15.1	14.9	15.0	-1.3	0.7

1. Figures for 1990 onwards are partly estimates and projections.
2. Capital income shares are calculated as the ratio of gross operating surplus (value added minus compensation to employees) to GDP at factor cost. Rates of return on capital are calculated as the ratio of gross operating surplus to the capital stock. For more detailed definitions see source.

Source: OECD, Economic Outlook No. 51.

Graph 15. **Rates of return in the business sector**
Percentages

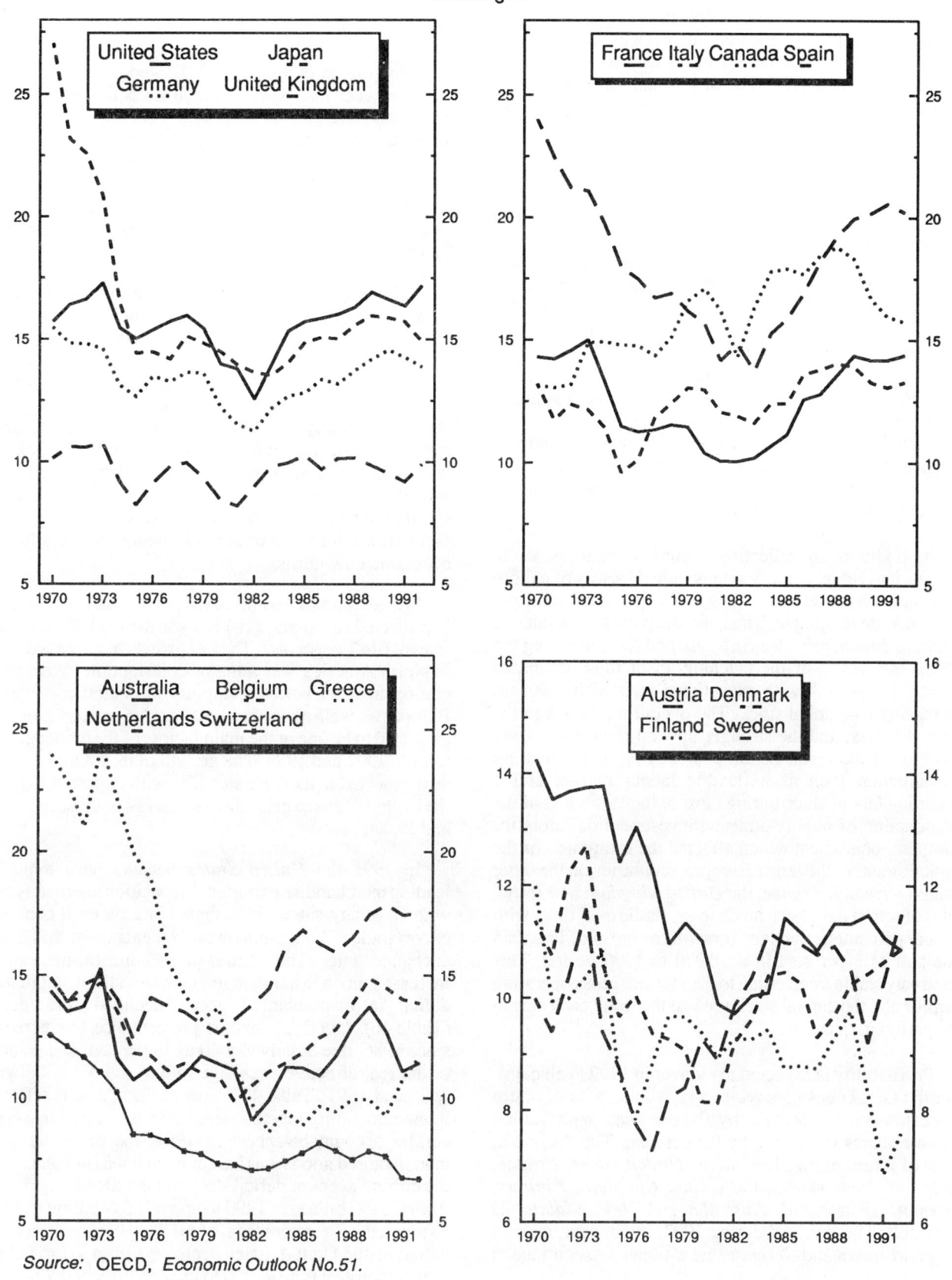

Source: OECD, *Economic Outlook No.51.*

in e.g. the treatment of unpaid family workers or in the inclusion of operating surplus of the housing sector complicate the calculation of gross operating surplus, while the inclusion of quality-adjusted investment deflators for certain industries in some countries or different national estimates of the average life of machines affect the estimates of the capital stock and hamper the international comparability of the resulting indicators.

Bearing these caveats in mind, longer-term trends in rates of return in the business sector are shown in Graph 15. The graph shows that rates of return in most OECD countries declined during the 1970s and reached their lowest point around 1982. From that year onwards rates rose up until the end of the 1980s, the start of the current period of decline. Despite these common tendencies, the graph also illustrates the substantial differences that exist between countries. While in 1991 the OECD-wide rate of return was 15 per cent, rates ranged from over 20 per cent in *Spain* to less than 10 per cent in the *United Kingdom, Finland* and *Switzerland*. Furthermore, there does not appear to be any convergence over time between countries. In contrast, after a period in the early to mid-80s where rates of return in most countries were between 10 and 15 per cent, rates diverged significantly.

In addition to reflecting common business cycle effects, individual country trends reflect factors of a more structural character that are specific to each country's economic development. Thus, the steep decline in rates of return in *Japan*, as well as in *Spain* and *Greece* during the 1970s is a result of the catching-up of these countries during that period, with exceptional rates of investment increasing the capital stock. The overall high rates in the *United States*, and the strongly upward trend from 1982 onwards is the result of the combination of a structural phenomenon such as a flexible labour market and a declining labour share during most of the 1980s and of the introduction of quality-adjusted investment deflators for computer equipment which affected the estimation of the capital stock. In the larger European countries on the other hand (*Germany, France,* the *United Kingdom* and *Italy*), rates of return have been much less volatile over time, with annual percentage declines (growth for Italy) of less than one half of a per cent in the 1970 to 1990 period. This relatively stable trend is due to the fact that gross operating surplus and the capital stock grew at the same pace during the period in question.

Profitability is expected to recover in 1992 (Table 45). For the OECD business sector as a whole, rates of return are estimated to increase by 0.7 per cent, with capital income shares increasing by 0.3 per cent. The decline in rates of return during 1991 in *the United States, France, Italy,* the *Netherlands*, the *United Kingdom, Finland, Sweden, Switzerland, Australia* and *New Zealand* is expected to be reversed during 1992. In contrast, rates of return in *Japan* and *Germany* are estimated to continue to decline.

C. Trade and competitiveness

Recent trends

The volume of world trade slowed down in 1991 for the third year in a row, although it continued to expand faster than output. The estimated 3 per cent growth in the volume of merchandise trade (2.5 per cent for the exports of the OECD area) in 1991 was the lowest since 1983. The recession in North America, the slowdown of the economic expansion in western Europe, together with the sharp contraction in central and eastern Europe were the main factors responsible for this disappointing performance.

Following a 13.5 per cent increase in 1990, the value of world merchandise trade grew by only 1.5 per cent in 1991 to US$3.5 trillion, the smallest gain since 1985. This sharply lower growth rate can be attributed to three factors: weaker volume growth, the "valuation effect" of the appreciation of the dollar against the ECU, and lower prices for some primary commodities [22]. For services (transportation, tourism, telecommunications, insurance, banking), preliminary estimates indicate that the deceleration in the growth of trade during 1991 in value terms was less than for merchandise trade, a performance consistent with the fact that services output is traditionally more resilient to economic downturns.

World trade picked up in the second half of 1991, and is projected to expand briskly over the next 18 months at rates of 6 to 7 per cent [23]. The fast growth of import volumes in North America was a major contribution to the acceleration to date, whereas imports in central and eastern Europe, as well as in the dynamic Asian economies are projected to be one of the main factors of the higher growth rates in 1992 and 1993. The growth of intra-OECD tade is also expected to increase steadily, with import volumes in the United States expanding twice as fast as those in Europe and Japan.

In 1991 the *United States* became once more the leading merchandise exporter [24], a position alternately held with Germany since 1986, depending on each country's export trade volumes and on movements in the dollar/DM exchange rate. The value of manufacturing exports increased much faster than imports, with the result that the deficit in manufactured goods declined substantially (Table 46). Good US export preformance has persisted since 1986, due largely to a 40 to 45 per cent depreciation of the real effective exchange rate of the dollar between 1985 and 1991 (Table 47). This performance is reflected in manufacturing merchandise trade, as well as in overall current account balances: in 1991, the trade deficit in manufactured goods was half of what it was in 1987, while the current account deficit declined drastically, shrinking from US$92 billion in 1990 to about US$9 billion in 1991. Expressed as a percentage of GDP, the current account deficit of the United States decreased from 1.7 to 0.2 per cent, although it is projected to increase to near 0.7 per cent

Table 46. **Trade in manufactured goods**[1]

	Exports					Imports					Balance				
	1987	1988	1989	1990	1991	1987	1988	1989	1990	1991	1987	1988	1989	1990	1991
United States	191.9	242.3	276.3	298.7	325.7	324.9	361.7	379.2	388.4	392.8	-133.0	-119.4	-103.0	-89.7	-67.2
Canada	59.2	75.3	78.9	87.0	87.3	74.9	93.1	98.2	98.4	101.3	-15.7	-17.8	-19.3	-11.4	-14.0
Japan	225.4	260.7	270.7	282.2	309.5	65.9	91.8	106.1	118.0	120.2	159.4	168.9	164.6	164.2	189.3
Belgium/Lux.	68.8	77.6	84.2	100.0	..	60.7	70.3	75.0	92.4	..	8.2	7.3	9.2	7.6	..
Denmark	16.0	17.2	17.9	22.7	23.0	19.3	19.8	20.3	24.5	24.9	-3.3	-2.5	-2.4	-1.8	-1.9
France	113.1	134.6	147.0	177.7	185.8	116.6	143.1	155.3	189.7	191.9	-3.5	-8.4	-8.2	-12.0	-6.0
Germany	270.2	297.1	313.9	369.4	369.2	165.6	188.2	204.8	263.0	302.8	104.6	109.0	109.1	106.5	66.4
Greece	3.9	3.5	4.3	4.6	..	8.3	8.9	11.7	14.4	..	-4.4	-5.4	-7.4	-9.8	..
Ireland	10.9	13.0	14.7	17.5	..	10.6	12.4	14.1	16.6	..	0.3	0.6	0.6	0.9	..
Italy	104.3	115.5	127.3	153.9	152.4	82.8	96.3	105.8	127.3	129.6	21.5	19.2	21.5	26.6	22.8
Netherlands	57.1	66.6	69.4	84.4	84.8	63.4	70.1	74.5	91.4	92.4	-6.3	-3.5	-5.1	-7.0	-7.6
Portugal	7.3	8.3	9.8	13.1	..	8.9	11.1	13.2	17.9	..	-1.7	-2.8	-3.5	-4.8	..
Spain	24.8	29.9	33.3	42.8	46.3	32.0	42.5	50.8	63.2	67.8	-7.3	-12.6	-17.4	-20.4	-21.5
United Kingdom	104.1	121.1	128.4	154.9	155.2	118.5	150.8	158.2	176.7	165.8	-14.4	-29.7	-29.8	-21.9	-10.6
Austria	24.3	27.9	29.1	37.2	37.6	26.7	30.4	32.5	41.2	43.0	-2.4	-2.5	-3.4	-4.0	-5.4
Finland	16.6	18.3	19.8	22.9	19.7	15.0	16.6	19.5	21.1	16.4	1.6	1.7	0.3	1.8	3.2
Norway	10.2	11.4	12.5	14.1	13.8	18.8	19.3	19.3	22.2	20.8	-8.7	-7.9	-6.8	-8.1	-7.0
Sweden	38.1	43.2	44.2	49.5	47.9	32.6	37.6	40.3	44.6	40.0	5.5	5.5	4.0	4.8	7.8
Australia	8.1	10.9	12.5	13.8	15.1	23.4	29.1	35.6	33.7	33.5	-15.3	-18.2	-23.1	-19.9	-18.4
New Zealand	1.9	2.7	2.9	3.1	3.3	6.0	6.1	7.3	7.8	6.8	-4.1	-3.4	-4.4	-4.7	-3.5

1. SITC rev. 2, product groups 5 + 6 + 7 + 8 + 9.
Source: OECD, *Monthly Statistics of Foreign Trade*, Series A.

Table 47. **Trade in manufactured goods: export market growth and relative export performance**

	A Import volume growth				B Export volume growth				C Export market growth[1]				D = C − B Relative export performance			
	Av. annual change 1970/90	1989/90	Change 1990/91	1991/92	Av. annual change 1970/90	1989/90	Change 1990/91	1991/92	Av. annual change 1970/90	1989/90	Change 1990/91	1991/92	Av. annual change 1970/90	1989/90	Change 1990/91	1991/92
United States	7.0	1.8	1.3	7.7	5.9	8.5	7.8	7.4	6.4	4.8	5.3	6.2	−0.5	3.6	2.4	1.1
Canada	6.6	−1.2	2.2	7.0	6.1	3.1	−1.0	8.1	6.9	2.5	2.0	7.5	−0.7	−0.6	−3.0	0.6
Japan	10.4	10.2	3.2	3.9	7.5	5.4	2.5	3.9	6.9	5.3	6.8	7.5	0.5	0.0	−4.0	−3.4
Belgium/Luxembourg	5.1	5.1	3.6	4.0	3.5	3.2	2.6	4.2	6.4	6.5	4.8	5.3	−2.7	−3.1	−2.1	−1.0
Denmark	3.1	4.1	5.4	5.4	5.6	5.9	5.2	4.8	6.1	5.6	1.8	3.8	−0.5	0.3	3.3	1.0
France	7.0	6.3	2.1	4.1	5.5	5.6	3.6	6.7	6.1	6.4	5.3	5.8	−0.5	−0.8	−1.6	0.8
Germany	7.1	13.0	12.6	5.2	5.0	1.2	−4.0	4.6	6.2	5.3	1.3	6.0	−1.1	−3.9	−5.2	−1.3
Greece	6.9	14.8	−1.1	4.7	9.6	−5.1	7.7	4.6	6.5	7.7	6.4	5.5	3.0	−11.9	1.2	−0.8
Ireland	6.7	7.2	−0.1	6.0	12.6	11.6	6.2	8.9	6.9	4.4	1.7	5.1	5.4	6.9	4.4	3.6
Italy	6.3	5.6	3.0	5.8	5.4	2.3	−0.1	3.7	6.5	6.9	5.0	5.7	−1.0	−4.3	−4.7	−1.9
Netherlands	4.3	1.0	4.3	4.2	6.1	6.3	4.4	5.8	6.4	6.9	4.8	5.2	−0.3	−0.6	−0.5	0.6
Portugal	7.6	14.2	5.2	6.8	9.8	14.4	1.9	6.0	6.5	5.9	3.7	5.3	3.1	8.0	−1.7	0.7
Spain	9.1	10.1	11.5	11.5	11.3	14.0	11.1	7.7	6.3	6.4	4.2	5.3	4.8	7.2	6.6	2.2
United Kingdom	8.2	1.0	−4.3	5.1	4.2	7.6	2.5	3.0	6.1	6.0	5.4	5.7	−1.8	1.5	−2.7	−2.6
Austria	7.4	12.2	7.9	6.4	7.2	10.5	7.3	3.9	6.4	8.1	5.5	5.7	0.7	2.2	1.7	−1.7
Finland	4.5	−4.9	−20.7	−7.6	4.6	4.4	−8.1	5.1	6.1	5.6	−1.2	5.9	−1.5	−1.1	−6.9	−0.7
Norway	4.8	11.2	−0.5	−1.1	3.3	6.3	0.5	−2.1	5.7	4.9	2.0	4.3	−2.3	1.3	−1.5	−6.1
Sweden	5.0	0.5	−8.3	−2.4	4.1	0.6	−1.0	1.9	5.9	5.2	2.2	4.6	−1.7	−4.4	−3.1	−2.6
Switzerland	4.3	2.7	−0.1	1.6	3.1	5.6	−0.7	3.0	6.7	7.4	5.7	5.9	−3.3	−1.7	−6.0	−2.7
Turkey	9.7	43.4	−0.6	8.3	21.3	3.5	6.9	7.1	6.2	6.5	9.5	5.7	14.2	−2.8	−2.3	1.4
Australia	6.2	−2.2	−1.7	3.6	7.9	16.5	19.8	6.7	7.8	7.9	5.5	6.5	0.2	8.0	13.6	0.2
New Zealand	4.6	8.6	−8.9	3.3	5.4	6.1	9.4	9.2	7.3	3.2	2.4	5.2	−1.8	2.8	6.8	3.8
G7 countries[2]	6.0	5.0	3.3	5.9	3.9	4.8	1.8	5.3	4.7	5.4	4.3	6.3	−0.7	−0.6	−2.5	−1.0
EC[2]	5.3	6.9	4.8	5.3	3.7	4.1	0.7	4.9	4.6	6.0	3.6	5.7	−0.8	−1.8	−2.8	−0.8
17 smaller OECD countries[2]	4.4	5.6	1.7	4.2	4.1	6.2	3.4	4.7	4.7	6.5	4.1	5.3	−0.6	−0.3	−0.7	−0.6
OECD total[2]	5.5	5.2	2.8	5.4	4.0	5.1	2.2	5.1	4.7	5.7	4.3	6.1	−0.7	−0.5	−2.0	−0.9
World[2]	4.8	5.7	4.6	6.2	4.6	5.6	3.8	5.9	:	:	:	:	:	:	:	:

1. The calculation of export market growth is based on the growth of import volume in each exporting country's markets, with weights based on manufacturing trade flows of 1987.
2. Average annual growth calculations for the period 1975-90.
Source: OECD, Economic Outlook No. 51.

Table 48. Competitive positions
Indices, 1987 = 100

	Average 1987-89	1990	1991	1992	Average 1987-89	1990	1991	1992
	Manufacturing unit labour costs in local currency				Export prices of manufactures in local currency			
United States	100	102	105	106	103	106	106	107
Canada	105	114	119	120	101	100	97	97
Japan	98	98	103	107	101	108	108	108
Belgium/Luxembourg	99	100	103	106	106	111	108	110
Denmark	101	106	107	108	103	107	107	108
France	97	98	102	103	104	105	105	104
Germany	100	103	107	112	102	104	105	107
Italy	103	116	125	130	105	116	119	122
Netherlands	98	98	101	103	103	104	103	105
Spain	105	121	127	132	105	107	106	108
United Kingdom	101	113	122	125	103	110	110	112
Austria	97	96	100	104	102	100	100	101
Finland	103	115	121	119	106	111	109	115
Norway	105	109	112	114	117	119	123	129
Sweden	106	129	136	137	105	113	113	113
Switzerland	102	109	117	122	104	111	115	122
Australia	108	125	129	132	106	105	98	99
New Zealand	104	114	118	119	113	123	125	133
Singapore	104	126	132	138	99	99	94	91
Taiwan	106	117	123	130	101	100	104	108
Korea	117	155	168	178	101	107	114	120
Hong Kong	110	142	157	172	102	106	108	111
	Relative unit labour costs in manufactures, in a common currency				Relative export prices of manufactures, in a common currency			
United States	94	85	81	79	97	93	91	90
Canada	110	122	125	119	104	104	103	98
Japan	98	81	88	91	101	95	101	102
Belgium/Luxembourg	97	98	95	95	101	106	103	104
Denmark	98	99	94	92	97	100	99	98
France	94	92	89	88	98	98	96	94
Germany	99	99	97	99	97	99	98	99
Italy	101	109	111	112	100	108	109	110
Netherlands	97	94	91	91	99	99	97	98
Spain	108	127	127	128	105	111	109	110
United Kingdom	103	107	111	110	102	103	103	103
Austria	95	92	91	92	99	95	93	93
Finland	103	112	107	92	104	109	102	96
Norway	102	97	94	94	112	110	111	115
Sweden	105	119	119	120	102	103	103	103
Switzerland	99	102	103	99	98	102	104	103
Australia	112	124	120	116	109	104	95	92
New Zealand	102	97	93	85	109	110	108	106
Singapore	106	132	139	142	99	103	102	97
Taiwan	115	128	129	132	107	108	112	115
Korea	130	167	166	170	108	112	114	118
Hong Kong	108	127	135	143	98	94	96	97

Source: OECD, *Economic Outlook No. 51.*

of GDP in 1992. Underlying this performance are favourable movements in relative costs and prices: in manufacturing, for example, both relative unit labour costs and relative export prices declined in 1991 and were projected to fall further during 1992 (Table 48). In addition, much of the improvement in the current account in 1991 reflected a one-time payment of US$43 billion in contributions by other nations to the Gulf War effort.

The manufacturing trade surplus in *Japan* increased in 1991, reversing a declining trend that had started in 1989. The value of manufacturing exports increased strongly while that of imports barely changed, leading to an increase in the surplus of over 15 per cent in value terms to reach nearly US$190 billion. The increase in the overall trade surplus can be traced in large part to the fall in imported energy prices and to the strong demand in other parts of east and south Asia for Japan's exports. The current account surplus also increased, and jumped from 1.2 per cent of GDP in 1990 to 2.1 per cent in 1991 -- still less than half the peak figure of 4.3 per cent in 1986. It is projected to increase further in 1992 and 1993. In terms of volume, the growth of both manufactured imports and exports declined significantly during 1991, but were projected for a mild recovery in 1992. Export markets for manufactured goods grew faster than the volume of exports, leading to a decline in Japan's relative export performance in manufactures trade (Table 47).

In the *European Community*, two of the four larger member countries continued to post manufacturing trade surpluses. The surplus in *Germany* declined drastically by over 37 per cent in 1991 to reach US$66 bilion, a reflection of stagnant manufacturing exports and a sharp increase in the value of manufacturing imports. In volume terms, manufacturing imports increased by 13 per cent in 1991, while exports declined by 4 per cent. As a result of the unification, the current surplus of 1990 turned into a deficit in 1991; expressed as a percentage of GDP, it went from a 2.9 per cent surplus in 1990 to a 1.2 per cent deficit in 1991, but is expected to decline in 1992 and further in 1993. The decline in the manufaturing trade surplus in *Italy* was more modest, and resulted from a fall in the value of manufactured exports and a slight increase in imports. In terms of volume, manufactured exports declined slightly in 1991 and imports increased; with the market for exports increasing in volume at a rate of 5 per cent, this resulted in a loss of relative competitiveness in manufactured trade. The manufacturing trade deficits in *France* and the *United Kingdom* halved in 1991, the result of exports rising faster than imports in France and of a fall in imports of manufactures in the United Kingdom. The relative export performance of both these countries declined in 1991, reflecting the fact that their export markets grew faster than the volume of their manufactures exports.

Of the smaller EC countries, *Denmark*, the *Netherlands* and *Spain* all increased their manufacturing trade deficits. Of the three, only Spain has an overall deficit in the current balance (2.9 per cent of GDP in 1991). The shrinking manufacturing trade surplus in *Belgium* and the expanding deficit in *Greece* are both reflected in their current balances (a surplus of 2 per cent of GDP in 1991 and a deficit of 2.2 per cent of GDP respectively). The current surplus in *Ireland* (nearly 5 per cent of GNP in 1991) reflects a pattern of manufacturing trade that remains almost balanced year to year, while the current deficit in *Portugal* (0.7 per cent of GDP in 1991) is partly due to a widening manufacturing trade deficit.

With the exception of *Finland* and *Sweden*, all of the remaining OECD countries posted manufacturing trade deficits in 1991. The deficit increased in *Canada* and *Austria*, while declining in *Norway, Australia* and *New Zealand*. In volume terms, both manufacturing imports and exports declined sharply in Finland because of the severe economic recession (by over 20 per cent and by 8 per cent respectively), and less so in Canada, Sweden and Switzerland. Manufacturing import volumes in Australia and New Zealand declined, while export volumes increased strongly and faster than the export markets of these countries, thus improving their relative export performance.

Structural aspects and sectoral patterns

Underlying these recent trends in trade performance and competitiveness are important structural shifts in the export market shares of OECD countries and in their pattern of specialisation and comparative advantage. In this context, trade in certain industrial sectors has attracted particular attention, as well as bilateral trade patterns between economic regions.

Bilateral trade patterns and export competitiveness

Graph 16 shows bilateral trade balances in the Triad for selected industries. The first panel of the graph shows the evolution of bilateral trade between the *United States* and *Japan*. With the exception of the aerospace industry, the United States is running a deficit with Japan in all high technology industries, as well as in motor vehicles. The surplus in aerospace has steadily grown since 1980 and was in 1990 running at around US$9 billion. The deficits in instruments and in electrical machinery, after growing initially up to 1986-87, had in 1990 stabilised at about US$4 and US$6 billion respectively. The deficit in computers increased steadily up to 1988 before stabilising to around US$6 billion. The effect of the appreciation of the yen since 1986 is visible in electronics (covering radio, TV, communication equipment & semiconductors) and in motor vehicles, where the increasing trend in the US deficit with Japan in these industries between 1980 and 1986 has since been reversed. In 1990, Japan had a surplus of about US$11 billion and US$28 billion respectively in these two industries.

Graph 16. **Bilateral trade balances: United States, Japan, EC**
$US billion

Source: OECD, STAN database.

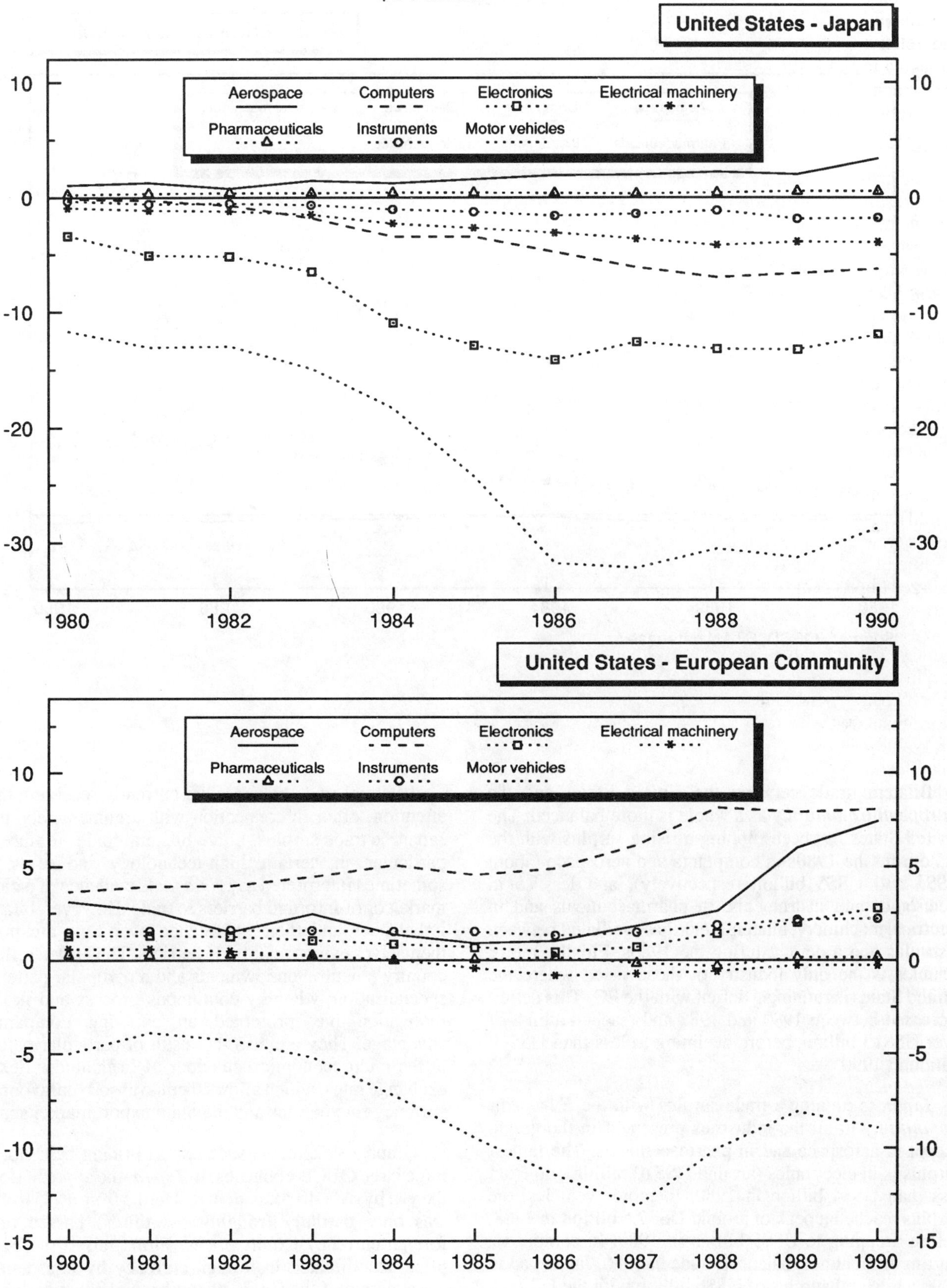

Graph 16 (cont).   Bilateral trade balances: United States, Japan, EC
$US billion

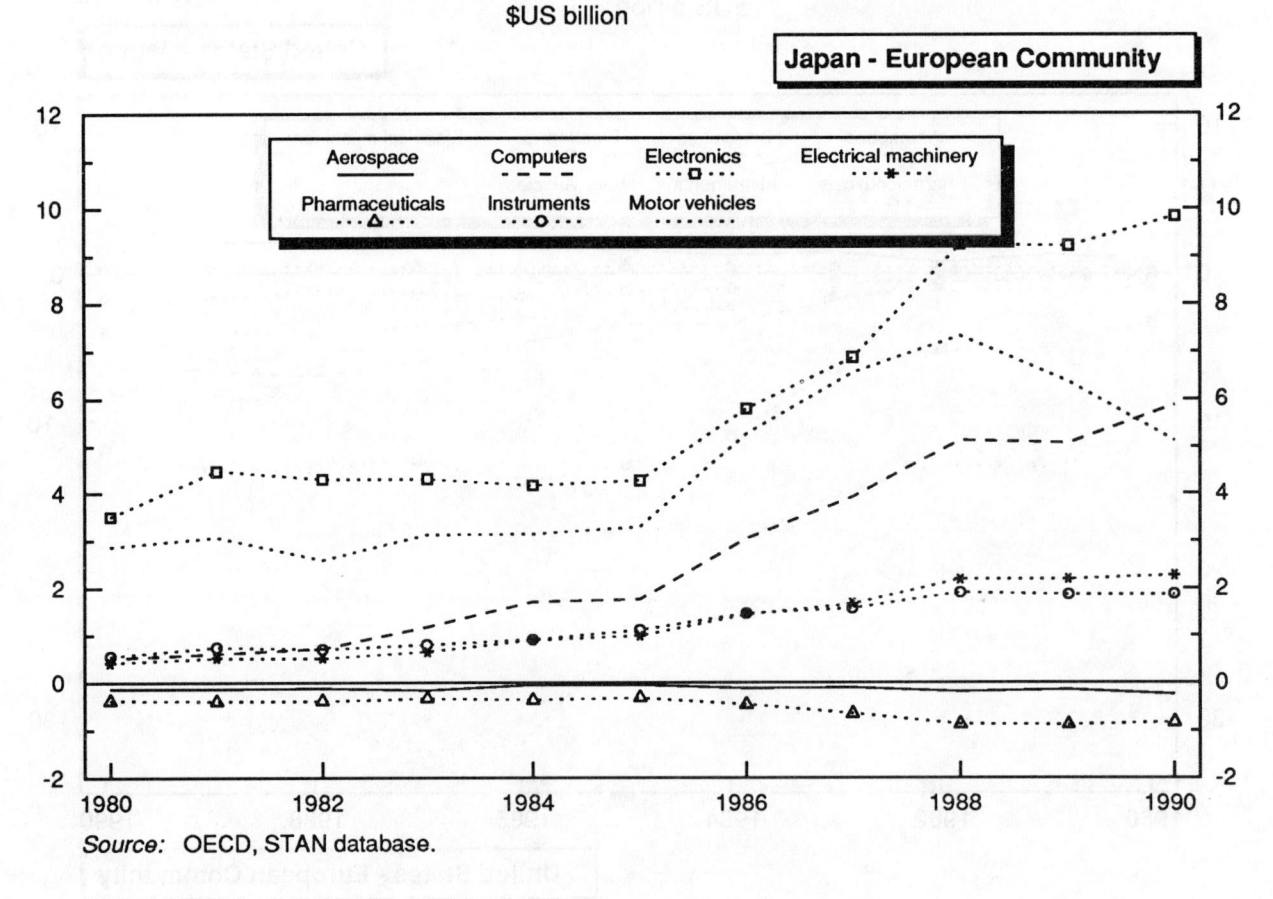

Japan - European Community

Source: OECD, STAN database.

Bilateral trade between the *United States* and the *European Community* as a whole is more balanced. The United States has been running a rising surplus with the EC during the 1980s in computers and aerospace (about US$6 and US$5 billion respectively), and less so in electronics and instruments. In pharmaceuticals and in electrical machinery, bilateral trade has oscillated between a surplus and a deficit during the 1980s. Finally, motor vehicles is the only industry of those listed where the United States is running a deficit with the EC. This deficit increased between 1980 and 1987 and reached a high of over US$15 billion, before declining to less than US$10 billion in 1990.

Japan is running a trade surplus with the *European Community* in all the industries presented in the graph, except in aerospace and in pharmaceuticals. The largest surplus is in electronics (around US$10 billion), up from less than US$4 billion in 1980. In motor vehicles, the surplus reached a peak of around US$7.5 billion in 1988, before dropping to US$5 billion in 1990. In computers, starting from almost balanced trade in 1980, Japan had in 1990 a bilateral surplus of US$6 billion with the EC.

Bilateral trade balances are currently receiving much attention, often in connection with arguments about the Japanese trade surplus. Large bilateral trade surpluses, in particular in certain high-technology industries, are sometimes interpreted as *prima facie* evidence of a closed market or of informal barriers to trade. However, bilateral imbalances and their persistence over time are not in themselves evidence of trade barriers. They often reflect a country's natural endowments and a particular pattern of specialisation, whereby continuous process and product innovation has promoted an evolving comparative advantage. They are also the result of particular patterns in the microeconomic behaviour of firms under flexible exchange rates, which allows them to absorb unfavourable currency fluctuations and maintain export market shares.

Graph 17 examines such export pricing behaviour in three large OECD countries. In *Japan*, the appreciation of the yen by over 40 per cent in real terms from 1985 to 1988 was only partially (roughly two-thirds) passed on to foreign-currency export prices. Firms raised the export price denominated in foreign currency by less than the appreciation of the yen (a phenomenon known as "partial

Graph 17. **Export prices and exchange rate movements**
Percentage changes from preceding year

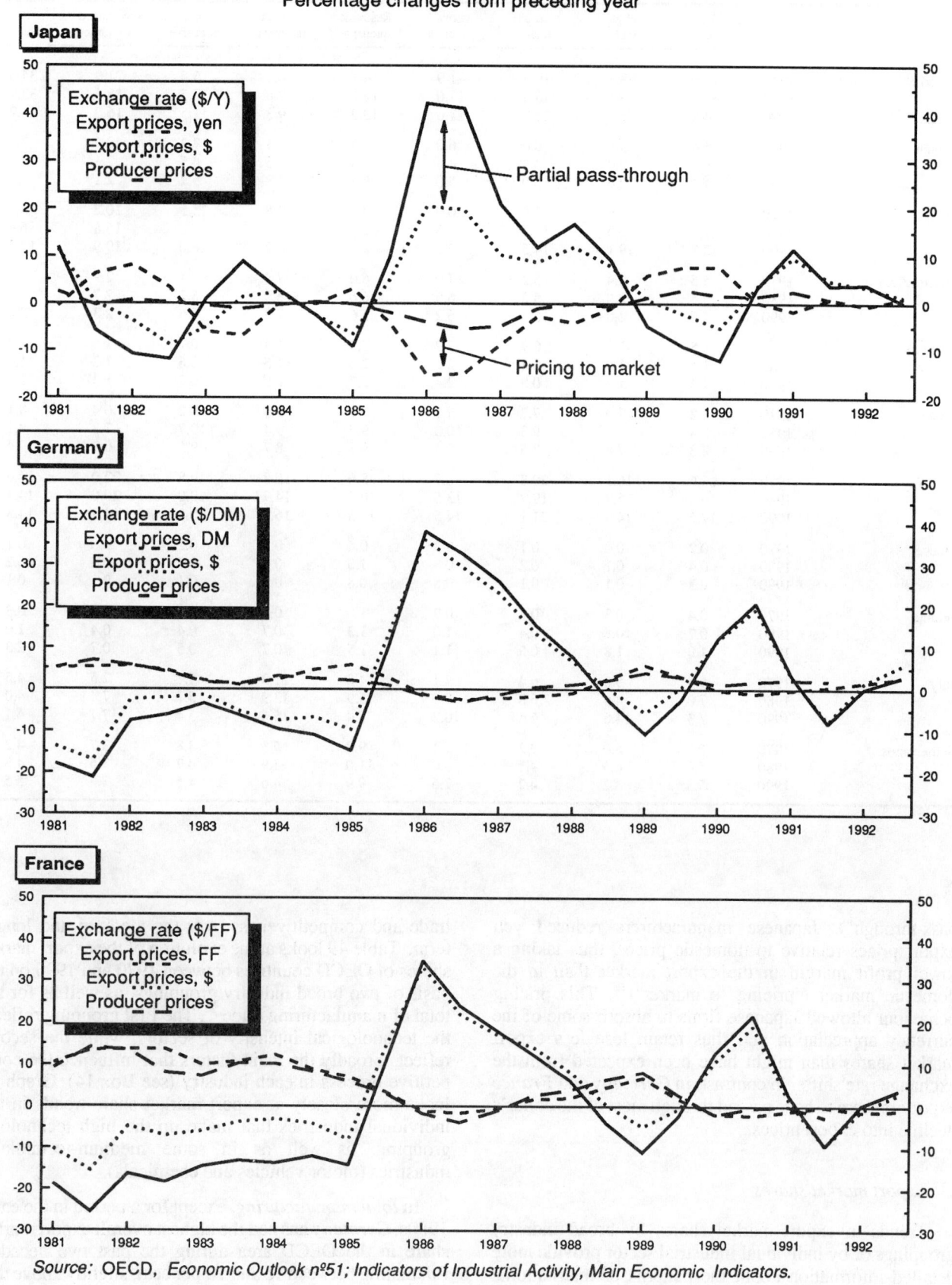

Japan

Exchange rate ($/Y)
Export prices, yen
Export prices, $
Producer prices

Partial pass-through

Pricing to market

Germany

Exchange rate ($/DM)
Export prices, DM
Export prices, $
Producer prices

France

Exchange rate ($/FF)
Export prices, FF
Export prices, $
Producer prices

Source: OECD, *Economic Outlook nº51; Indicators of Industrial Activity, Main Economic Indicators.*

Table 49. **Export market shares by type of industry**[1]

		Total manuf.	High tech.	Medium tech.	Low tech.	Resource intensive	Labour intensive	Scale-intensive	Specialised-supplier	Science-based
United States	1970	17.8	28.3	19.6	11.9	14.1	10.2	15.5	21.9	34.5
	1980	15.7	25.1	16.6	11.0	12.2	12.6	12.5	18.6	32.1
	1990	14.8	23.7	13.2	11.0	13.3	9.3	11.5	16.3	26.7
Canada	1970	6.4	3.6	8.0	6.0	12.7	2.1	7.3	3.2	3.7
	1980	4.2	2.0	4.4	4.8	8.4	1.5	4.5	2.1	2.0
	1990	4.4	2.6	5.0	5.0	8.8	1.9	5.7	2.1	2.3
Japan	1970	9.7	12.0	7.6	10.9	3.2	12.8	13.5	10.2	6.1
	1980	11.7	15.3	12.4	8.8	2.6	8.6	17.6	15.8	6.6
	1990	12.8	19.1	14.5	5.7	2.3	6.2	16.0	19.9	12.2
Belgium/Lux.	1970	5.5	2.4	5.2	7.0	6.0	7.4	7.1	2.9	2.3
	1980	5.4	2.6	5.5	6.6	6.6	8.0	6.2	2.7	3.1
	1990	5.0	2.0	5.8	6.2	5.6	7.9	6.6	2.3	2.6
Denmark	1970	1.5	1.1	0.9	2.2	2.9	1.4	0.7	1.5	1.0
	1980	1.4	1.0	0.8	2.2	2.6	1.5	0.6	1.2	1.0
	1990	1.4	1.1	0.8	2.4	2.7	1.8	0.7	1.3	1.1
France	1970	8.2	7.0	7.7	9.1	7.6	9.5	9.2	6.4	8.1
	1980	9.4	7.9	9.3	10.3	9.7	9.4	10.7	7.8	8.7
	1990	8.8	7.8	8.5	9.8	9.8	8.7	9.5	6.7	9.4
Germany	1970	16.6	16.1	20.8	12.7	8.0	15.8	19.8	22.0	14.6
	1980	16.8	15.9	19.7	13.5	10.7	14.9	20.0	20.0	14.7
	1990	17.5	14.6	21.1	14.5	11.3	16.8	20.9	19.9	14.3
Greece	1970	0.2	0.0	0.1	0.3	0.4	0.2	0.2	0.0	0.1
	1980	0.4	0.1	0.2	0.8	1.0	0.7	0.2	0.1	0.2
	1990	0.3	0.1	0.1	0.8	0.8	0.9	0.1	0.1	0.1
Ireland	1970	0.4	0.3	0.1	0.7	1.0	0.5	0.1	0.1	0.3
	1980	0.7	0.8	0.4	1.0	1.3	0.7	0.4	0.4	1.0
	1990	1.0	1.8	0.5	1.1	1.5	0.7	0.5	0.7	2.3
Italy	1970	6.5	5.0	6.4	7.1	4.8	11.9	5.1	7.5	4.5
	1980	7.0	4.6	6.3	8.9	5.9	13.9	5.7	7.4	4.0
	1990	7.3	4.6	6.6	10.2	6.4	16.6	5.4	7.7	4.1
Netherlands	1970	5.1	5.0	3.2	7.1	9.0	5.3	3.8	3.7	4.2
	1980	5.6	4.5	4.1	8.0	11.0	3.9	4.7	3.5	4.3
	1990	5.3	4.2	4.2	7.6	9.9	4.6	4.5	3.3	5.5

pass-through"). Japanese manufacturers reduced yen export prices relative to domestic prices, thus taking a lower profit margin in the export market than in the domestic market ("pricing to market")[25]. This pricing behaviour allowed Japanese firms to absorb some of the currency appreciation and thus retain lose less export market shares than might have been expected from the exchange rate shifts. In contrast, in *Germany* and *France* exporters seem to have passed through most of the dollar's decline into export prices.

Export market shares

Trends in export market shares by broad industry groupings or by individual industrial sector provide more detailed information about the patterns of international trade and competitiveness over the medium and longer term. Table 49 looks at the evolution of the export market shares of OECD countries between 1970 and 1990 on the basis of two broad industry groupings, as well as for the total of manufacturing trade[26]. The first grouping reflects the technological intensity of sectors, while the second reflects broadly the main factors that influence the competitive process in each industry (see Box 14). Graph 18 looks more closely at export market share trends in the individual industries that make up the high technology grouping, as well as in some medium-technology industries (motor vehicles and chemicals).

In *total manufacturing*, except for a period in the early 1980s, *Germany* has had the highest overall export market share in the OECD area during the past two decades, fluctuating between 16 and 18 per cent, slightly above that

Table 49. **Export market shares by type of industry**[1] *(cont'd)*

		Total manuf.	High tech.	Medium tech.	Low tech.	Resource intensive	Labour intensive	Scale-intensive	Specialised-supplier	Science-based
Portugal	1970	0.4	0.2	0.2	0.8	0.9	1.1	0.2	0.2	0.2
	1980	0.4	0.2	0.2	0.8	0.7	1.1	0.2	0.2	0.2
	1990	0.7	0.3	0.3	1.6	1.0	2.5	0.4	0.4	0.1
Spain	1970	1.0	0.4	0.6	1.6	1.8	1.3	0.8	0.6	0.3
	1980	1.7	0.8	1.5	2.5	2.3	1.9	2.1	1.1	0.7
	1990	2.3	1.2	2.4	3.0	3.1	2.4	3.1	1.3	1.2
United Kingdom	1970	9.2	9.6	10.7	7.4	7.1	10.6	8.6	10.2	10.8
	1980	8.8	11.2	9.6	7.1	7.8	10.1	7.1	9.2	14.4
	1990	7.5	9.2	7.3	6.9	6.3	7.3	7.0	7.4	11.1
Austria	1970	1.4	1.0	1.0	1.9	1.6	2.3	1.2	1.4	0.4
	1980	1.5	1.1	1.2	2.1	1.6	2.3	1.4	1.7	0.6
	1990	1.9	1.4	1.7	2.4	2.0	2.6	1.7	2.2	0.8
Finland	1970	1.1	0.2	0.4	2.2	3.5	0.8	0.5	0.5	0.1
	1980	1.3	0.5	0.6	2.4	3.2	1.2	0.7	0.7	0.3
	1990	1.2	0.6	0.8	2.2	3.1	0.8	0.8	1.1	0.4
Norway	1970	1.1	0.3	1.0	1.6	2.6	0.5	1.2	0.5	0.2
	1980	0.9	0.4	0.8	1.2	1.9	0.4	0.9	0.5	0.3
	1990	0.8	0.4	0.7	1.3	2.2	0.4	0.8	0.4	0.4
Sweden	1970	3.3	2.4	2.7	4.1	4.7	1.9	3.2	3.5	1.8
	1980	2.7	2.3	2.4	3.3	3.7	1.9	2.5	3.1	1.6
	1990	2.5	2.1	2.2	3.1	3.8	1.6	2.3	2.8	1.8
Switzerland	1970	2.6	4.8	2.7	1.6	1.3	3.0	1.4	3.5	6.4
	1980	2.7	3.2	3.1	1.4	1.3	3.8	1.5	3.7	3.6
	1990	2.8	2.7	3.3	1.7	1.3	4.3	1.7	3.7	3.2
Turkey	1970	0.1	0.0	0.0	0.1	0.1	0.1	0.0	0.0	0.0
	1980	0.1	0.0	0.0	0.2	0.1	0.3	0.1	0.0	0.0
	1990	0.5	0.1	0.2	1.3	0.6	1.9	0.4	0.1	0.1
Australia	1970	1.4	0.2	0.9	2.3	4.4	0.8	0.7	0.3	0.3
	1980	1.1	0.3	0.8	1.9	3.7	0.6	0.4	0.3	0.4
	1990	0.7	0.2	0.5	1.4	2.5	0.7	0.3	0.2	0.3
New Zealand	1970	0.6	0.0	0.1	1.3	2.2	0.3	0.0	0.0	0.1
	1980	0.4	0.1	0.1	1.0	1.5	0.5	0.1	0.1	0.0
	1990	0.3	0.1	0.1	0.9	1.5	0.3	0.1	0.1	0.0

1. Calculated on the basis of current US dollars. For the sectors in each type of industry, see Box 13.
Source: OECD, STAN database.

for the *United States*. *Japan*, third on the list, has experienced more fluctuation, attaining over 15 per cent in the mid-1980s from about 11 per cent during the 1970s but falling below 13 per cent in 1990. The share of *France* has remained stable at slightly over 8 per cent while the *United Kingdom* has lost ground steadily from over 9 in the early 1970s to 7.5 per cent in 1990. The shares of *Italy* and *Belgium* remained stable at about 7 per cent and 5 per cent respectively.

Although their share remains very small in total OECD manufacturing exports, significant growth in export market shares can be seen in *Ireland, Spain, Greece* and *Turkey*. Ireland and Spain have more than doubled their share from 1970 to 1990, with increases across the board in most manufacturing industries. The single most significant increase was in computers in Ireland (from below 0.2 per cent to nearly 5 per cent of the OECD market from 1970 to 1990), while over the same period Spain increased its export market shares in motor vehicles and aerospace over 10-fold. Greece nearly doubled its export market share of total manufacturing but remains at 0.3 per cent of the OECD market. Turkey experienced the highest relative growth, raising its export market share to slightly more than 0.5 per cent in 1990 from 0.1 per cent in the early 1970s. In these last two countries the increase was largely due to the growth in the textiles industry. In contrast, besides those in the US and the UK, losses in market shares occurred in *Australia* and *Canada*, and to a lesser extent in *Norway* and *Sweden*.

Box 14. Classifying international trade

The analysis of trends in the composition of manufacturing exports necessitates an appropriate classification of products and industries. This report uses two such classifications: one based on the R&D intensity of industries, and the other based on the major factors thought to affect competitiveness in particular industries.

The first classification distinguishes industries into groups on the basis of the criterion of R&D intensity in the OECD area as a whole (generally defined as the ratio of business enterprise R&D to sales -- see box 12 in the R&D section above). Industries are then grouped into high, medium and low technology groups. These groups include the following industries:

High technology	Aerospace, computers, electronics, parmaceuticals, instruments and electrical machinery;
Medium technology	Motor vehicles, chemicals, non-electrical machinery, rubber and plastics, non-ferrous metals, other manufacturing and other transport;
Low technology	Stone and glass, food, drink and tobacco, shipbuilding, petroleum refining, ferrous metals, fabricated metal products, paper and printing, wood, furniture and textiles.

While this classification is widely used, it suffers from a number of shortcomings. First, while high technology industries share a number of common characteristics, industries in the medium and low technology groupings are very heterogeneous. Secondly, this classification leads to a tendency to assume that a specialisation in high technology exports is economically desirable in itself at the exclusion of any other form of trade. While high technology industries have seen a growing world market in the past twenty years (see Part 4 of this report on structural change), many countries have built very successful export profiles by specialising on what are traditionally considered medium or low technology sectors (for example Germany in cars and machinery or Italy in textiles).

An alternative classification used in this report[1] is based on the primary factors believed to affect the competitive process in each activity. Industries are grouped into the five following groups:

Grouping	Major factors affecting competitiveness	Industries
(i) **Resource-intensive**	Access to natural resources	Food, beverages, tobacco, leather, wood, paper, petroleum refining, cement and clay
(ii) **Labour-intensive**	Labour costs	Textiles, apparel, footwear, furniture, non-ferrous and fabricated metals
(iii) **Scale-intensive**	Length of production runs	Printing, industrial chemicals, rubber and plastics, pottery and glass, iron and steel, railroad equipment, shipbuilding, cars and other transport
(iv) **Specialised-supplier (differentiated goods)**	Tailoring products to varied demand characteristics	Non-electrical machinery excl. computers, electrical machinery excl. telecoms and semiconductors
(v) **Science-based**	Rapid application of scientific advance	Pharmaceuticals, computers, telecommunications and semiconductors, aircraft, scientific instruments, and other chemicals.

These distinctions are not water-tight. Moreover, competitiveness depends often on a mix of characteristics -- e.g. applying scientific advance is also important in activities which produce differentiated goods. Nevertheless, this classification provides a link between the way product groups are defined and the main types of economic benefits that are derived from trade. Thus, trade in resource- and labour-intensive products brings the allocation of resources within countries more closely into line with the international pattern of factor endowments. Trade in scale-intensive products allows firms to increase plant size and lengthen production runs, thus reducing costs. Trade in differentiated goods increases variety and thus benefits consumers without sacrificing the advantages of large-scale production. Finally, trade in science-based industries spreads the high fixed costs of R&D over a larger market, while ensuring the rapid diffusion of new products.

1. See OECD (1987), *Structural Adjustment and Economic Performance*, in particular chapter 7.

The *high technology* industries acounted for 16 per cent of OECD total manufacturing exports in 1970, rising to 23 per cent in 1990. Within this group, there has been considerable movement and redistribution in terms of export market shares, especially between the *United States* and *Japan*. In 1970, the US had over 28 per cent of the OECD high-tech export market, including 60 per cent in aerospace and 37 per cent in computers. In 1990, its share in aerospace had dropped to below 47 per cent and in computers to 26 per cent, contributing to an overall decline to below 24 per cent of the high-tech export market. During the period in question, Japan's share increased by over 7 percentage points to reach over 19 per cent in 1990. While its share in aerospace and pharmaceuticals remains very small, its market share increases in electronics, computers and electrical machinery have been significant. In the European countries the change has been less drastic, although *Germany*'s decline is noteworthy.

European countries are principally responsible for eating into the share of the US in the *aerospace* export market, particularly *Germany, France, Italy* and *Spain*, which increased their combined share by nearly 18 percentage points to just below 30 per cent over the 1970-90 period. The share of the *United Kingdom* in aerospace fluctuated between 12 per cent and 20 per cent in the 1970s and 1980s to reach 11 per cent in 1990. In the same period *Canada*, with over 8 per cent of this market in 1970, lost nearly 4 percentage points.

In the *computers & office machinery* industry, *Japan*'s gain of over 14 percentage points to 22 per cent of the OECD market, has primarily been at the expense of the share of the *US*, which fell from 37 per cent to 26 per cent between 1970 and 1990. The shares of most European countries declined as well, and notably that of *Germany*, which fell from 16 per cent to below 10 per cent. Although their shares remain small, strong European newcomers to this market are *Ireland*, increasing from 0.2 per cent in 1970 to 5 per cent in 1990, and *Spain*, whose share grew from 0.5 per cent to over 1 per cent over the period.

In *electronics* (radio, TV, communication equipment & semiconductors) *Japan*'s gain of 7 percentage points has clearly been more at the expense of the share the European countries than that of the US, since the latter maintained approximately 20 per cent of the export market over the years. The *UK, Germany, France* and the *Netherlands* combined lost just below 7 percentage points, going from 35 per cent in 1970 to slightly over 28 per cent in 1990.

Germany has consistently held the largest export market share in *electrical machinery*, with roughly 22 per cent of the market throughout the 1970s and 1980s. In 1990, *Japan*'s share overtook that of the US to attain the second largest share at 18 per cent, up about 7 percentage points since 1970, while the *US* dropped from 17 per cent to 14 per cent during these two decades. Other important exporters of electrical machinery are *France, Italy* and the *UK*, accounting for roughly 25 per cent of OECD exports combined.

Germany's share of total OECD *pharmaceutical* exports has fallen from nearly 20 per cent in 1970 to 16.5 per cent in 1990, although it remains the main OECD exporter in this industry, followed closely by *Switzerland*, traditionally holding slightly over 13 per cent of the market. The *US* has fallen behind Switzerland with 12 per cent, down from nearly 17 per cent in 1970. Other important OECD exporters of pharmaceuticals in 1990 were the *United Kingdom* (12 per cent), *France* (11 per cent), *Italy* (5 per cent) and the *Netherlands* (4 per cent). Their shares have only fluctuated slightly over the past two decades.

The *scientific instruments* industry has been more volatile. The *US* share of OECD instruments exports has fluctuated between 20 per cent and nearly 30 per cent in the 1970s and 80s; that of *Germany* between 15 per cent and 20 per cent; *Japan*'s between 7 per cent and almost 19 per cent. In 1990, the shares of these three countries were 22, 19 and 16 per cent respectively, although all slightly in decline compared to previous years. While the shares of the *UK, France*, the *Netherlands* and *Italy* have remained relatively stable, *Switzerland* has incurred a sizeable loss of market share from over 14 per cent of the export market in 1970 to 5 per cent in 1990.

Exports of *medium technology* industries accounted for 44 per cent in total manufaturing in 1990, barely higher than the 42 per cent share in 1970. Within the group, the shares of the *US* and of *Canada* have declined, that of *Japan* has increased while the variation in the European countries was small. *Germany* is the main OECD exporter in medium technology industries, with 19 to 21 per cent of the market between 1970 and 1990. The US, also accounting for about 20 per cent in 1970, had in 1990 slightly over 13 per cent, while the share of Japan nearly doubled from 7.6 per cent to 14.5 per cent over the same period. The combined shares of the *UK, France, Italy* and *Spain* have remained stable at close to 25 per cent, with the UK suffering some market share losses and Spain making gains. Over these two decades Canada's share has declined from 8 per cent to 5 per cent.

Within the medium-technology group, in *motor vehicles*, the *US* and *Japan* have experienced the largest changes in export market shares, while the changes in Europe have been generally smaller. The US share of OECD motor vehicle exports fell from over 18 per cent in 1970 to below 11 per cent in 1990. Meanwhile, Japan's share tripled to nearly 22 per cent in twenty years. Other countries that lost market share were the *UK* (falling from 10 to 5 per cent) and *Canada* (from 16 to 9 per cent). The shares of *Italy, France* and *Sweden* decreased as well, although to a lesser degree. *Germany*'s roughly 23 per cent market share remained intact over the twenty year period, although it briefly fell below 20 per cent in the mid 1980s. The share of *Belgium* grew slightly from just over

Graph 18. **Export market shares**

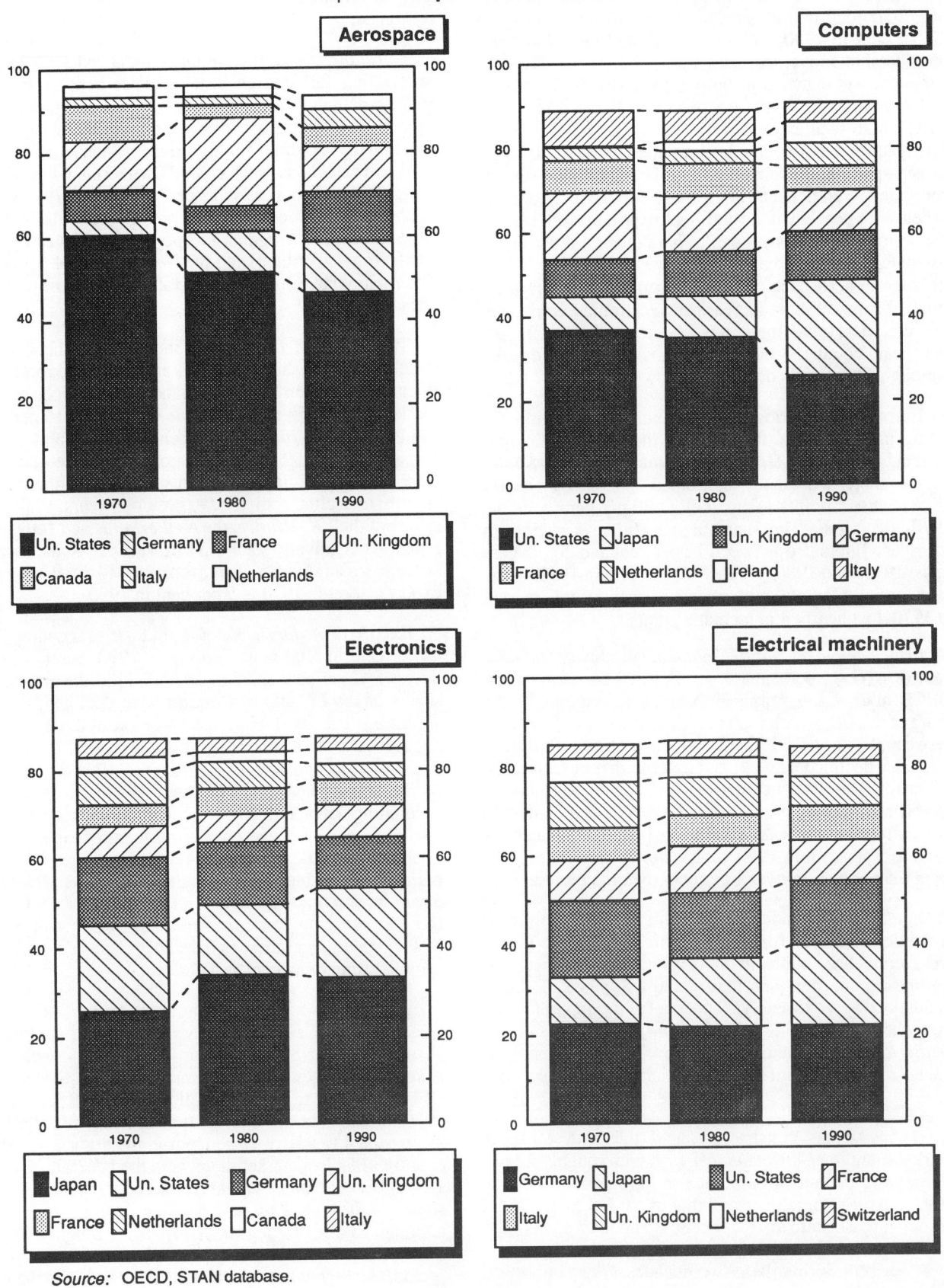

Aerospace

Computers

Electronics

Electrical machinery

Source: OECD, STAN database.

Graph 18 (cont). **Export market shares**

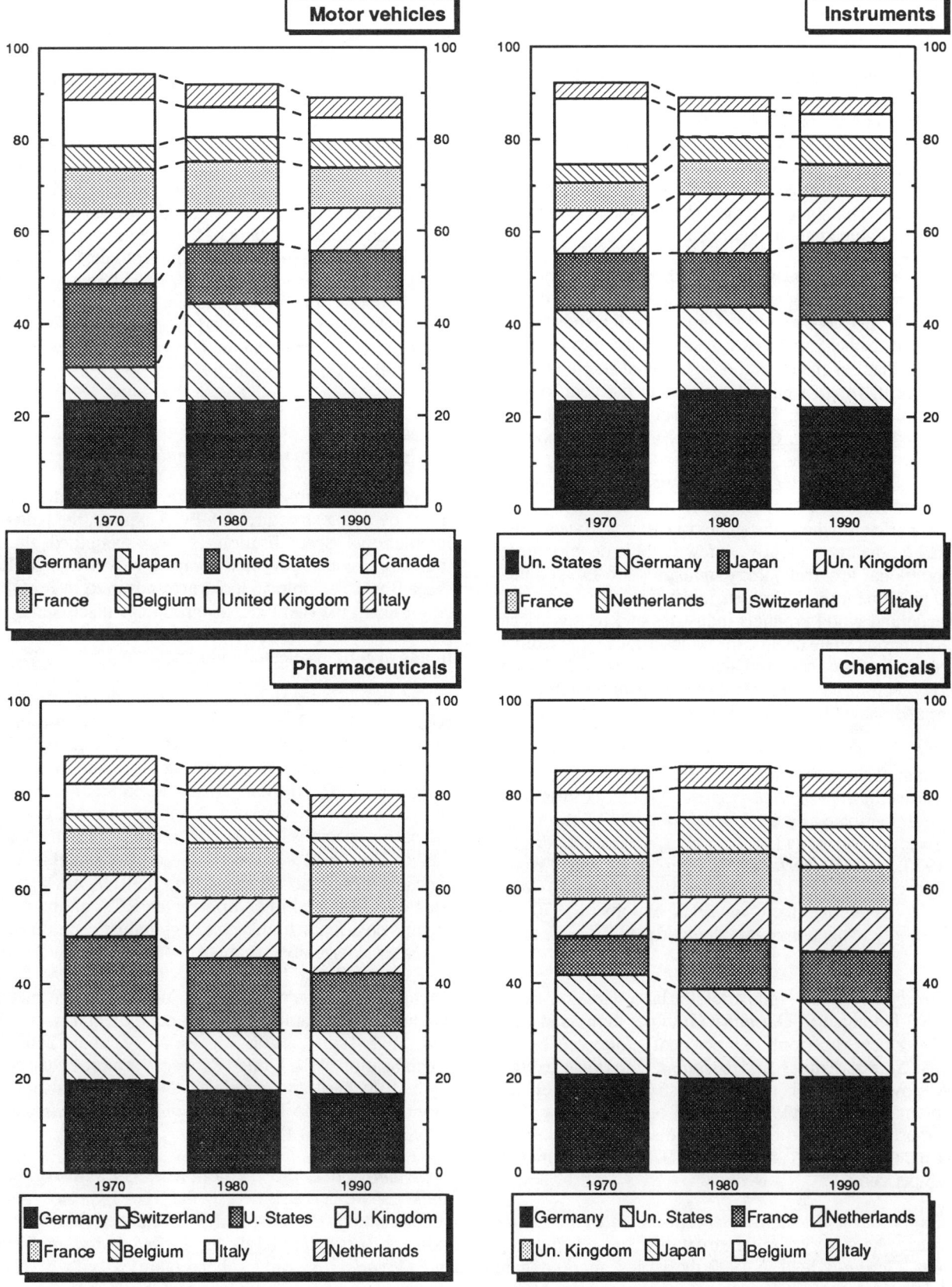

Motor vehicles

Legend: Germany, Japan, United States, Canada, France, Belgium, United Kingdom, Italy

Instruments

Legend: Un. States, Germany, Japan, Un. Kingdom, France, Netherlands, Switzerland, Italy

Pharmaceuticals

Legend: Germany, Switzerland, U. States, U. Kingdom, France, Belgium, Italy, Netherlands

Chemicals

Legend: Germany, Un. States, France, Netherlands, Un. Kingdom, Japan, Belgium, Italy

Source: OECD, STAN database.

5 per cent to just below 6 per cent over this period. Motor vehicle exports in *Spain* had remarkable relative growth, increasing the country's share of the market 11-fold to 3.8 per cent in 1990.

The *chemicals* industry was less volatile, with no major redistribution between countries, except for the *US* which lost about 5 percentage points and fell behind *Germany* to 16 per cent of the market in 1990. Germany's share has remained stable with approximately 20 per cent of the market, while slight gains were made by *Japan, France* and *Spain*. The shares of the *UK* and the *Netherlands* remained stable at about 9 per cent.

Low technology exports are a shrinking part of total OECD manufacturing exports, falling from 41 per cent in 1970 to 32 per cent in 1990. Three overall trends can be discerned in these industries over the past two decades. The *US* share of the market has remained stable at about 11 per cent, *Japan*'s has fallen from 11 per cent to 6 per cent while, in general, the European countries moderately increased their shares. Of the larger European economies, only the share of the *UK* decreased marginally. The combined shares of *Germany, France, Italy* and *Spain* increased from 30 per cent in 1970 to over 37 per cent in 1990, while elsewhere, the shares of *Canada, Sweden* and *Australia* declined slightly. A few notable developments in individual low-technology industries are Japan's near total movement out of exports in the food, beverages and tobacco and wood products industries and its significant export market share decline in textiles, footwear & leather. Germany's share increased across the board in low-technology sectors, and notably in the food (from 5.5 to 11 per cent) and paper (from 7 to 13.5 per cent) industries.

Turning now to the alternative classification based on the main factors shaping competitiveness in individual industries, in the *resource-intensive* group, exports were in 1990 dominated by the *United States* (13.3 per cent), followed by *Germany* (11.3 per cent, up from 8 per cent in 1970), the *Netherlands* (9.9 per cent) and *France* (9.8 per cent, up from 7.6 per cent in 1970). *Canada,* which with 12.7 per cent of the total OECD exports in 1970 was second only to the US saw its share drop to 8.8 per cent in 1990.

In *labour-intensive* industries, the largest market shares in 1990 belonged to *Germany* (16.8 per cent) and Italy (16.6 per cent, up from 11.9 per cent), followed by the *United States, France* and *Belgium. Japanese* exports have moved out of this type of industry: the 12.8 per cent export market share in 1970 -- second only to Germany's -- was more than halved by 1990. The same is true of UK exports: the 10.6 per cent share in 1970 declined in 1990 to 7.3 per cent.

Exports in *scale-intensive* and in *specialised-supplier* industries have very similar structures. In both industry groups, *Germany* held in 1990 the largest market share with 20 per cent of OECD exports (unchanged since 1970).

It was followed by *Japan* who has made significant market share gains, doubling is share in the specialised supplier group to reach that of Germany, and by the *United States* who has lost market share in both industry groupings. The other noteworthy trend is the decline of the *UK* share in the specialised supplier group from 10.2 per cent in 1970 to 7.4 per cent in 1990.

Finally, exports in *science-based* industries (a group that largely overlaps with the high technology group) are dominated by the *United States* which held in 1990 26.7 per cent of the market. This is the highest market share held by any country in any of the five industry groupings, but represents a significant decline from the 34.5 per cent share in 1970. *Germany* held in 1990 14.3 per cent of the export market, practically unchanged in the last twenty years, whereas *Japan* doubled its share to 12.2 per cent in 1990, thereby overtaking the *United Kingdom* which also increased its share marginally.

Revealed comparative advantage

While export market share trends provide a description of the evolving structure of OECD exports, the pattern of international specialisation is best examined through indicators such as revealed comparative advantage (RCA -- see Box 15). Table 50 looks at trends in RCA for OECD countries in the two industry groupings discussed above, and Graph 19 examines revealed comparative advantage trends in certain selected industries.

In the *high technology* industry group, only four countries had in 1990 a relative specialisation such that their RCA indicator was above 100: *Ireland* (with 181), the *United States* (161), *Japan* (149), and the *United Kingdom* (123). Of these, Ireland's remarkable evolution (its RCA in 1970 was just 72) is due to that country's increasing specialisation in the exports of computers, while that of the United States is largely attributable to the specialisation in aerospace, where its RCA has generally been over 300, and in computers (an RCA of about 200). Japan's position in high technology industries is due to net increases in its relative share of exports in computers (from an RCA of 81 in 1970 to one of 175 in 1990) and in electrical machinery. Its competitive advantage in semi-conductors and communications equipment has remained high and stable, with an RCA of about 260. The specialisation of the United Kingdom is more even accross all high-technology industries. Noteworthy also is the halving in the RCA for *Switzerland* in this industry group between 1970 and 1990.

In *aerospace*, the *US* dominance in terms of export market share is confirmed by the RCA indicator: at over 300, it remains the most highly specialised country in this industry. It is followed by the *United Kingdom, France* and *Canada,* the only other countries with a relative comparative advantage in this sector.

> **Box 15. Revealed comparative advantage in manufacturing**
>
> Revealed Comparative Advantage (RCA) is an indicator of trade showing relative specialisation and performance. For a given country and industry (or industry grouping), it is defined in this report as the share of the exports of the industry in the total manufacturing exports of the country divided by the share of total OECD-wide exports of the industry in total OECD manufacturing exports. The RCA for the German car industry for example would be expressed as the share of German car exports in German manufacturing exports relative to the share of OECD car exports in total OECD manufacturing exports.
>
> By definition, the average value of RCA for a particular industry in the OECD area is 100. Values greater than 100 indicate that a country's exports are relatively specialised in that industry. As an example, in 1990 the exports of the US aerospace industry were US$35 billion in current prices, while total manufacturing exports for the US were US$325 billion. For that same year, total OECD aerospace exports were US$76 billion, and total OECD manufacturing exports at US$2 201 billion. Thus in 1990 US aerospace exports represented 10.8 per cent of its total manufacturing exports, whereas for the OECD as a whole they represented only 3.4 per cent. The resulting value of RCA for the US aerospace industry was 315, indicating that, relative to its total manufacturing exports, US exports in aerospace are over three times greater than the OECD average.
>
> The export structure of a particular country reflects its endowments, whether in natural resources, capital, labour or technology. The RCA indicator provides information about this structure and about a country's specialisation in particular industries or industry groupings. It helps to identify the areas of strengths and of weaknesses, as these are revealed by past export performance. As the indicator is expressed relative to a benchmark such as the OECD average, it has built-in international comparability. The evolution of the indicator over time allows an analysis of the changing patterns of exports and thus of structural changes in the economy. Changes in its value reflect relative shifts in specialisation between industries, rather than outright increases or declines in export market share. Thus, used in conjunction with other trade indicators such as export market shares, it provides a good indication of competitiveness and international specialisation for countries.
>
> As is the case with every indicator, RCA has a number of limitations. First, it is by construction backward-looking. It provides information about the type of specialisation in the exports of a particular country and hence about its revealed comparative advantage in the past, but not directly about any potential shifts in that advantage in the future. Secondly, and common to other trade indicators, RCA misses intrafirm exchanges which transcend national borders. An increasing part of the production and assembly of certain goods is carried out in several countries by the same firm. To the extent that the ensuing intrafirm exchanges are not accurately accounted for in trade statistics (e.g. due to intrafirm pricing which does not reflect market prices), RCA will miss out on an important component of a country's comparative advantage. Finally, another limitation is related to the calculation of RCA in current prices. Changes in its value for an industry could then simply reflect relative export price shifts between different countries. To the extent however that export prices for the products of a given industry tend to clear internationally, distortions will be limited to the short term and to cases where industries in certain countries have dominant positions internationally.

In *computers*, the RCA trend for *Ireland* is remarkable, rising from below 50 to 500 between 1970 and 1990. Computer exports were thus 5 times more important in total Irish manufacturing exports than for the OECD as a whole. Other countries with a comparative advantage in this industry are the **United States** (with an RCA of about 175 in 1990), **Japan** (with the same RCA but a near doubling since 1970), the **United Kingdom** and the **Netherlands**.

In *electronics*, **Japan**'s relative specialisation (an RCA of 260, practically unchanged since 1970) marks it from all other countries, with only the **United States, Ireland** and **Austria** rising above 100, and the **United Kingdom** and **Sweden** just below it.

Switzerland remains highly specialised in *pharmaceuticals*, although its comparative advantage in that industry has declined in the last twenty years. A number of countries had in 1990 RCA values exceeding 100 in this industry, notably **Ireland, Denmark,** the **United Kingdom, Sweden, France** and **Austria** who has had the steepest shift in comparative advantage since 1970. Finally, in *instruments*, Switzerland remains the country with the highest specialisation, but its comparative advantage differential has collapsed: its RCA of 550 in 1970 has been replaced by a more modest 175 in 1990.

Six OECD countries have a specialisation in *medium technology* industries: **Canada, Japan, Belgium, Germany,** the **United Kingdom** and **Switzerland**. All had in

Table 50. **Revealed comparative advantage in manufacturing exports**[1]

		High tech.	Medium tech.	Low tech.	Resource-intensive	Labour-intensive	Scale-intensive	Specialised supplier	Science-based
United States	1970	159	110	67	79	58	87	123	194
	1980	160	106	70	78	80	79	118	204
	1990	161	89	74	90	63	78	110	181
Canada	1970	55	124	93	197	32	114	50	57
	1980	48	105	114	199	37	107	50	47
	1990	58	115	114	199	43	130	49	53
Japan	1970	124	78	113	33	132	139	105	63
	1980	130	106	75	22	73	151	135	56
	1990	149	113	44	18	48	125	156	95
Belgium/Lux.	1970	44	95	127	109	135	129	52	42
	1980	49	102	123	122	149	115	50	58
	1990	40	116	124	113	159	132	47	53
Denmark	1970	73	62	149	197	97	50	97	69
	1980	77	58	161	195	111	46	92	77
	1990	78	59	171	195	128	51	92	82
France	1970	86	94	112	93	117	112	79	99
	1980	84	99	109	103	100	114	83	93
	1990	90	98	112	111	99	109	77	107
Germany	1970	97	125	76	48	95	119	132	88
	1980	95	117	80	64	89	119	119	88
	1990	83	121	83	65	96	119	114	82
Greece	1970	15	60	174	221	115	96	10	35
	1980	18	39	210	247	184	43	15	44
	1990	18	33	252	250	294	39	18	18
Ireland	1970	72	22	191	274	136	25	26	85
	1980	117	58	143	183	109	58	53	145
	1990	181	54	107	150	66	48	68	232
Italy	1970	78	99	109	74	185	78	117	69
	1980	66	91	128	84	199	81	106	57
	1990	63	90	140	87	227	74	106	56
Netherlands	1970	98	63	139	175	103	75	72	82
	1980	80	73	143	195	69	84	62	77
	1990	80	79	142	186	87	84	62	104

1990 RCA indices between 100 and 120 (121 for Germany) and have exhibited little movement in the last twenty years. The greatest shift towards this type of exports was in Japan, while the United States and the United Kingdom were two countries whose export structure moved away from medium technology. Comparative advantage in *motor vehicles*, one of the largest industries in this group, has shifted a lot between countries, with Canada, Japan and *Spain* the three OECD countries showing the highest relative export specialisation in the sector in 1990. The largest shifts in comparative advantage have occurred in Spain, Japan and *Austria,* while the RCA index fell most sharply in *France,* the *United States* and the United Kingdom.

In the *low technology* group, it is in smaller OECD economies such as *Greece, Portugal* and *New Zealand* that comparative advantage lies. The export specialisation of these countries in low technology industries has grown stronger in the 1970-90 period. Of the larger OECD countries, only *France, Canada* and *Italy* have RCA indices above 100, and it is only in Italy that this type of export specialisation has increased since 1970. The sharpest shift away from low technology exports has been in *Japan,* which, starting with an RCA index of 113 in 1970 ended up in 1990 with an index of 44.

The alternative five-group industry classification shows a more differentiated picture of the structure and

Table 50. **Revealed comparative advantage in manufacturing exports**[1] *(cont'd)*

		High tech.	Medium tech.	Low tech.	Resource-intensive	Labour-intensive	Scale-intensive	Specialised supplier	Science-based
Portugal	1970	46	37	186	194	256	35	34	34
	1980	58	37	194	164	268	42	44	42
	1990	47	42	220	140	346	54	53	20
Spain	1970	37	63	163	184	132	82	56	32
	1980	47	86	142	133	112	120	62	42
	1990	53	102	132	134	104	134	59	52
United Kingdom	1970	105	117	81	78	115	94	112	118
	1980	127	109	80	88	115	81	104	163
	1990	123	97	91	83	97	93	98	147
Austria	1970	70	73	140	115	165	84	99	30
	1980	74	79	136	103	151	89	107	39
	1990	75	93	128	109	140	92	118	43
Finland	1970	20	36	197	304	69	48	44	6
	1980	40	46	193	255	96	53	58	26
	1990	54	64	186	258	64	67	94	30
Norway	1970	29	90	138	232	43	104	42	18
	1980	41	90	140	216	48	98	54	38
	1990	42	87	161	267	45	95	48	44
Sweden	1970	74	84	127	145	58	98	109	54
	1980	83	87	122	137	68	91	115	60
	1990	83	89	124	150	65	90	111	71
Switzerland	1970	185	105	61	50	117	55	134	248
	1980	122	115	54	48	142	57	138	136
	1990	94	116	59	46	150	60	129	111
Turkey	1970	11	46	190	250	207	36	11	33
	1980	10	36	217	143	349	54	15	8
	1990	23	32	251	124	363	78	24	18
Australia	1970	17	67	166	322	57	51	20	25
	1980	27	71	169	328	58	37	23	40
	1990	32	75	185	343	98	46	29	41
New Zealand	1970	4	10	230	405	63	4	7	21
	1980	12	22	232	346	119	15	14	9
	1990	15	32	257	428	92	23	20	12

1. Revealed comparative advantage (RCA) for a particular industry (or industry grouping) is defined as the ratio of the share of the country's exports in that industry in its total manufacturing exports to the share of total exports by that industry (or industry grouping) in OECD manufacturing exports. With exports denoted by X, for a country k, the RCA of an industry i is given by: $100 \cdot ([X_{ik}/\Sigma_i X_{ik}]/[\Sigma_k X_{ik}/\Sigma_{i,k} X_{ik}])$.

Source: OECD, STAN database.

evolution of apparant comparative advantage in OECD manufacturing exports. With the exception of the G7 group of countries (*France* excluded) and of *Switzerland*, all OECD countries had in 1990 RCA indices exceeding 100 in *resource-intensive* industries, while the greatest relative specialisation was with the resource-rich countries of *Australia, New Zealand, Norway* and *Finland*. Of these, only in the case of Finland has there been a -- relatively modest -- shift away from this type of exports. Apparent comparative advantage in the *labour intensive* group of industries lay in 1990 with smaller OECD countries such as *Turkey, Greece* and *Portugal*, whose RCA index increased markedly in this type of exports between 1970 and 1990, as well as with *Italy*, unique among larger countries for exhibiting the same shift towards this type of manufactured exports. *Spain, Belgium, Canada, Japan*, France and *Germany* were the only OECD countries with a relative export specialization in *scale-intensive* industries.

In the *specialized-supplier* group, apparant comparative advantage in 1990 was in all the G7 countries (and

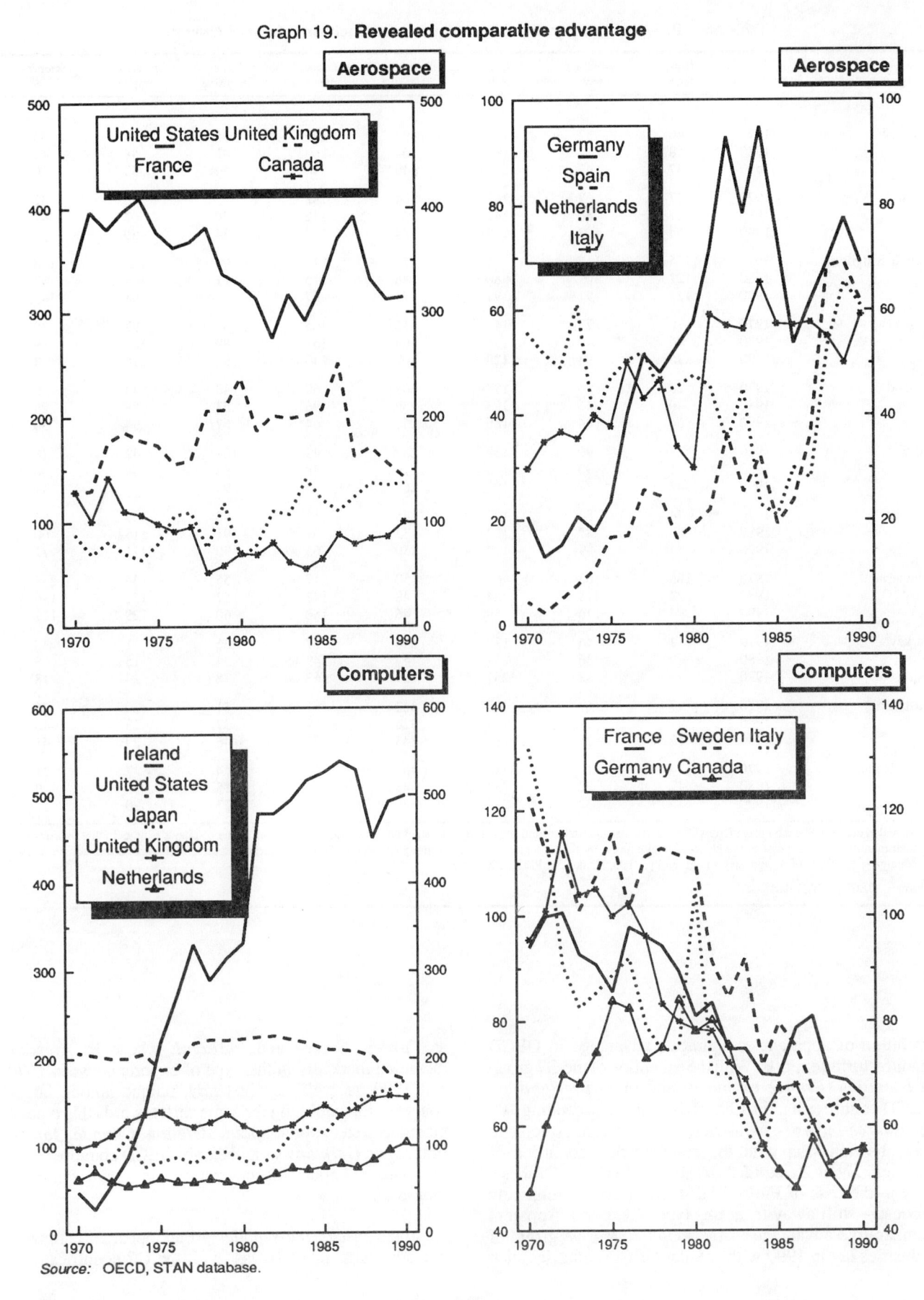

Graph 19. **Revealed comparative advantage**

Aerospace (United States, United Kingdom, France, Canada)

Aerospace (Germany, Spain, Netherlands, Italy)

Computers (Ireland, United States, Japan, United Kingdom, Netherlands)

Computers (France, Sweden, Italy, Germany, Canada)

Source: OECD, STAN database.

Graph 19 (cont). **Revealed comparative advantage**

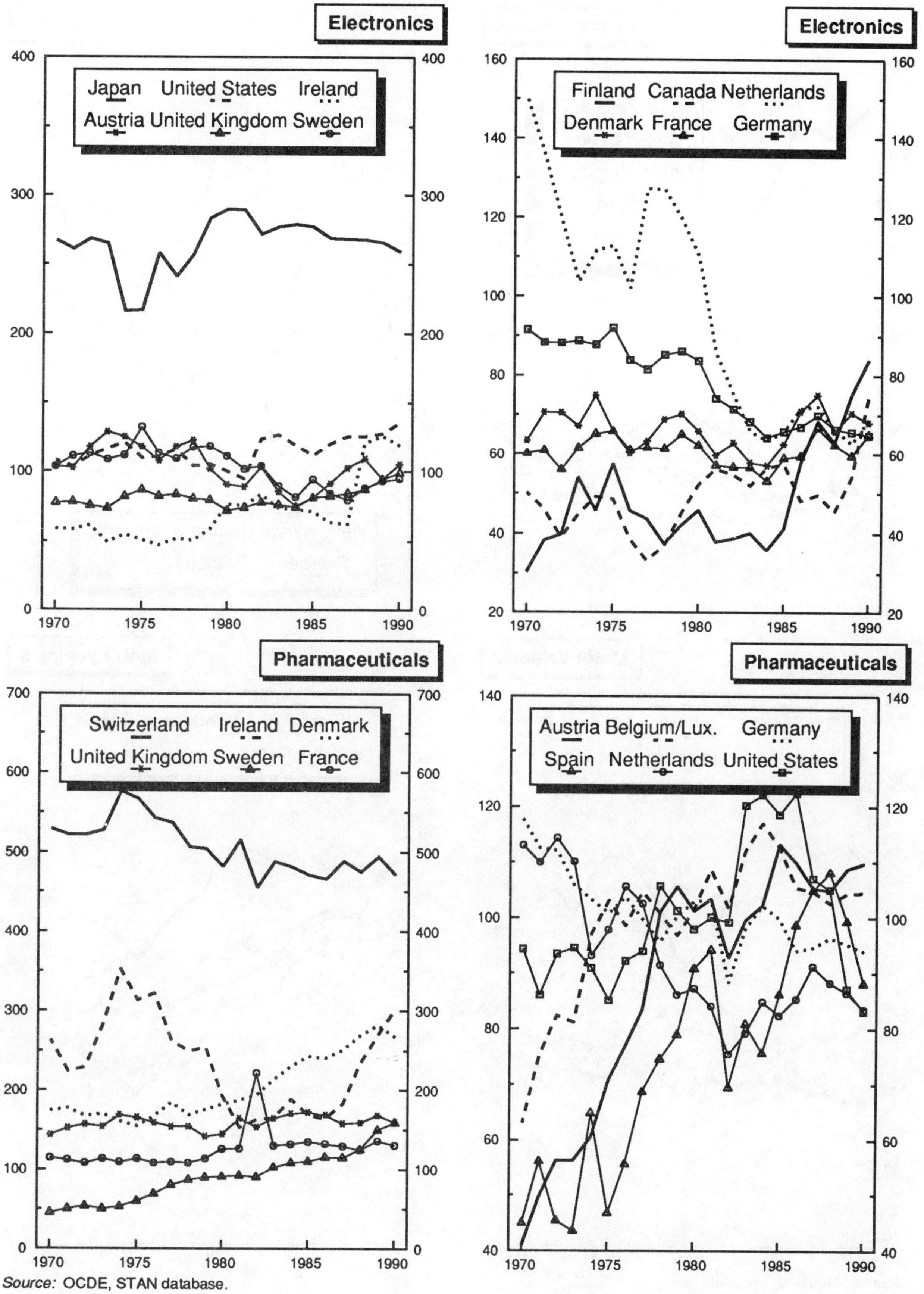

Source: OCDE, STAN database.

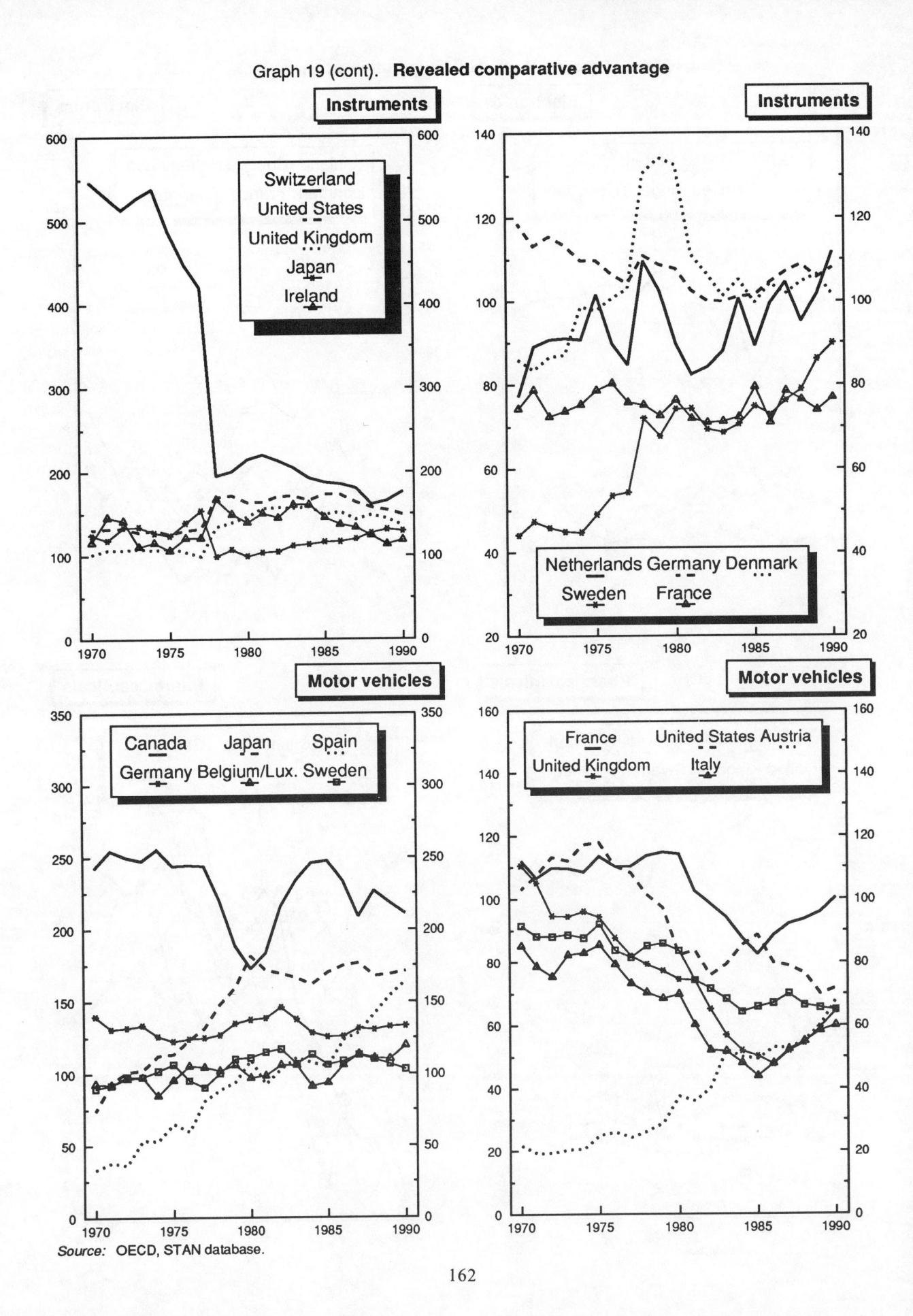

Graph 19 (cont). **Revealed comparative advantage**

Source: OECD, STAN database.

especially *Japan*), as well as in ***Austria, Sweden*** and ***Switzerland***. Finally, in the *science-based* group of industries, the RCA index in 1990 exceeded 100 in ***Ireland***, the ***United States, France***, the ***Netherlands***, the ***United Kingdom*** and Switzerland. Of these countries, the largest shift towards this type of export was in Ireland (from an RCA index of 85 in 1970 to one of 232 in 1990), while it was in Switzerland that the structure of exports moved away the most from science-based sectors (from an RCA index of 248 in 1970 to one of 111 in 1990).

In summary, the export market shares and revealed comparative advantage indicators examined under the two alternative clasification systems reveal some important structural shifts in the composition of OECD manufacturing exports. Of the large OECD countries, the ***United States*** has lost market share in all industry categories, but conserves an important comparative advantage in high technology or science-based industries. ***Japan*** has moved out of low technology and labour-intensive industries towards medium and high technology sectors, or towards specialised-supplier and science-based industries. ***Germany*** has increased or held market share accross the board, while its export specialisation remains unchanged, concentrated around medium technology, or scale-intensive and specialised-supplier industries. Market shares and comparative advantage in ***France*** have varied little, while ***Italy*** is the only large country whose exports have moved in the direction of low technology, labour intensive industries, reinforcing both market share and specialisation. ***Canada*** has lost market share in all industry groups, while its export specialisation remains centered around resource and scale-intensive industries.

In the smaller OECD countries, three patterns emerge. The first is that of more mature economies such as ***Austria, Switzerland*** and the ***Nordic*** countries. They have in general held on to their export market shares and export specialisation patterns, although in some cases (as with Switzerland) their comparative advantage in some industry groups (high technology, science-based) has been largely dissipated. The second pattern is that of countries such as ***Ireland*** and ***Spain***, which have made remarkable market share gains, and whose comparative advantage has clearly moved in the direction of medium and high technology industries, while also maintaining some specialisation in resource and labour intensive sectors. The third pattern is that of countries such as ***Greece, Portugal*** and ***Turkey***, which while making some market gains (especially in the case of Portugal and Turkey), they have at the same time reinforced their specialisation in labour-intensive, low-technology industries.

NOTES AND REFERENCES

1. For a more detailed discussion of the macroeconomic situation on the OECD area, see OECD (1992), *OECD Economic Outlook No.51*, Paris.
2. See *OECD Economic Outlook, op.cit.*
3. See *OECD Economic Outlook, op.cit.*
4. OECD (1992), *The Steel Market in 1991 and the Outlook for 1992*, Paris.
5. US Department of Commerce (1992), *US Industrial Outlook 1992*.
6. Commission of the European Communities (1992), *Panorama of EC Industries 1991-92*.
7. US Department of Commerce (1992), *US Industrial Outlook 1992*.
8. OECD (1992), *OECD Employment Outlook*, Paris.
9. For a more extended treatment of this issue see *OECD Employment Outlook, op.cit.*
10. US Department of Commerce (1992), *Plant and Equipment Expenditures and Plans*, April.
11. Finnish Ministry of Finance (1991), *Economic Survey of Finland*.
12. See Ford, R. and Poret, P. (1991), "Business Investment: Recent Performance and Implications for Policy", *OECD Economic Studies No.16*, Spring.
13. See Ford, R. and Poret, P. (1991), *op.cit.*
14. A net foreign investment balance is negative (positive) when the inflows of capital to a certain country exceed (are less) than capital outflows.
15. See US Department of Commerce (1991), "US Business Enterprises Acquired or Established by Foreign Direct Investors in 1990", *Survey of Current Business*, May, pp. 30-39.
16. The figures in Tables 37 and 38 are not directly comparable with the flow data compiled from balances of payments.
17. See US Department of Commerce (1991), *Survey of Current Business*.
18. Data from the Japanese Ministry of Finance.
19. See Hunya, G. (1992), "Foreign Direct Investment and Privatisation in Central and Eastern Europe", paper presented at the Vienna Institute for Comparative Economics Studies Seminar, April.
20. Figures from the *East-West Joint Ventures Newsletter*, March 1992.
21. *United Nations World Investment Report* (1991).
22. General Agreement of Tariffs and Trade -- GATT (1992), *Council Overview of Developments in International Trade and the Trading System: Annual Report by the Director General*.
23. *OECD Economic Outlook, op.cit.*
24. General Agreement of Tariffs and Trade -- GATT (1992), *op.cit.*
25. See OECD (1991), *OECD Economic Surveys: Japan*, as well as Marston, R. (1990), "Price Behaviour in Japanese and US Manufacturing", NBER Working Paper No.3364.
26. Export market shares are calculated from the OECD/ESDNA NEXT database, and converted to current US dollars using current exchange rates.

Part 4

**STRUCTURAL CHANGE AND INDUSTRIAL PERFORMANCE:
GROWTH DECOMPOSITION IN SEVEN OECD ECONOMIES**

A. Introduction

This part of the report analyses structural change in seven OECD countries in the decade and a half since the first oil shock [1]. Countries covered are *Australia*, *Canada*, *France*, *Germany*, *Japan*, the *United Kingdom* and the *United States*. Together, these seven countries were responsible for 84 per cent of OECD GDP and 71 per cent of OECD exports in 1989. Changes in the detailed industrial structure of each economy are examined, as well as the extent and determinants of real growth rates. The aim is to describe and compare the observed patterns of change in the sectoral composition of each economy and to characterise them in policy relevant terms by:

- developing measures of the extent of change;

- characterising the extent in terms of the direction of change; and

- analysing both the extent and direction in terms of the factors associated with the change.

The last two decades were accompanied by extensive economic change in OECD economies, causing some analysts to characterize this period as one of an economic transition -- changing from one state to another [2]. Although market economies are always evolving in response to changes in the economic environment, the magnitude of the changes and the challenges they represented were particularly large: two oil shocks, two major recessions, substantial changes in the size and nature of international trade, the liberalisation of global capital markets, and the development of microelectronic technologies and their widespread diffusion, were a few of the more important events. These changes coincided with a slowdown in growth where the real increase in OECD GDP was half as fast during this period as it was from 1950 to 1973 [3] and the growth rate of productivity fell from a yearly average of 5 per cent to less than 2 per cent [4].

In response to these changes, industrial structures in most countries have altered significantly, reflecting structural, as opposed to cyclical, shifts in the composition of output, employment, and trade. Nevertheless, the magnitude and nature of these shifts differed significantly from one country to another. An accurate picture of these changes is a prerequisite to understanding the current state and likely development of national economies in the 1990s. In particular, it is important to address the following type of policy-related questions:

- Which were the sectors experiencing growth across countries and what factors were associated with this growth? Was the growth export driven or was it due to strong domestic demand or the displacement of imports? Or was it spurred on by technological change? What characteristics were common to expanding industries?

- What were the sectors of decline across countries? What events were aligned with this decline: falling exports? increased import penetration? a downturn in domestic demand? or an adverse shift in technology? What characteristics did declining industries share?

- Which economies experienced the most and least structural change? How did the factors associated with the change differ across countries? What does this imply for structural change in the 1990s?

The importance of such questions has increased as countries have recognized that structural flexibility and speed of response to changing economic environments are significant determinants of growth. The attention given to the reform and co-ordination of microeconomic policies, as a complement to macroeconomic policies, has grown accordingly. This part of the report describes the characteristics of these structural shifts and changes in growth, showing how the industrial profiles of OECD economies have changed over the last decade-and-a-half.

B. Analytical framework

Defining structural change

Although the term "structural change" is widely used, neither its meaning nor measurement are precisely defined. In practice structural change covers a number of different concepts and a variety of measures. In broad terms, structural change encompasses two different themes: compositional structural change and institutional structural change.

Compositional structural change refers to changes in the industrial composition or profile of an economy: changes in the output or employment shares accounted for by different industries, for example, or changes in the mix of factor inputs used by industries (see Box 16). Its main characteristic is that it examines individual industries; the capital and labour inputs they use; and the way in which industries are connected to one another, both domestically and internationally. Its strength is that it provides a detailed picture of how the structure of an economy and its interlinkages have evolved over time. Its weakness is that it points only indirectly to policy actions. Indicators of compositional change measure the outcomes of structural change, whereas policy is more concerned with the underlying causes and in particular the nature and

> **Box 16. Gross output and value-added measures of structural change**
>
> Changes in gross output (factory shipments) and value-added (the contribution of an industry to GNP) are the two most common variables used to measure structural change. Interpreting them requires a knowledge of their limitations.
>
> ***Gross output*** represents factory production or shipments [1]. It is relatively simple to measure and interpret, being the unit price of an industry's product multiplied by the number of units produced [2]. It is also relatively easy to convert from current to constant prices. However, gross output includes the value of all inputs that were purchased from other industries as well as the value added to these inputs by the using industry. When aggregated across the whole economy significant double counting occurs in gross output measures. For example, the output of the steel industry is counted both by the steel industry which produced it and also by the motor vehicle industry that used steel as an input. In terms of measuring structural change this can be misleading since an industry's level of output can rise through increased throughput of intermediate inputs with little additional value being added. Nevertheless, the inclusion of intermediate inputs serves two purposes: (i) it preserves the links that exist between industries, revealing the interdependencies that exist; and (ii) it retains a profile of the mixture of inputs used by an industry. Changes in this profile are a broad reflection of technological change which is an important factor in analyzing structural change.
>
> ***Value-added*** by definition is equal to an industry's gross output minus intermediate inputs. Summed across all industries, it yields GNP. Unlike output, value-added represents the net addition an industry contributes in its production process and does not result in double counting. Combined with the fact that GNP is a widely followed indicator of economic activity, this makes it an attractive variable for measuring structural change. However, value-added is difficult to convert to constant prices. Without constant prices it is not possible to separate the effects of real structural change (i.e. changes in the volumes of output) from differential inflation when comparing the evolution of different industries. Some difficulties are conceptual; others are technical and reflect deficiencies in the available data. Because the calculation of value-added requires separate price indexes for both the inputs and the outputs, the problems associated with converting value-added to constant prices are substantially larger than for (gross) output. At the detailed industry level of this study, it has not been possible to assemble internationally comparable and internally consistent value-added data.
>
> The analysis of structural change here is based on gross output.
>
> 1. Precise definitions differ from country to country and may include changes in stocks, work done on own account, services rendered etc. See OECD (1991), *Industrial Structure Statistics*, Paris.
> 2. The model used in this report is based on producer's prices as opposed to purchaser's prices and as a result does not include the transaction costs associated with selling the product such as transportation, insurance, or wholesale and retail trade margins.

magnitude of constraints to structural adjustment. Any observed compositional change is likely to have a range of causal factors. Interpretation generally requires that a number of compositional indicators be considered together, along with information on the likely underlying economic determinants.

Institutional structural change is concerned with the behaviour of labour and financial markets, the traded goods market, and the operation of the public sector. Analysis typically focuses on labour and capital market rigidities (including exchange rate regimes); tariff and non-tariff barriers; and the regulatory and public infrastructure environment in which firms operate. The characteristic of institutional structural change is that it examines broad markets not necessarily restricted to any one industry and is concerned with deviations from competitive market behaviour. The institutional factors associated with such deviations are assumed to be among the primary constraints to structural adjustment. The strength of institutional structural change indicators is that they are directly related to policy actions. Their weakness is that they are often difficult to derive and in many cases must be obtained as the result of modelling, itself an indirect process.

Compositional and institutional structural change are complementary concepts. Robust policy analysis of structural change requires both. In each, the emphasis is on medium term change, including the response to significant shocks, rather than the short term fluctuations associated with business cycles.

The focus here is on compositional structural change and how the division of economic activity by industry sector has changed over the decade and a half from the first oil crisis in 1973 to the mid 1980s. The aim of compositional change is to describe the observed patterns of change and to characterise them in policy relevant terms. Although it does not examine the institutional factors behind the compositional changes, it does identify the broad sources of change for each industry: export growth, growth in domestic demand, import substitution and changes in the pattern of inter-industry linkages in the economy (referred to as the economy's "technology"). In doing so it represents an extension of previous compositional work [5] and a complement to previous institutional analyses carried out in the OECD.

Measuring compositional structural change

Two different compositional indicators are used to analyze the extent of structural change: the annual growth rate of (real) output in each industry and the share of national (real) output accounted for by each industry. Even though both the annual growth rate and share indicators are based on the same underlying data, their interpretation differs. The annual growth rates of output are absolute measures of change whereas share indicators measure change relative to the average rate of growth for the economy as a whole. The change in an industry's share of total output is analogous to increases or decreases in slices of a pie. An industry might be expanding but if the economy as a whole is growing more rapidly the industry's share will decline. Growth rates suffer from being sensitive to the initial size of the industry in a particular country: relatively small industries tend to be more volatile than large, generally mature industries. Shares are less sensitive to the volatility of small industries: a gain of 1 per cent in the share of total output represents a fixed quantity and is independent of the size of the industry.

In summary, the measurement of structural change in this study is based on integrating three elements:

- compositional measures of the extent of change;

- characterisation of the extent in terms of the direction of change; and

- analysis of both the extent and direction in terms of the factors associated with growth and decline that represent the path of change followed to reach the present industrial structure.

Decomposing structural change using input-output tables

The changing pattern of linkages between industries is itself one of the major manifestations of structural change (see Box 17). At any one moment, the interlinkages specify how the outputs of each industry in the economy are used as inputs in other industries (as well as in final demand). This snapshot of the input mixes used by each industry is often referred to as the "technology" or "production recipe" of the economy and the changing connections between industries is then interpreted as technical change. As economies become technologically more sophisticated and there is increasing division of labour and specialisation, the inter-industry links generally grow more complex. Such technical change is a distinctly different process from changes in final demand and is not captured at all by conventional compositional indicators of structural change.

Input-output models of the economy explicitly capture the interconnections between different industries. By their construction, they show how the output of each industry in the economy flows to various uses: as intermediate inputs into other industries; as goods for final consumption by households and governments; as goods for domestic investment; and as goods for exports. As used in this study, they also specify how imports are used as intermediate inputs and final goods. At the same time, they describe the input mix of each industry: how much of the outputs of other industries was used to produce a unit of own output.

Changes in the pattern of intermediate consumption correspond to changes in the interlinkages between industries (i.e. changes in the input-output coefficients)

Box 17. Capturing the indirect effects of structural change: US steel

As the level of international trade has grown it has become intertwined through complex and often not obvious interrelationships with nearly every industry. In such cases, indicators of direct trade performance, such as the ratio of imports to shipments, represent only part of the effect. For example, the US Department of Commerce using input-output methodology has estimated that imports of steel into the US were US$4.8 billion in 1984, but the steel embedded in other imported items were valued at US$8.5 billion, nearly double the direct effect. Thus imports of cars made of steel affect not only the US auto industry, but also the US steel industry -- a connection that is not made with conventional indicators. The reverse is also true: the steel industry exported directly only 1.7 per cent of its output in 1984, but when the indirect effect is accounted for the ratio rises to 21.7 per cent [1].

1. US Department of Commerce (1984), "Trade Ripples Across US Industries", Office of Business Analysis, Working Paper, January.

> **Box 18. Technical change in input-output analysis**
>
> An example of what is meant by technological change as shifts in intermediate inputs can be seen in the motor vehicle industry where in the US from the mid-1970s to the mid-1980s, the iron and steel content of a car fell by 30 per cent while the amount of plastics and composites increased by 33 per cent [1]. Such changes in the use of materials and the adoption of new processes alter the mix of intermediate inputs in the motor vehicle industry and subsequently affect the supplying industries. In these cases decreases would be felt in the steel and electricity sectors and an increase in the plastics industry.
>
> Although these shifts in inputs are commonly labelled technological change, they could also arise as a result of substitution among inputs due to relative price changes. These might in turn be due to changes in relative labour costs, or external factors such as an oil shock. They may also reflect improved allocative efficiencies following institutional changes in labour or financial markets, in the regulatory environment, or in trade instruments such as tariffs. Alternatively, they may be due to a changing mixture of industries at a level of aggregation that is lower than the one being analyzed. For example, a change in the inputs of the motor vehicle industry might not be due to a "true" change in technology but might be due to the fact that the motorcycle component of motor vehicles has grown relative to truck production. This inability to precisely identify technical change does not have an impact on the construction of the indicators developed here; it does however mean that the technology factor in decomposition analyses must be interpreted with caution.
>
> 1. Williams, R., Larson, E. and Ross, M. (1987), "Materials, Affluence, and Industrial Energy Use", *Annual Review of Energy*, p.120; and Motor Vehicle Manufacturers Assoc., *Facts and Figures*, various issues.

and following normal convention will be called "technical change" (see Box 18) [6]. By systematically varying each one of these factors at a time while holding the others constant, the total change in an industry's output between any two years can be decomposed into those parts attributable to changes in each of the factors [7]. This allows an analysis which not only quantifies the loss or gain in output made by an industry, but also how that change came about in terms of movements in each of the underlying factors.

The change in an industry's output or employment can therefore be decomposed according to the factors that have contributed to the change:

Change in output = change due to domestic final demand
+ change due to exports
+ change due to imports of final products
+ change due to imports of intermediate inputs
+ change in technology (input-output coefficients)

Table 51 illustrates a typical decomposition of constant price gross output for manufacturing. In *Australia*, for example, manufacturing gross output grew in real terms at an average annual rate of 1.6 per cent. The dominant positive source for this growth was expansion of domestic final demand, i.e. expansion of consumption by households and government together with business investment. Had there been no other influences, this expansion would have generated a manufacturing growth rate of 2.2 per cent. The growing substitution by imports for domestically produced manufactures reduced the growth rate significantly. Finally, technical change in the Australian economy resulted in less intensive intermediate use of manufactures as inputs into other industries. This technical change decreased the average annual growth rate by 0.5 per cent. Actual gross output growth is equal to the sum of all of the five effects: adding across all the sources of change yields the observed output growth rate of 1.6 per cent [8].

The picture is quite different for *Canada*. Real manufacturing output grew at a rate of 2.2 per cent with expansion in exports being the dominant factor, demand for domestic products generated a relatively small 0.4 gain in the growth rate. These gains were reduced by 1.0 per cent by imports of intermediate and final goods. Though technical change did decrease the manufacturing growth rate, its effect was relatively small. In contrast, in the *United Kingdom* growth in domestic final demand and exports were relatively weak while import penetration was a major factor in the overall low growth rate. Import penetration was also an important factor all the other countries except *Japan* where it was negligible. But in each of these countries, either domestic demand expansion or export expansion provided a counterbalancing force.

As is clear from these examples, the same industry may be driven by different forces in different countries. This reflects a range of underlying causal factors. Shifts in final demand are linked to a host of exogenous variables such as prices, demographics, tastes and income levels as well as government policies. As the level and composition of

Table 51. **Sources of growth in real output for manufacturing**

	Period (base year)	Av. annual growth rate (per cent)	Source of growth				
			Domestic final demand expansion	Export expansion	Imports of final goods	Imports of interm. goods	Technology (change in I/O coeff.)[1]
Australia	1974-86 (1984)	1.6	2.2	0.5	−0.3	−0.3	−0.5
Canada	1981-86 (1981)	2.2	0.4	3.0	−0.5	−0.5	−0.2
France	1972-85 (1980)	1.3	1.0	1.6	−0.5	−0.5	−0.2
Germany	1978-86 (1980)	1.0	0.6	1.8	−0.4	−0.6	−0.3
Japan	1970-85 (1975)	4.4	2.7	2.0	0.0	−0.1	−0.3
United Kingdom	1968-84 (1980)	0.2	0.8	1.0	−0.7	−0.8	−0.2
United States	1972-85 (1982)	1.6	2.2	0.6	−0.4	−0.4	−0.5

1. I/O: Input/Output.
Source: OECD, STAN input-output database.

domestic consumption changes, industries respond by adjusting their output and employment. Other things being equal, industrial production in economies that have large internal markets would be expected to be more sensitive to changes in domestic consumption than production in small, outward-oriented economies.

Similarly, the level and commodity composition of a country's exports depend on many factors. These include the country's natural resources and endowments of human capital, exchange rates, trade policies and the openness of markets, and the rates of economic growth in those markets to which the country in question is exporting. It will also depend on factors specific to each industry such as the level of unit labour costs, the rate of long term investment and expenditures on innovation.

The degree of import penetration depends more directly on the level of internationalisation of a country and the rate of trade exposure of its industries. In the growth decomposition tables, a negative value associated with imports in a particular industry indicates that purchases of imports have increased, reducing the potential output growth of the domestic industry. A positive value represents a displacement of imports -- the rate of import penetration for a particular industry has declined, causing an increase in the output of the domestic industry.

Although conventionally counted as part of final demand, a significant portion of imports are also used as intermediate inputs (e.g. steel, oil) in domestic production processes. Depending on currency fluctuations, regulations, relative prices and various other factors, producers will substitute imported inputs for domestically supplied inputs, affecting the output and employment of the domestic industry. As production facilities expand around the globe with increases in foreign direct investment, transplant facilities, and intrafirm trade, the impact of this factor on structural change will increase in importance. As in the case of imports of final products, usually the effect of this factor will be negative, reducing the potential level of domestic output. However, in some instances a positive value can occur, indicating a displacement of imports.

Intermediate inputs tend to be raw materials, semi-finished goods, and business services. They are provided by suppliers to an industry which transforms them, using capital and labour inputs, into the industry's output. This combination or mix of inputs represents the industry's production recipe since it reflects not only the ingredients used to make its product, but also the know-how involved in combining these inputs into a final product. As discussed above, the pattern of input mixes across all industries is called the "technology" of the economy. An increase in the use of inputs relative to total output is an indicator of increased specialization of the production process; industries are "out-sourcing" more of their inputs. The causes may be many. Relative prices may change, favouring raw materials over capital and labour. Diseconomies of scale may encourage leaner organisational structures. Conversely, a decrease in the use of inputs as a proportion of output indicates that more processes are being undertaken "in-house", possibly to capture economies of scale. Alternatively, scientific innovations may lead to increased production efficiencies in the use of raw materials which result in fewer inputs are required to produce the same level of output. Whatever the case, these production recipes are a reflection of the technology of the economy and are subject to all the forces of technological change.

C. Results of the growth decomposition

The decomposition of structural change is based on three general questions: What were the engines of growth? What were the sectors of decline? and which economies experienced the most and least structural change? Shifts in real output, together with changes in absolute growth rates, are analysed to identify those industries that have experienced the most and least adjustment over the period. The two types of measures provide differing but complementary pictures of how the countries examined have moved towards service and high-technology manufacturing and away from construction, low-technology manufacturing, and in some countries, medium technology manufacturing and natural resource intensive industries.

What were the sectors of growth across countries?

On the basis of gains in share of total output, the expanding sectors in the seven countries were the service sectors, led by the financial services group (consisting of finance & insurance and real estate & business services) and technologically sophisticated manufacturing, particularly the production of computers and communication & semiconductor equipment. Three groups of countries emerge, with Japan and the US being in one group; France, Germany, the UK, and to a lesser extent Canada representing a second group; and Australia in a third category exhibiting movement towards services, but no positive shifts in manufacturing.

The first group: Japan and the US

Japan represents the most pronounced example of this pattern of structural change. Its high-technology sector experienced the largest gain in share of total output from 1970 to 1985, jumping by 7.2 share points (Graph 20). This was the single largest gain of any sector in any of the countries analysed and was the factor why Japan was the only country to register a positive increase in manufacturing's share of total output. The gain in share of the high-technology group has been consistent and growing since 1975 with 60 per cent of the positive gain in share occurring from 1980 to 1985. The decomposition of the high-technology output growth reveals that every factor contributed to this growth, but exports, domestic demand and technological change were the major factors, each respectively contributing 47, 36, and 15 per cent of the growth from 1970 to 1985. The bulk of the export led growth occurred during the 1980 to 1985 period, probably a reflection of the low value of the yen compared to other currencies, especially the US dollar. Although a relatively smaller factor, the effect of imports on Japan's high-technology sector was positive, signifying a displacement of imported high-technology goods with domestically produced products. Most of the high-technology gain in share was due to the computer & office machinery and communication & semiconductor industries.

Japan also witnessed shifts in total output towards some service sectors during the 1970 to 1985 period with both the financial services and the community, social, & personal services (CSPS) groups experiencing gains of 1.7 and 1.5 share points respectively [9]. The gain in financial services was entirely due to the real estate & business services component of this group which saw growth primarily in the 1970 to 1975 period. CSPS's gain in output share from 1970 to 1985 was due to an increase in the share held by the government producers industry and to a lesser extent the social & personal services industry. For government, domestic final demand was the catalyst behind the change while changes in technology affected social & personal services.

The medium-technology manufacturing group was the remaining Japanese sector to increase its share of total output from 1970 to 1985. Its relatively small increase of one percentage point conceals the fact that large, offsetting changes were occurring within the sector: while exports boosted its share by three percentage points and technology contributed 0.4 points of an increase, changes in domestic final demand led to a 2.3 share point drop. The overwhelming bulk of this sector's gain occurred from 1975 to 1980 and was attributable to the motor vehicle industry.

In the *United States*, as in Japan, the sectors experiencing the greatest positive gain in share of total output from 1972 to 1985 were the financial services and the high-technology manufacturing sector (Graph 20). Unlike Japan, the magnitude of the change attributable to the high-technology sector was much smaller, 2.4 versus 7.2 share points, making it the second largest source of output gain for the US behind financial services which grew by 2.5 points. Sixty nine per cent of the growth in the financial services group was concentrated in the real estate & business services industry. The output increase in this industry was associated with growth in domestic final demand and to a much lesser extent increases due to exports and technology. The growth was largely concentrated in the 1977 to 1985 period.

Output growth in the US high-technology sector was driven by domestic final demand for its products with exports playing a smaller, supporting role. The output share gain would have been a half-point higher were it not for imports of both intermediate and final high-technology goods. Nearly all of the growth occurred between 1977 to 1985 and was largely driven by the computer & office machinery and communication & semiconductor equipment industries. Imports particularly affected the electronic machinery and communication & semiconductor equipment industries.

Three service sectors other than the financial services group had increases in total output from 1972 to 1985: community, social & personal services (+1.9), wholesale & retail trade and hotels & restaurants (+1.6), and transportation, storage & communication (+0.7). The growth in community, social & personal services group was all in the social & personal services part which includes private education and health care services. The other industry in this group, government producers, lost share over this time period. The increase in share was due both to increases

Graph 20. **Changes in share of real output**

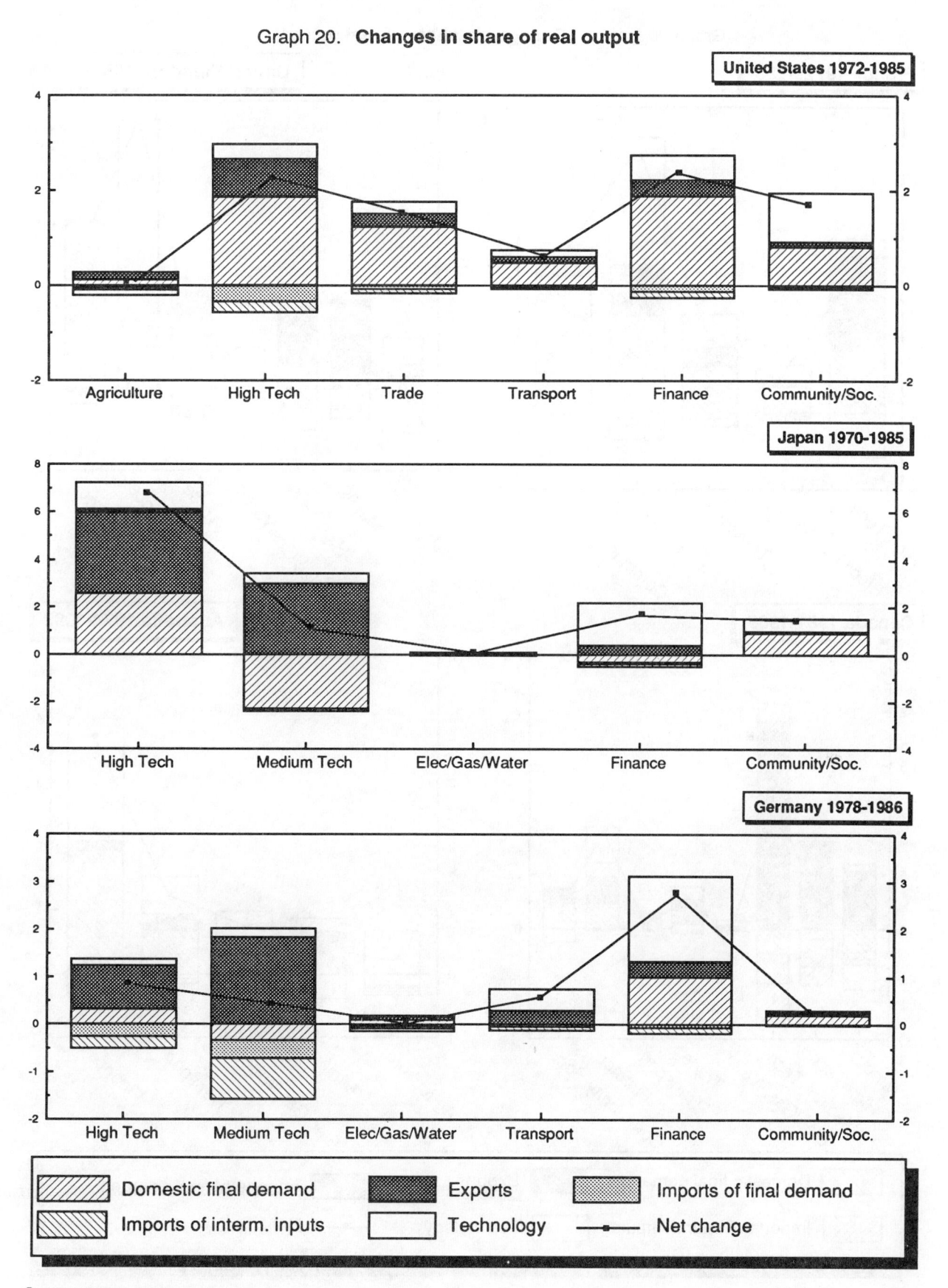

United States 1972-1985

Japan 1970-1985

Germany 1978-1986

Legend:
- Domestic final demand
- Exports
- Imports of final demand
- Imports of interm. inputs
- Technology
- Net change

Source: OECD, STAN database.

Graph 20 (cont). **Changes in share of real output**

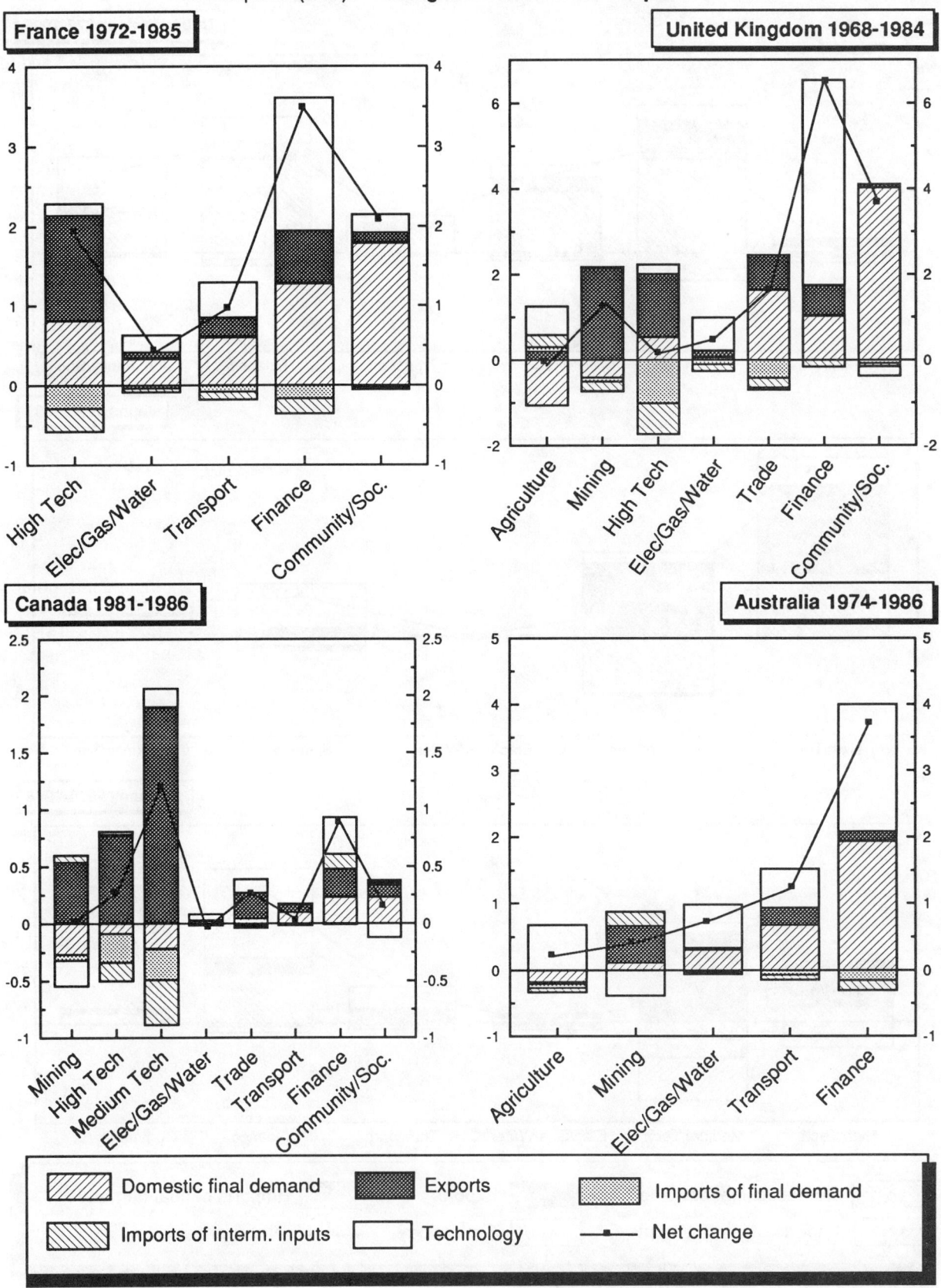

Source: OECD, STAN database.

associated with domestic final demand and to technological change. Within the trade and hotels groups, the increase in share was located in the wholesale & retail trade industry which benefited from technological changes from 1972 to 1977 while from 1977 to 1985 the growth was due to domestic final demand [10]. Over four-fifths of the growth in the transportation & communication sector from 1972 to 1985 is due to increases in the communication services industry [11]. This growth was relatively constant over both periods and can be attributed to both changes in domestic final demand and technology, with technology playing a more important role in the early period while demand dominated the latter period.

The second group: France, Germany, the UK, and Canada

The shifts in output structure towards high-technology manufacturing and financial services found in Japan and the US are also evident in the European countries and Canada, although the magnitude of the changes is less pronounced.

It was in *France* that the structural change occurring from 1972 to 1985 most resembled that of the first group: strong growth in the financial services group's output share, coupled with an increase in the share of community services, followed by a moderate gain in output share by the high-technology group (Graph 20). The shift of output towards financial services (finance, insurance, real estate, and business services), consisting of a gain of 3.2 percentage points, was one of the largest of all of the countries in the analysis. It gained largely because of technological change (other industries made more intensive use of this industry's output) and because of increases in domestic demand for this industry's output as a final product [12]. Domestic demand was particularly important from 1980 to 1985.

Although not as pronounced as the shift in Japan or the US, France had the third largest shift in output structure towards high-technology industries of the seven countries, gaining 1.7 percentage points from 1972 to 1985. This ranking holds even if only 1977 to 1985 changes are considered. This increase was largely due to gains achieved through exports and changes in domestic demand; nevertheless, this net gain does not reflect the fact that imports of both intermediate and finished goods reduced the share held by this sector by half-a-point. The increase in this sector was led by the communication & semiconductor equipment industry which saw consistent growth over the complete period. This output growth came from exports and domestic final demand and to a lesser degree changes in technology. The next two most important contributors to this gain were the aerospace and pharmaceuticals industries.

The transportation, storage & communications sector was the remaining French sector to significantly gain in its share of total output, increasing by 1.1 points from 1972 to 1985. Over four-fifths of the gain was in the communication services industry. This industry benefited primarily from domestic demand for its product and to a lesser extent by technological changes that resulted in more intensive use of the product as an intermediate input.

For *Germany*, only the 1978 to 1986 period was available for analysis, but even over this limited time period there was a significant change in the structure of total output with the financial services group gaining nearly three share points (Graph 20). Three-quarters of this gain in financial services is concentrated in the real estate & business services industry, with only one quarter of the gain connected to the finance & insurance industry. Most of this increase in real estate & business services was driven by technological change with domestic demand playing a secondary role -- on average, industries made more intensive use of business services such as legal advice, accounting, advertising, engineering & computer services and business consulting.

Consistent with the pattern found across most of the countries in our sample, the second largest shift within Germany was in the high-technology sector. Unlike Japan, the US and France, the gain was a relatively small nine-tenths of a share point. The bulk of the gain was due to exports which were three times as important as domestic demand. Part of the reason why the share gain was not larger was because imports, of both intermediate and final products, resulted in a loss of half-a-point. The share gain in this sector was almost evenly split between computers & office machinery and electrical machinery (which includes communication & semiconductors for this country). Electrical machinery was the source of most of the exports. The transportation, storage & communications sector gained in its share of total output in Germany, largely because of changes in technology which increased the use of transportation and communication services as inputs. Technology was nearly twice as important as the next most important factor: exports.

The medium-technology manufacturing group also gained share in Germany during this period, albeit by a small four-tenths of point. This small net change masks the competing forces at work in this sector. Strong exports and a relatively weak technology effect collectively boosted the share by two points but this was counterbalanced by imports and slack domestic demand which drove it down by 1.6 share points. Three industries -- motor vehicles, rubber & plastic, and chemicals (which includes pharmaceuticals for this country) -- contributed to this growth, with the motor vehicle industry responsible for half of the positive share gain. Motor vehicles benefited from exports while the share gain associated with rubber & plastics was more evenly attributable to both exports and technological change. Chemicals also depended on exports for its increase in share, although most of this gain was negated by imports, resulting in a small 0.1 point gain for this industry.

The *United Kingdom* led the seven countries in its shift in total output towards the financial services group, gaining over 6 percentage points, but failed to register much of an increase in high-technology manufacturing (+0.5). As shown in Graph 20, most of the other sectors that had an increase in share were services (community, social & personal services and wholesale & retail trade and hotels & restaurants), except for the 1.4 point gain registered by the mining sector. The sharp output gain by the financial services group was almost evenly split between the two component industries of finance & insurance and real estate & business services. Over half of the overall gain by this group occurred in the last 5 years of the 1968 to 1984 period. Technological change was the driving force behind the increase in the financial services group, responsible for three-quarters of the overall output growth. As in other countries, this reflects the increased intensity of use by UK business of service inputs such as computer processing, engineering services, advertising, and legal services.

Two other UK service sectors -- community, social & personal services (CSPS); and wholesale & retail trade and restaurants & hotels -- increased their shares of total output by 3.7 and 1.7 points respectively. For CSPS, the gain came almost entirely from the government producers industry for which domestic final demand was important, especially during the 1968 to 1979 period. Within the trade, restaurants & hotel group over 90 per cent of the 1968 to 1984 growth in output share came from the wholesale & retail trade industry where the source of the increase was domestic final demand and to a lesser extent exports. Three-quarters of the gain of this sector occurred from 1979 to 1984.

Reflecting the discovery of oil in the North Sea, the UK is unique among the countries discussed so far in registering an output share gain in its mining sector of 1.4 points. All of the increase was associated with export expansion and was evenly divided between the 1968 to 1979 and the 1979 to 1984 periods.

The last UK sector to record an increase in share was the high-technology manufacturing group. Although a relatively weak half-point gain, this net measure does not reveal the large offsetting forces at work: exports, domestic demand, and to a lesser degree technology increased this sector's share by over two points, while imports of both final and intermediate goods caused the sector to lose 1.7 points. Of the net growth that did occur, all of it occurred from 1979 to 1984. The dominant industries in descending order of importance were communication & semiconductors, computers & office machinery, and aerospace. The sectors most affected by the penetration of imports were electrical machinery and communication & semiconductor equipment.

Although included in the moderate change tier, *Canada* had a pattern of output growth sequenced differently from that in other countries. From 1981 to 1986, medium-technology manufacturing had the largest gains (+1.2) with financial services gaining the second largest increase in share over the period (+0.9). The trade & hotels group and high-technology manufacturing also gained, but these increases were relatively small (+0.3 respectively). Extended comparisons from 1971 to 1986 are not possible for Canada because of technical problems associated with the conversion of the data into constant prices, but even when the comparisons are made within the 1971 to 1976 and 1981 to 1986 periods, the same trends prevailed. The exception was that the output share held by high-technology dropped during the earlier period.

The increase in output share by the medium-technology manufacturing group from 1981 to 1986 in Canada was almost entirely due to exports with a very small positive contribution made by changes in technology. As can be seen from Graph 20, all the other factors, including domestic final demand, were negative. Of those industries within this group generating a positive contribution, 93 per cent of the gain was attributable to the motor vehicle industry, where 94 per cent of the growth was associated with exports. This pattern is consistent with that for 1971 to 1976, except that domestic final demand exerted a positive impact on growth in the earlier period.

Output shifts towards the service sector in Canada from 1981 to 1986 appeared in the financial services and trade & hotels groups. The more significant increase of 0.9 points occurred in financial services, where nearly two-thirds of this growth came from the finance & insurance industry which benefited almost equally from increases linked to domestic demand, exports, and technology. Within trade & hotels, the output growth came entirely from the expansion of the wholesale and retail trade industry, gaining from changes in domestic demand, exports, and technology. In each case, these shifts towards services were already underway in the 1971 to 1976 period.

High-technology manufacturing was the last significant group to increase its share from 1981 to 1986 in Canada and like the medium technology sector, the growth was due exclusively to exports which was limited by imports. Of those industries within the high-technology group that witnessed positive growth over the period, 72 per cent of the growth originated in the computer & office machinery industry, while most of the remainder (21 per cent) came from the communication & semiconductor equipment industry. This was a reversal of the earlier period when the high-technology group lost part of its share of total output because of weak exports and strong imports.

The third group: Australia

Structural change in *Australia* from 1974 to 1986 followed a much different pattern than in the other six countries (Graph 20). None of the manufacturing groups experienced any gains in their share of total output. Positive shifts were concentrated in the service sectors, particularly financial services and transportation & communications. These were coupled with moderate gains in the electric, gas & water services and the mining groups. Financial services posted a large gain of 3.7 share points which emanated entirely from the real estate & business services since the finance & insurance industry saw a drop in share. The growth in real estate & business services was primarily due to technological change which boosted output: domestic final demand was a secondary factor. Increases in the transportation & communication services group were roughly split between the two component industries, transportation & storage and communication services, which both benefited from domestic demand and technological change. Electric, gas & water services' share also grew because of domestic demand and technological shifts, although two-thirds of the gain was associated with technology: businesses were using more inputs of electricity, gas, and water relative to other inputs.

Australia's mining sector saw a modest growth in share of half-a-point. Most of this came from exports, although the displacement of imports (intermediate) and to a lesser extent domestic final demand also contributed to the increase. Mining would have increased its share further had it not been for negative effects associated with changes in technology. Australia's agriculture also had a small gain of 0.3 per cent in share over the period solely due to technological change -- all the other factors were negative.

Leading industries of change within the group of countries as a whole

The significance of high-technology manufacturing industries, such as computers and communication & semiconductor equipment, and of sophisticated services, like communication services and real estate & business services, becomes more apparent when analysed using real annual growth rates at the industry level. Table 52 shows the ranking of the ten industries with the fastest rate of output growth for each of the seven countries over the various time periods available [13]. Most striking is the number one ranking of computers & office equipment for six of the seven countries [14]. Every country in our sample had the communication services industry listed among its ten fastest growing industries. Similarly, six out of seven countries had the communications & semiconductor equipment industry listed [15]. Although causality can not be established, a clustering of industries is apparent across countries: of those six countries which had the computer industry listed as number one, five out of the six had the communications & semiconductor equipment industry listed among the top three industries and four out of the six had communication services in the top five. When analysed over only the latter period from the mid-70s to the mid-80s, aerospace joins this cadre with five out of the six countries having the aerospace industry among the top five fastest growing industries.

Nevertheless, the decomposition reveals that the sources of output growth varied from country to country. Domestic final demand was the primary force behind the growth in the computer & office machinery industry, except for *Canada* and *Germany* where exports dominated. For communication & semiconductor equipment the reverse was true: exports led the growth in four of the six countries with domestic demand being the main factor only in the *United States* and *Australia*. Of the five countries listing aerospace in the top-ten during the latter mid-1970s to mid-1980s period, all three of the European countries, the *UK*, *France* and Germany, had aerospace growth due to exports, possibly to each other via the Airbus consortium. In *Japan* and the United States, aerospace output growth was associated with domestic demand. Only in the case of communication services was domestic final demand the common source of growth for all seven countries.

Other common industries in the top-ten ranking included real estate & business services, pharmaceuticals, finance & insurance, and rubber & plastic products. Real estate & business services appeared in the top-ten of six of the seven countries and was due to domestic demand in every country except *Germany* and the *UK* where technological change was the primary factor [16]. Finance & insurance was listed for each country except *Australia* and *Japan*. Its growth was solely associated with domestic demand. Similarly, the pharmaceuticals industry was largely driven by domestic demand, except in Japan where technological change was the primary factor. Lastly, the rubber & plastic industry made the top-ten for five of the seven countries, but the primary factor responsible for this growth differed from exports in *Canada* and Germany, to domestic demand in Japan and the United States, to technological change in the United Kingdom.

Even though the ranking for each country reveals many common industries, the uncommon industries give insight into particular comparative advantages. For example, only in the *UK* and in *Australia* does output growth in the mining industry place it in the top group. Australia was also unique in having the agriculture and non-ferrous metal industries among the top-ten, reflecting its strong natural resource base. *Germany* was the only country to list electrical machinery while *Canada* was the sole county to have the wood, cork, and furniture industry in the top-ten. Only Canada, Germany, and *Japan* had the motor vehicle industry in the top group. For each of these countries, exports was the dominant factor behind the growth in their motor vehicle industries. The *United States* and Canada were the only two countries to list the wholesale & retail trade and hotel & restaurant industry in the top group, possibly because of their large geographic size.

In summary, the two "engines of growth" for nearly all of the seven countries analysed were financial services and high-technology manufacturing. Gains by the financial services group was dominated by growth in the real estate

Table 52. **Ten highest output growth industries and dominant factor**[1]

	Australia 1974-86	Canada 1981-86	France 1972-85	Germany 1978-86	Japan 1970-85	United Kingdom 1968-84	United States 1972-85
1.	Real estate *DFD*	Computers *Exports*	Computers *DFD*	Computers *Exports*	Computers *DFD*	Computers *Exports*	Computers *DFD*
2.	Communications *DFD*	Motor vehicles *Exports*	Communications *DFD*	Aerospace *Exports*	Pharmaceuticals *Tech.*	Real estate *Tech.*	Electronics *DFD*
3.	Utilities *DFD*	Electronics *Exports*	Electronics *Exports/DFD*	Communications *DFD*	Electronics *Exports/DFD*	Electronics *Exports*	Communications *DFD*
4.	Non-ferrous *Exports*	Real estate *DFD*	Pharmaceuticals *DFD*	Real estate *Tech.*	Motor vehicles *Exports*	Finance and insurance *DFD*	Instruments *DFD*
5.	Instruments *DFD*	Pharmaceuticals *DFD*	Aerospace *Exports*	Finance and insurance *DFD*	Communications *DFD*	Mining *Exports*	Social services *DFD*
6.	Pharmaceuticals *DFD*	Plastics *DFD*	Finance and insurance *DFD*	Plastics *Exports*	Instruments *DFD*	Government *DFD*	Finance and insurance *DFD*
7.	Transport services *DFD*	Finance and insurance *DFD*	Social services *DFD*	Electrical machinery *Exports*	Aerospace *Tech*	Pharmaceuticals *DFD*	Trade *DFD*
8.	Mining *Exports*	Communications *DFD*	Utilities *DFD*	Motor vehicles *Exports*	Real estate *DFD*	Communications *DFD*	Real estate *DFD*
9.	Agriculture *DFD/Exports*	Trade *DFD*	Instruments *Exports*	Transport services *Exports*	Government *DFD*	Utilities *DFD*	Plastics *DFD*
10.	Electronics *DFD*	Wood *Exports*	Government *DFD*	Social services *DFD*	Plastics *DFD*	Plastics *DFD*	Aerospace *DFD*

1. In the table, *Tech.* is technical change; *DFD* is domestic final demand. Growth rates used are constant price gross output.
Source: OECD, STAN input-output database.

& business services industry component. The primary factor behind this industry's growth was technological change: businesses increasingly made more intensive use of this industry's output as an input into their own production processes [17]. Some analysts have speculated that the growth in this industry is not true growth but is simply a reflection of industries, particularly manufacturing, buying services from outside suppliers that they used to produced internally -- a phenomenon called unbundling [18]. Detailed analyses of the business services industry in the US and UK have reached a different conclusion, attributing the growth to changes in the economic environment such as increased reliance on information made possible by new information technologies, increased government regulations, and more complex systems of production that require changes in the nature of production using these new inputs [19].

The output growth of high-technology manufacturing industries was largely a result of heightened domestic demand and exports, although technological change was also a positive factor. The growth in demand and exports is a reflection of the rapid technological advances made in this sector which opened up new markets for products that barely existed in the early 1970s. This growth was fuelled by precipitous price declines such as the 35 per cent annual drop in the unit cost of random-access memory since 1970 [20]. As a result, purchases of technologically sophisticated goods expanded so that over 40 per cent of US durable equipment purchases in 1986 were for information technologies (e.g. computers, communications, instruments), double the 1979 level and nearly 4 times the 1972 level [21].

What were the sectors of decline across countries?

General decline in low and medium technology manufacturing; and construction

Based on changes in real gross output shares, every country had significant losses in low-technology manufacturing and in construction, and several had declines in medium-technology manufacturing. These declines in

Table 53. **Sources of change in real output shares for manufacturing**

		Total change in output share (per cent per year)	Source of change				
			Domestic final demand expansion	Export expansion	Imports of final goods	Imports of interm. goods	Technology (change in I/O coeff.)
Australia (1974-86)	Manufacturing	-4.70	-0.59	-0.24	-1.18	-0.98	-1.72
	High technology	-0.40	0.16	0.03	-0.36	-0.39	0.16
	Medium technology	-1.52	-0.58	0.25	-0.47	-0.53	-0.19
	Low technology	-2.80	-0.17	-0.52	-0.36	-0.07	-1.69
Canada (1981-86)	Manufacturing	-0.66	-1.63	3.11	-0.89	-0.89	-0.36
	High technology	0.31	-0.09	0.78	-0.25	-0.16	0.03
	Medium technology	1.17	-0.22	1.90	-0.27	-0.40	0.16
	Low technology	-2.14	-1.33	0.43	-0.37	-0.33	-0.54
France (1972-85)	Manufacturing	-3.98	-2.00	4.49	-2.34	-2.92	-1.21
	High technology	1.72	0.81	1.34	-0.29	-0.29	0.15
	Medium technology	-0.52	-0.46	1.63	-0.76	-0.95	0.02
	Low technology	-5.18	-2.35	1.52	-1.29	-1.68	-1.38
Germany (1978-86)	Manufacturing	-2.32	-1.34	3.52	-1.32	-2.11	-1.07
	High technology	0.87	0.31	0.94	-0.26	-0.25	0.13
	Medium technology	0.44	-0.34	1.84	-0.37	-0.86	0.18
	Low technology	-3.63	-1.31	0.74	-0.69	-0.99	-1.38
Japan (1970-85)	Manufacturing	1.36	-4.05	6.78	0.01	-0.36	-1.02
	High technology	7.25	2.58	3.41	0.11	0.04	1.11
	Medium technology	1.02	-2.29	3.00	0.01	-0.12	0.43
	Low technology	-6.92	-4.34	0.38	-0.11	-0.29	-2.55
Un. Kingdom (1968-84)	Manufacturing	-11.57	-2.76	1.70	-4.18	-5.33	-1.00
	High technology	0.49	0.52	1.49	-1.02	-0.72	0.21
	Medium technology	-4.09	-0.40	0.65	-1.84	-2.66	0.16
	Low technology	-7.97	-2.88	-0.44	-1.32	-1.96	-1.38
Un. States (1972-85)	Manufacturing	-3.08	0.86	1.56	-1.74	-1.68	-2.07
	High technology	2.40	1.87	0.80	-0.34	-0.24	0.31
	Medium technology	-1.52	0.05	0.34	-0.77	-0.66	-0.47
	Low technology	-3.95	-1.05	0.42	-0.63	-0.78	-1.91

Source: OECD, STAN input-output database.

manufacturing, both in terms of shares and growth rates, were concentrated in the ferrous metals, textiles, petroleum refining, and fabricated metal product industries. However, the pattern of manufacturing decline, and the sources for it, varied significantly between different countries (see Table 53). While all countries experienced declining output shares in the low technology group, in only four (Australia, France, the UK and the US) was this accompanied by decreasing shares for the medium technology group. A very similar pattern of structural change in employment occurred except that due to productivity gains the declining shares were accentuated.

Losses concentrated in low-technology manufacturing: Japan, Germany, and Canada

Japan's low-technology sector experienced the second largest loss of output share of all of the seven countries. The major industries that led this decline in the share of low-technology manufacturing in Japan from 1970 to 1985 were textiles (textiles, footwear, & leather), steel (ferrous metals), and petroleum refining. Textiles was the source of most of the decline, responsible for about a quarter of the low-technology drop. The drop was due to declines in domestic demand, exports, and changes in technology and was relatively constant over the whole period. Ferrous metals was responsible for over a fifth of the overall decline, but nearly half of this drop in output share occurred from 1980 to 1985 due to technological changes. Lastly, petroleum refining contributed 13 per cent of the sector's decline, but this only occurred after 1975 -- the first post-oil-shock data point for Japan. Most of the decline in the share of petroleum refining was due to technological change and to a lesser extent due to domestic final demand. Overall, the declining output share of low-technology manufacturing in Japan was associated primarily with shifts in domestic final demand and secondarily with changes in technology.

Germany's 1978 to 1986 decline in low-technology manufacturing output was more evenly attributed to three factors: changes in domestic final demand, technology, and the combined effect of imports of final and intermediate goods. The main industries which caused the declining share of output were ferrous metals (22 per cent of the low-technology drop) and the food, drinks, & tobacco industry (19 per cent of the sectoral decline), although decreases in the share held by the textiles, wood, cork & furniture, and petroleum refining industries were also significant. As in the case in Japan, technological change was the primary factor behind the declining output share of the ferrous metals industry, but unlike , imports of intermediate inputs was an important secondary factor in the decline of the German ferrous metals industry.

As was the case in Germany, **Canada**'s decline in the share of output produced by low-technology industries between 1981 and 1986 was associated with adverse movements in domestic final demand, although every decomposition factor, except exports, contributed to the decline. This decline was principally due to drops in petroleum refining (47 per cent of the sector's decline), although the food, drinks, & tobacco and ferrous metals industries also had large decreases in share. These declines were consistent with 1971 to 1976 trends, except that during the earlier period petroleum refining's share was constant, gaining a tenth of a share point. As in Germany, the share of Canadian employment associated with low-technology manufacturing experienced the largest drop (1.1 points) of any sector.

Losses in both low- and medium-technology manufacturing: France, the UK, the US, and Australia

Of the four countries in the second group, **France** is most like Japan, Germany, and Canada because the medium-technology sector only lost half an output share point from 1972 to 1985. This small net lost conceals the fact that while exports boosted the sector by 1.6 points, the other factors combined to lower the share by 2.1 points. Industries like motor vehicles and other non-electrical equipment had positive output share gains in the 1972 to 1977 period which turned negative in the 1977 to 1985 period because of imports (final and intermediate) and slack domestic demand. The fall in relative output in France's low-technology sector was the third largest of the seven countries and was concentrated in the three industries commonly experiencing decline: petroleum refining, textiles, and ferrous metals. Technological change was the primary factor associated with the decline in the ferrous metals and the petroleum refining industries while imports and domestic final demand affected the textile industry in France.

The **United Kingdom**'s 1968 to 1984 loss of output share in both the low- and the medium-technology manufacturing was the largest of any of the seven countries. The low-technology share losses were due to all of the decomposition factors, especially domestic final demand and the combined effect of intermediate and final imports. Unlike the other countries, the petroleum refining industry was not a prime declining industry. Instead, the large low-technology losing industries were fabricated metal products, ferrous metals and textiles. Nearly all the decline in fabricated metals occurred from 1968 to 1979 while the other two industries' decline was more even over the whole period. The UK's medium-technology manufacturing output share loss was concentrated in the motor vehicle and non-electrical machinery industries. For both of these industries the bulk of the decline occurred in the 1979 to 1984 period due to a downturn in exports and domestic demand. This is in contrast with the earlier 1968 to 1979 period where the loss for these industries was primarily due to imports of final and intermediate goods.

In the **United States**, the share of gross output held by low- and medium-technology manufacturing also fell from 1972 to 1985, although the decline was less significant than

Table 54. **Ten lowest output growth industries and dominant factor**[1]

	Australia 1974-86	Canada 1981-86	France 1972-85	Germany 1978-86	Japan 1970-85	United Kingdom 1968-84	United States 1972-85
1.	Shipbuilding *Tech.*	Shipbuilding *DFD*	Petroleum refining *Tech.*	Wood *Tech./DFD*	Mining *Tech.*	Other transport *Tech.*	Ferrous metals *Tech.*
2.	Non-elec. machinery *I-FD.*	Petroleum refining *DFD/Tech.*	Other transports *Exports*	Ferrous metals *Tech.*	Shipbuilding *DFD*	Fabricated metals *Tech.*	Other transports *DFD*
3.	Electrical machinery *I-int.*	Aerospace *I-FD*	Ferrous metals *Tech.*	Textiles *I-FD*	Wood *Tech.*	Shipbuilding *DFD*	Other manufacturing *I-FD*
4.	Ferrous metals *Exports*	Other transports *I-FD*	Textiles *I-FD*	Mining *Tech.*	Textiles *Tech.*	Non-ferrous metals *I-int.*	Non-ferrous metals *Tech.*
5.	Motor vehicles *Tech.*	Ferrous metals *Tech.*	Shipbuilding *DFD*	Shipbuilding *Exports*	Agriculture *Tech.*	Motor vehicles *I-FD*	Mining *Tech.*
6.	Chemicals *I-int.*	Non-elec. machinery *Exports*	Construction *DFD*	Petroleum refining *I-int*	Other transport *Tech.*	Ferrous metals *I-int.*	Stone, clay, glass *Tech.*
7.	Fabricated metals *Tech.*	Electrical machinery *I-int.*	Fabricated metals *I-int*	Stone, clay, glass *Tech.*	Stone, clay, glass *Tech.*	Transport services *Tech.*	Non-elec. machinery *I-FD.*
8.	Wood *Tech.*	Construction *Tech.*	Stone, clay, glass *I-int.*	Fabricated metals *Tech.*	Petroleum refining *Tech.*	Textiles *I-FD/I-int.*	Textiles *I-PF/I-int*
9.	Stone, clay, glass *Tech.*	Hotels and restaurants *Tech.*	Mining *Tech.*	Construction *Tech.*	Ferrous metals *Tech.*	Non-elec. machinery *I-int/I-FD*	Wood *Tech*
10.	Aerospace *Tech.*	Fabricated metals *Tech.*	Wood *I-int.*	Instruments *I-int*	Transport services *I-int.*	Instruments *I-FD*	Shipbuilding *I-FD*

1. In the table, *Tech.* is technical change; *DFD* is domestic demand; *I-int* is imports of intermediate goods; and *I-FD* is imports of final demand goods. Growth rates used are constant price gross output.
Source: OECD, STAN input-output database.

the losses incurred in France and the UK. Technological change was the primary factor associated with the low-technology decline, particularly in the ferrous metals industry -- the industry contributing the largest loss of share in this sector. Changes in technology and shifts in domestic demand also caused the petroleum refining industry to recede, although this did not occur until after 1977. The impact of imports (final and intermediate) on the low-technology sector was most pronounced in textiles, particularly in the 1977 to 1985 period. The US medium-technology sector's share of output did not decline as steeply, although the impact of imports was as large as the effect on low-technology industries, making it the primary factor associated with the decline of this sector. The effect of imports was restricted to the 1977 to 1985 period, causing some industries like motor vehicles and chemicals that had share gains from the 1972 to 1977 period to register share losses. Some of these losses can be attributed to the high value of the dollar, which caused declines in export-oriented manufacturing and encouraged the greater use of imported intermediate inputs.

In *Australia*, the largest loss in share of total output from 1979 to 1986 was in the low- and medium-technology manufacturing sectors. Unlike the other six countries, the industry contributing most to the low-technology sector loss of share was the food, drinks, & tobacco industry. This was primarily due to shifts in domestic final demand and slack exports. Similar to other countries, Australia also had significant drops in the ferrous metals and fabricated metal products industries. These sectors declined because of technological change. The motor vehicles and non-electrical machinery industries led the decline of Australia's medium-technology sector which fell because of adverse changes in every decomposition factor except exports.

Technical change and import penetration in the low growth industries

The decline of some smaller industries like shipbuilding and wood, cork & furniture is evident from the ranking of the lowest output growth rate industries by country in Table 54. Listed among the bottom-ten growing industries in terms of output for every country, the shipbuilding sector was ranked within the top five slowest industries for six of the seven countries. The ferrous metals industry was also among the ten slowest industries for every country. Other common slow output growing industries include fabricated metal products; wood, cork & furniture; and other transportation equipment (trains, motorcycles and specialised transportation equipment, such as tanks). A clustering of steel using industries -- shipbuilding, ferrous metals, fabricated metal products, and other transportation equipment -- among the bottom-ten industries is apparent. Although the list is still predominantly manufacturing it includes some other sectors such as agriculture; mining; construction; hotels & restaurants; and transport & storage. The list changes remarkably little when the focus is on employment growth rates: the ferrous metals, textiles, and shipbuilding industries were among the bottom-ten for at least six of the seven countries.

While the pattern in Table 54 varies across countries what stands out is the dominance of technical change and imports (both final and intermediate) as the most frequent factors of change. Technology appears at least twice as often as import substitution in *Australia*, *Germany* and *Japan*. Technology and import substitution appear with about the same frequency in *Canada* and the *United States*; import substitution appears more often than technology in *France* and the *UK*.

Which economies experienced the most and the least structural change?

Although the sectors and industries experiencing positive and negative structural change were generally similar, the magnitude and nature of the change differed significantly among the seven countries. The question of which countries experienced the most and the least structural change is examined in two ways:

- by overall or summary measures of structural change;
- and by a description of the primary cause of the output growth in the ten fastest and the ten slowest growing industries.

The aggregate picture obtained from these indicators reveals that each country has had a unique experience: some countries gained manufacturing share while others experienced a decline; some were driven by exports, others were dependent on domestic final demand for growth.

Summary measures of structural change

Table 55 contains a ranking of countries by the rate of compositional change index introduced above. Results have been annualised to correct for the fact that different time periods have been used for different countries [22]. The

Table 55. **Index of structural change of output**
Annualised percentage change

	Index of structural change
Japan (1970-85)	1.04
United Kingdom (1968-84)	1.02
Canada (1981-86)	0.91
United States (1972-85)	0.76
Germany (1978-86)	0.72
Australia (1974-86)	0.68
France (1972-85)	0.68

Source: OECD, STAN input-output database.

higher the index, the greater the realignment of shares of output that the country has experienced.

Japan, the *UK*, and *Canada* experienced the most structural change with the mix of total output being rearranged by more than one percentage point per year in Japan and the UK. A more moderate rate of change occurred in the *United States* and *Germany* while *Australia* and *France* had the lowest annual levels of change. However, while useful as a measure of the overall extent of structural change, the index provides no indication of the direction of change or initial starting position. Without additional information on these two points, it cannot be interpreted as a measure of relative adjustment performance. More structural change may not be desirable if it is counter to global trends of industrial expansion and contraction (although niche markets may provide opportunities in declining industries). Similarly, extensive structural change may simply reflect a catch-up process in a country whose initial industrial structure was poorly matched to global growth opportunities. A country whose initial structure was better adapted to the economic environment may not need much structural change.

Graph 21 provides a second indicator of structural change based on the cumulative effect that each decomposition factor had on a particular country's output shares from the mid-1970s to the mid-1980s. Unlike Table 55 which summed share changes across industries ignoring the underlying effects of the decomposition factors, the graph sums the share change for each country across the various factors, ignoring the industry specific share changes. While Table 55 indicates the shifts occurring between industries, Graph 21 represents the net share changes due to domestic final demand, exports, imports of intermediate inputs, imports of final products, and technology. Because the graph is of total output share change for each country, the positive and negative portion of the bar must be equal, summing to zero, but the overall length of the bar indicates the magnitude of the share change caused by the different factors. To adjust for the different time periods for the various countries, an annualised index

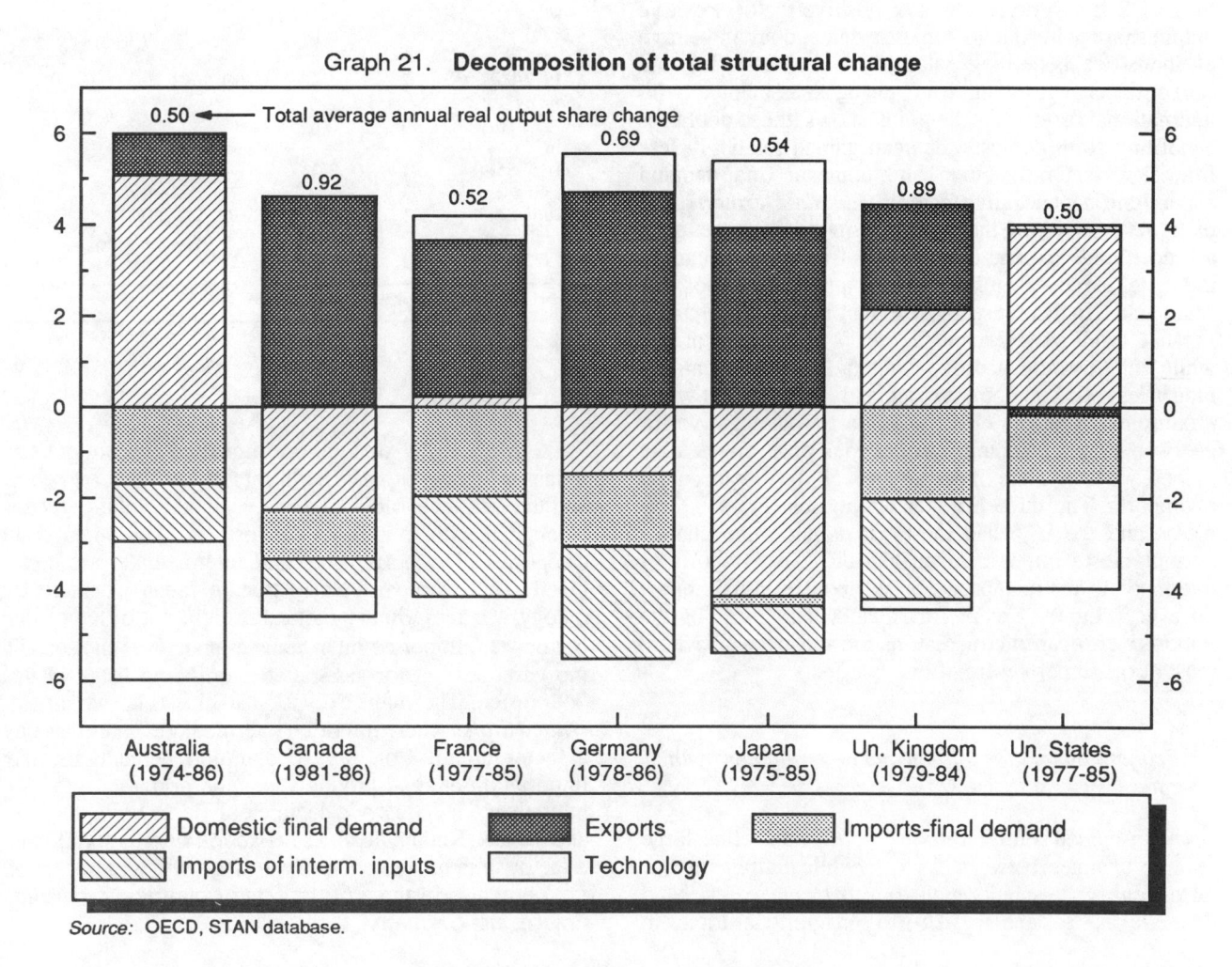

Graph 21. **Decomposition of total structural change**

Source: OECD, STAN database.

using the same formula as the index in Table 55 has been calculated and placed above each country's bar. This index represents the overall average annual change in output shares that occurred due to the combined effects of all of the various factors.

Using this scheme, *Canada* and the *UK* experienced the greatest structural change while *Germany*, *France*, and *Japan* had more moderate shifts and the *United States* and *Australia* had the least. Interestingly, Canada and the UK ranked in the top regardless of which scheme was used to construct the index. Strictly in terms of changes in the relative ranks, Japan and the US showed the most change from one index to another with each country falling by three positions from the industry based index (Table 55) to the factor based index (Graph 21). This suggests that each of these countries had relatively significant industrial realignments compared to the other countries but have seen relatively fewer adjustments due to changes in the broad factors.

Graph 21 also reveals that the relative importance and the sign of the factors differed significantly across countries. Domestic final demand was an important positive factor only in *Australia*, the *UK* and the *United States*. In the US it was nearly the sole positive factor. Positive output share gains due to domestic demand are indicative of industries benefiting relatively more from internal economic changes than from changes associated with international factors. As the graph shows, those countries benefiting from domestic demand gained relatively less from exports. On the other hand, domestic final demand was a significant negative factor in *Canada*, *Germany*, and particularly in *Japan*, indicating that internal changes such as declining expenditures on infrastructure caused industries to recede while exports resulted in large positive share gains. In this sense, those industries gaining share in Japan, Canada, *France*, and Germany were export driven while in Australia and the United States the gaining industries relied on domestic demand. In the UK, it was a mixture of both. The effect of imports was negative for every country -- no country's industries were, on net, able to increase their share of output through the displacement of imports. The three European countries (France, Germany, and the UK) had the most output share change attributable to imports. Japan had the least. Imports of intermediate and final products had about an equal impact on every country except for Japan where most of the imports were of an intermediate nature and in the US where most of the imports were of final products.

Primary factors for top-ten and bottom-ten growth rates

As discussed before, shifts in output shares reflect large relative changes between sectors, while output growth rates identify the smaller industries that have experienced dramatic changes and are likely to be significant forces in the future. Although there was a large amount of similarity across countries in which industries were included in the top-ten and bottom-ten rankings, Table 56 reveals that factors associated with these output share gains and losses were also very similar. Domestic final demand was the primary factor for at least five out of the ten industries with rapid output growth in every country except *Germany* where exports was the dominant factor. In other words, domestic demand was in most cases the most important factor in stimulating quickly growing industries. Exports were also important, particularly in Germany and *Canada*. Technological change was less significant, but was the primary factor in two of the ten top-ten industries in *Japan* and the *UK*.

Table 56. **Primary sources of change for the ten fastest and the ten slowest output growth industries (fast/slow)**

	Domestic final demand	Export expansion	Imports of final products	Imports of intermediate inputs	Technology
Australia (1974-86)	8/0	2/1	0/1	0/2	0/6
Canada (1981-86)	5/2	5/1	0/2	0/1	0/4
France (1972-85)	7/2	3/1	0/1	0/3	0/3
Germany (1978-86)	3/0	6/1	0/1	0/2	1/6
Japan (1970-85)	6/1	2/0	0/0	0/1	2/8
Un. Kingdom (1968-84)	5/1	3/0	0/3	0/3	2/3
United States (1972-85)	10/1	0/0	0/4	0/0	0/5

Source: OECD, STAN input-output database.

A wider array of factors dominated the bottom-ten industries' low output growth rates. Except for *France* and the *UK*, technological change was the primary factor associated with low-growth industries, even when both categories of imports, final and intermediate, are combined. This was particularly true in Japan where technology was the primary factor for eight out of ten of the bottom-ten. Imported intermediate inputs was the second most frequent factor associated with being listed in the bottom-ten. The main exception to this rule was in the *United States* where imported intermediate inputs was not a factor at all. Contrary to common perceptions, the importation of final products was the primary factor for more than one industry's decline only in *Canada*, the US, and the UK. Rather, declines in exports were as significant a factor in contributing to the low growth as imports of final products in three of the seven countries: *Australia*, France, and *Germany*.

Current states and trajectories for the future

The previous cross-country comparisons of changes in output shares and differences in output growth rates reveal the direction and pace of structural change, but do not indicate the current industrial composition of each country's economy. These are best shown in a series of XY graphs (Graph 22) which show the composition of each country's economy through a two-dimensional plot where the X axis indicates the current (1984 to 1986) share of total gross output a particular sector holds while the Y axis shows the annual rate of growth that sector has experienced from the mid-1970s to the mid-1980s. The upper right-hand corner of each graph is an area of rapid growth and a high relative share of total output; the lower left-hand corner represents slow growth and a low share. By plotting the current share (measured in current prices) and the recent growth rate, and listing the overall growth rate in parentheses, the current composition and its current growth path or trajectory are revealed. Although the past is never a very accurate predictor of the future, it is an essential starting point for considering what the future will resemble like and where the relative momentum for growth can be found.

Natural Resources. Of the seven countries, *Australia*, the *UK*, and *Canada* had the largest share of their output devoted to natural resource (agriculture and mining) intensive industries, although given the high growth rates of Australia and the UK, they looked poised for further gains while Canada's and *France*'s natural resource sectors are likely to retain a relatively constant share in the future (Graph 22). Already with rather low shares dedicated to the natural resource sector, *Japan*'s and *Germany*'s share is likely to fall further in the future given the low growth rates of the past. Even for those countries such as Canada and Australia which are considered to have natural resource oriented economies, less than a twelfth of the economy's output is dedicated to this sector.

Services. By the mid-1980s every country had more than half of their output originating in the service sector. Nevertheless, there were nearly ten share points separating *Australia*, the most service oriented country, with *Japan* -- the least, even though both countries were tied for having the highest growth rates. This recent high growth suggest that the Australian economy will continue to shift to services while Japan will probably retain a constant share. Given the growth rates of 2 to 3 per cent in *Canada*, *Germany*, *France*, and the *United States*, it is also likely that the service sector's share of total output will grow slowly in the future. The same is probably true for the *UK* although speculation about the UK is made more difficult by the available data points which cover a short, recessionary period.

Manufacturing. A near mirror image of the services graph is evident in the manufacturing graph where *Japan*'s economy is the most oriented towards manufacturing and has sustained the highest recent growth rate, suggesting that this sector will continue to gain share in the future [23]. Given its recent growth rate, *Canada* will probably retain or slightly increase its share of manufacturing, but the manufacturing sector will probably continue to recede in *Australia*, the *United States*, *France*, and *Germany*. The *UK*'s manufacturing sector will probably decline also, but the negative growth rate which is reflective of the recessionary period plotted is not an accurate indicator of the future. Nevertheless, even when the growth rates for the entire period (early-1970s to mid-1980s) are plotted for France, Japan, the UK, and the US, the relative positions of the countries do not change, only the growth rates differ: the US and France both gain about half-a-percentage point, the UK gains 1.75 points, and Japan drops 1 point.

High-Technology. The graph for the high-technology portion of manufacturing reveals a similar pattern with *Japan* maintaining the highest share and the highest growth rate while *Australia* has the lowest share and the lowest growth rate. Nevertheless, the five remaining countries realigned significantly from the manufacturing shares pattern, with the *United States* slightly in the lead, *France*, *Germany*, and the *UK* following, and *Canada* with the lowest share of the five, but a relatively strong growth rate. The remarkable aspect of the graph is the wide gap in growth rates between Japan and the other six countries: Japan had nearly twice the growth rate of the next closest country, the United States. Table 52 shows that these differences have less to do with domestic demand for final high-technology products as opposed to exports, imports, and technological change. Nearly half of Japan's high-technology growth rate was associated with exports; Japan was the only country of the seven where import displacement of both final and intermediate high-technology products took place; and it was the only country to derive significant gains in the high-technology sector through greater use of high-technology products as inputs into other production processes. It appears likely that all countries, except possibly Australia, will have a greater percentage of their total output coming from the high-technology sector in the future. This will be especially true for Japan where the high-technology growth rate is nearly four times the economy average.

D. Conclusions and policy implications

By their nature, indicators of compositional structural change point only indirectly to policy actions. Normative conclusions cannot be drawn from simple summary measures of the extent or rate of compositional structural change without additional information regarding the direction of change, the path followed from the previous industrial structure and the associated economic and institutional factors. While this report does not deal with institutional issues, its analysis of both direction and broad sources of change provide a number of indirect insights and a better awareness of the nature of structural adjustment in the last two decades.

Graph 22. **Performance comparisons by industry group** [1]

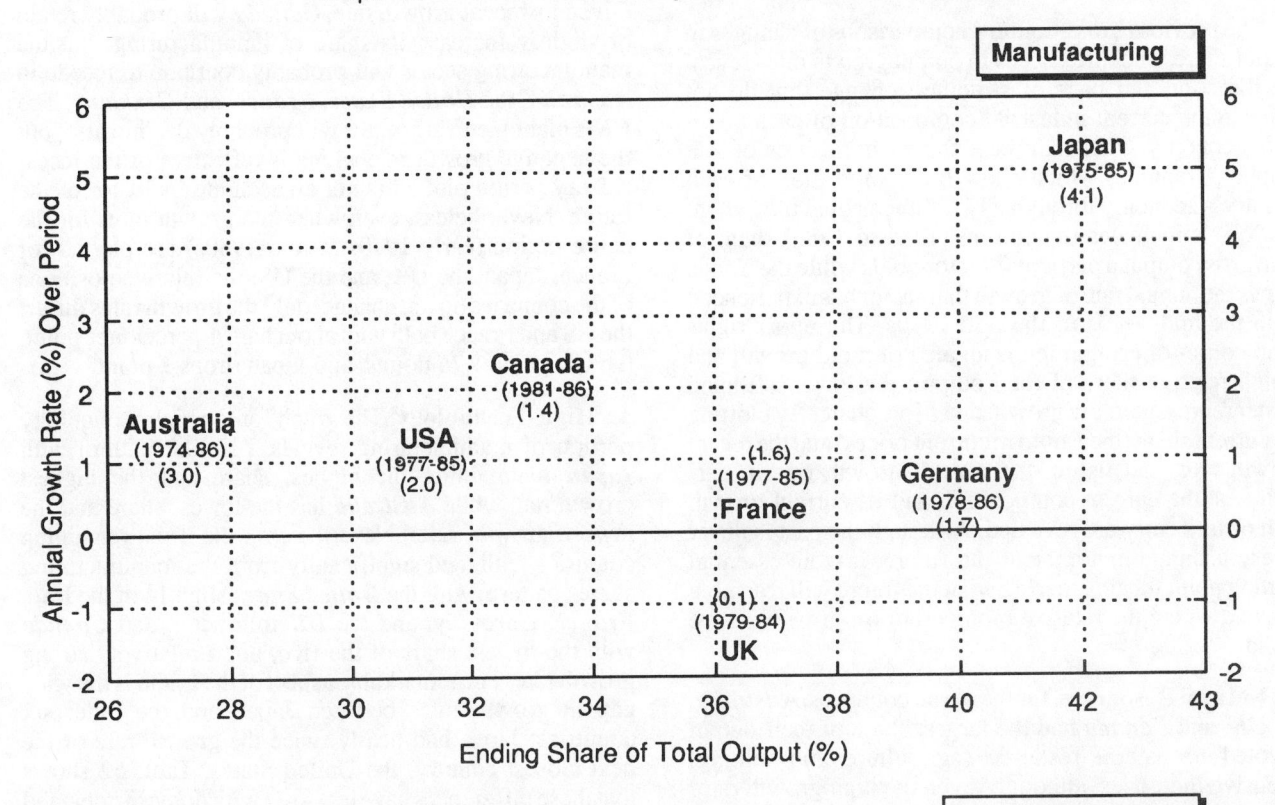

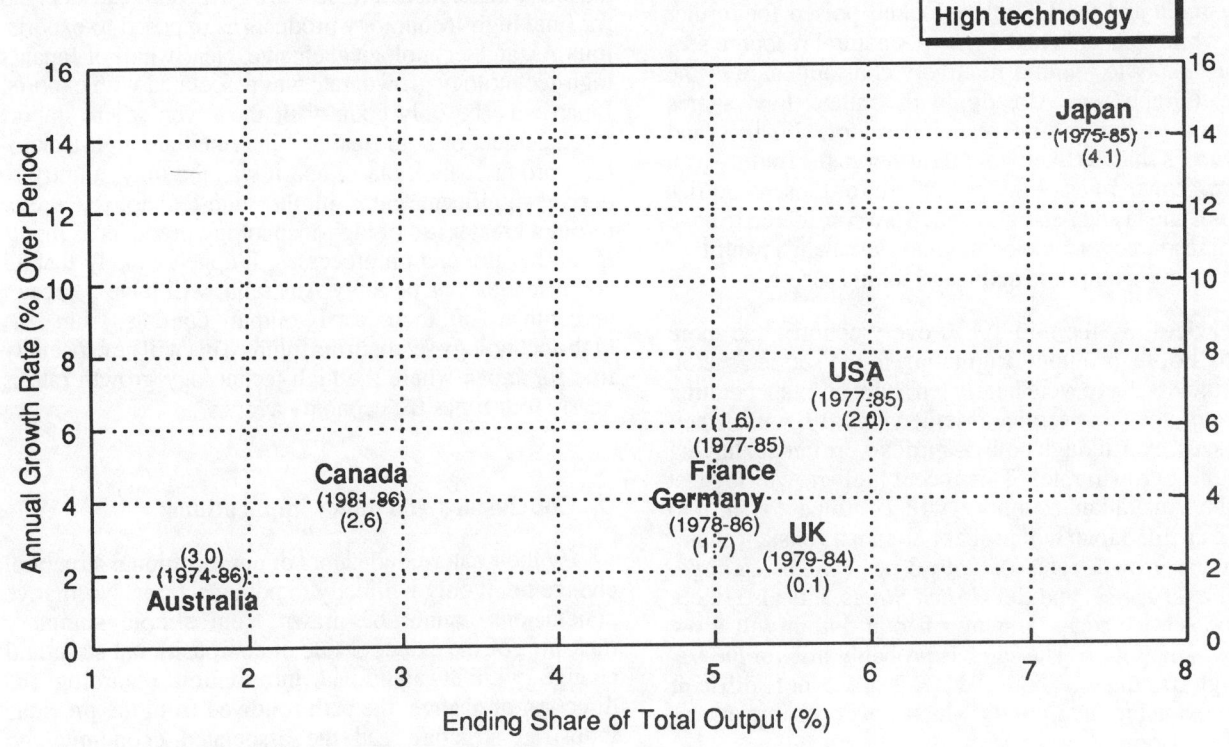

Manufacturing

(Annual Growth Rate (%) Over Period vs. Ending Share of Total Output (%))

- Japan (1975-85) (4.1)
- Canada (1981-86) (1.4)
- Australia (1974-86) (3.0)
- USA (1977-85) (2.0)
- France (1.6) (1977-85)
- Germany (1978-86) (1.7)
- UK (0.1) (1979-84)

High technology

(Annual Growth Rate (%) Over Period vs. Ending Share of Total Output (%))

- Japan (1975-85) (4.1)
- USA (1977-85) (2.0)
- France (1.6) (1977-85)
- Canada (1981-86) (2.6)
- Germany (1978-86) (1.7)
- UK (1979-84) (0.1)
- Australia (1974-86) (3.0)

1. Economy-wide growth rates are in parentheses.
Source: OECD, STAN database.

Graph 22 (cont). **Performance comparisons by industry group**[1]

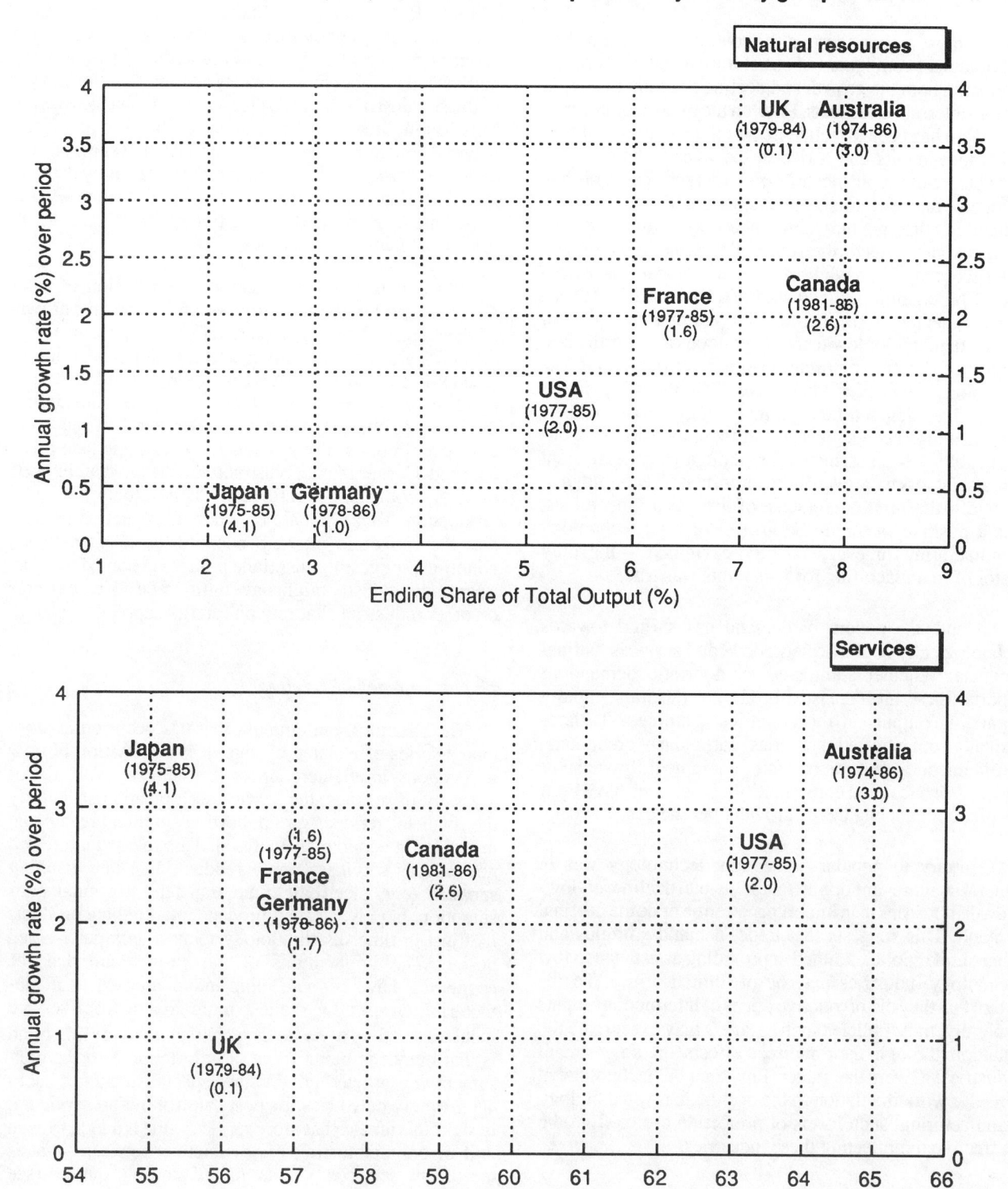

Natural resources

Scatter plot — Annual growth rate (%) over period vs Ending Share of Total Output (%):
- UK (1979-84) (0.1): ~7, 3.7
- Australia (1974-86) (3.0): ~8, 3.7
- France (1977-85) (1.6): ~6, 2.0
- Canada (1981-86) (2.6): ~8, 2.0
- USA (1977-85) (2.0): ~5.5, 1.2
- Japan (1975-85) (4.1): ~2, 0.3
- Germany (1978-86) (1.0): ~3, 0.3

Services

Scatter plot — Annual growth rate (%) over period vs Ending Share of Total Output (%):
- Japan (1975-85) (4.1): ~55, 3.3
- Australia (1974-86) (3.0): ~65, 3.3
- France (1977-85) (1.6): ~57, 2.6
- Canada (1981-86) (2.6): ~59, 2.5
- USA (1977-85) (2.0): ~63, 2.5
- Germany (1978-86) (1.7): ~57, 2.2
- UK (1979-84) (0.1): ~56, 0.8

1. Economy-wide growth rates are in parentheses.

Source: OECD, STAN database.

The role of technology

Foremost among these is the role of technology. The technological component of structural change is a critical element in both the growth and decline of industries. This has two interrelated aspects. First, on the intermediate input side, there has been a decline in the intensity of use of low technology inputs and a rise in the intermediate use of technologically sophisticated goods and services. This has changed the patterns of interconnections between industries; that is, the input mixes of industries -- in input-output language often referred to as the "technology" of an economy. As a whole, the technological sophistication of production has increased and this marks a fundamental change in the nature of countries' economies. Falling demand for low technology goods as intermediate inputs has been an important factor in the decline of low technology industries themselves. Conversely, rising intermediate demand for high technology goods and services has also been significant in the expansion of technologically advanced industries (though in general, final demand factors were even more important). Technological change, in the input-output sense of changes in input mixes, was a positive factor in the growth of high technology manufacturing in every country examined -- the only sector of manufacturing for which this was true.

Second, the pattern of demand has shifted towards technologically sophisticated goods and services as final products. Whether stimulated by domestic demand or exports, these are consistently among the most rapidly expanding outputs in the countries examined. Technologically sophisticated industries, particularly computers, communication & semiconductor equipment, financial & business services and communications services have been the predominant engines of growth over the past 15 years.

Contrary to popular perception, technology was in general a more important factor in the decline of low-growth industries than import penetration or domestic final demand. This suggests that trade, demand stimulus and other similar policies aimed at providing assistance to low technology industries may be of limited utility. To the extent that they distort relative prices of intermediate inputs generally, trade policies such as tariffs may exacerbate the situation through their indirect effects on downstream industries. Given the rather fundamental technological forces at work in relation to the decline in low technology manufacturing, such forms of protection are likely to be ineffective in protecting these industries.

The fact that technologically sophisticated industries are important on both the intermediate inputs side and the final demand side suggests that both the production and use of advanced technology should be seen as complementary policy objectives. In other words, technology diffusion should be seen as the policy complement to technology development.

The role of domestic final demand and of exports (in addition to technological change) as factors behind the expansion of technologically sophisticated goods and services suggests that some combination of strong home market and a global presence may be important for growth in these industries, and thus for structural change overall. This has implications for a range of domestic and international policies. At the most general level, it suggests that a sound macroeconomic environment and healthy demand are basic elements in effective structural change. At the same time it emphasises the positive structural adjustment role of reducing trade barriers.

Associated with this is the global diffusion of technology. Exports were also an important factor in the growth of the high-technology sector, reflecting the transfer of technology to other countries and the global sourcing of technologically sophisticated inputs by businesses. In a more general sense, for those four countries (France, Japan, the UK, and the US) for which extended data sets were available, imports of high-technology intermediate products had a larger impact on structural change than imports of final products -- a reflection of the global nature of production. These global networks of production emphasize the economic interdependences that exist between countries, suggesting that trade policies designed to assist a particular industry might have unforeseen adverse effects on other industries that rely on foreign suppliers.

The ascendency of services

The structural realignment that has occurred is more than a series of isolated change. It is a reflection of how the economy as an interconnected system has evolved. For a variety of reasons, the service sectors, and particularly the financial services group, have taken on a greater role in the seven economies analysed. This role is manifested not only as services supply products like new banking services (e.g. electronic fund transfers) for final consumption, but also as they produce intermediate products like just-in-time distribution systems or computer-aided design. The implications of this growth are that the economies have become more interconnected as manufacturing firms now request more inputs from service industries and visa-versa. One characteristic of this trend is that output is being more closely tailored to the consumers via targeted advertising, special financing packages, timely deliveries, or post-sale follow-up servicing. In short this means that more service value is added to each unit of output blurring the distinction between what is meant by services versus manufacturing output (see Box 19).

In terms of analyzing structural change, the clean lines separating the economy into sectors will probably have less meaning in the future. Instead of emphasizing one sector over another (e.g. "manufacturing matters") the focus of economic development policy should be on

> **Box 19. The blurred lines between manufacturing and services**
>
> The distinction between "manufacturing" and "services" has begun to blur, limiting the utility of the separation. One of the quintessential manufacturing enterprises, General Motors (GM), illustrates the point. In terms of inputs, one of the single largest suppliers to GM is not a steel or glass company, but a health care provider, Blue Cross-Blue Shield. This input cost GM over US$2.2 billion in 1983 and covered over 2 million people -- roughly 1 per cent of the US population [1]. In terms of output, one of the largest GM "products" is financial services. GM finances the purchase of many of the cars it makes. In 1985, over 20 per cent of GM's profits were from GM's finance division, GMAC. After sales service standards such as 24-hour roadside repairs have also risen, so that the service component of GM's cars has increased [2].
>
> As economies become more complex, so services have become an increasing input into manufacturing processes and vice versa. Firms may choose to internalise such inputs or to purchase them. While this may alter whether the firm is classified to manufacturing or services for statistical purposes, it does not change the mix of inputs that go into the final product. As this statistical blurring increases, it becomes more important to look beyond the immediate classification of the firm and to consider the complete production chain.
>
> 1. Kinter, H. and Smith, E. (1986), "General Motors: Provides Health Care Benefits to Millions", *American Demographics*, April.
> 2. Quinn, J. and Gagnon, C. (1986), "Will Services Follow Manufacturing into Decline?", *Harvard Business Review*, November/December, p.101.

systemwide gains that maximize the efficiency of the integration of different industries. From this point of view basic economic infrastructure improvements such as transportation, communication, and education systems that connect the different sectors are likely to become more important. This perspective suggests that if the components of the system, namely the different industries of the economy, are considered together rather than in isolation, policies might be redirected to where they offer the maximum return. From the perspective of overall productivity growth as well as containment of inflation, increases in service sector productivity would appear to be at least as important as those in manufacturing, despite past emphasis on the latter. For example, in the US, over half of the purchaser's price of durable household furnishings and nearly half of the sale price of apparel is attributable to trade and distribution margins [24]. Given this, efficiency gains in wholesale & retail trade or transportation are likely to have a larger impact on reducing the cost of the final product than changes in the manufacturing process. A major problem for policy analysis in such areas is the lack of suitable data. This suggests the need for better data and measurement techniques for the service sector so that more informed decisions can be made.

The 1970s and 1980s were a period of restructuring particularly in the low-and medium-technology manufacturing sectors due to technological change and imports. In comparison, the service sector, particularly financial services, experienced relatively strong growth due to domestic demand and technological changes. Looking ahead to the future, a similar type of restructuring like that which occurred in manufacturing may happen in the service sector during the 1990s with potentially more significant results given the large number of jobs in this sector. The current Australian, UK, and US recessions that started in the service sector have undoubtedly reduced some inefficiencies and over capacity, and have underscored the fact that this sector is not immune to cyclical fluctuations. Counter-cyclical policies that tend to be oriented towards the manufacturing sector should be re-examined with the special characteristics of the service sector being kept in mind.

Continued exposure of the service sector to international competition will contribute to this restructuring. GATT figures show services to be the fastest growing segment of traded products in 1990, representing 22 per cent of all trade. Combined with the attention services have received in the Uruguay round of GATT and some of the recent bilateral trade disagreements that have emerged, this suggests that the ascendency of services will cause a reorientation of trade policy. This reorientation will have to take into account the fact that significant amounts of services are not traded at all, but are delivered by foreign affiliates. The share of foreign direct investment (FDI) dedicated to services in the four major foreign direct investing countries (France, Japan, the UK and the US) increased from 1980 to 1988, so that by 1988 about 40 per cent of the stock of outward FDI was in services [25]. As the composition of trade moves from manufactured goods that can be traded at an arms-length to services which are delivered through direct investments, a re-examination of the rules and procedures that have governed trade may be required.

The uneven effect of policies at the industry level

The decomposition analysis illustrates how the relative importance of the factors associated with structural change -- export growth, domestic demand growth and so on -- differ from one industry to another. Some industries like high-technology manufacturing are primarily driven by exports. Others such as communication services are affected predominantly by growth in domestic markets. Still others like textiles are most sensitive to imports, while industries such as petroleum refining are susceptible to technological change.

Because of this variation, policies not generally thought of as being industry-specific are nevertheless likely to have uneven impacts across different sectors. This includes general macroeconomic policies, for example those concerned with exchange rate levels or domestic demand management, or broad industry policies such as tax incentives for R&D or investment. Even policy measures in principle available to all sectors are in practice quite industry-specific if they are used by only a small number of industries. If this differential effect of policies is not taken into account they might lead to unexpected outcomes.

Uneven impact across industries leads to differing adjustment costs. These include costs related to the dislocation that accompanies structural change, such as retraining and other costs associated with frictional unemployment as well as possible regional shifts in infrastructure investment demands. Such costs may have a high political impact and policies designed to mitigate them may need to take into account the sectoral differentiation that exists. By providing policy makers with a quantitative picture of how sensitive individual industries are to the factors associated with structural change, the decomposition analysis provides a rough framework for tracking the impact of policies.

Unexpected effects may also arise as a result of the interconnections inherent in a modern economies. Policies designed to promote one industry might have effects on other industries. For example, efforts to promote the development of a domestic semiconductor industry through import protection generally lead to rises in semiconductor prices. This affects all those industries that use semiconductors as intermediate inputs. It may also lead to increases in the prices of goods that embody semiconductors with consequent effects on other downstream industries. Price changes may lead to increased imports in goods embodying semiconductors and thus alter the balance of trade. The point here is not to argue for or against such policies but to observe that before they are implemented it is important to account for their potential effects not only on the industries directly concerned but also on the rest of the economy. Many of the indirect interconnections are likely to involve imports and exports. These interconnections, many of which are hidden, suggests that the divisions between domestic and international economic policies are increasingly artificial and that future industrial polices will require their increased integration.

Differences between countries

The analysis reveals that the current composition of the seven countries economies and the structural change that occurred to achieve this state differ significantly across countries. Australia, the US, the UK, and France are more service sector oriented than Japan, Germany, and Canada. Japan's economic growth has been export oriented, European countries have had a high degree of exposure to imports, while Australia and the US have been affected relatively more by domestic final demand. These differences are partly due to natural, indigenous factors: given the large US market, it is not surprising that the US is more inward looking while the relatively small size of the European countries and Japan necessitates a more outward stance. Nevertheless, some of the differences in the structural changes that have occurred between the countries is also a reflection of different policies, some of which retard and some of which facilitate structural adjustments to changes in the economic environment.

A number of policy instruments are in place ranging from tariff barriers to direct subsidies to implicit bilateral agreements that cause the magnitude and nature of structural change to differ between countries. The most efficient means of securing responsiveness to changing opportunities is through exposure to international trade, and it is true that trade barriers, especially tariffs, have decreased in the 1970s and 1980s. Nevertheless, export subsidies, direct industry subsidies, non-tariff barriers such as voluntary export agreements, and retaliatory measures (anti-dumping) have proliferated during the 1980s, causing distortions and differences in the nature of structural change. By the mid-1980s, non-tariff barriers affected 27 per cent of the industrialized countries imports with over 250 voluntary restraint agreements in existence [26].

While these defensive policies appear to be giving way to more positive policies aimed at helping firms adapt, political pressures from influential industries and competing domestic issues such as environmental and national security concerns threaten to limit these gains. The political reality of the situation is that change is most easily accommodated when economic growth is strong. With a strong overall growth rate structural adjustments can be realized with a minimum of sacrifice. The key is to strengthen the responsiveness to changes in the economic environment, by opening up other avenues of growth and easing the transition through the active promotion of investment, training and retraining for new jobs, the privatisation and deregulation of industries, and the reduction of aid to ailing firms.

NOTES AND REFERENCES

1. This part of the report is an edited version of OECD (1992), "Structural Change and Industrial Performance: A Seven-Country Growth Decomposition Study", document, Paris.

2. See OECD (1989), *Economies in Transition: Structural Adjustment in OECD Countries*, Paris, and US Congress, Office of Technology Assessment (1988), *Technology and the American Economic Transition*, OTA-TET-283, Washington DC, Government Printing Office.

3. OECD (1987), *Structural Adjustment and Economic Performance*, Paris, p.18.

4. OECD (1988), "Changing Industrial Structures in OECD Countries", document, Paris.

5. See OECD, "Changing Industrial Structures in OECD Countries", *op. cit.*

6. Leontief, W. (1985), "The Choice of Technology," *Scientific American*, Vol. 252, No. 6; and Carter, A. (1970), *Structural Change in the American Economy*, Boston, MA: Harvard University Press.

7. In fact a sixth term is generated which represents a sum of interactive terms. As opposed to a residual, the interactive terms are well defined and represent the simultaneous change of two or more of the five identified factors.

8. The sixth term which represents the sum of interactive terms has been allocated across the five factors.

9. For the basis of comparisons between countries the results for community and social services includes only two industries, government producers and social and personal services.

10. This may be due to the fact that the 1985 data point for the US is not a benchmark table and thus is less likely to reflect changes in the allocation of margins and in technological change.

11. For an in depth input-output analysis of the US communications sectors, see DRI/McGraw-Hill (1990), "The Contribution of Telecommunication Infrastructure to Aggregate and Sectoral Efficiency", November.

12. The separation of this sector into its requisite industries is not possible for France because of data limitations.

13. Although the time periods differ, comparisons using data from the mid-70s to the mid-80s for France, Japan, the UK, and the US, have a relatively small effect on the ranking and almost no impact on which industries make the top-ten. The major exception to this rule was the UK. The 1979 to 1984 period included four industries in the top-ten that are not included in the 1968 to 1984 period: aerospace, agriculture, chemicals, and non-ferrous metals. These replaced government producers, pharmaceuticals, electricity, gas & water, and rubber & plastics.

14. To some degree the wide variation in growth rates is attributable to differences associated with the conversion of this sector's output into constant prices.

15. It is likely that all seven countries would have listed this industry among the top-ten, but because this industry is included with the electrical equipment industry in Germany its growth rate could not be calculated.

16. Because of data limitations real estate & business services was included in the finance & insurance industry for France. If this had not been the case, it is likely that real estate & business services would have been listed in the top-ten by each of the seven countries.

17. The exception to this case is the United States where domestic final demand was the dominant factor behind the growth in real estate and business services. This is probably because of the inclusion of real estate which saw dramatic gains during this period in the US due to domestic demand and business services which grew due to technological changes. See Kutscher, R. (1989), "Structural Change in the USA, Past and Perspective: Its Implications for Skill and Educational Requirements", *Economic Systems Research*, Vol.1, No.3, p.33.

18. Blades, D. (1987), "Goods and Services in OECD Countries," *OECD Economic Studies*, No. 8.

19. Tschetter, J. (1987), "Producer Services Industries: Why are they Growing So Rapidly?", *Monthly Labor Review*, December; Barker, T. (1990), "Sources of Structural Change for the UK Service Industries 1979-84", *Economic Systems Research*, Vol.2, No. 2, p.180; and Quinn, J. (1989), "Serving the Service Industry", *Issues in Science and Technology*, Summer.

20. Noyce, R. (1977), "Microelectronics", *Scientific American*, Vol.237, No.3, September, p.67.

21. US Department of Commerce, Bureau of Economic Analysis, *Survey of Current Business*, National Income and Product Accounts, table 5.7, p.74.

22. The index defined above is calculated for the entire time period and then divided by the number of years involved. It has also been multiplied by 100 to express change in percentage terms.

23. The data plotted are gross output, not net output or value-added. The double-counting of production in gross output figures is particularly pronounced in manufacturing because of its extensive use of intermediate inputs; the shares of total output held by manufacturing will therefore be inflated.

24. US Department of Commerce (1977), "The Input-Output Structure of the US Economy, 1977", *Survey of Current Business*, table B, p.46.

25. Julius, A. (1990), *Global Companies and Public Policy*, Pinter, London, p.31.

26. See OECD, *Structural Adjustment and Economic Performance*, op.cit., pp.18-38, and OECD, *Economies in Transition*, op.cit., ch.4.

Part 5

GLOBALISATION: DEVELOPMENTS AND POLICY ISSUES

Chapter I

RECENT DEVELOPMENTS

A. Introduction

Globalisation is being driven by technological change, continued long-term growth in foreign investment and international sourcing, and the recent extensive formation of new kinds of international links between firms and countries. This combination is increasingly integrating national economies and changing the nature of global competition.

Technological change underpins globalisation. Rapid declines in the cost of international communications of all kinds, and expanding potential to co-ordinate design, production and distribution in computer-controlled supply networks are encouraging global production and global business. At the same time, in many industries increased R&D costs and shorter innovation time-scales must be recouped over larger production runs and more markets. This has encouraged inter-firm technological alliances to spread R&D costs, promoted international acquisitions and expanded foreign investment. The need to gain access to markets, take advantage of differences in costs of supply, and increase flexibility have all contributed to globalisation, encouraged by investment liberalisation and financial market deregulation.

Foreign direct investment has grown rapidly over a long period. It outstripped growth in production and trade through the 1970s and 1980s, particularly from 1985, although it declined sharply in 1991 except for continuing investment in fast-growing Asian economies, a revival of investment in Latin America and some new flows into Central and Eastern Europe. (For more details, see Part 3, Chapter II.F on international investment). In addition, there are now more sources of investment. Japan, Europe and the Dynamic Asian Economies are taking much larger shares of outward investment. Inward investment increased dramatically into the **United States** and into **Europe**, but inward flows are still relatively minor in **Japan**. Overall, new investment has been mainly within East Asia, western Europe and North America, with greater balance between the three parts of the Triad as sources of investment.

International trade has been the engine of growth post-World War II, but it is being increasingly transformed by the globalisation of production activities. An increasing share of trade is between and within firms related by equity holdings or linked through tightly controlled sourcing and supply relations, and traditional arms-length trade is decreasing in importance. This is reflected in the rising importance of intra-industry and intra-firm trade during the 1980s, driven by increasing foreign investment, narrowing specialisation and complex patterns of international sourcing.

Other more subtle forms of globalisation, not necessarily leading to the re-location of technological and industrial activities, are also increasingly important. These include minority equity holdings and cross-holdings by industrial firms, the establishment of jointly-owned subsidiaries and formation of a wide range of inter-firm non-equity agreements in development, production and marketing. These form increasingly dense and complex inter-firm networks. They are also transforming the dynamics of foreign direct investment, the behaviour of MNEs, the patterns of location of different industrial activities (R&D, production, supply and marketing) and having important effects on the nature of competition. However, many of these changes and their impacts are difficult to measure, or are poorly measured.

The combination of these changes is raising a host of policy questions. These range from defining national interest as firms and industries become increasingly global and national economies are increasingly inter-linked, the role of policies to support R&D and their impacts on the global distribution of technology, how national competitiveness is shaped by global firms, their linkages with local suppliers and small firms and impacts on national efficiency, employment and the foreign balance, and the development of competition policy at international level. While not all of the wider structural changes in industry are solely attributable to globalisation, globalisation is focusing attention on structural change and crystallising the most challenging issues linked with technological advance, changes in competitiveness and comparative advantage, and in competition.

This chapter examines some of these changes and discusses some aggregate measures of globalisation. Many of these measures focus on foreign direct investment, for which detailed data exists. But there are many aspects of globalisation which will only be understood through collection and examination of new internationally comparable data and case studies.

The chapter begins by discussing firm-level globalisation strategies. There follows a description of aggregate trends in foreign direct investment, acquisitions, green-field investment, minority investment and inter-firm agreements. This is succeeded by a discussion of R&D activities in foreign-controlled firms. Finally some of the impacts of globalisation on the level of foreign ownership, trade and international sourcing are examined, finishing with competition and concentration. Most of this summary examines the position of host (receiving) countries, rather than of the sources of investment. Policy issues are discussed in the light of these features of globalisation in Chapter II.

B. Globalisation of firms

At firm level industrial globalisation is characterised by:

- the increasing share of foreign activities in the total activities of many industrial and commercial enterprises;

- the shift from local and national markets to world markets, via foreign direct investment, from exporting to operating in foreign markets, combined with careful differentiation between regional or local markets within overall world-wide strategies;

- the search for globally optimum patterns of location -- often associated with increased regional concentration -- increasing the importance of international sourcing;

- the rapid increase in global strategic alliances and partnerships to develop new products and, increasingly, in production;

- management strategies which optimise resource use across all activities, not only in individual national markets or products.

These firm-level trends are increasing the share of foreign-owned firms in many countries, and increasingly integrating and merging national economies.

A firm is globalised when it organises operations along the chain from R&D and innovation, finance, through production and distribution to final sales to maximise its returns on a global scale [1]. This requires spreading final sales and operations across many markets, and world-wide co-ordination of activities. Competition in one country significantly affects operations in others. This kind of firm strategy is being adopted increasingly as firms disperse their activities widely. Firms in high technology industries, such as aerospace, computers, electronics and chemicals, and some assembly industries such as automobiles, are often global, because R&D costs are high and there are economies of scale in world-wide operations.

Not all international firms operate with global strategies however. Many still pursue multi-domestic strategies. They divide their operations into distinct national markets which are largely independent from each other, but which may involve complex patterns of co-ordination and control between the independent units. Final service and consumption industries strongly influenced by cultural and institutional traditions, such as retailing, deposit banking, food and beverages and other consumer goods, are of this type, as well as some process industries producing intermediate products (building materials, paper pulp).

Many large international firms operate mixed strategies, carefully differentiating national and regional markets so that they can take advantage of local external economies in production and distribution, while tightly co-ordinating their core activities (R&D, technology, planning, finance and other key management functions) at global level. Many more firms, particularly smaller ones, only operate domestically (which may include limited exporting), conducting the overwhelming share of their activities in one national market, but a market which is increasingly an arena of global competition.

Firms set up operations in foreign countries because of their advantages and for strategic reasons. These include [2]:

- Superior technology, organisation, production or marketing methods developed in the home country, which can be effectively used elsewhere (for example a firm's innovations and production organisation are superior to those of foreign competitors);

- Location advantages in the host country (for example access to key raw materials, lower production, transport or marketing costs, avoiding trade restrictions, diversification of supply, but also increasingly to take advantage of the R&D resources, skill base and technological infrastructure in the host country);

- Advantages from conducting operations internally within the firm on a global scale (for example R&D, marketing or component production) rather than buying goods and services through arms-length transactions in external markets;

- Imitative behaviour. Firms in the same industry often follow each other into the same market, clustering foreign direct investments together in a short time period [3]. This may be driven by geographical diversification or opportunities for new businesses;

- De-regulation of financial markets and the formation of global ones encouraged new forms of international investment financing, coupled with new opportunities following the elimination of controls and barriers to foreign investment in many countries.

These driving forces have resulted in increasing globalisation of industrial and commercial activities of all kinds. The remainder of this chapter focuses on various aspects of globalisation of manufacturing industry.

Manufacturing has been the most active sector for international investment, acquisition and merger activity and has a major share of strategic alliances, as well as witnessing rapid increases in international sourcing of inputs.

C. The patterns of foreign direct investment

Although new forms of global expansion are probably increasingly important, the growth and structure of foreign direct investment gives the best-documented measure of globalisation. Aggregate foreign direct investment grew much more rapidly than either foreign trade (the traditional international "engine" of growth) or domestic product in the 1970s and 1980s. It showed particularly rapid growth from 1985-89, but slowed down in 1990 and declined in 1991 along with the global downturn in late-1990 and 1991 (see Part 3, Chapter II.F on international investment for more details).

The boom in foreign direct investment was driven by three major forces:

- *Market expansion*. In the OECD area, foreign investment has been driven by opportunities to locate in the ***United States*** and rationalisation in the ***European Community*** before the 1993 Single Market have driven recent foreign investment. Over 80 per cent of all foreign investment went to OECD countries in the 1985-90 period and most of this went to the ***United States*** and to the ***European Community***. There has also been an investment boom in the Dynamic Asian Economies (notably ***Singapore*** and ***Taiwan***, but increasingly in a broad range of South-East Asian countries) to locate in rapidly growing economies. Recently there has been a revival in investment in Latin America as their prospects improved, and investment has begun to flow into Central and Eastern Europe. ***Japan*** became the largest single source of foreign investment from 1988 onwards, although it is considerably less important than the ***European Community*** countries combined, and the ***United States*** declined in relative importance as a source of foreign investment as Japan and Europe increased and the richer Asian economies became important sources of investment in the Asian area.

Table 57. **World stocks of inward direct investment**

	Amount (billion US$)			Distribution (per cent)		
	1967	1980	1989	1967	1980	1989
United States	9.9	83.0	400.8	9.4	16.5	28.6
Canada	19.2	51.6	103.0	18.2	10.2	7.3
Japan	0.6	3.3	9.2	0.6	0.7	0.7
European Community	24.8	186.9	483.9	23.3	37.0	34.5
of which:						
France	3.0	21.1	59.0	2.8	4.2	4.2
Germany	3.6	47.9	101.5	3.4	9.5	7.2
Italy	2.6	8.9	50.9	2.5	1.8	3.6
Netherlands	4.9	19.2	47.9	4.6	3.8	3.4
Spain	0.4	9.1	42.1	0.4	1.8	3.0
United Kingdom	7.9	63.0	138.8	7.5	12.5	9.9
Other Europe	6.6	25.4	56.0	6.3	5.0	4.0
of which:						
Sweden	0.5	1.7	5.4	0.5	0.3	0.4
Switzerland	2.1	14.3	31.7	2.0	2.8	2.3
Australia	4.9	28.1	69.3	4.6	5.6	4.9
South Africa	7.2	15.1	11.1	6.8	3.0	0.8
Developing countries	32.3	111.1	269.6	30.6	22.0	19.2
of which:						
Latin America	18.5	62.2	103.9	17.5	12.3	7.4
Africa	5.6	13.1	29.8	5.3	2.6	2.1
Middle East	3.2	4.3	12.1	3.0	0.9	0.9
East Asia	5.1	31.5	123.8	4.8	6.2	8.8
All countries	105.5	504.5	1 402.9	100.0	100.0	100.0

Source: Adapted from U.S. Department of Commerce, *Foreign Direct Investment in the United States,* August 1991, Appendix 4-1.

- *Rapid technological change* coupled with falling communications costs. Firms have developed new advantages based on technological strengths (for example in electronics and information technology) and organisational developments (new management techniques and structures built around advanced manufacturing technology);

- *Competitive pressures* to operate in all of the major integrated regions evolving in East Asia, Europe and North America (the "Triad") [4]. Recent Japanese investment by leading electronics and automobile firms is of this kind.

The most important long-term development has been the expansion of the share of the total foreign investment stock held by OECD countries. Two-thirds of the world total is in the *United States* and Europe (Table 57). The share of developing countries and regions in the total stock of foreign direct investment has fallen dramatically to less than 20 per cent of the total, due to instability and poor market prospects, although flows to Latin America have revived recently. The notable exceptions to this downward trend have been in South-East and East Asia, where market-oriented development policies, coupled with very high rates of economic growth have fed a foreign investment boom and an increasing share of total investment.

The *European Community* replaced the *United States* as the main destination for direct investment from 1989 onwards (the EC held this position in the 1970s also). Opportunities for market expansion and rationalisation inside the Single Market attracted investment from the United States and other European countries, and investment from *Japan* and the Dynamic Asian Economies (particularly *Taiwan* and *Korea*) expanded rapidly. Around one half of outward investment by EC firms now goes to other EC countries, including over one-half of these flows from *France*, *Germany* and *Italy*. The exception is the *United Kingdom*, where both inward and outward investment has tended to be much more global and less concentrated on Europe. A little less than one-half of US outward investment also goes to the EC, particularly the *United Kingdom* and the *Netherlands*. Although Japanese investment in Europe is rising rapidly, the stock is still only one-quarter of the US total, and only around one-quarter of total Japanese investment goes to Europe.

Foreign investment tends to follow market opportunities and market prospects, rather than create them. This helps to explain the slowness of new investment in central and eastern Europe. Foreign investment has been hampered by the collapse in demand, few viable firms to purchase and difficulties in valuing assets and deciding property rights, the slow process of developing take-over and merger rules and regulations governing foreign investment, poor infrastructure and the slow development of capital markets.

D. Acquisitions, mergers and green-field investments

Foreign investment can be through acquisitions of existing firms to strengthen market positions or expand commercial activities or through construction of new plants and facilities ("green-field" investment). Acquisitions result in an immediate shift in ownership coupled with some potential to improve performance. Production and patterns of supply and sales are unlikely to change radically, although they may become more international. Green-field investment will have a delayed impact on production and employment and is likely to involve new international patterns of sourcing and sales.

Acquisitions are most common in countries where stock markets are extensively used as sources of finance (for example in *Canada*, the *United Kingdom* and the *United States*. In many cases established firms became available to foreign investors as part of re-structuring and the sale of peripheral businesses following previous domestic acquisitions. Acquisitions as a mode of entry into new markets are less common in countries where the banking system has built long-term financing arrangements with industrial firms (for example in *Germany* and *Japan*).

Acquisitions account for almost 85 per cent of foreign investment outlays in the *United States* in the 1980s through to 1990. Around 60 per cent of recent cross-border investment in the *European Community* has been acquisitions, and foreign acquisitions have shown a rising trend in *Canada* to make up over one-half of new foreign investment. Home-country influences play a part in the choice between acquisition or green-field investment. For example, firms from the United States, *France* and the *United Kingdom* have been much more active in foreign acquisitions in the EC than German and Japanese firms. (Table 58 shows increasing cross-border acquisitions in the EC.)

Finally, a significant share of total acquisitions in both the *European Community* and the *United States* have been in process industries where there are important economies of scale in production and/or marketing (food-processing, pulp and paper, chemicals) and advantages in spreading large R&D costs over larger sales volumes (chemicals). These industries have relatively low imports and high local content and have lower direct impacts on the foreign balance than assembly industries such as machinery, motor vehicles and electronics, which source components and sub-assemblies globally.

E. Minority investments, joint ventures, inter-firm agreements and networking

A range of minority or non-equity investments have also grown rapidly. International minority investments have grown strongly in the *European Community* for example. These may be a prelude to majority acquisitions,

Table 58. **Industrial deals of the 1 000 largest firms in the European Community**

Number of operations and geographical breakdown[1]

	1982/83	1983/84	1984/85	1985/86	1986/87	1987/88	1988/89	1989/90
				Mergers and acquisitions of majority holdings				
Number of operations	117	155	208	227	303	383	492	622
National share[2]	50.4	65.2	70.2	63.9	69.6	55.9	47.4	38.7
Community share[3]	32.5	18.7	21.2	22.9	24.8	29.2	40.0	41.3
Non-Community share[4]	17.1	16.1	8.7	13.2	5.6	14.9	12.6	19.9
				Acquisitions of minority holdings				
Number of operations	33	54	67	130	117	181	159	180
National share[2]	60.6	68.5	67.2	67.7	71.8	63.5	64.2	40.6
Community share[3]	27.3	14.8	14.9	15.4	17.9	20.4	23.3	34.4
Non-Community share[4]	12.1	16.7	17.9	16.9	10.3	16.0	12.6	25.0
				Establishment of jointly-owned subsidiary				
Number of operations	46	69	82	81	90	111	129	156
National share[2]	50.0	46.4	48.8	42.0	32.2	40.5	43.4	26.2
Community share[3]	17.4	15.9	18.3	24.7	17.8	27.9	27.9	35.3
Non-Community share[4]	32.6	37.7	32.9	33.3	50.0	31.5	28.7	38.5

1. Data collected from the specialist press regarding operations involving at least one of the 1 000 largest firms of the Community, ranked according to their financial data.
2. Operations of firms from the same Community member state.
3. Operations of firms from different Community member states.
4. Operations of firms from Community member states and third countries which affect the Community market.

Source: Commission of the European Communities, *Report on Competition Policy*, various issues.

as they have been common in industries such as food and beverages, chemicals, electrical engineering and electronics, where acquisitions are also common and where there is active rationalisation (Table 58). The automobile industry is another industry which has a large number of international minority cross-holdings. The links between US, Japanese and Korean producers are long-standing, but new cross-holding and sourcing arrangements are building up in Europe, with some notable examples being developed with Japanese producers.

Joint ventures are often set up to develop new technologies, as well as to exploit new markets, and this form of inter-firm arrangement has also become increasingly common. In Europe they tend to be clustered in R&D-intensive industries, particularly chemicals and electrical engineering, with increasing Japanese and US participation as a way of facilitating their market entry.

However, by some measures, minority holdings have become less common forms of foreign direct investment. For example, for US multinational companies the share of employment in majority-owned affiliates has tended to grow relative to minority-owned affiliates (ownership between 10 per cent or more and 50 per cent or less of total equity), and this trend was a general one across all major countries and regions of investment. The share of total employment in minority-owned affiliates shrank from over 25 per cent in 1977 to less than 23 per cent in 1989. For inward investment to France the relative importance of majority-owned foreign firms also grew, and the share of employment in minority-owned firms (between 20 per cent or more and 50 per cent or less) declined from 21 per cent in 1978 to 11 per cent in 1988 [5]. These data suggest that there has been an ongoing process of rationalisation and growth of majority holdings, but that this was parallelled by a build-up in new strategic minority holdings, often below the lower limits defined as a "controlling interest" in official statistics.

The growth of international inter-firm agreements, often building on older informal scientific and technological networks, has been a significant development of the 1980s. These agreements are also creating dense networks of links between firms and between firms and technological institutions. They mainly aim at technological development, but they increasingly involve production and marketing to reap benefits of development. These networks are an important component of international and national systems for innovation and they may have significant long-term impacts on technological development and applications of new technologies. Inter-firm agreements concentrate in a few industries which are globalised and R&D-intensive, such as electronics, aerospace, telecommunications and computers, as well as automobiles, and often focus on core technologies (information technology, biotechnology and new materials). Most agreements are between firms from the Triad, with agreements most common between firms within the EC, between EC and North American firms and then between EC and Japanese firms [6].

Such agreements enable firms to participate in global technological development, without necessarily shifting the geographical location of R&D. The principal motives for technological co-operation appear to be: (i) the search for technological complementarities in areas where firms have limited expertise; (ii) reductions in the innovation time-span and increases in efficiency to get new products and processes to markets; and (iii) market access and re-structuring in mature technologies and slow growth industries. Little analysis of their long-term economic significance and impacts on foreign investment, industrial structure and concentration has been carried out [7].

F. Foreign investment, R&D and technology generation

Because of the importance of foreign investment by large, leading firms in technologically advanced industries, they may make an important contribution to R&D and technology generation in host countries. There are four intersecting factors which determine the location of R&D in global firms:

- *Centralisation*. Economies of scale in R&D and its strategic importance favours centralisation of R&D as a "headquarters" function [8];

- *Diversification*. The segmentation of global markets into three major regions in Asia, North America and Europe encourages globalised firms to set up R&D activities in each, to spread risks and gain access to complementary research resources, R&D staff and institutions;

- *Entry strategy*. R&D tends to lag green-field investment. Acquisitions tend to maintain existing R&D and may increasingly be aimed at capturing R&D resources (for example in biotechnology in the *United States*);

- *Country-specific factors*. New-comers to foreign investment tend to perform less R&D away from home. Global enterprises from smaller countries (the *Netherlands, Sweden, Switzerland*) tend to perform more R&D in foreign countries because of their limited domestic resources, and the necessity of drawing on new developments in major R&D-performing countries.

Inter-firm technology agreements may also encourage firms to concentrate resources, either by allowing R&D to remain at headquarters, or alternatively by creating joint teams which operate in one part of the Triad.

All of these factors are driving new global patterns of R&D. In the *United States,* for example, expenditures on R&D as a share of gross output are higher for foreign manufacturing affiliates located in the United States than the average for all manufacturing (7.6 per cent in foreign affiliates compared with the average of 6.5 per cent in 1987). This is explained by the high level of direct investment in R&D-intensive industries, and particularly by the acquisition of R&D-intensive firms by foreign investors. It also reflects the attractiveness of the United States as a R&D location, due to its stock of skilled manpower and large market [9].

In the *United Kingdom* the shares of R&D expenditures and manufacturing output by foreign-owned firms are also similar (although the R&D share is somewhat lower), suggesting that a few countries are being used as important R&D bases within the Triad. This also reflects relatively high foreign investment in R&D-intensive industries, and the contribution that foreign R&D-intensive firms make to overall national R&D-intensity. Foreign-controlled R&D is also important in countries where there are relatively lower levels of indigenous industrial R&D. In *Australia, Canada, Ireland* and *Spain*, foreign-controlled enterprises perform a large share of manufacturing R&D, reflecting the important role of foreign firms in high-tech manufacturing industry (compare Tables 59, 60 and 61). However, the share of R&D carried out by foreign firms is often less than their share of industrial output in the same industry, and R&D activities of foreign firms are rarely dramatically higher than those of indigenous firms in the same industry. Reasons include centralisation of R&D functions at home where the research networks and infrastructure are most dense, the preference for government research contracts to be allocated to national firms, and poorly developed globalisation of small research-intensive service firms.

The pattern of international investment of *Sweden's* large global firms illustrates the lag in the transfer of key R&D functions. The eighteen companies with most employees outside of Sweden had over 60 per cent of total employees abroad in 1989. Close to 40 per cent of expenditures on buildings and machinery were outside of Sweden, but only 16 per cent of R&D expenditures were abroad [10]. However, R&D performed outside of Sweden is growing rapidly due to limits on domestic resources, and to acquisition of foreign R&D resources as part of international expansion. Similarly it is estimated that globalised companies of the *Netherlands* performed 55 per cent of their R&D abroad in 1990, although this may be less than foreign production and employment in these firms.

Major investing countries also transfer R&D abroad with a lag. US manufacturing affiliates abroad have the equivalent of one-third of parent firm employment and sales, but R&D expenditures are only 10-12 per cent of parent expenditures and R&D employment only 15 per cent of parent firm totals. These shares have remained stable over time and over broad industry groups, suggesting that US corporations have developed long-term globally optimum patterns of production, investment and R&D activities with a large share of R&D remaining at home (see Tables 62 and 63). There are however significant R&D activities of US firms in Germany and Japan compared with the general pattern of overseas activities of US firms. For Japan, a survey for fiscal 1989 showed that an amount equivalent to only 0.8 per cent of total business enterprise R&D was performed abroad, although this is expanding [11]. Overall, despite the contribution of foreign-owned firms to indigenous technological development, international transfer of R&D activities may lag employment and output. But networks of technology alliances may globalise R&D efficiently without shifts in the location of R&D activities which run counter to the achievement of economic scale. There is also extensive international scientific collaboration outside strategic alliances and direct investment, for example between research universities or facilities and foreign firms.

Table 59. **Share of R&D expenditures of foreign-controlled firms in total business enterprise R&D expenditures**

Percentages

	1981	1989
United States		
Manufacturing	5 (1980)	11 (1988)
Canada		
Manufacturing	..	52
All business	44	38
Japan		
Manufacturing	4 (1980)	3
France	17 (1977)	12
Ireland		
Manufacturing	59	59 (1988)
All business	52	52
Netherlands		
All business	..	13 (1990)
Spain		
All business	..	39 (1988)
United Kingdom		
Manufacturing	15	17
Finland		
All business	3	..
Sweden		
Manufacturing + mining	7	14
Australia		
Manufacturing	51 (1976/77)	45 (1986/87)
All business	52	32

Source: OECD, compiled from national sources.

G. Impacts of globalisation

Penetration of foreign firms

High levels of foreign investment and expansion of established foreign firms have increased the relative importance of foreign ownership in most OECD countries.

Table 60. **Share of foreign enterprises in manufacturing employment**[1]
Percentages

	1970	1980	1987	1988	1989
United States[2]	3.2 (1974)	5.8	7.7[3]	8.9	10.0
Canada	44.3	37.8	34.0 (1986)	..	..
Japan	..	1.6	1.0	..	1.1
Denmark	..	..	12.4 (1986)	..	..
France[2]	17.9 (1975)	18.5	21.6	22.3	..
Germany[2]	22.4 (1972)	16.6	15.5	15.4	18.1
Ireland	26.7 (1973)	36.3 (1983)	..	44.2	..
Italy	18.3 (1977)	15.8	15.9 (1986)[4]	17.2	..
Portugal[2]	..	..	17.7 (1984)	..	..
United Kingdom	10.3 (1971)	14.9 (1981)	13.0	13.0	14.8
Austria	23.4	..	24.9 (1985)[2]	..	..
Finland[2]	4.3 (1975)	4.0[2]	6.0[1]	5.5[2]	5.3[2]
Norway[2]	12.4 (1973)	11.2	9.6	9.7	..
Sweden	4.5	6.4	10.2	13.5	14.0
Turkey[2]	..	..	8.4	..	..
Australia[2]	23.6 (1972/73)	26.3 (1982/83)	23.8 (1986/87)	..	..

1. Includes minority holdings (equity holdings >10 or >20 per cent up to 50 per cent) for countries indicated. Percentages are calculated as a share of production from the annual census of production in most cases. This may overstate the share of foreign firms, if small firms (<20 employees) are excluded from the annual census, as small firms are predominantly domestic.
2. Includes joint ventures and minority participation (<50 per cent). Values for France are unweighted by share of minority ownership.
3. From U.S. Department of Commerce, *Survey of Current Business*, 1990, 1991.
4. Estimates.
Source: OECD, from data supplied by national authorities and national sources.

Table 61. **Share of foreign enterprises in manufacturing turnover**[1]
Percentages

	1970	1980	1987	1988	1989
United States[2]	..	5.1	11.4[3]	12.7	14.9
Canada	57.2 (1972)	50.6	48.6	..	..
Japan	..	4.7	2.3	..	2.4
Denmark	..	..	13.3 (1986)	..	..
France[2]	21.6 (1975)	26.6	26.9	27.5	..
Germany[2]	25.1 (1972)	23.2	21.0	20.5	21.7
Ireland	..	46.1 (1983)	52.2	55.1	..
Italy	23.8 (1977)	19.2	22.0 (1986)[4]	22.3	..
Norway[2]	18.0 (1973)	17.0	11.6	12.9	..
Portugal[2]	..	..	23.6 (1984)	..	..
United Kingdom	14.2 (1971)	19.3 (1981)	20.0	20.2	23.5
Austria	25.2	..	..	..	..
Finland[2]	4.0 (1975)	3.4	5.4	5.0	5.1
Sweden	6.7 (1972)	7.9	11.1	14.7	15.0
Turkey[2]	..	..	14.6	..	..
Australia[2]	28.7 (1972/73)	33.5 (1982/83)	32.0 (1986/87)	..	..

1. Includes minority holdings (equity holdings >10 or >20 per cent up to 50 per cent) for countries indicated. Percentages are calculated as a share of production from the annual census of production in most cases. This may overstate the share of foreign firms, if small firms (<20 employees) are excluded from the annual census, as small firms are predominantly domestic.
2. Includes joint ventures and minority controlled (<50 per cent). Values for France are unweighted by share of minority ownership.
3. From U.S. Department of Commerce, *Survey of Current Business*, 1990, 1991.
4. Estimates.
Source: OECD, from data supplied by national authorities and national sources.

Table 62. **Sales, employment, capital expenditure and R&D by US majority-owned foreign affiliates as a percentage of US parent firm totals**

	Sales			Employment			Plant and equipment expenditures			R&D expenditures			R&D employment		
	1977	1982	1989	1977	1982	1989	1977	1982	1989[1]	1977	1982	1989	1977[2]	1982	1989
Chemicals and allied products	34.4	32.6	40.8	39.3	35.9	38.1	26.6	23.8	42.2	12.1	10.7	11.8	18.6	17.1	20.0
Machinery, except electrical	37.0	35.4	56.0	35.3	30.5	39.8	53.7	41.0	41.8	5.0	4.1	6.0	16.3	11.6	14.5
Electrical and electronic	32.6	20.2	27.2	53.8	35.2	44.3	26.0	13.4	20.7	14.0	10.1	15.2	23.8	12.9	13.6
Transport	30.0	31.8	31.9	33.3	35.1	28.7	21.5	31.7	26.5	12.4	15.1	15.5	12.1	14.6	13.0
Other	21.5	23.2	25.0	28.6	30.5	26.9	19.3	17.4	28.1	10.3	12.1	11.9	17.6	21.1	12.8
Manufacturing total	27.8	27.4	32.7	34.3	32.7	32.0	26.4	23.9	31.5	10.7	10.4	11.4	16.7	15.1	14.5
All industries	38.2	32.5	32.4	30.7	27.6	27.3	26.4	23.9	29.5	10.7	10.4	12.1	15.5	15.3	15.3

1. Capital expenditures.
2. R&D scientists and engineers.
Source: Foreign affiliate data by industry of affiliate, parent data by industry of parent. Calculated from U.S. Department of Commerce, *U.S. Direct Investment Abroad, 1977*, April 1981; *U.S. Direct Investment Abroad, 1982*, December 1985; *U.S. Direct Investment Abroad, 1989* (preliminary results), October 1991. 1989 parent data for all non-bank parents, 1977 and 1982 parent data for non-bank parents of majority-owed non-bank affiliates.

Table 63. **Research and development expenditures of foreign affiliates of US MNEs as a percentage of total MNE group expenditures**

	1966	1977	1982	1989
All industries	6.5	10.0	8.8	10.8
Petroleum	7.0	11.7	10.7	6.9
Manufacturing	6.6	8.6	8.8	10.3
Food and kindred products	11.1	14.1	16.4	15.5
Chemical and allied products	7.6	11.7	10.8	10.6
Primary and fabricated metals	4.6	4.3	4.0	7.5
Machinery except electrical	6.9	5.3	5.2	5.7
Electrical/electronic equipment	6.0	3.4	3.3	13.2
Transportation equipment	5.1	10.1	13.0	13.4
Other manufacturing	10.7	10.6	10.1	10.3
Other industries	2.8	29.8	7.9	16.2

Source: Data for 1966 are reported in Petrella, R., "Internationalisation, Multinationalisation and Globalisation of R&D", mimeo, October 1991. Other years calculated from US Department of Commerce, *US Direct Investment Abroad, 1977*, April 1981; *US Direct Investment Abroad, 1982*, December 1985; *US Direct Investment Abroad, 1989*, (preliminary results), October 1991.

However, there are wide differences among OECD countries in the share of turnover and employment in foreign-controlled firms (see Tables 60 and 61). Section C above and Part 3, Chapter II.F on international investment give details of the broad changes in flows and stocks of foreign investment. This section concentrates on the cumulative importance of this investment and foreign ownership and on the activities of foreign-owned firms.

The share of foreign-owned subsidiaries in manufacturing turnover is:

- over 30 per cent in *Australia, Belgium, Canada* and *Ireland*;

- 20-30 per cent in *Austria, France, Germany, Portugal* and the *United Kingdom*;

- 10-20 per cent in *Denmark, Italy, Norway, Sweden, Turkey* and the *United States*;

- less than 10 per cent in *Finland* and *Japan*.

Penetration has increased particularly rapidly in the *United States*, reflecting strong inflows of foreign investment in the 1980s, and in *Sweden,* both from a low base. In the European Community, it has increased rapidly in *Portugal* and *Spain* following large inflows of foreign investment and has continued to grow significantly in *Ireland*. With the boom in foreign investment from the latter part of the 1980s, the relative importance of foreign ownership increased again in larger European countries (*France, Germany, Italy, United Kingdom*) which already had 15-25 per cent of manufacturing output in foreign-owned subsidiaries in the 1970s but which showed low growth of foreign investment and penetration in the early 1980s. The share of foreign-controlled output has declined from previous high levels in *Australia* and *Canada*.

In most countries the chemical, pharmaceutical, automobile, electronics and computer industries have the largest flows of investment and the highest shares of foreign ownership (see Table 64). However there are some

Table 64. **Industrial sectors with the highest share of production by foreign enterprises**[1]

	Canada (1987)	France (1988)	Germany (1989)	Italy (1989)	United Kingdom (1989)	United States (1989)	Japan (1989)
1.	Automobiles 85%	Computers 71%	Computers 78%	Computers 63%	Computers 65%	Other manuf. 30%	Chemicals 11%
2.	Chemicals 76%	Chemicals 45%	Chemicals 39%	Electronics 55%	Automobiles 56%	Non-met. products 29%	Machinery/equ. 2%
3.	Non-met. products 55%	Electronics 33%	Food, beverages 21%	Chemicals 30%	Chemicals 37%	Chemicals 27%	Basic metals 1%
4.	Machinery/equ. 44%	Non-met. products 27%	Automobiles 20%	Food, beverages 15%	Electronics 30%	Basic metals 22%	Other manuf. 0.6%
5.	Other manuf. 35%	Machines 24%	Basic metals 17%	Machines 12%	Basic metals 22%	Electronics 19%	Paper, printing 0.5%

1. Production from foreign-owned enterprises and enterprises with foreign participation as a share of total production in industry in each country. Values may be overestimated in some cases, see notes to Tables 60 and 61. Production refers to turnover, output or sales depending on the source. For Japan only 2-digit ISIC data available.

Source: OECD, Industry Division.

differences between countries in the industries which have the highest levels of foreign ownership, with for example resource-intensive process industries which need to be located near to markets (cement, glass, chemicals, metal refining) prominent amongst industries in the *United States* with extensive foreign ownership.

The pattern of penetration of foreign firms will also be shaped by the industries and countries which are the new investors, and which are adding most rapidly to the global stock of foreign ownership. *Japan* has been the most important new investor through the 1980s and 1990, but there has also been significant new investments from *France*, and the EFTA countries have invested extensively in the European Community.

New globalisation strategies are re-shaping investment patterns established by previous waves of investors from countries such as the *United States*, the *United Kingdom* and *Germany* which have been investing in foreign markets more consistently over a longer period. The growth of employment in foreign affiliates of Japanese firms in North America and Europe has averaged around 15 per cent per year in the 1980-90 period as Japanese firms

Table 65. **Employment in foreign affiliates**
Thousand

	Japan			Germany			United States		
Subsidiaries in:	1980	1990	Annual Growth (%)	1980	1990	Annual Growth (%)	1980	1990	Annual Growth (%)
Asia	401	484	1.9	133	177	2.9	829	1 416	8.0
North America	82	368	16.2	393	498	2.4			
Canada							914	945	0.5
Europe	33	127	14.5	711	1 100	4.5	2 767	2 708	–0.3
Rest of world	186	177	–0.5	506	553	0.9	2 131	1 552	–4.4
World	701	1 157	5.1	1 743	2 328	2.9	6 640	6 621	–0.04
Manufacturing	605	922	4.3	1 312	1 638	2.2	4 429	4 189	–0.8
Share of employment (%)	(86.3%)	(79.7%)		(75.3%)	(70.4%)		(66.7%)	(63.3%)	

Source: OECD, calculated from *Survey on Japanese Business Activities Abroad*, MITI, Japan; *Monatsberichten der Deutschen Bundesbank*, Bundesbank of Germany; Benchmark Surveys, U.S. Department of Commerce (Nonbank Affiliates of U.S. Nonbank Parents). Survey coverage may vary between countries.

expanded rapidly there. Japanese firms have been expanding global employment at approximately twice the rate of German firms (detailed data on overseas employment in UK subsidiaries are not available, but the total is probably about twice that in German foreign subsidiaries). Employment in US subsidiaries remained steady in the 1980s and US parent firms retained a stable share of total US manufacturing (See Tables 62 and 65). This suggests that US global firms have reached an optimum balance between their foreign and domestic operations.

Foreign firms tend to have a higher share of output and value added than their share of employment, higher average labour productivity and higher average wages. This is due to technological and organisational advantages of foreign firms, the advanced industries that they often operate in, and their larger average size. They are also often more capital intensive than domestic firms. These differences between foreign firms and domestic ones generally hold across most OECD countries, and across most industries.

International trade: general impacts

A high and increasing share of international trade is within related firms or between firms involved in contracting and supply of components and inputs into final production. A declining share involves traditional arms-length trade. Foreign affiliates are more oriented towards international trade than domestic firms (Table 66). They have a high proportion of intra-firm imported inputs for final assembly and sale, while also importing technology, machinery and equipment and services from parents. For example, in 1988 over three-quarters of merchandise imports by foreign-owned affiliates in the *United States* came from the foreign parent group, and close to 40 per cent of foreign-owned affiliate exports went to the foreign parent group [12].

The share of total national trade due to direct investment is high. For the *United States* and *Japan* values are [13]:

- *United States* (1986) exports to affiliates plus exports by foreign-owned firms were 55 per cent of total merchandise exports, imports from US affiliates abroad plus imports by foreign-owned firms were 52 per cent of merchandise imports;
- *Japan*'s (1983) exports to affiliates plus exports by foreign-owned firms were 41 per cent of total merchandise exports, imports from Japanese affiliates abroad plus imports by foreign-owned firms were 57 per cent of merchandise imports.

There is a wide range of industry-specific patterns of globalised production. For example, the chemical industry (by some measures the most highly globalised industry) has higher levels of local inputs because process production is based on bulk feed-stock, whereas electronics and automobiles have high international flows of components and assemblies and world-wide sourcing.

These data illustrate the trade propensity of globally operating firms, where components and finished products are shipped in complex patterns between affiliated groups and contracting and supplying firms. The contribution of foreign investment to the overall national trade balance (and total balance of payments through invisibles and capital movements) is of major importance, making direct control of the external balance by traditional policies more complex, if not unworkable, and conventional trade balance data misleading in some countries.

Intra-industry trade

One of the facets of globalisation is increased trade within the same broad industry or product group. This trade pattern reflects the increasingly oligopolistic structure of markets, with firms engaged in fierce competition at home seeking outlets overseas, the differentiation of products that follows the more diverse tastes in advanced economies, and is often related to international investment and overseas production, intra-firm trade, and international sourcing of inputs by global firms (see Box 20).

Graph 23 shows the evolution of intra-industry trade since 1970 in the OECD area. The highest IIT indices in 1990 can be found in the *United Kingdom, France and Austria* (where over three-quarters of total trade is accounted by intra-industry transactions), followed by *Spain, Belgium, Germany,* the *United States,* and the *Netherlands. New Zealand, Australia, Japan* and *Turkey* are the four countries with the lowest IIT indices in 1990, with less than a third of their total trade representing transactions within the same broadly defined product group. For almost all countries, the proportion of total trade that is accounted by intra-industry transactions has increased significantly in the period 1970-90. The exception is *Norway*, where the share of intra-industry trade in

Table 66. **Trade intensity of foreign affiliates in manufacturing**

	Exports/turnover (%)		Imports/turnover (%)	
	Foreign	All industry	Foreign	All industry
United States (1989) all industries, % of gross product (1987)	9.0 31.7	.. 7.2	11.3 94.5	.. 11.5
Japan (1989)	7.3	..	45.4	..
France (1988)	30.7	27.9	..	..
Ireland (1988)	86.1	63.6	..	..
Finland (1989)	36.8	32.5	..	..
Sweden (1989)	41.2	34.0	..	..

Source: OECD, compiled from national sources.

Box 20. Globalisation and intra-industry trade

The process of globalisation involves a transformation of international patterns of production and trade. In an attempt to identify empirically some dimensions of this phenomenon, a number of characteristics need to be examined. These include the pattern of international sourcing of intermediate and capital inputs, the international diffusion of technology, international investment and the formation of international networks for the production and distribution of goods and services, and intra-firm and intra-industry trade.

Definition and measurement. Intra-industry trade (IIT) is a measure of two-way trade within the same industrial or product classification. An example of intra-industry trade is where Japan exports laptop computers to the United States, while the US exports mainframe computers to Japan. For a particular product or industry i, IIT is defined as the value of total trade (X_i+M_i) remaining after subtraction of the absolute value of net exports or imports, $|X_i-M_i|$ [1]. In order to be able to compare between countries and industries, the measure is expressed as a percentage of each industry's combined exports and imports. A measure of *inter*-industry trade is then expressed as $100[|X_i-M_i|/(X_i+M_i)]$ and the *intra*-industry trade measure is given by $100(1-[|X_i-M_i|/(X_i+M_i)])$. The index varies between 0 and 100. If a country exports and imports roughly equal quantities of a certain product, the IIT index is high. If it is mainly one-way trade (whether exporting or importing), the IIT index is low. For aggregation purposes, the measure can be summed over many industries [2].

Interpretation. There are a number of explanations for the phenomenon of intra-industry trade which help in the interpretation of IIT indices. The first is based on economies of scale and *product differentiation* [3]. Trade opens up the possibility of specialisation in order to reap economies of scale in production. As consumption is however spread over all product varieties, a country will simultaneously export and import similar products, leading to a situation of two-way trade in highly differentiated products even among countries where the factors of production are similar. In this context, the IIT index is an indicator also of the capacity of a given country to structurally adapt in order to be able to realise the benefits involved in increasing specialisation and product variety. This type of adaptation is not easily accounted for by "conventional" trade theory as it is significantly different to industrial specialisation whereby countries develop "strong points" based on comparative advantage -- often involving major inter-sectoral reallocations of production factors [4].

A second explanation focuses on *market structure* and traces the primary cause for intra-industry trade to the growth of oligopolistic markets in industrialised countries. Oligopolistic firms usually seek to increase market share by methods other than price competition. In addition to product differentiation, their strategy can include seeking outlets abroad for surplus output, giving rise to intra-industry trade. Eventually, however, exports may give way to overseas production, with the result of increased foreign investment by firms in each other's home markets (what is sometimes referred to as intra-industry foreign direct investment) [5]. In this sense, intra-industry trade also explains the growth of foreign direct investment. The two can be regarded as different methods whereby firms expand internationally in response to the oligopolistic character of markets in advanced industrialised economies.

1990 (an index of 42) was below that of 1970, and one of the lowest among OECD countries. Turkey and New Zealand have had the fastest growth in this type of trade in the last twenty years, with annual growth rates of 9 and 5 per cent respectively. This shift in the structure of trade is also pronounced in the *United Kingdom, Spain,* the *United States, Finland, Greece* and *Japan* (in the 1980-90 period).

The main factors that affect the level of intra-industry trade are reflected in the positions of different countries in the graph. High IIT indices should be expected in countries with high per capita incomes and greater economic development. High or rising per capita incomes increase demand for variety and bring about trade in differentiated products. The degree of economic integration between countries also tends to affect intra-industry trade, with countries belonging to regional trading zones (such as the EC member states) exhibiting high IIT indices, especially when they are at a similar stage of development. Low IIT indices should in contrast be expected in countries that are geographically far from the areas where the bulk of world demand and trade is concentrated and in countries that have a very high specialisation in one group of products (for example natural resource-based economies) or a high import dependence on others.

Box 20 *(cont).* **Globalisation and intra-industry trade**

Another explanation focuses on the *international sourcing of inputs*. An indicator of intra-industry trade, expressed at an aggregate level or at the level of individual industries, captures trade in finished goods for consumption as well as trade in intermediate and capital goods which are used as inputs in production. In addition therefore to indicating the degree of product differentiation, IIT indices can also be indicators of the extent to which companies source a proportion of their inputs internationally and of the evolution of that sourcing over time. The IIT index can be interpreted as a globalisation indicator, since it provides information about the changing strategies of firms and the shifting international patterns of production.

A final explanation is based on *intra-firm trade* and on the existence of global firms. In many industries firms operate by having production facilities in a number of countries, often specialising in different components of the completed product in each country. They then engage in substantial intra-firm transfers, often at prices that are different from those charged by other companies acting as suppliers ("transfer pricing"). The growth of such firms and the increasingly dense networks of production and sourcing that they create internationally is one dimension of globalisation. To the extent that the IIT index captures some of this type of trade, it is an indicator that helps quantify this aspect of globalisation.

These explanations are not mutually exclusive. Any given IIT index will describe all four phenomena. Disentangling them is not possible without external information about the share of traded products that are intermediate inputs or the share of trade that is intra-firm. The tables in the text calculate IIT indices without attempting to separate these components.

1. See Grubel, H.G., and Lloyd, P.J., (1975), *Intra-industry Trade*, London.
2. For aggregation purposes, the unadjusted aggregate (*UA*) measure of intra-industry trade is given by:

$$UA = 100 \frac{\sum(X_i + M_i) - \sum|X_i - M_i|}{\sum(X_i + M_i)}$$

Alternatively, the adjusted average (*AA*) measure can be employed, which adjusts for aggregate trade imbalances of countries and is given by:

$$AA = UA \frac{\sum(X_i + M_i)}{\sum(X_i + M_i) - |\sum X_i - \sum M_i|}$$

See OECD (1987), *Structural Adjustment and Economic Performance*, Paris, p.284. Note also that these measures are sensitive to the degree of aggregation involved.
3. See OECD (1990), "The role of indicators in structural surveillance", ESD Working Paper No. 72, Paris.
4. See OECD (1989), *Economies in Transition: Structural Adjustment in OECD Countries*, Paris.
5. See Grimswade, N. (1989), *New Patterns of Trade, Production and Investment*, Routledge.

Table 67 takes a closer look at the pattern of intra-industry trade in the G-7 group of OECD countries, by examining their bilateral transactions in differentiated products belonging to the same broad group. The table shows that in the case of the *United States*, the relatively high share of intra-industry trade in total trade is fairly evenly distributed with its different trading partners. Effects of geographical proximity seem to be important, as over 70 per cent of its total trade with *Canada* in 1990 was intra-industry trade, a slight increase from the 1970 share. With the large EC countries, over 60 per cent (50 per cent with Italy) of US bilateral trade is intra-industry, a share that has risen since 1970 in all cases. With *Japan*, the share of US intra-industry trade in 1990 was less than 50 per cent, although it showed a strong increase since 1970.

The comparatively lower overall share of intra-industry trade for *Japan* has a large variance depending on the trading partner. Thus, while in 1990 only 9 per cent of its trade with *Canada* was intra-industry (unchanged from the 1970 share), the share of intra-industry trade in the total Japanese trade with *Germany* was a high 77 per cent, a significant increase from the 1970 level. Of the other large EC countries, Japanese intra-industry trade is large with the *United Kingdom,* although the index fell in the 1980s.

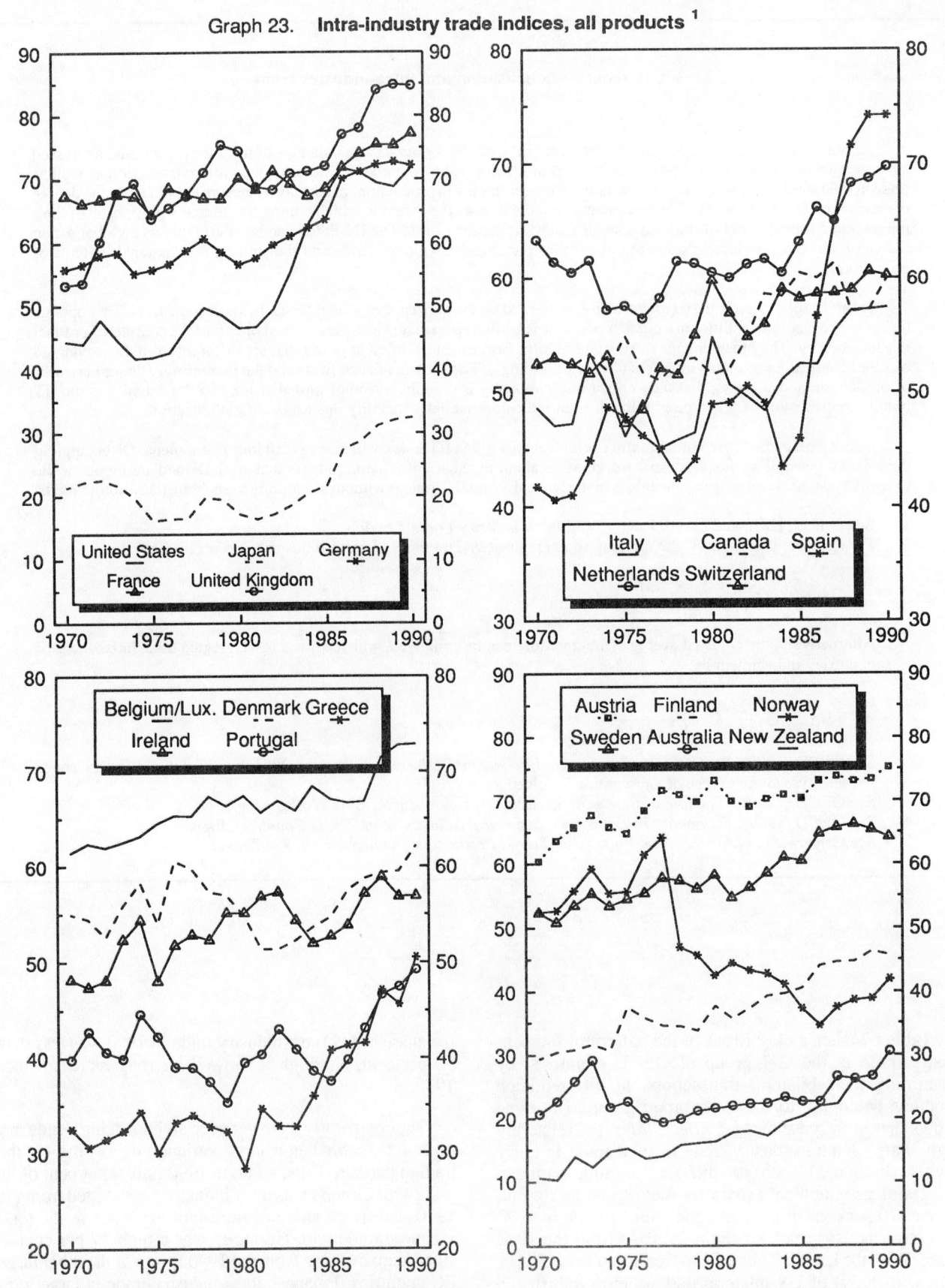

Graph 23. **Intra-industry trade indices, all products** [1]

1. Grubel-Lloyd indices calculated on SITC (Rev.2) 3-digit level; adjustment is made for aggregate trade imbalances. See box.
Source: OECD, ESDNA/NEXT database; Industry Division.

Table 67. **Bilateral intra-industry trade indices, total products**[1]
G-7 countries

		Japan	Germany	France	United Kingdom	Italy	Canada
United States	1970	32	44	52	52	34	63
	1980	31	48	59	55	42	71
	1990	48	64	69	63	56	71
Japan	1970		54	62	45	50	9
	1980		69	47	66	41	12
	1990		77	31	62	44	9
Germany	1970			72	77	55	16
	1980			83	59	54	24
	1990			88	76	66	31
France	1970				66	63	19
	1980				69	59	30
	1990				81	71	39
United Kingdom	1970					61	36
	1980					75	39
	1990					75	38
Italy	1970						14
	1980						22
	1990						24

1. Figures are calculated from SITC Rev. 2, 3-digit product categories and are adjusted for overall trade imbalances. See Box 20.
Source: OECD, ESDNA/NEXT database; Industry Division.

It is low with *France*, where in addition it has fallen from 62 per cent in 1970 (the highest of all G-7 trading partners) to 31 in 1990 (the lowest with the exception of bilateral IIT with Canada).

Germany, France and the *United Kingdom* have very similar structures of bilateral intra-industry trade with very high rates (over 90 per cent) between them and somewhat lower rates with *Italy*, due largely to their similar economic structures and their participation in the European Community. Of these four large EC countries, intra-industry trade is least important between Germany and Italy (66 per cent in 1990). Germany also has a high proportion of intra-industry trade with the *United States* (64 per cent in 1990, substantially higher than in 1970). The structure of bilateral intra-industry trade for *Canada* is similar to that of Japan, in the sense that it exhibits the same type of large variance according to trading partner (intra-industry trade is important for Canada-US trade, not important for Canada-Japan trade where it is less than 10 per cent). Canadian bilateral intra-industry trade with the large EC countries is highest with France and lowest with Italy.

Table 68 summarises intra-industry trade by product group for the G-7 countries. The table confirms that intra-industry trade is more important in manufactured products than it is for primary commodities. In particular, IIT indices tend to be highest in the chemicals, manufactured goods, machinery & transport, and miscellaneous and other manufacturing products groups in most G-7 countries. In these groups products tend to be the most differentiated, and there is also high levels of foreign direct investment in industries producing these products (see Table 64). In contrast, intra-industry trade in food, beverages and tobacco, raw materials and mineral fuels tends to be low, since the likelihood of inter-industry specialisation increases with the standardisation of the product, and these products tend to be supplied from resource-based economies in return for more highly elaborated products.

Nevertheless, despite this broad tendency for IIT trade to be highest in manufactured goods, country-specific factors remain very important in determining the weight of this type of trade. In the *United States,* for example, with the exception of the beverages & tobacco and the mineral fuels product groups, intra-industry trade accounted in 1990 for more than half of all trade in all other product groups (45 per cent in the miscellaneous manufacturing group). *Canada*, on the other hand, reflecting its natural-resource base, had in 1990 the highest proportion of intra-industry trade in the beverages & tobacco group (over 90 per cent), followed by the mineral fuels group (73 per cent).

Of all the countries in the G-7 group, *Japan* is the one with the lowest overall IIT index and the most variance in the level of intra-industry trade between product groups. It is also unique among countries in having a comparatively low level of intra-industry trade, while being a highly developed economy specialising in manufacturing products, the product group where most intra-industry trade is concentrated. This low overall IIT index is mainly due to the country's import dependence in raw materials, food and energy. Less than 10 per cent of trade in these product groups is due to intra-industry transactions. These low figures bring down the overall IIT index for all products. Nevertheless, it is also true that while IIT indices in some manufactured goods such as chemicals are nearer to those for other G-7 countries, the IIT index is very low for the machinery and transport product group, reflecting the large Japanese trade surplus in these products. A low overall IIT index and the low indices in certain manufacturing product subgroups may suggest evidence of a closed market. There exists however no direct evidence that intra-industry trade is higher in industries where trade barriers are lower, or conversely that a high IIT index is evidence of trade and non-trade barriers. Low IIT indices with a high variance between product groups may instead simply reflect a particular pattern of specialisation.

Of the four large European Community G-7 countries, *France* and *Germany* both combine high overall IIT indices with a concentration of intra-industry transactions in manufacturing products. In 1990, intra-industry transactions were less than half of total trade in only two product

Table 68. **Intra-industry trade in the G-7 countries by product group**[1]

SITC	0 Food and live animals	1 Beverages and tobacco	2 Raw materials except fuels	3 Mineral fuels	4 Oils and fats	5 Chemicals	6 Manufactured goods	7 Machinery and transport	8 Miscellaneous manufacturing	9 Other nec
United States										
1970	22	19	42	19	19	53	60	47	41	61
1980	25	26	39	6	16	64	62	57	50	63
1990	51	25	56	17	68	74	62	71	46	81
Japan										
1970	15	26	3	3	43	56	19	30	43	62
1980	12	7	4	1	55	64	24	17	47	77
1990	10	9	7	4	40	66	43	27	43	72
Germany										
1970	32	37	29	28	53	59	70	50	63	76
1980	47	52	35	23	60	69	76	55	69	76
1990	59	57	43	28	69	75	81	66	71	82
France										
1970	46	62	47	21	48	81	73	76	77	4
1980	50	35	53	23	66	73	80	76	83	27
1990	60	30	53	26	75	72	83	83	77	92
United Kingdom										
1970	19	38	22	32	17	66	62	56	77	58
1980	40	53	34	94	43	71	79	73	83	64
1990	46	70	34	84	40	76	76	83	77	77
Italy										
1970	23	47	21	6	30	78	54	71	33	79
1980	24	43	22	27	43	81	59	70	35	61
1990	36	46	25	31	62	71	64	69	40	64
Canada										
1970	30	43	25	58	42	39	35	63	46	40
1980	28	82	34	45	18	36	40	67	47	36
1990	39	91	32	73	51	55	52	68	45	89

nec: not elsewhere classified.
1. See Box 20 for methodology.
Source: OECD, ESDNA/NEXT database; Industry Division.

subgroups in each country: in raw materials and mineral fuels in Germany, and in beverages & tobacco and in mineral fuels in France. In the *United Kingdom*, which has the highest overall IIT index in the OECD area, intra-industry trade is particularly important in machinery & transport and in mineral fuels (accounting for more than 80 per cent of overall trade), and accounts for more than three-fourths of all manufactured products trade. It is least important in raw materials and oils, where however it still accounts for over one-third of total trade. Finally, intra-industry trade in *Italy* is near 70 per cent of overall trade only in the chemicals and machinery & transport subgroups; in contrast, inter-industry trade dominates largely in food, raw materials and mineral fuels.

H. International sourcing for final production

A further indicator of the growth of globalisation is the increasing international sourcing of intermediate inputs for final production (see Box 21). Although purchases from abroad need not necessarily be intra-firm, a considerable share is between firms linked through equity holdings. Detailed analysis of the patterns of sourcing (intra-firm and unrelated sourcing) from the early 1970s to the mid-1980s shows [14]:

- international linkages through sourcing of intermediates have grown in importance relative to domestic sourcing;

- motor vehicles, computers, aerospace, communications and semiconductors, textiles and petroleum refining were more internationally oriented than other industries;

- *Canada* has the highest level of foreign sourcing of intermediates amongst major OECD economies, the *United States* and *Japan* the lowest, and the importance of imported products differs widely across countries;

- the Triad of western Europe, North America and Japan are the principal partners trading in inputs, and geographical proximity continues to be important in the patterns of sourcing.

> **Box 21. International sourcing and the "nationality" of products**
>
> Many finished products are becoming multinational composites with their design, components, assembly and supporting services coming from various countries. This makes the "nationality" of products -- like that of firms -- an increasingly elusive concept in the case of numerous goods and services.
>
> The multinational composition of products can be illustrated by a US automobile, the Pontiac La Mans, which is sold a General Motors' product. Of the approximately US$10 000 received by the company from the sale of one of the automobiles:
>
> --$3 000 goes to South Korea for assembly operations and labour;
> --$1 750 to Japan for engine, transaxles and electronics components;
> --$ 750 to Germany for styling and design engineering;
> --$ 400 to Taiwan, Singapore and Japan for small components;
> --$ 250 to the United Kingdom for advertising and marketing; and
> --$ 50 to Ireland and Barbados for data processing.
>
> The remainder -- less than US$ 4 000 -- is received by General Motors for the payment of its various costs and for dividends to the company's shareholders.
>
> *Source*: Reich, R. (1991), *The Work of Nations*, Alfred A. Knopf, New York.

There are strong similarities between patterns of sourcing and foreign investment. Industries which are most penetrated (with the highest shares of manufacturing output and employment in foreign-controlled firms) are the most likely to purchase their intermediate inputs internationally. This suggests that firms which invest abroad will organise production on a global basis and purchase inputs internationally. This relation is particularly strong for *Canada, France* and the *United Kingdom* amongst the G-7 countries, all of which have relatively high levels of foreign control in industry [15].

In countries where there are lower levels of penetration (*Germany, Japan* and the *United States*), the patterns of international sourcing are not strongly related to production associated with inward investment. A few industries are also exceptions to these generalisations. Textiles and clothing have high levels of international sourcing and low levels of international investment, and non-metallic mineral products have low levels of international sourcing and high levels of investment. But overall, the higher the level of international investment, the more intensive is international sourcing.

These trends have particular implications for small and medium-sized firms. They are major suppliers to large firms, and there are increasing pressures on large firms to purchase more goods, intermediates and services from outside. This provides opportunities for small firms to form long-term sub-contracting and supply linkages with large global firms. But it also means that these linkages will be increasingly international, and will face increasing competition from international suppliers -- posing competitive challenges for small firms.

I. Competition and concentration

Global industrial structures are undergoing rapid change due to competition from new entrants and changes in the nature and pervasiveness of barriers to entry. Changes in concentration, however, do not necessarily provide evidence of changing competition and performance. Entry and exit and mobility of firms in global markets, and the impacts of international sourcing and supply arrangements are complex and cannot be analysed easily. Inter-firm agreements are also changing the parameters of competition and adding a further dynamic element. However in the absence of more detailed analysis, trends in concentration can give a crude guide to changes in competitive conditions [16].

As globalising firms begin operations in foreign markets they may have major effects on industrial structures in their host countries and globally. A foreign firm entering a new market for the first time can either increase concentration by adding one new large producer to a fragmented market, or reduce concentration in a concentrated market. The effect also depends on whether entry and subsequent expansion is through acquisition, which may increase concentration by improving performance of the acquired firm, or through green-field investment which increases total resources in an industry and may reduce concentration initially. National concentration may be unchanged through acquisition, but global concentration increased. Because foreign investment is often in newer, expanding industries, it may tend to increase concentration, but there are also numerous examples where foreign entry has decreased concentration in established, highly-concentrated industries.

For example, in Europe in the early 1980s, the level of concentration correlated with the degree of foreign participation, but this was mainly due to the larger size of foreign investments (foreign participation tends to be in more concentrated industries) and the minimum economic scale needed to justify these investments. There was no apparent causal relation between foreign investment and changes in concentration [17].

There has been renewed interest in the process of structural change and concentration. This is due to rapid changes in many product and service markets and the entry of new foreign competitors, particularly in the *United States* and Europe, and re-structuring of global markets as new competitors begin to operate in two or three parts of the Triad. At national level in the United States, following a period of declining concentration, it appears to be increasing in industries such as banking, domestic appliances, air transport, auto tyres and software. But new foreign entrants are also reducing concentration in automobiles and computers for example. In Europe, although concentration has been relatively high in individual countries, the production share of the top firms at European Community level in many industries is lower than in *Japan* and the United States. There has however been a trend towards increasing concentration in the *EC*. The sharp increase since the mid-1980s of international cross-border and extra-European investment and acquisitions has been driven by the opportunities to gain a larger share of the combined European market, and reap economies of scale and other efficiencies.

At global level there is no simple picture of the competition and consolidation processes which are taking place. In industries as diverse as automobiles, computers, pharmaceuticals and international construction, the top firms do not appear to be increasing their global market shares, but there have been many changes in the identity and nationality of the top firms. However in some narrower segments, for example in electronic components, there has been concern over the declining number of key suppliers, and the emergence of a very limited group of suppliers from only one or two countries.

Chapter II

INDUSTRY POLICY ISSUES

In many areas the thrust of globalisation is out-running the capacity of national policies and the international framework to deal with opportunities and problems that it raises. This is partly due to diverging aims and time horizons and lack of co-ordination between national policies which can positively re-shape industrial globalisation (investment, technology, labour market, regional, trade and competition policies, as well as industry policy). At national level it may be necessary to more comprehensively consider how globalisation is re-shaping industry and industrial adjustment, and take better account of the dynamic impacts of globalisation in re-orienting competitiveness policies. At international level, frictions arising from globalisation and different national policy approaches are suggesting areas where policy convergence or further international co-operation frameworks could be useful.

This chapter discusses briefly policy areas which are receiving increased attention and which in many cases are the subject of international frictions.

The international distribution of technology and R&D. R&D and technological resources are concentrated in the major Triad countries, with a large share of these resources in a limited number of large globalised firms in a few leading industries. The same firms are most often involved in inter-firm technology agreements and strategic alliances. The concentration of technological resources in a limited number of leading firms in each industry in a few regions is raising barriers to entry for many smaller firms and excluding some countries from participation in high technology activities [18].

Smaller firms and lagging countries must develop effective strategies to link with leading firms and regions. Government policies which promote rapid diffusion of new technologies can be effective in aiding modernisation and improving the technological level of firms. In some generic technologies there may also be benefits from greater international co-operation in development, coupled with effective diffusion to spread applications widely. The growing importance of foreign-controlled firms in many industries and increased international investment and strategic alliances of major national firms, gives an increasingly international dimension to all policies designed to improve national technological performance.

New patterns of ownership, production and sales. New global patterns of production and sourcing are being created as firms optimise their organisation to build operations with global economies of scale to service differentiated regional markets. With increasing globalisation of operations, economic and political forces outside of the home country become more influential. Firms may have their headquarters in a country but the majority of their operations outside of it, and need to take foreign policy changes extensively into account. On the other hand foreign-owned firms may have more operations in an industry than domestic firms, and be the major focus of domestic policy. Policy measures in third countries can have important impacts on both domestic and foreign-controlled firms and impacts on the domestic economy through shifts in the location of firm activities or changes in their emphasis. Extensive technological networking and production joint ventures can shift benefits of national R&D efforts to other countries, or vice versa. The OECD Right of Establishment and National Treatment instruments deal with some aspects of these issues to ensure that foreign and national firms are given equal treatment, but increasing globalisation is bringing more dilemmas regarding the treatment of foreign and national firms which may only be handled satisfactorily by further development of the multilateral framework.

Direct investment. Almost all governments at various levels actively pursue inward foreign investment, and it is often the target for investment subsidies and special treatment. OECD work, for example on investment incentives and disincentives, has contributed to transparency in an area where there are always threats of competition to provide increasingly expensive subsidies to inward investors. Incentives to attract physical and intangible investment by foreign investors may need better international harmonisation. The development of internationally comparable indicators of globalisation are a necessary part of work aimed at improving transparency and bringing international multilateral discipline to avoid unnecessary subsidisation.

International trade. In many globalised industries there has been increasing use of a wide range of voluntary restraints, "grey-area" non-tariff barriers and anti-dumping measures to restrict what are seen as disruptive trade flows and protect strategic industries and firms. These measures are particularly common in a few globalised R&D-intensive industries and in automobiles. They have tended to be backward looking and have often slowed adaptation and been expensive to consumers. The key policy issue is how to ensure that new kinds of trade restraints are not leading to extensive managed trade, that they are not unnecessarily distorting and that they will assist forward-looking re-structuring.

Much international trade is between affiliated firms and between firms with long-term purchase and supply arrangements. Many aspects of these new trade patterns have not been explored. Better indicators of intra-firm trade, combined with data on domestic and foreign production by national firms are needed to provide global indicators of national production and trade, global trade balances and global production balances.

Linkages and local content. Linkages between global firms and local suppliers and the diffusion of new technology and management practices into local firms are of growing importance. These linkages often grow slowly, and many governments have introduced local content requirements and support domestic firms to develop their supply capabilities and meet stringent supply requirements. However, achieving global economies of scale and efficiencies through international sourcing may be incompatible with developing high levels of local content in all countries. The complexity of global production and supply patterns and diversity of specialised components which make up many assembled products make local content requirements and related rules increasingly difficult to apply, and a source of continuing international frictions between countries, and between countries and global firms.

Location of local capabilities. High value added and advanced activities tend to form into distinct self-reinforcing local clusters of firms and institutions which attract foreign firms and develop international linkages. However there are major differences between countries and regions in the distribution of strong points of industrial specialisation. The policy issue is how to identify long-term potential strengths, build local resources and local competitiveness (through the technological infrastructure, support to firm development, encouraging technology diffusion) and link these to global networks of industrial sourcing and foreign investment. Policies for infrastructure, training and business support services need to take into account rapidly changing patterns of sourcing and production.

Competitiveness and competition. Much of industry policy is designed to improve competitiveness by encouraging the entry of new competitors (foreign firms and new firms), lowering barriers to entry (addressing market failures in the supply of capital and services) and reducing investment costs. It may also seek to promote scale economies in R&D, production or marketing by encouraging collaboration and allowing mergers. These measures attempt to improve the functioning of the supply side of industry, and to the extent that they lower barriers to entry, increase the number of competitors and generally increase competition. They will also improve consumer welfare by lowering costs and increasing choice. However, as firms operate increasingly internationally, policies to promote competitiveness must increasingly take into account potentially distorting impacts of domestic support measures (for new competitors and new production capacity for example), measures which reduce costs to firms and domestic measures that encourage greater scale, as they may reduce international competition. Purely national approaches to promoting competitiveness across firms and industries without unnecessarily distorting competition are increasingly difficult to implement, and are a further area warranting increased attention.

National, regional and global concentration may be changing due to the ongoing series of international acquisitions, mergers and investments to gain economies of scale and market access. International inter-firm agreements by large firms in R&D-intensive sectors which are not possible at national level may also be changing the nature of competition. Government promotion of co-operation in R&D and related areas is contributing to these trends. Barriers to entry are probably increasing due to the increasing scale of R&D and technological development. The structure of industry is also being changed by the development of new national and international sourcing arrangements, many of which are linking users and suppliers more tightly into long-term contacting arrangements because of quality and flexibility requirements of modern production. These areas require further analysis to explore their implications for industry policy and competition policy, and to elucidate the ways that policy is modifying these new global structures of production and sourcing.

NOTES AND REFERENCES

1. Porter, M. (1990), *The Competitive Advantage of Nations*, Macmillan, London.

2. Dunning, J.H. (1988), *Explaining International Production*, Unwin Hyman, London.

3. Knickerbocker, F. (1973), *Oligopolistic Reaction and Multinational Enterprise*, Harvard Business School.

4. Ohmae, K. (1985), *Triad Power. The Coming Shape of Global Competition*, Free Press.

5. US Department of Commerce (1981), (1985) and (1991), *US Direct Investment Abroad*, Benchmark Surveys for 1977, 1982 and 1989 (preliminary results); and Ministère de l'Industrie et de l'Aménagement du Territoire (1991), *L'implantation étrangère dans l'industrie au 1er janvier 1989*, Paris.

6. Developments drawn from a report prepared for the OECD by Jaffe, J. (1991), "Trends in world-wide inter-firm agreements", INSEAD, mimeo, 1991. For a summary of technology-based agreements see Hagedoorn, J., (1990), "Globalisation in the computer industry: Inter-firm technology co-operation", prepared for an OECD Experts' Meeting. Earlier work is summarised in Chesnais, F. (1988), "Technical co-operation agreements between firms", *STI Review No.4*, OECD, Paris.

7. For an analysis of some of the effects of formal joint ventures by the OECD, see OECD (1987), *Competition Policy and Joint Ventures*, Paris.

8. For a similar analysis of the sources of large-firm patenting in the US, see Patel, P., and Pavitt, K. (1990), "Large firms in the production of the world's technology: An important case of 'non-globalisation'", mimeo.

9. US Department of Commerce (1991), *Foreign Direct Investment in the United States*.

10. Industridepartementet (1991), *Svenskt näringsliv och näringspolitik*, Svenska Dagbladets Förlags AB.

11. Calculated from US Department of Commerce, *US Direct Investment Abroad*, 1977, 1982 and 1989; and JETRO.

12. US Department of Commerce (1991), *Foreign Direct Investment in the United States*.

13. Julius, A. (1990), *Global Companies and Public Policy: The Growing Challenge of Foreign Direct Investment*, RIIA/Pinter Publishers, London.

14. For more detail see OECD (1992), "The international sourcing of intermediate inputs: Canada, France, Germany, Japan, the United Kingdom and the United States", document.

15. Data on direct international sourcing compared with domestic sourcing (reference 14) were re-aggregated to match the data available for penetration by foreign enterprises (share of output, turnover or sales by foreign-controlled firms). These data sets on international sourcing and penetration for each country, covering all of manufacturing industry, were then ranked in descending order. Spearman rank correlation results are (countries are listed in descending order of foreign penetration of manufacturing industry shown in Table 61):
Canada (1986 data) $r=0.53$
(N=10 industries -- significant at 1 per cent level)
France (1985 data) $r=0.46$
(N=11 industries -- significant at 2.5 per cent level)
United Kingdom (1984/87 data) $r=0.52$
(N=10 industries -- significant at 1 per cent level)
Germany (1985 data) $r=0.12$
(N=11 industries -- not significant)
Japan (1985/87 data) $r=0.10$
(N=9 industries -- not significant)
United States (1986 data) $r=-0.07$
(N=12 industries -- not significant)

16. One finding of the work carried out for the OECD Technology/Economy Programme was that special attention from government should be given to the phenomenon of "concentration as a world process and whether a global competition policy is needed and how it might be implemented". See OECD (1992), *Technology and the Economy: The Key Relationships*, Paris, Chapter 10, p. 209. See also CEC, *Report on Competition Policy*, Brussels/Luxembourg, various issues; and OECD (1991), "Development of new indicators of competitiveness", Note by Canada to the OECD Working Party No.9 of the Industry Committee.

17. Fishwick, F. (1982), *Multinational Companies and Economic Concentration in Europe*, Gower, Aldershot.

18. O'Doherty, D. (ed.), (1990), *The Cooperation Phenomenon. Prospects for Small Firms and the Small Economies*, Graham & Trotman, London.

Part 6

**TRENDS IN INDUSTRY AND POLICY MEASURES
IN NON-MEMBER COUNTRIES**

Chapter I

RECENT TRENDS AND POLICY MEASURES IN THE NEWLY INDUSTRIALISED ECONOMIES OF ASIA

A. Recent trends in manufacturing industry

The macroeconomic context

In 1991 the Newly Industrialised Economies of Asia (Asian NIEs) performed well despite the poor state of the world economy and the persisting slowdown of the growth of international trade in goods and services (which increased by 3 per cent compared with 5 per cent in 1990). East Asia is the region of the world in which trade is increasing the most rapidly: Hong Kong ranks tenth in world trade, followed by Taiwan (in twelfth place), Korea (in fourteenth place) and Singapore (in seventeenth place).

Prices rose rapidly in Hong Kong (by 11.6 per cent) and in Korea (by 9.5 per cent) but moderately in Taiwan (3.6 per cent) and Singapore (2.6 per cent); the currencies of the latter two countries appreciated (see Table 69).

Table 69. **GNP growth rate and consumer price inflation in Asian NIEs**

Percentage change from preceding year

	Real GNP			Consumer price index		
	1989	1990	1991	1989	1990	1991
Korea	6.1	9.3	8.4	5.7	8.6	9.7
Taiwan	7.6	5.0	7.3	4.4	4.1	3.6
Hong Kong	2.3	2.8	3.9	10.1	9.8	12.0
Singapore	9.2	8.3	6.7	2.4	3.4	2.5

Source: OECD, *Economic Outlook No. 51*; National Sources: Bank of Korea, Council for Planning and Economic Development (Taiwan), Economic Development Board (Singapore); Hong Kong.

Macroeconomic policies were sometimes slow to tackle the causes of inflation: the bottlenecks resulting from several years of rapid growth, rapid wage increases, the emergence of current account surpluses, and soaring property prices. By and large, manufacturing prices rose less than the prices of services.

In *Korea*, economic growth slowed only very slightly in 1991 (8.4 per cent compared with 9 per cent in 1990); the main components of growth were investment (up by 12.8 per cent, though down on the 18.4 per cent growth rate in 1990), consumption and exports (9.4 per cent). Financial services (up by 13 per cent) and construction (up by 12.8 per cent) were the most dynamic sectors, whereas manufacturing growth slowed to 7 per cent. The pick-up in export growth (9.6 per cent in 1991, as against 4.6 per cent in 1990) was less than that in import growth (17.4 per cent), where purchases of equipment (up by 18.9 per cent) and petroleum products showed the largest increases. The worsening of the trade balance and the balance on services, which was partly due to the increase in the number of Korean tourists travelling abroad, contributed to the quadrupling of the current account deficit from US$2.2 billion in 1990 to US$8.8 billion in 1991, the equivalent of 3.2 per cent of GNP (Table 70).

The Seventh Korean Plan (1992-96) that was published in 1991 is based on the assumption that world output will grow by 3.2 per cent and international trade by 4.9 per cent, and that Korean GNP growth will average 7.5 per cent. On these projections, Korea's GNP per capita could be US$ 11 000 in 1996, which would represent an annual increase of 11.5 per cent (in current US dollars). Manufacturing is projected to be the most dynamic sector of the Korean economy, with average annual growth of 9.8 per cent between 1992 and 1996. The plan provides for a gradual reduction in the current account deficit and the emergence of a surplus equivalent to 2.5 per cent of GNP at the end of the period.

Hong Kong's improved growth in 1991 (3.9 per cent compared with 2.4 per cent the previous year) was due to a surge in re-exports (up by 26 per cent) and of investment (up by 10.2 per cent); in contrast, domestic exports were flat (up by 0.4 per cent). The manufacturing sector, which has declined in importance as production facilities have been relocated to China, recorded only slight growth, and the growth of the construction sector slowed as several projects were completed; on the other hand, tourism, which had been hit by the Gulf War, strengthened during the second half of the year. Prices increased by 11.6 per cent but the index of export prices rose by only 3 per cent, a

Table 70. **Trade and current balances in Asian NIEs**
Billion US dollars

		Korea	Taiwan	Hong Kong	Singapore
Exports	1986	33.9	39.5	35.4	22.4
	1987	47.3	53.2	48.4	28.6
	1988	60.7	60.4	63.2	39.3
	1989	61.2	66.4	73.2	44.7
	1990	63.2	67.2	82.1	52.7
	1991	69.5	76.2	98.0	59.2
Imports	1986	29.7	22.6	35.3	23.6
	1987	41.0	32.6	48.4	32.5
	1988	51.8	46.5	64.2	43.8
	1989	56.7	50.1	72.5	49.7
	1990	65.1	54.7	82.4	60.9
	1991	76.5	62.9	98.8	66.3
Trade balance	1986	4.2	16.9	0.1	-3.0
	1987	6.3	20.6	0.0	-3.9
	1988	8.9	13.9	-0.8	-4.5
	1989	4.5	16.3	1.0	-5.2
	1990	-1.9	12.5	-0.3	-8.2
	1991	-7.0	13.3	-0.8	-7.1
Current balance	1986	4.6	16.2	..	0.0
	1987	9.7	17.9	2.9	0.5
	1988	14.2	10.1	2.8	1.3
	1989	5.1	12.0	5.1	2.5
	1990	-2.2	10.8	3.5	2.1
	1991	-8.8	12.0	2.5	4.2

Sources: For Korea, Hong Kong and Singapore, Direction of Trade, IMF and national sources for the current balance; Hong Kong does not publish balance of payments statistics; for Taiwan, *Council for Planning and Economic Development.*

difference which helps to explain the intensity of sub-contracting between Hong Kong and the regions of southern China. Because the Hong Kong dollar is pegged at a fixed rate to the US dollar, the monetary authorities cannot use interest rates to fight inflation. Among the instruments used to curb inflationary pressures were the decision to raise the quotas for foreign workers (see below), and higher property taxes. The colony's trade deficit widened due to the fact that imports of goods rose more rapidly (up by 19 per cent in real terms) than exports (domestic exports and re-exports up by 16.6 per cent). However, the surplus on invisibles still allowed the colony to show a current account surplus estimated at HK$19.4 billion (US$2.7 billion).

In *Singapore,* growth slowed gradually in 1991 to 6.5 per cent compared with 8.3 per cent in 1990. Investment and exports were the engines of growth; the buoyancy of exports, which was quite remarkable given the international context, was partly due to the sound state of the economies belonging to the Association of South East Asia Nations (ASEAN), to which 29 per cent of exports were directed. The construction sector was the most dynamic (up by 21 per cent in 1991 compared with 7.2 per cent the previous year) on account of the large increase in the number of infrastructure projects; in contrast, the growth of the financial sector slowed (5.4 per cent compared with 12.7 per cent in 1990), as did also that of the manufacturing sector (5.3 per cent compared with 9.5 per cent the previous year). The trade deficit fell, and the improvement in the invisibles balance helped to increase the current account balance (from US$2.1 billion to US$4.2 billion in 1991). Accumulated reserves stood officially at US$32.9 billion, which meant that Singapore had the highest reserves per head in the world.

In 1991 the Economic Development Board (EDB) published the Strategic Economic Plan which was drawn up in close co-operation with the private sector. This plan sets out various development scenarios and very long-term growth objectives. Under the plan, Singapore will have joined the ranks of the industrialised countries by 2020; by 2020 its income per capita will be equal to that of the Netherlands, and in the optimistic scenario, will have caught up with that of the United States by 2030. To attain these objectives, and to overcome two of the major constraints on the country's development -- the smallness of its territory and the size of its population --, the plan aims to promote the expansion of a "growth triangle" consisting of the Singapore, Johore (Malaysia) and the Riau archipelago (Indonesia) in which Singapore firms could locate their activities and integrate more closely with the ASEAN. The plan also calls for a major restructuring of service activities, which have not received as much foreign investment as industry and whose productivity is still low.

In *Taiwan*, growth improved sharply to 7.2 per cent in 1991 compared with 5.1 per cent in 1990. The growth of exports, and especially exports to China, and the increase in major infrastructure projects (with public investment rising by 24 per cent) and the pick-up in private investment (up by 4 per cent after an 8 per cent decline in 1990) contributed to this recovery. The trade surplus and the current account surplus widened and contributed to the appreciation of the currency. With reserves estimated at US$82.4 billion in December 1991 (according to the Central Bank of China), Taiwan has the largest reserves in the world, ahead of Japan. This financial strength made it possible to announce an extremely ambitious programme (US$300 billion) of spending on infrastructure.

Published in 1991, the Sixth Development Plan (1991-96) envisages average annual growth of 7 per cent, which would bring Taiwan's GNP per capita up from US$7 990 in 1990 up to US$13 975 by 1996. Over the period, investment would grow by an average of 12.5 per cent. Import growth would outstrip export growth, thereby making it possible to reduce the trade balance (from US$11 billion in 1991 to US$4 billion in 1996).

Two major decisions were taken in 1991 that are likely to transform the economic situation of the Asian NIEs in coming years:

- In July 1991, China withdrew its objections to the construction of a new airport in Hong Kong and, in agreement with the United Kingdom, requested the Hong Kong Government to start work on the project. This major project (costing US$10 billion) is being undertaken with an eye to the colony's future after 1997 (when Britain's lease runs out), and reflects the growing links between "the Three Chinas", i.e. Hong Kong, Taiwan and the People's Republic of China, the latter two countries having been admitted to APEC (Asia Pacific Economic Co-operation).

- In September 1991, the two Koreas were admitted simultaneously to the United Nations, and in December of that year they signed a reconciliation agreement. The thaw in relations between the two countries could have major repercussions in the region. The United Nations Development Programme (UNDP) is already studying the feasibility of a development project in the Tumen delta, which could allow the natural resources of North-East Asia to be tapped. In addition to the two Koreas, China, Mongolia, Japan and Russia would be involved in the project.

These developments, which have opened up "new frontiers" for the Asian NIEs, should help to sustain their growth in coming years while reinforcing their economic integration into Pacific Asia.

Industrial trends

Despite its progression in Hong Kong and Taiwan, industrial growth in the Asian NIEs was lower than in previous years. For some years, labour-intensive activities (textiles, clothing and footwear) have been badly hit by wage increases and firms are finding it difficult to recruit workers. The trend of unit labour costs varies quite markedly from one country to another. They are estimated to gave risen rapidly in Korea, where the average wage increase in manufacturing, measured in US$, was 24 per cent (higher than productivity gains), and also in Singapore (17 per cent); in contrast, unit costs probably fell slightly for the first time in Taiwan despite a wage increase of 18 per cent (measured in US$).

In *Korea*, manufacturing growth, as measured by changes in the index of production, slowed in 1991 (6 per cent compared with 9 per cent the previous year -- see Table 71). The intermediate goods sector recorded remarkable growth (24 per cent for refining, 13 per cent for the iron and steel industry); in contrast, the transport equipment, mechanical engineering and electronics industries grew less rapidly than in 1990, and the growth of the textiles and clothing industries continued to slow, declining by 3 per cent and 6 per cent respectively.

In *Hong Kong*, the industrial production index rose by 2 per cent, after a 1 per cent decline in 1990. The main constraint is the slowdown of the supply of labour, and industrialists are tending increasingly to sub-contract part of their production to China. In 1991 the textile, clothing and electronic industries grew slightly, in contrast with the decline in 1990; the growth of the mechanical engineering industry was more marked.

Table 71. **Production indices in Asian NIEs**

	1986	1987	1988	1989	1990	1991
Total manufacturing						
Korea	122	146	166	171	186	199
Hong Kong	100	116	123	124	123	113
Singapore	65	77	91	100	110	116
Taïwan	100	111	115	119	117	124
Food						
Korea	109	120	133	142	150	160
Hong Kong	100	108	122	127	142	144
Singapore	88	89	97	100	98	102
Taïwan	100	104	106	103	109	110
Textile						
Korea	120	134	138	134	133	129
Hong Kong	100	114	111	117	115	101
Singapore	78	89	96	100	94	100
Taïwan	100	105	94	97	92	97
Clothing						
Korea	115	140	138	131	126	119
Hong Kong	100	113	112	113	111	101
Singapore	78	92	98	100	93	92
Taïwan	100	103	86	84	76	75
Paper						
Korea	147	166	177	188	195	..
Hong Kong	100	126	153	167	182	181
Singapore	67	89	98	100	106	109
Taïwan	100	106	110	121	126	132
Petroleum refining						
Korea	106	125	145	155	197	..
Singapore	90	84	88	100	113	117
Taïwan	100	119	129	139	125	126
Iron and steel						
Korea	122	131	146	164	186	..
Singapore	88	92	97	100	108	102
Taïwan	100	107	120	127	140	140
Mechanical						
Korea	138	181	203	226	259	280
Hong Kong	100	132	159	161	162	167
Singapore	60	70	85	100	108	120
Taïwan	100	118	134	135	139	146
Electronics						
Korea	153	216	272	271	290	319
Hong Kong*	100	136	136	131	133	128
Singapore	54	71	91	100	113	114
Taïwan	100	123	136	143	141	153
Transport equipment						
Korea	123	161	200	211	260	284
Singapore	63	68	82	100	111	116
Taïwan	100	123	125	144	144	160

* Consumer electronics.
Sources: Korea: Industrial production indices unadjusted for seasonnal variation in *Monthly Statistics*, December (10 months 1991 – 1985 = 100). Taïwan: *Industry Free China* (1991 = 11 months). Hong Kong: *Monthly Digest of Statistics* (October 1991); the evolution is measured by the first six months report of 1990. Singapore: *Economic Survey*, 1991, Economic Development Board.

In *Singapore*, manufacturing growth, which had slowed in 1990, fell sharply in 1991 (5.3 per cent compared with 9.5 per cent in 1990). The most marked slowdown was in iron and steel output -- due to the slowdown of private construction -- and in the electronics industry -- due to the difficulties encountered by disk drive manufacturers. Singapore was particularly hit by the slowdown of personal computer sales in the United States. More traditional industries such as textiles and ship-building repairs performed better.

In *Taiwan*, industrial growth picked up again in 1991: the manufacturing output index rose by 6 per cent after its 2 per cent decrease in 1990. The improvement was above average in the electronics industry (8 per cent), the transport equipment sector (which benefited from a surge in the domestic market), and the textile industry, which is expanding its exports to China. In contrast, growth slowed in the intermediate goods industries (iron and steel, and refining).

Trade in manufactured goods

With the exception of Singapore, the exports of the Asian NIEs consist essentially of manufactured goods, while the bulk of their purchases of industrial products consists of capital goods and semi-finished products.

Trade with the United States. The bilateral surpluses of *Korea* and *Singapore* with the United States have narrowed or disappeared: according to Korean statistics, Korea's surplus has given way to a deficit, due to the slowdown of exports and a fairly steep increase in imports resulting from the liberalisation of its customs regime (see Table 72). The rise in *Hong Kong*'s surplus stemmed from the surge in re-exports, since domestic exports to the United States fell by 9.2 per cent. *Taiwan*'s surplus with the United States increased slightly. However, it should be noted that the increase in China's bilateral surplus with the United States can be partly explained by the fact that Taiwan has shifted a considerable proportion of its production to China (see below) and that Hong Kong firms sub-contract work to China.

Singapore signed a bilateral trade and investment agreement with the United States in January 1992. In *Taiwan* the machine tool manufacturers association rejected a US proposal to extend for a further two years the voluntary export restraint agreement. Bilateral negotiations are under way between China and the United States with a view to ensuring that property rights over the computer software and hardware exported from Taiwan are respected.

Trade with Europe. The Asian NIEs' exports to Europe rose quite rapidly in 1991. The European Com-

Table 72. **Trade balances of Asian NIEs**
Billion US dollars

		Korea	Taiwan	Hong Kong	Singapore
With the United States					
Exports	1988	21.4	23.4	15.6	9.4
	1989	20.9	24.0	18.5	10.1
	1990	19.3	21.5	19.8	11.2
	1991	18.5	26.8	22.3	11.6
Imports	1988	12.7	13.0	5.3	6.9
	1989	15.8	12.0	5.9	8.3
	1990	16.9	12.2	6.6	9.8
	1991	19.1	14.2	7.3	10.4
Balance	1988	8.7	10.4	10.3	2.6
	1989	5.1	12.0	12.6	1.8
	1990	2.4	11.2	13.2	1.4
	1991	−0.6	12.6	15.3	1.2
With Japan					
Exports	1988	12.0	8.8	3.9	3.4
	1989	13.4	9.1	4.5	3.8
	1990	12.6	9.1	4.7	4.6
	1991	12.8	9.3	5.3	5.2
Imports	1988	15.9	14.8	11.9	9.7
	1989	17.4	16.0	11.9	10.3
	1990	18.5	15.3	13.2	12.2
	1991	21.5	19.1	16.3	14.1
Trade balance	1988	−3.9	−6.0	−8.0	−6.3
	1989	−4.0	−7.0	−7.4	−6.5
	1990	−5.9	−6.2	−8.5	−7.6
	1991	−8.7	−9.8	−11.0	−8.9
With the European Community					
Exports	1988	8.1	9.8	9.9	6.1
	1989	7.4	11.0	11.1	6.9
	1990	8.8	10.2	13.9	9.2
	1991	9.8	12.1	16.1	10.0
Imports	1988	6.1	6.0	6.6	6.5
	1989	6.6	5.9	7.1	7.5
	1990	8.4	7.1	8.1	9.7
	1991	9.8	7.5	9.8	9.9
Trade balance	1988	1.9	1.6	3.3	−0.4
	1989	0.8	2.3	4.0	−0.6
	1990	0.4	3.1	5.89	−0.5
	1991	0.0	4.6	6.3	0.1

Source: Direction of Trade, IMF; national sources for 1991 and Taïwan.

munity denounced *Korea*'s very high customs tariff on whisky imports, the purpose of which is to protect local producers of alcoholic beverages, and anti-dumping measures could be taken against imports of weighing scales from *Singapore* and Korea. The European Community and Korea reached an agreement in their dispute over the protection of property rights. Korea agreed to grant the same protection to European pharmaceuticals and agrochemicals that it gives to US products, while the European Community is to restore the benefit of the Generalised System of Preferences (GSP) to Korean exports, which it had suspended from 1987.

Trade with Japan. The Asian NIEs' trade deficit with Japan worsened in 1991. Their investment in automation resulted in a steep increase in purchases of Japanese capital goods, while their exports to Japan grew more slowly. In *Korea*, the worsening deficit prompted the government to publish a plan to promote local sourcing of 4 000 mechanical and electronic components. The government is to give firms financial incentives to buy from local suppliers. Bilateral discussions are under way to reduce the deficit.

Trade with other Asian economies. The trade of Asian NIEs with other Asian economies, especially China and the ASEAN countries, has intensified during the past three years, partly as a result of the NIEs' direct investment in the region.

Korea has established consular relations with China, and contacts between the two countries have been facilitated by the introduction of ferry services between them. Trade between the two countries amounted to US$4 billion in 1991, and an increasing number of Korean firms are investing in China. Trade with the People's Democratic Republic of Korea, non-existent 3 years earlier, amounted to US$200 million in 1991; the Korean authorities have estimated the potential trade between the two countries at US$9 billion.

In recent years relations between *Taiwan* and China have evolved from confrontation to co-operation, and their bilateral trade increased steeply to US$5.8 billion in 1991 (up by 43 per cent on 1990). After several months' deliberation, the Taiwanese government authorised indirect imports of semi-finished products from China, while stressing that they would be allowed in only provided that they did not harm local manufacturers; the aim in allowing them in is to help make Taiwanese exports more competitive. Finally, in January 1992, *Singapore* signed a treaty which provided for the creation of a free-trade area between the ASEAN countries.

B. Recent industrial policy measures

Measures to promote industrial investment

Increasing investment together with export growth have been the main engines of the Asian NIEs' growth. Most of the measures to promote industrial investment aim to encourage firms to move into high-technology sectors. In *Korea*, the government has asked banks to raise the proportion of loans for industrial investment in total loans outstanding from 50 to 55 per cent. In *Singapore*, the government has announced that taxes will continue to be reduced, and has lowered the tax on corporate profits by one percentage point to 30 per cent.

Measures to promote R&D, innovation and technology diffusion in industry

The Asian NIEs increasingly see the promotion of R&D as being essential to maintaining their competitiveness in international markets, all the more in that their spending on royalties has risen rapidly in recent years: in the case of Korea, they increased ten-fold between 1982 and 1991, from US$116 million to 1 184 million, while over the same period imports of capital goods tripled.

In *Korea*, the state's participation in the long-term plan for the development of science and technology has been scaled down, but the objective of devoting the equivalent of 5 per cent of GNP to R&D remains unchanged (Table 73). Under this plan, several major projects are to be implemented, in particular the development of a 256 Megabyte DRAM and a 1 000 Megabyte DRAM, high-definition television and ISDN networks; four scientific, technological and industrial estates will be built in Pusan, Taegu, Chonju and Kangnung, which will be able to accommodate between 200 and 300 firms specialised in software engineering and design. The government plans to invest US$13 billion in R&D by 2001, and has announced that state enterprises will launch co-operation programmes with other countries in the areas of very high-density components, new materials, pharmaceuticals and chemicals.

Table 73. **Science and technology investment plans in Korea**

	1992	1996	2001
Investment (billion wons)	5 539	9 570	28 755
Percentage of GNP	2.6	3.5	5.0
Public sector (percentage)	28	32	35
Private sector (percentage)	72	68	65
Employment in R&D (thousands)	66	112	..

Source: Ministry of Science and Technology, Korea.

In *Hong Kong*, the government has founded a science and technology university, and has announced a plan to set up an industrial and technological development institute.

In *Singapore*, the continuation of a high rate of growth necessitates, given the specific constraints on the city state, a constant inflow of foreign investment and also an increase in R&D. R&D spending, which currently represents only 1 per cent of GDP, is set to rise to 2 per cent of GDP in 1995. Between now and then the government plans to set up a fund of US$1.2 billion that will be used to provide tax and financial incentives to promote industrial research by firms. The number of R&D personnel is set to rise from 7 000 at present to 10 000 in 1995. A new body, the National Science and Technology Board, has taken steps to promote R&D activities, among which the introduction of grants for higher education and research, the setting-up of a Research and Development Assistance Scheme with a budget of S$80 million over a five-year period, to be disbursed in the form of loans and subsidies; a two-year tax deferral has been introduced for firms eligible for "pioneer" status that engage in R&D. The state has also announced the creation of a fourth national polytechnic.

In *Taiwan*, R&D spending represents the equivalent of 1.6 per cent of GNP (1991), and it is planned to raise it to 2.5 per cent in 1996. The R&D programmes implemented by the state since the 1970s have aimed to stimulate the creation of industries considered to be of strategic importance. The research undertaken by the Industrial Technology Research Institute (ITRI) has compensated for the lack of R&D by the private sector. In recent years the state has chosen to co-operate more closely with private firms on long-term research programmes such as that for the development of submicronic technology, launched in 1988. In the next five years the National Science Council plans to allocate NT$300 billion (US$11 billion) in aid to the private sector to develop ten industries and eight technologies that are considered to be priority areas. Half of this amount will be invested in basic research, the rest in industrial applications. Any team that brings together a local research centre and a firm will be eligible to apply for funding.

In this context, the Council for Economic Planning and Development (CEPD) has called upon the private sector to participate in fifty-six R&D projects and in the development of twenty-seven products; the government could finance up to half of the cost of the projects that are selected, the remainder being funded in the form of loans. Projects will have to be in one of the ten industries that the CEPD considers to be "emerging": communications, information technology, consumer electronics, precision and automation equipment, new materials, specialty chemicals and pharmaceuticals, aerospace, health care and pollution control equipment. US$503 million will be made available to promote the development of the semiconductor industry (integrated circuits, LCDs and dynamic memories). The Ministry of Economic Affairs (MOEA) plans to build three general R&D centres, one in the north, one in the centre and one in the south of the country, to provide a better environment for industry. It has also announced the construction of a central laboratory for textiles, and another for biotechnologies.

Labour-related measures

The shortage of labour, which until recently affected only *Singapore* and *Hong Kong*, is now a constraint on the industrial development of the Asian NIEs as a whole. The situation will get worse because the growth of the labour force will slow and because there is hardly any unemployment. These pressures on the labour market have prompted a debate on whether the immigration of foreign labour should be encouraged or not. *Korea,* which was a net exporter of labour during the 1970s, became a net importer in 1991; in both Singapore and Hong Kong, where the shortage of labour is the most acute, immigration has become one of the variables of industrial adjustment.

The pressures on the labour market are reflected in wage levels, which are continuing to rise rapidly (between 10 and 15 per cent in 1991). Minimum wages, which are well below average wages, are US$410 in Taiwan and US$275 in Korea; Singapore has the highest hourly wage in the region (US$3.09), compared with US$2.85 in Hong Kong.

In *Korea*, a survey by the Ministry of Labour of industrial enterprises estimated that there was a shortage of 220 000 workers (or 9 per cent) and that 250 000 managerial and administrative jobs had not been filled. This shortage results in illegal immigration from south-east Asia and China (with an estimated 50 000 illegal immigrant workers). The government has announced that a package of 7 400 billion won would be set aside to help firms to finance automation (compared with 4 900 billion won in 1991). The Ministry of Labour has announced that the 44-working week decided in 1990 would be extended from 1992 to firms with less than 300 employees. It has launched the first plan for industrial safety, since the accident rate in industry is very high -- 2 336 fatal accidents in 1990, a rate of 1.6 per cent. The goal is to bring it down to 1 per cent by 1996.

In *Hong Kong*, the growth of the labour force is slowing while emigration is rising (43 000 people have left the colony each year compared with 21 000 between 1981 and 1985); the number of immigrants represents only 30 per cent of the number of emigrants. Employment in manufacturing has fallen but labour productivity has risen fairly rapidly. In 1991, when the rate of underemployment was 1.8 per cent during the last quarter, the government decided to raise the quota of foreign workers from 13 800 in 1991 to 25 000 in 1992.

In *Singapore*, despite the labour shortage (in some sectors the average monthly labour turnover is 5 per cent), the government has decided to tighten the rules on the employment of unskilled foreign workers and to ease those on the temporary immigration of skilled workers. A foreign labour quota has been set for the shipbuilding and repairs industry, which employs just over a quarter of all foreign workers (80 000 out of 300 000). The percentage of foreign workers could rise to 67 per cent from July 1992 (compared with an informal ceiling of 50 per cent), though this figure will include workers employed by sub-contracting firms. The construction industry (which employs 120 000 foreign workers) will be authorised to employ three foreign workers for every Singaporean worker (instead of two as at present). The tax on the employment of foreign workers will be raised to S$400 (US$247) for unskilled workers and to S$250 for skilled workers (respectively S$250 and S$350 in the shipbuilding industry). The government has also announced a slight change in the breakdown of the contributions to the Central Provident Fund; the employer's contribution has been raised by one point (from 16.5 to 17.5) and the employee's contribution has been cut by half a point (from 23 per cent to 22.5 per cent). Ultimately, the aim is a contribution equivalent to 40 per cent of wages, split equally between employers and employees. A supplementary health insurance programme (MEDI-FUND, complementing MEDISAVE -- the hospital insurance scheme) will provide social cover to the whole population.

In *Taiwan*, where the rate of underemployment is under 2 per cent, the government is encouraging automation in industry. The Industrial Development Bureau (IDB) and the Government Development Fund have set aside resources (NT$13 billion) to provide subsidised loans to firms that want to bring in automation.

Measures directed at industrial sectors

In *Korea*, the programme for the promotion of the development of high-definition television has been scaled down from 15 billion to 9.8 billion won for 1992. The Ministry of Industry is to encourage semiconductor manufacturers to regroup in two industrial areas to the south of Seoul, and an association of manufacturers and research centres is to be set up. Incentives are to be introduced to help firms to raise the rate of integration of the shipbuilding industry from an average of 75 per cent to 80-90 per cent.

In *Singapore,* the petrochemicals industry, which accounts for 4 per cent of GDP, is considered to be a priority sector. In the medium term, it is planned to double or even triple investment in the industry, and the government is envisaging the construction of a petrochemical complex on a site of 2 000 to 3 000 hectares, which will require massive investment to upgrade infrastructure. Since independence, ship-building has been one of Singapore's basic industries. To strengthen the industry's position, the EDB has identified several strategic areas on which it believes industry should focus such as switching to those markets in which Korean and Japanese competition is not as strong (ship redesign, construction of oil platforms and medium-sized specialised vessels).

Singapore's Economic Strategic Plan lists fourteen key sectors for the economy: international trade, transport, precision engineering, information technology, petroleum and petrochemicals, construction, heavy engineering, finance and tourism. The aim is not so much to target these sectors, since they account for 72 per cent of Singapore's GNP, but rather to identify their different requirements; they are all sectors that are set to become areas of excellence in the future.

In *Taiwan*, the Industrial Development Bureau has published a development plan for the textile industry, according to whose projection it could account for 15 per cent of exports by 2000. Among the major constraints on the development of the sector are: relatively high wage levels, the appreciation of the Taiwanese currency, the lack of internationally recognised brands, the process of relocation of the industry to low-wage countries, and the fact that exports of clothing are too heavily geared to the US market, while those of textile fibres are too heavily concentrated on the Chinese market.

The Ministry of Economic Affairs (MOEA) is drawing up a new sectoral plan for the automobile industry. In previous years, the customs tariff on automobile imports was cut from 65 to 30 per cent; in the next few years, it will continue to fall though there will continue to be a difference of 10 percentage points between the tariff on imports of assembled vehicles and that on imports of sub-assemblies. Authorisations for imports of assembled vehicles (with the exception of those from Japan, which are banned) will be considered on a case-by-case basis, and the government will continue to promote the expansion of domestic production while requiring a rate of local integration of 50 per cent.

Measures to support small and medium-sized enterprises

In *Korea*, despite the measures that were taken to support them in the past, many SMEs are having difficulty adapting to the new constraints resulting from the rapid rise in wages. In response, the government has prepared a plan whereby over a period of ten years, 200 firms will be selected annually for intensive assistance in technology. In the next five years, thirty industrial zones will be purpose-built for SMEs. To make it easier for them to borrow, the government has authorised small firms to use property belonging to third parties as security.

In *Singapore*, SMEs do not play a very prominent role in industry; however, between 1985 and 1990, their average productivity rose twice as fast as that of industry as a whole (respectively 11 and 5 per cent). The Economic Development Board has announced a remodelling of the system of aid to investment. The Small Industry Finance Scheme has been replaced by the Local Enterprise Finance Scheme, which no longer covers only SMEs (defined as firms with assets of under S$8 million), but also firms that are considered to be local (i.e. in which the foreign stake is under 30 per cent) and with assets of up to S$12 million. The loans that will be offered by the Local Enterprise Finance Scheme (totalling S$353 million) should make it possible for firms to install automated systems (CAD, numerically-controlled tools). Another programme, Local

Industrial Upgrading, which is managed by the Economic Development Board, is designed to strengthen the sub-contracting ties between local firms and the twenty-five multinational firms that have accepted to take part in the programme.

Regulatory reform and competition policy

In *Korea*, the rate of economic concentration is particularly high. A study by the Fair Trade Commission estimated that the number of conglomerates rose from thirty-two with 509 subsidiaries in 1987, to sixty-one with 915 subsidiaries in 1991. Steps are to be taken to encourage large enterprises to introduce their subsidiaries onto the stock exchange. Only 64 of the 198 subsidiaries of the five largest groups are listed. The regulations on cross-shareholdings between subsidiaries are to be strengthened and measures are to be taken to stop the practice whereby firms within the same group provide loan guarantees to one another.

With a view to curbing the diversification of the *jaebuls* (major groups), which it considers to be excessive, the government has asked them to concentrate on three activities. To encourage them to do so, it has decided to abolish the credit ceiling imposed on major enterprises, for projects that come under the three activities. In addition, following the lifting of the ban on investments in petrochemicals in 1988, and faced with a crisis of overcapacity in this sector, the government has decided to ban the construction of new steam-cracking and caprolactam units between now and 1995.

With respect to privatisation, the state enterprise privatisation programme in Korea was launched in 1987. It concerned the national steel industry (POHANG STEEL CO) and the electricity generation industry (KEPCO). Suspended because of the sluggish state of the stockmarket, it has been relaunched with the announcement by the government of the sale of state holdings in KEPCO, KOREA TELECOM, the Citizen National Bank, the Industrial Bank of Korea and the Korea Exchange Bank.

Singapore has announced that the Public Utilities Board (water and electricity) and Telecoms will be privatised. It has partially privatised Singapore Electronics and Engineering Limited (a subsidiary of Singapore Technologies). The state remains the majority shareholder, the share of the capital that can be held by foreign investors being set at 15 per cent (but no individual foreign investor can acquire more than 5 per cent). At the same time, the Economic Development Board has joined forces with several large foreign enterprises to set up a firm that will invest in the construction of a silicon foundry that will be operational in 1993. The state's participation in this project is dictated more by commercial reasons than by the desire to promote industrial integration.

In *Taiwan*, the government has passed a "Fair Trade" Act to combat monopolistic practices and unfair competition. Under the Act, prior authorisation will be required for a merger when the enterprise resulting from it will have a market share of more than a third, or when one of the partners to the merger will have a market share of over a quarter. The state enterprises concerned by the Act -- in the construction, iron and steel and electricity generation sectors -- have been given five years to comply with its provisions, following which they will have to compete with private firms.

In addition, the government has announced that the privatisation programme begun in the mid-1980s will be resumed. Six state enterprises will be privatised in 1992, and twenty-two in the medium term. It has been estimated that the state will collect $24 billion from the privatisations.

Measures related to international trade and investments

In *Korea*, the government has announced the liberalisation of the import regime for 43 products which up to now were subject to quotas. Further to this liberalisation, which takes effect in 1992, the number of products still subject to quotas will be 240 (out of 10 274 customs positions), of which 10 manufactured products.

The government has liberalised investment by abolishing the bans that existed in various sectors, including that on investment in the power generation sector. Foreign stakes in the capital of Korean firms that are quoted on the stock exchange are to be limited to 10 per cent of the total share issue, and no individual foreign investor will be allowed to acquire more than 5 per cent of the capital, and not more than 3 per cent in certain sectors considered to have a strategic importance (transport and utilities). In addition, the conditions governing foreign investment by Korean footwear firms have been liberalised. Hitherto, only five firms had been authorised to move their production offshore per country. To encourage investment in Vietnam and China, the government is participating in the setting-up of free zones in these countries, which will be reserved to Korean firms.

Hong Kong has announced that it is adopting the Harmonized System for exports and imports as from 1 January 1992. This should facilitate both the description and classification of goods, and the analysis of statistical data.

In *Singapore*, the role of the Economic Development Board (EDB) is to promote foreign investment. The creation of EDB Investment Holdings in 1991 was part of the reorganisation of the EDB's activities, as well as reflecting an evolution in the nature of the institution. EDB Investment Holdings will put up venture capital (S$100 million) and will participate financially in projects that transfer technology to Singapore; its role will be different from that of other state holdings (Temasek is under the authority of the Ministry of Finance, Sheng Li Holdings under that of the Defence Ministry, and Singapore Investment Corp is under that of the Monetary Authority of Singapore).

As part of its efforts to promote a "growth triangle", the government is participating in the construction of industrial zones in Johore and on the island of Batam (Indonesia) and has announced development projects in the Bintam (tourism) and the Karimum (ship repairs) islands.

In *Taiwan*, when the investment law expired, the government confirmed that it would maintain its policy of seeking to attract foreign investors, but that henceforth it would give priority to investment in the manufacturing sector. In view of the worsening trade deficit with Japan, the government could consider proposing a number of restrictions on Japanese investment in the consumer goods sector. In addition, the government has ratified the law revising customs tariffs, which was proposed by the Ministry of Finance and relates to 2 000 customs positions. Tariffs are to be cut on average by 7.95 per cent. The largest decrease will be in tariffs on automobiles (down from 42.5 per cent to 30 per cent), while there will be no tariffs on imports of equipment for protecting the environment. The average customs tariff has thus been cut to 6.5 per cent. Finally, in its effort to facilitate the internationalisation of Taiwanese enterprises, the government is participating in the construction of industrial zones in Central America and south-east Asia. It has announced the construction of an industrial zone for Taiwanese electronics firms in Ireland. The government's position with regard to Taiwanese investment in China has evolved. It plans to encourage Taiwanese firms to make such investments while requiring that at the same time they invest the same amount in Taiwan itself.

Regional development measures

In *Taiwan*, tax incentives will be given to enterprises that invest at least NT$5 billion in eight economically-backward provinces (Miaoli, Yunlin, Chiayi, Taitung, Pingtung, Hualien, Penghu and Nantou). These incentives can represent up to 20 per cent of the investment. In view of the opposition that greenfield projects meet with from environmental groups, the government has published a plan to build a vast industrial estate (15 700 hectares) in the Yulin region on land that has been reclaimed from the sea. Work is to start in 1992. Several state enterprises have announced that they will build new projects on the estate.

Industry-related environmental policies

In *Korea*, imports of gases that deplete the ozone layer will require the prior authorisation of the Ministry of Industry. In *Hong Kong*, the government has announced that a tax of 0.75 per cent will be levied on all chemicals (whether imported, manufactured locally or re-exported). The proceeds from this tax will be used to finance an integrated waste processing facility. Finally, in *Singapore*, the government has published a very ambitious plan for the environment -- "Singapore's green plan, towards an environment city" -- the aim of which is to make the city state a model for environmental planning. Among the plan's objectives are: to eliminate CFCs by the year 2000, to reduce SO_2 emissions in the year 2000 to their 1991 level, and to reduce air pollution to below 50 in the Pollutant Standard Index, which is based on the criteria of the US Environmental Protection Agency. Other objectives are: to incinerate 85 per cent of solid waste and to maintain carbon oxide emissions below the average recorded in the OECD countries.

Chapter II

RECENT TRENDS AND POLICY MEASURES IN THE COUNTRIES OF CENTRAL AND EASTERN EUROPE

A. Introduction

For the past two or three years, Poland, Hungary and the Czech and Slovak Federal Republic (CSFR) have been engaged in a far-reaching programme of structural reform aimed at creating the basis for a market economy, a vast undertaking in terms of the number, range and importance of the reforms to be carried out[1]. These reforms are affecting practically every aspect of the institutional and legal systems governing the three economies. They involve the dismantling of many components of the previous system, the setting up of new institutions, and the establishment of a legal infrastructure necessary to the operation of a market economy.

In terms of the restructuring of industry, while the tactics and specific policy choices often differ from one country to another, the strategy of reform for all countries is guided by three objectives [2]:

- The creation of a competitive industrial structure through privatisation, the break-up of monopolies and the suppression of direct state control on the management of firms;

- The creation of an incentive system that follows market rules by re-establishing the role of prices as resource allocation signals, abolishing subsidies and reforming tax and investment finance mechanisms; and

- The introduction of the incentives and disciplines of the world market through trade liberalisation, openness to foreign investment, and the adoption of an exchange rate policy that creates a clear link between domestic and world prices.

The realisation of the structural reform programmes under way is largely conditioned by the success of the macroeconomic stabilisation policies put in place. These are coming under increasing pressure in all three countries under consideration, in part because continuing output declines are reducing tax revenues and thus make budget deficits harder to control, and also because rising unemployment is eroding popular support for stringent stabilisation programmes (Tables 74 and 75). Such pressures are most apparent in Poland, where after substantial progress in 1990, during 1991 the budget shifted into growing deficit, wage growth accelerated, and the rising unemployment put pressure on the government to shift its emphasis towards "economic recovery". Similar problems, though on a much more modest scale, can be observed in the CSFR, while even in Hungary, which started on the transition process early on, severe problems of budgetary control are evident in 1992 [3].

Table 74. **Output of central and eastern European countries**

Percentage change from preceding period

	GDP				Industrial production		
	1989	1990	1991[1]	1992[2]	1989	1990	1991[1]
Bulgaria[3]	−0.4	−9.1	−17.0	−8.0	1.1	−10.0	−12.0
CSFR[3]	1.0	−0.4	−16.0	−5.0	1.0	−3.7	−4.5
Hungary	−0.2	−3.3	−10.0	0.0	−1.0	−10.0	−12.0
Poland	0.0	−11.6	−9.0	−2.0	−0.5	−24.2	−11.8
Romania[3]	−4.0	−7.4	−14.0	−8.0	−2.1	−22.0	−20.0

1. Estimations.
2. Projections.
3. Pre-1991 figures refer to net material product.
Source: OECD, *Economic Outlook No. 51;* Industry Division.

Progress in structural reform has been slower than expected and this has in turn contributed to the difficulty of maintaining a stable macroeconomic environment. The reform of the tax system has turned out to be a slow process, and has thus not contributed as much as expected to easing budgetary strains. Continuing soft budget constraints on many enterprises have undermined the scope for effective monetary policies: in the absence of a real threat of bankruptcy, credit does not decline in response to higher interest rates while at the same time a tightening of monetary policy can have the perverse result of misallocating the scarce financial resources available by leading to a reduction of credit to smaller firms and to the emerging private sector.

Table 75. **Inflation and unemployment in central and eastern European countries**

	Unemployment				Inflation			
	Per cent of labour force				Percentage change over previous period			
	1989	1990	1991	1992[1]	1989	1990	1991	1992[1]
CSFR	0.0	1.0	6.8	12.0	1.4	10.0	58.0	15.0
Hungary	0.5	1.6	7.5	10.0	17.1	28.4	35.0	26.0
Poland	0.3	6.1	11.5	19.0	251.1	585.8	70.0	50.0

1. Projections.
Source: OECD, *Economic Outlook No 51*.

Privatisation plans, although proceeding, have in many cases run up against institutional bottlenecks, while there is continuing uncertainty about the right balance to achieve between domestic and foreign capital. A wide range of labour market policies are being put in place, and are constantly revised in order to better adapt them both to the rise in unemployment and to the budgetary constraints that countries are facing. Trade policies have been largely liberalised, and a number of association agreements have been signed. Despite remaining trade barriers from OECD countries, exports to the OECD area have increased (especially in the case of the CSFR and Hungary) and partly offset the collapse of CMEA trade; sharp import increases continue however to put a considerable strain on current accounts, especially in Poland. A continuing reduction of import barriers from OECD countries is essential in this respect for further progress to be made on this front.

Perhaps more so than in the case of OECD countries, in the case of the central and eastern European countries in transition, macroeconomic policies and structural reforms which improve the efficiency of resource allocation are inextricably bound together. Macroeconomic stabilisation policies are binding constraints on most initiatives which attempt to improve the functioning of product or factor markets, while macroeconomic stabilisation is only effective when an institutional and legal framework is in place. In this context, industrial policy has important roles to play. The first is to contribute to the elimination of the sources of several market failures that are still present: excessive monopolisation and "soft budget constraints" for enterprises in product markets, price controls on labour or the lack of a well-functioning capital market. This means that there is an urgent need to put into place the institutions that are a prerequisite to a viably functioning market economy.

A second role is to provide catalysts and to help accelerate industrial development. This consists of helping develop material and intangible infrastructures such as transport and telecommunications, R&D and training facilities, or technical and product quality standards. In addition, industrial policy in these countries operates in an economic environment that is characterised by incipient markets and credit constraints, and where macroeconomic policies and structural reforms are not always interacting as in mature western economies. Industrial policy initiatives have in this context the potential to accelerate the adjustment process by amplifying market incentives for enterprises with the greatest potential, while sanctioning non-performing ones. While the experience of OECD countries suggests that the concept of sectoral comparative advantage is not a useful guide for policy choices, the promotion of the restructuring of a limited number of viable firms regardless of industry may be a possible option in certain circumstances [4].

B. Recent trends

In *Poland*, the government decided in late 1989 to opt for a radical shift to a market economy. Since the introduction of the Economic Transformation Programme in the beginning of 1990, the economic system has undergone a series of drastic changes. These changes have given rise to already perceptible positive effects, such as the disappearance of shortages and the rapid development of the small private sector, services in particular. At the same time however, the transition process has also brought along a period of sharp output decline caused by the process of macroeconomic stabilisation and by the inevitable delay in adjusting supply to the new incentive structure that is still not fully in place. The positive developments of the economic reforms are currently overshadowed by a sharp rise in unemployment, high (but declining) inflation, falling real wages and an erosion of purchasing power suffered by households.

Poland's GDP fell by 11.6 per cent during 1990 and by an estimated 9 per cent in 1991 [5]. After falling by over 24 per cent in 1990, industrial production (manufacturing and mining) declined by nearly 12 per cent in 1991, and manufacturing production by 12.3 per cent. Large declines in the index of production were registered in transport equipment (33.8 per cent), instruments (25.4 per cent) and iron and steel (23.9 per cent). Between the beginning of

1989 and August 1991, sales, productivity and profitability fell for all industrial sectors. At the same time, there appear to be wide variations in the profitability of enterprises within broadly defined industries. For instance, in 1990, about one third of all firms in the textile and leather products industries showed losses, while the remaining two thirds made profits. Furthermore, a breakdown by industry branch suggests that there is no simple relationship between these indicators. For instance, the non-ferrous metals sector had the highest profit margin of all sectors in 1991, but experienced one of the steepest declines in sales and productivity, while price increases in this sector were also among the lowest. In contrast, the fuel and energy sector had one of the highest rates of price increase, but about half of all enterprises in this sector experienced losses in 1990 [6].

The economic transformation under way is apparent in the structural changes occurring in Polish industry. These include the development of a private industrial sector, the break-up of monopolies, trade liberalisation, and liberalisation of foreign direct investment. Considerable progress has been made towards establishing a market economy, particularly in product markets. Product prices have been largely freed, and firms now operate virtually without subsidies. Significant gains to the economy have also been made as a result of trade liberalisation. Following the measures taken in order to liberalise trade, Polish industry entered the world market very rapidly. During 1991, the value of all exports of industrial products rose significantly, even though at the same time the value of total production fell (see Table 76). Also, since 1989, the proportion of trade with the CMEA and with non-CMEA countries changed dramatically. While there has been an important acceleration in exports to non-CMEA countries, the EC in particular, the absolute value of trade with CMEA countries has fallen. At the same time, the balance of payments surplus achieved in 1990 has become an important deficit in the first half of 1991. Comparing the first eight months of 1991 to 1990, foreign trade calculated in current prices showed a large increase in imports while exports decreased, and terms of trade deteriorated from 100 to 86.9 per cent.

Hungary is more advanced than other central and eastern European countries (CEECs) in its transition to a market economy. Economic reforms began early, the country was an early adherent to international institutions (GATT, IMF, the World Bank), and was the first to attract foreign investment. This early start combined with a stable political situation has given Hungary a number of advantages. It must now manage these advantages through the transition period.

Hungary's GDP dropped by 3.3 per cent in 1990, and the estimated fall during 1991 was 10 per cent. The trade balance swung from surplus in 1989 and 1990 into deficit in 1991. Import competition was particularly severe in consumer goods, machinery and transport. Exports have performed well, increasing by over 40 per cent in convertible currencies (current prices) in 1991, after 15 per cent growth in 1990. The export boom is to a certain degree due to increased marketing efforts and to exports from foreign investments in Hungary, which account for about 20 per cent of 1991 exports. Preliminary official statistics indicate that industrial production declined by one-third between 1989 and 1991, with acceleration of the decline in 1991. It is expected to fall again in 1992. The declines are most marked in basic metals, machinery and transport, and textiles, clothing and footwear (Table 77) [7]. Employment in manufacturing industry fell by 28 per cent between 1989 and 1991, and may fall even further if competitiveness and productivity are to be improved to ensure long-term industrial performance.

The difficulties in the adjustment process of Hungarian industry can be attributed to a variety of factors, many of them common to all countries in the transition process. In general, the manufacturing sector has been relatively over-developed and excess resources are now shifting to under-developed service activities. Inefficient state-owned enterprises have to cope with increased competition, the collapse of CMEA export markets, reductions in state subsidies and credit support, and the application of strict financial controls. As a result, uneconomic and loss-making production units are now being closed down or cut back, and large production units are being split up. The collapse of subsidised energy supplies and the switch to world energy prices has made energy-intensive industries uncompetitive. Export industries lost former markets in eastern Europe and the ex-Soviet Union (machinery, pharmaceuticals, transport equipment), while import-competing industries are facing dramatic increases in imports (in particular of consumer goods and motor vehicles) during a period in which total domestic demand has fallen. Finally, industries specialised in the production of investment goods are experiencing substantial declines in domestic investment rates.

Table 76. **Export growth and current balances in central and eastern European countries**

	Export growth to the OECD area			Current balances		
	Percentage change from previous year in ECU terms			(billion $)		
	1989	1990	1991	1989	1990	1991[1]	1992[2]
Bulgaria	–3.8	14.6	7.8	32.1	–1.2	–0.9	–1.4
CSFR	6.8	16.0	1.8	40.7	–1.1	0.4	–0.5
Poland	13.8	15.0	24.9	15.1	0.7	–2.1	–2.0
Romania	–3.2	3.4	–39.1	–11.6	–1.7	–1.0	–1.3
Former USSR	1.3	16.9	2.8	8.2	1.1	2.0	–3.0

1. Estimations.
2. Projections.
Source: OECD, *Economic Outlook No 51.*

Table 77. **Industrial production in Hungary**
Volume indices

	1986	1987	1988	1989	1990	1991	1986	1987	1988	1989	1990	1991
	Previous year = 100						1985 = 100					
Mining	99.9	99.6	96.3	94.8	82.8	89.1	99.9	99.5	95.8	90.8	75.2	67.0
Electricity supply	102.1	104.4	100.1	102.2	102.9	92.0	102.1	106.6	106.7	109.1	112.3	103.3
Basic metals	102.8	100.9	104.3	104.4	85.7	67.3	102.8	103.7	108.2	113.0	96.8	65.1
Machinery, transport	103.7	104.7	100.0	100.2	83.1	65.1	103.7	108.6	108.6	108.8	90.4	58.9
Building materials	102.3	106.9	101.6	98.4	97.5	67.0	102.3	109.4	111.1	109.4	106.7	71.5
Chemicals	101.4	106.1	101.3	96.1	93.9	81.5	101.4	107.6	109.0	104.7	98.3	80.2
Light industry	101.1	102.9	10.2	95.2	88.9	75.1	101.1	104.0	104.2	99.2	88.2	66.3
of which:												
Timber	104.0	107.4	102.0	103.9	99.4	81.6	104.0	111.7	113.9	118.4	117.4	96.0
Paper	109.7	106.2	104.2	95.8	95.1	77.0	109.7	116.5	121.4	116.3	110.6	85.2
Printing	106.0	106.8	103.0	103.7	88.8	79.9	106.0	113.2	116.6	120.9	107.4	85.8
Textiles	99.1	102.7	101.2	95.5	84.5	65.8	99.1	101.8	103.0	98.4	83.1	54.7
Leather, shoes	106.2	99.8	91.5	87.4	86.2	73.6	106.2	106.0	97.0	84.8	73.1	53.8
Clothing	91.9	99.8	101.7	88.5	89.9	87.7	91.9	91.7	93.3	82.5	74.2	65.1
Other industry	97.1	101.2	95.7	88.0	84.1	61.7	97.1	98.3	94.0	82.8	69.6	42.9
Total industry	102.1	103.9	100.5	98.6	88.9	75.3	102.1	106.1	106.6	105.1	93.5	70.4

Source: Calculated from *Yearbook of Economic Statistics, 1990,* Hungarian Central Statistical Office, 1991. Preliminary data from Central Statistical Office for 1991. Data from units with 50 or more employees.

Enterprises have to renew investment, modernise, improve their productivity performance and generally sharpen their competitiveness, which has declined throughout the 1980s. As many as one-half of large state-owned enterprises are probably potentially competitive, provided that they will be restructured, reduce their debt burden and improve management, financial, and marketing skills. The Law on Bankruptcy came into force on 1 January 1992, and changing market conditions will rapidly eliminate unviable firms. However, severe short-term economic difficulties, combined with erosion of the skill and technical base, may also terminally weaken potentially competitive state-owned enterprises, in particular if exports and domestic markets remain weak.

The *CFSR* has made substantial progress in its transition from central planning mechanisms to a market-based economic system. Most importantly, macroeconomic stability in the face of liberalisation has been preserved. Despite an initial surge in prices, an inflationary spiral of wage-price increases has been avoided. The relatively stable macroeconomic environment has set the stage for the necessary restructuring at the microeconomic level which is a central part of the overall transition process. In this context, there has been an important reduction in budgetary subsidies, and their partial replacement with transfer payments (Table 78). Yet, the economic reforms have been accompanied by a sharp drop in output (an estimated 16 per cent during 1991). Consequently, the CFSR has experienced its first measurable unemployment in four decades. In addition, real wages have fallen considerably during the past two years. Nevertheless, through restraint in nominal wage increases, inflation has been kept relatively under control. The inflation rate increased from 10 per cent in 1990 to a peak of 58 per cent in 1991, but is expected to fall again to 15 per cent in 1992.

Before its reform, the CSFR was highly dependent on trade with the other countries of the socialist bloc. In 1989, over 60 per cent of trade was with other CMEA countries, about half of which with the USSR. Since then, the share of trade with other CMEA countries has declined sharply, falling to around 40 per cent in 1991. This strong orientation of the CSFR towards CMEA markets has led to reduced competitiveness on international markets. Losses on CMEA trade been partially compensated by gains in other markets. Export growth to the OECD area has been strong recently, with convertible-currency exports increasing by 29 per cent in the first quarter of 1992.

Before the economic reforms were initiated, manufacturing industry in the CSFR was oriented towards capital intensive, mass-production industries, with only a small amount of output coming from high technology industries. Over the years, there was an important shift away from light manufacturing industries, and in 1990 they accounted for no more than 22.6 per cent of the value added in manufacturing industry. Manufacturing industry as a whole experienced a severe shock in 1991, although its magnitude affected the various industries in a different proportion. The level of industrial output during the first

Table 78. **Budgetary subsidies in the CSFR, 1985-91**

Billions of current koruny

	1985	1986	1987	1988	1989	1990	Budget 1991
Total subsidies[1]	80.0	85.4	88.7	96.1	122.1	111.8	45.2
As % of GDP[2]	11.8	12.3	12.5	13.0	16.1	14.0	4.2
As % of government expenditures	20.9	21.7	21.6	21.6	26.4	24.1	9.1
Subsidies to enterprises	40.8	39.2	41.1	47.7	59.2	51.9	45.2
of which: agriculture	23.9	23.7	22.5	26.3	35.0	30.0	23.9
Subsidies to households (negative turnover tax)	26.6	28.6	29.8	29.8	49.1	49.2	0.0
of which:							
Dairy	8.9	9.1	9.6	9.4	13.0	13.1	0.0
Meat	4.3	4.4	4.5	4.5	11.9	12.0	0.0
Coal & gas	5.5	6.8	7.3	7.5	7.1	7.2	0.0
Foreign trade subsidies	12.6	17.6	17.8	18.6	13.8	10.7	..

1. Total budgetary subsidies include subsidies paid by national committees (residential heating, housing and urban transport) as well as current transfers to enterprises from the state budget.
2. The GDP ratios in 1991 refer to projected GDP with assumptions of real GDP growth –12 per cent and inflation +55 per cent.

Source: Federal Ministry of Finance.

half of 1991 was only about 80 per cent of the level the previous year. Only coal mining experienced an increase in output. In every other industry output fell, and in certain cases there even was a total collapse in output. The industry with the highest fall in output was apparel, where production in the first half of 1991 was only 63.3 per cent of the level of output during the first half of 1990. Other industries experiencing a sharp drop in production were non-ferrous metals, leather and footwear, and textiles. Industries where production was considerably less affected include energy, paper, and iron and steel.

C. Recent industrial policy measures

Privatisation measures

The privatisation of state-owned enterprises is probably the most important process at work in the economic restructuring of the CEECs. The most widely used forms of privatisation in the three countries under consideration to date include purchase by foreign investors and, mainly for small scale assets, auction sales and restitution to former owners. Given their relative immaturity, the contribution of stockmarkets to the privatisation process has so far been limited. Mass privatisation programmes appear to be essential in the continuation of the privatisation process, as domestic savings are low or non-existent, and, especially in Hungary and the CSFR, many of the best assets have already been privatised.

In *Poland*, the privatisation programme adopted in July 1990 aims to accomplish by 1993 the transfer of half of the industrial state-owned assets to private owners and to have an ownership structure identical to that of an average EC country by 1995. The Ministry of Ownership Changes (MOC), the institution which bears the main responsibility for privatisation, distinguishes between privatisation through "transformation" and privatisation through "liquidation". In the first case, the state company remains an entity throughout the privatisation process, while in the second case, the company is dissolved and its assets are leased or sold to the owners of a new, private company. Enterprises privatised through transformation are initially converted into joint stock companies whose shares are owned by the Polish Treasury. Following this intermediate or "commercialisation" stage between public and private ownership, the shares are sold in one of the following three ways: (i) public offering, i.e. traditional stock offering; (ii) trade sale, where a company is sold to a single investor through competitive bidding; or (iii) mass privatisation, whereby the shares are initially allocated to employees, the government and National Investment Funds. Privatisation through liquidation, intended for the smaller to medium size firms, can occur in two ways. The assets of insolvent enterprises are sold off to private enterprises or individuals and the proceeds go to the creditors. Alternatively, enterprises that are solvent are "liquidated" under Article 37 of the Law of Privatisation by contributing assets and liabilities to a joint venture with a domestic or foreign partner or by selling assets and liabilities to a new firm established by management and workers (buy-out).

The privatisation programme appears to be behind schedule. Privatisation has gone fastest in cases where capital requirements were low and the firms' main assets consisted of the expertise of the employees. The privatisation of medium to large industrial enterprises (numbering over 8 000) has been much slower than anticipated. By the end of 1991, only 26 medium and large companies had been "transformed" through direct sales (16), public offering (8) and leverage buy-outs (2), while the mass privatisation scheme, initially destined to affect 800 to 1 000 companies, had not yet been launched. The target for its first phase, which is planned to last through the autumn of 1992, has now been reduced to 400 firms. The privatisation of small to medium size firms has been comparatively successful. By the end of 1991, around 500 firms had been privatised, mostly through liquidation and sale to a new company set up by management and workers as provided for by Article 37 of the Law of Privatisation. In addition, some 600 firms had been liquidated under Article 19 of the Law on state-owned enterprises. In principle this involves the auctioning of assets, but the process sometimes lacks transparency (see Table 79).

Table 79. **Summary of progress in privatisation in Poland**

	31.12.90	30.6.91	31.12.91	30.3.92
Total number of state-owned enterprises	8 453	8 591	3 228	8 273
Small/medium enterprises privatised by liquidation:	59	343	950	1 123
Under Article 37[1,2]	37	170	416	488
Under Article 19[3]	22	173	534	635
Companies converted to joint-stock companies awaiting privatisation	159	162	244	504
Capital privatisation *including:*	1	13	26	32
Leveraged buy-outs	1	1	2	2
Public flotation	..	6	8	8
Trade sales	..	5	16	22

1. Of which approximately 90 per cent through leasing.
2. In 1991 including industry (85 firms), trade (79), contruction (185).
3. In 1991 including industry (170 firms), trade (47), contruction (86).
Source: Dynamika Prywatyzacji, Ministry of Ownership Changes, Warsaw, Nos. 6 and 8, 1992.

The emergence of institutional bottlenecks is likely to become a major obstacle to the achievement of the privatisation programme's target to place most of the economy in private hands by 1995. The centralised approach to privatisation poses the problem of the processing capacities of the MOC, which may be unable to deal effectively with the growing number of applications for liquidation.

In *Hungary*, the private sector accounts for about 30 per cent of GDP, with 50 000 private legal entities and 11 000 joint ventures with foreign partners, chosen through competitive bidding. Roughly 80 per cent of industrial production still comes from state-owned enterprises. State property was transferred to the State Property Agency (SPA) following its creation in 1990 to manage privatisation. The complexity of sorting out fair and efficient ways of transferring control of state property has made the process slower than anticipated. About two-thirds of the 2 200 large state-owned enterprises have yet to begin their move towards privatisation. So far, foreign investors have played a major role in the privatisation process. Manufacturing, and more specifically consumer goods companies have been the first to be privatised and are now largely in the hands of western multinationals. Privatisation in other sectors, and in particular in utilities, is more complicated. In addition to a lack of the necessary legal and administrative framework, companies in this sector are much less financially attractive for foreign investors.

Alongside privatisation through foreign investment, a range of other approaches have been tried. These include several SPA-initiated privatisation programmes. The first rivatisation programme involved the "model privatisation" of 20 large state-owned enterprises with a good track record. The second concerned "shell" state holding companies where property rights had been transferred. There is also a self-privatisation programme involving around 300 smaller state-owned enterprises, organised with the aid of external consulting firms. The SPA is furthermore privatising small businesses under the Pre-Privatisation Law. Leases and ownership in retail trade, catering and consumer services are being auctioned. Around 10 000 small businesses are potentially for sale but existing rental contracts have limited availability to 3 000. They are reserved exclusively for Hungarian citizens, and subsidised loans are available. In May 1992, several new measures to further encourage domestic participation in the privatisation process were announced. They include discrimination in favour of domestic investors over foreign companies in the case of similar bids and easy payment terms for domestic investors.

In the *CSFR*, the private sector accounted in 1990 for less than half a per cent of non-agricultural output [8]. Private sector development is therefore linked more closely to the success of privatisation than in Hungary or Poland, where the private sector accounted for more than 10 per cent of GDP at the outset. Privatisation is divided into small and large-scale. The former involves the auctioning of small business units primarily to domestic investors and is proceeding at a rapid pace. Between January and October 1991, the privatisation of 13 000 firms under the law for the privatisation of small enterprises (October 1990) had been completed. The government then decided to revise its initial target of 120 000 firms to be privatised under this law to 23 000 and to sell the remaining enterprises under the law for the privatisation of large-scale enterprises (February 1991). The latter law initially provided for the privatisation of about three quarters of the 5 500 large state-owned enterprises. The remainder will remain in state control or will be liquidated. The mechanisms available for large-scale privatisation are direct sales (generally involving a foreign partner), restitution and the extensive use of vouchers. Large-scale privatisation will be carried out in several waves, each involving several bidding rounds. The first wave was initiated in May 1992 with vouchers that have been on sale for a nominal fee since October 1991.

The recent political developments in the CFSR have created some uncertainties concerning the continuation of the voucher programme. Although the second wave of mass privatisation is likely to take place as expected in the Czech lands, the newly elected political leaders in the Slovak Republic may opt for alternative mechanisms for privatisation, where attracting foreign capital will probably be considered a priority. So far, however, Slovak enterprises have attracted only 10 per cent of foreign investment in the CFSR.

Creation of financial markets

One of the essential elements in the transition to a market economy is the creation of a competitive financial market. A financial system where interest rates and lending and borrowing decisions are largely driven by market forces is a *sine qua non* condition for the efficient allocation of domestic savings. There are several institutional and structural obstacles that need to be eliminated in order to liberalise financial markets. They include inadequate regulatory and supervisory systems, underdeveloped money and securities markets, the overhang of bad assets in the portfolio of banks, and insufficient competition between financial institutions. For example, in most CEECs banks are allowed to operate as universal banks, i.e. undertake activities on both the lending and deposit side. In practice, however, current financial systems have remained highly monopolistic as the markets are dominated be a limited number of state-owned banks and there is very little competition from non-bank financial intermediaries. Among the CEECs, Poland, Hungary, and the CSFR have made most progress in the creation of market-based banking systems. All three countries introduced Central Bank legislation and several other new banking laws [9].

In *Poland*, the financial system was a focus for reform efforts after 1989. It began with the creation of a two-tier banking system, composed of the National Bank of Poland, which plays the role of central bank and supervises the banking system, and commercial banks, which serve individuals and public and private enterprises. A capital market, initially consisting of a stock exchange, started functioning in April 1991. Nine commercial banks were created out of the former National Bank of Poland, but remain state banks. There are plans to privatise two of them in 1992. Private banks are still small and local, and they include several new banks created as joint ventures between private and state capital. At the end of 1991, five foreign banks were operating in Poland.

The government is taking measures to develop a regulatory framework for the banking system, particularly with respect to bank supervision. New laws adopted in March 1992 give the president of the central bank relatively far-reaching powers in supervisory matters, and establish wider powers for the banks while at the same time establishing clear prudential limits. Eventually, a new legal framework will be put into place, but there have been delays in its preparation [10].

Overall, Poland is only slowly developing a market-oriented financial system. Newly established commercial banks are still far from behaving like efficient financial intermediaries for industrial restructuring. This is due to their lack of experience in fields such as industrial risk assessment and project appraisal; uncertainties surrounding government plans to tackle the overall debt problem; and the recent sharp increase in the share of non-performing assets in their portfolios. As a result, many potentially productive firms are deprived of the funds needed for restructuring, while some of the scarce credit resources are wasted on non-viable firms. Competition among banks is also limited. The nine commercial banks are still largely dominant within the regions where they operate. Most new banks are small and concentrate their lending where the commercial banks have not yet sought to develop their activities.

In *Hungary*, the independence of the central bank was formally stipulated in 1991. The State Banking Supervisory Agency, subordinate to the government, is responsible for the supervision of the banking section as provided for by the recently adopted "Banking Law". The development of a market-based banking sector and the introduction of more effective central banking operations in Hungary are hampered by the large volume of bad assets. In the 1990 audits, a total of 36 billion forints in bad loans were identified. Of this amount, the government is providing guarantees for 10 billion; 6 billion are to be covered by banks' existing reserves; and for a further 10 billion new reserves are to be built up out of banks' high earnings and restrictive dividends policy [11]. Since 1990, however, the volume of bad assets has grown steadily, and there appears to be a need for additional measures. This potential need is reinforced by the prospect of bankruptcy among the major clients of the three largest state-owned commercial banks.

In the *CSFR*, a two-tier banking system was introduced in January 1990 with the enactment of legislation which separated central bank and commercial banking functions. The central or State Bank was provided with the means to conduct monetary policy and with regulatory authority over the commercial banks. Also, the legal framework for the creation of new domestic and joint venture banks was established. In the fall of 1991, there were 37 newly licensed banks, including savings banks, but they only accounted for a small share of total deposits and credits.

The two most pressing structural problems confronting the CSFR financial system at the moment are a deficient capital base and a lack of competition between banks. These two problems are interrelated and, to a certain extent, there exists a trade-off in solving them. Lack of competition, allowing for high borrowing-lending spreads, results in large banking profits; and this can have a positive effect on strengthening their capital base. However, this would also imply high costs of investment and low returns to savings, discouraging both at a time of economic reforms, when high investment and savings are urgently needed.

Labour-related measures

The transformation of the centrally planned economies has brought along a dramatic rise in unemployment. Before the reforms, a large component of the labour force was concentrated in heavy and energy-intensive industries, while the service sector was heavily under-represented. Most job losses in 1990 and 1991 occurred in manufacturing industry. Employment in this sector fell by 11 per cent, 13 per cent and 28 per cent in the CSFR, Poland and Hungary respectively. Although the share of services in total employment has increased, it may take some time before the services sector will absorb part of the jobs lost in other sectors. Only in the CSFR was moderate growth of employment in tertiary activities registered in 1990, but the following year service sector jobs fell in all three countries. Finally, despite the progress made with privatisation, the state sector remains the principal source of employment. So far, employment growth in the private sector has not been sufficient to offset job losses in the state sector.

A wide range of labour market policy measures have been put in place to cope with the rise in unemployment and to improve management [12]. In all three countries under consideration, unemployment social insurance schemes have been introduced. The benefits are of a limited duration that varies from six to eighteen months. With the rapid growth in unemployment, the schemes have been revised several times in order to improve their fiscal sustainability. In fact, unemployment benefits account for most of the public expenditure on labour market programmes. Budget estimates for 1992 show that between 17.5 per cent (Poland) and 30 per cent (the CSFR) of these expenditures will be used for "active labour market policies". These policies involve several instruments to promote re-integration into the labour force. They include training programmes, subsidised employment schemes, loans to unemployed to start up their own business activities, and job-creation and public-work programmes. The latter consist of temporary, low paid and relatively unskilled jobs, offered preferentially to those unemployed who have exhausted their rights to unemployment benefits.

In *Poland*, the number of registered unemployed increased from 56 000 in January 1990 to 2.2 million in March 1992, or 13 per cent of the labour force. Although part of this growth in unemployment can be attributed to mass registration of school leavers, most of it is due to displaced workers. Mass lay-offs accounted for almost one-fourth of the total unemployed in December 1991.

The initial Polish unemployment benefit scheme, established in 1989, was open-ended. Limits to the duration of the schemes (12 or 18 months, with a declining gross replacement ratio) were introduced in December 1991. The government has also designed several active labour market policies such as training and public-work programmes for the unemployed. Under a scheme to promote employment in community services, labour offices partly cover wage costs and social security contributions sustained by the employers and provide them with small grants in cases where they offer a contract of unlimited duration. In addition, firms hiring people registered as unemployed receive special credits.

In *Hungary*, official figures for unemployment show a rise in job-seekers from 23 000 in January 1990 to 478 000 in March 1992. The country was the first CEEC to define a legal basis for active labour market policies with the introduction of the Employment Law in the mid-1980s. This law was revised in March 1991 to remedy certain shortcomings of measures implemented so far. Job-creation programmes involving preferential loans and grants to firms undertaking investments, used extensively until 1991, were abolished because of their high costs and limited effectiveness. Instead, subsidised unemployment schemes targeting the long-term unemployed were put into place. Public work programmes, started in 1987, reached about 11 500 participants -- or 2.5 per cent of the unemployed -- by the end of 1991. The country's unemployment benefit scheme provides for benefits with a maximum duration between 6 and 18 months.

In the *CSFR*, unemployment is not evenly spread throughout the Federal Republic. By October 1991, unemployment as a percentage of the labour force was almost three times higher in the Slovak Republic than in the Czech Republic. This differential in unemployment rates is partly due to the past forced industrialisation in the Slovak Republic, where a greater dependency on the Soviet Union was developed, particularly in the armaments industry. The Slovak Republic was thus more adversely affected by the collapse of the CMEA export market, while the Czech Republic is more oriented towards new export opportunities, mainly in western European countries. The CSFR as a whole experienced a rise in unemployment from 13 000 in June 1990 to 523 000 in January 1992. Partly as a result of deregistrations following changes to the labour law which shortened the maximum duration of benefits to six months, this number had fallen to 503 000 three months later.

Policy measures to cope with unemployment in the CFSR include public-work programmes and subsidies given to firms recruiting school-leavers. Unemployed starting up their own business can receive up to their yearly unemployment allowance, or more if further positions are created. Training and retraining schemes for the unemployed exist, but there were few incentives to actually attend training as the difference between training benefits and unemployment benefits has in the past been very small. This situation may have changed since in January 1992 the level of unemployment benefits was lowered to 50-60 per cent of previous earnings while training benefits remained at 70 per cent of previous earnings.

Measures to support small and medium-size enterprises

The development of a private small and medium-sized enterprise (SME) sector is an essential requirement to successful transition to market economies. SMEs are key players in a market structure of production and distribution, as they respond quickly to market signals and promote competitiveness. Despite its small size, the SME sector is developing rapidly in response to legislative and policy changes. This will improve the quality and efficiency of domestic goods and services, build entrepreneurship and contribute to employment and new job creation.

In *Poland*, although before the reforms industry was less characterised by very large enterprises than in other CEECs, it was still marked by a lack of SMEs in comparison to market economies. In 1988, 19.6 per cent of all employees were working in manufacturing (excluding mining and construction) enterprises of less than 500 employees, and only 1.4 per cent of employment in manufacturing was in firms with less than one hundred employees. The basic legal conditions for private entrepreneurship, such as property rights and company law, now exist, but there are several remaining administrative and legal obstacles. Restrictions on the use of real estate that encumber mortgage lending and excessively bureaucratic company registration procedures are examples of the latter. There is also good ground for arguing for further support to SMEs, because of "market failures" in the supply of technology, finance, and commercial services to SMEs, and because of the limited access of SMEs to exports markets and government procurement contracts. In the area of finance, for instance, lending institutions are often reluctant to incur the administrative costs of small loans and are frequently unwilling to risk uncollateralised loans altogether. A number of local initiatives aimed at providing basic advisory and support services required by the growing number of new, inexperienced firms have been taken. These include local advisory and support services offered by a number of Independent Chambers of Commerce, and advisory services for self-employment and individual initiatives provided by about 50 employment centres of the Ministry of Labour and Social Policy.

In *Hungary*, the total number of small enterprises showed a rapid increase from 1989. In 1991, the share of employment in enterprises with less than 300 employees was estimated to be 16 per cent, and, in 1990, the share of employment in private or state-owned enterprises with less than 500 employees was estimated to be 37 per cent. In industry the number of plants has shown rapid growth, with the formation of new, smaller units and the break-up of vertically integrated state-owned enterprises. The number of small industrial enterprises with less than 21 employees grew particularly fast, tripling in 1990. Most small enterprises, however, are active in services and commercial trade. Less than one in five small enterprises are in manufacturing industry.

The formation of new enterprises is hampered by a number of difficulties, such as financial problems (high interest rates), poor infrastructure, declining demand, and lack of market knowledge. Between one quarter and one third of all small enterprises are believed to be loss-making. To overcome some of these problems -- notably lack of finance -- a number of support mechanisms and funds have been established. SME assistance and financing schemes are co-ordinated by the Small Business Administration. The Hungarian Foundation for Enterprise Promotion has a more operational role providing assistance. It operates a subsidised lending programme through the banking system and currently is the most important source of credit for SMEs. So far, however, its success rate has been rather low. Of 4 000 enterprises receiving initial assistance, it was estimated early in 1992 that only about 40 per cent were still operating.

In the *CSFR*, between 1956 and 1980, the share of manufacturing employment accounted for by firms with fewer than 500 employees had fallen from 13.6 to 1.4 per cent. In 1990, only about 5 per cent of industrial enterprises had fewer than one hundred employees. The government has taken several measures to promote SMEs. New legislation adopted in 1990 supporting the development of the private sector includes a law on private business activities giving the citizens the right to establish their own business, and a law regulating the taxation of small enterprises. The Ministry of Labour and Social Affairs has launched a plan for SME development which involves the establishment of regional business centres that will provide assistance to people setting up an enterprise.

Finance is a particularly severe problem facing SMEs and potential entrepreneurs in the CFSR. An example of the type of financial institution that could serve as an instrument for promoting the development of SMEs is the Slovak Guarantee Bank. This bank, which began operating in September 1991, has a mandate to make financial resources accessible to SMEs. As it provides guarantees for loans made by commercial banks, it will substantially reduce the risks associated with loans to new firms.

Developments in the area of R&D and technology diffusion

Before transition, technological development in the CEECs was seriously undermined by the centralised structure of the national systems of innovation, the absence of competition, and the fact that supply conditions were not responsive to changes in demand. In most cases, innovative behaviour was largely motivated by a desire to reduce input costs, and virtually no consideration was given to efforts to improve quality or product structure. The present technology gap with industrialised countries is characterised by an outdated capital stock and a shortage of high quality equipment and services. There are, to different degrees, several weaknesses in these countries' innovation systems which must be corrected during the transition period. They include a low overall efficiency, due to the lack of economic incentives to innovate; insufficient infrastructural support for innovation; and inadequate organisation of the science and technology system (excessive centralisation of research activities in national institutions, to the detriment of in-house research activities). Another weakness is the sectoral bias in the allocation of R&D resources that mirrors the distorted sectoral structure of production and employment (in particular, the modest role played by the consumer durable goods sectors as technology developers, adapters or purchasers).

In *Poland*, compared to world innovation patterns, R&D activity is relatively concentrated on machinery for mining, handling and lifting; iron and steel, agriculture and chemicals. Traditionally, the country has had a weak patent activity. During the period 1982-88, there were only 395 Polish inventions with patent applications in at least two countries. In 1989, no more than 16 patents were granted by the United States to Poland, as compared to 34 and 131 respectively for the CSFR and Hungary. Expenditures on R&D and for improving manufacturing techniques are also relatively low. Expenses on all forms of "technical progress", including R&D, were 1.4 per cent of sales value in 1988 and 0.8 per cent in 1989 (in many OECD countries, R&D expenses alone represent over 2 per cent of the value of manufacturing output). After 1989, investments in technical applications and R&D were cut further in the budget squeeze. The share of such investments by state-owned enterprises in total sales rose, but this was due to a decline in sales rather than to an increase in absolute R&D expenditures, which fell. Cutbacks in science and technology investments constitute a barrier to restructuring as they reduce the ability to more widely disseminate improved technology. In the long run, Poland's competitiveness will depend on rebuilding a solid technology support system.

In *Hungary*, gross domestic expenditure on R&D as a percentage of GDP declined steadily during the 1980s, before falling sharply in 1989 and 1990. Nevertheless, the number of patents (over two thousand) granted to Hungarians between 1982 and 1989 by at least two countries reveals a clear superiority with regard to Poland and the CSFR. The country's research effort is divided relatively evenly between the state sector and the business sector. In 1989, the latter funded and carried out 45 per cent of Hungarian R&D. This is comparable to the situation in the OECD area, except that in Hungary the business sector is still largely nationalised and thus controlled by the Ministry of Industry and Commerce. The share of the state budget in R&D funding fell from 23.2 per cent during 1980-85 to 16.5 per cent in 1988, and then rose to 23.7 per cent in 1990. This recent increase however is due to the fact that most enterprises, experiencing economic difficulties since 1988, have considerably decreased their R&D expenditure, while state funding remained stable [13].

Hungary's desire for greater openness towards the West over the last few years has resulted in the establishment of close co-operation with industrialised countries in the areas of science, technology and industry. Co-operation agreements with about 15 countries have been signed, including the United States and the largest EC countries. The Hungarian Academy of Sciences has signed co-operation agreements with around 60 scientific institutions in about 35 countries.

In the *CSFR*, the innovation system has focused strongly on the engineering sector, in particular textile machinery, gears and transmission equipment, robotics, and machinery for the rubber and plastics industry. A number of changes have been introduced recently to the national R&D system. Before 1989, the majority of R&D organisations were controlled and financed by Federal bodies according to the requirements of the State Plan. At the end of 1991, the vast majority of R&D organisations were managed by the state authorities of the Czech and Slovak Republics. In terms of financing of science and technology activities, the state continues to play an important role at Federal and Republic levels. At the Federal level, the Ministry of Economy, which coordinates R&D projects, designated in 1991 thirteen "problem areas" for funding out of its appropriations. Most projects are in energy and transport (together accounting for 50 per cent of Federally supported projects), informatics and the environment. Similar priority areas have been defined at Republic level, with projects in the fields of health and nutrition accounting for the largest share in both the Czech and the Slovak Republics [14].

Industry-related environmental policies

One of the challenges of the transition process in the CEECs is to reduce the present levels of environmental pollution. Environmental concerns were rarely, if at all, taken into account in the centrally planned policies aimed at rapid industrialisation, and pollution levels in the CEECs, in particular in densely populated areas, have become extremely high. The worsening economic situation is likely to have further repercussions on the environment. Environmental considerations dictate the immediate closing of certain plants, but short term economic and social considerations often dictate the opposite. Polluters are often in a better-than-average financial situation, they constitute an important source of hard currency, and employees can form an effective lobby. Yet, there may be several beneficial effects to the environment resulting from economic restructuring. Several sectors with high levels of pollution are declining in significance, and the fall in production in these sectors will result in an absolute decrease in emissions of pollutants. Further environmental improvements are likely to arise from the elimination of subsidies and proper pricing of inputs (energy in particular), the enforcement of regulations and the introduction of environmental charges, taxes and fines. These developments may be reinforced by technological improvements accompanying the inflow of foreign capital, as well as by the quality requirements resulting from already signed international agreements on pollution control and those arising from the closer relationship with the EC.

There is an urgent need for a clear and stable regulatory framework on environmental issues which are closely connected to manufacturing industry. This is particularly important in cases of environmental liabilities which may be acquired in the process of privatisation and foreign investment, and which have to be taken into account when assessing the long-term viability of a state-owned enterprise. Preliminary results of a survey on industrial investment and environmental issues [15] suggest that large western companies look closely at environmental matters in their industrial investment decisions. Unresolved issues relating to environmental liability and environmental standards present important impediments to western direct investment in CEECs. The issue of liability arising from past practices, for example liability for the clean-up of soil contamination or uncertainty about emission standards, appears to be the most important environmental issue for investors.

In *Poland*, a combination of factors, such as the importance of heavy industry, inadequate environmental safeguards, and the low price of coal (coal accounts for 79 per cent of primary energy consumption), have resulted in a degree of air and water pollution that borders on ecological disaster. According to World Bank estimates, the overall income losses associated with environmental degradation are in the range of 2.5 to 3.0 per cent of GDP. The government aims to factor environmental considerations into the restructuring process and it has adopted a National Environmental Policy. This policy, the first of its kind to have been developed in central and eastern Europe, sets out specific objectives for the short (3-4 years), medium (10 years), and long (25 years) term. However, given the economic difficulties and the ensuing pressure on Polish enterprises and public funds, it may become very hard to achieve these objectives.

In *Hungary*, air pollution is a major problem. A third of the population lives in areas with unacceptably high levels of air pollution. It is estimated that 40 per cent of this pollution is caused by industry, another 40 per cent is caused by transport, and 20 per cent by heating. Water pollution constitutes another important issue. Most of the country's groundwater supplies are polluted as a result of intensive use of fertilisers and pesticides in agriculture and the poor standards of water treatment. According to the World Bank, the cost of all environmental damage in Hungary amount to 3 to 4 per cent of GNP, and the health costs of treating pollution related illnesses alone are 35 billion forints. Environmental protection is the joint repsonsibility of several ministries, including the Ministry of Environmental and Regional Development and the Ministry of Industry and Trade. The latter has an environmental protection unit charged with the integration of environmental considerations into industrial policy. Several proposals concerning regulatory and institutional arrangements for environmental protection are currently under development. These include proposals to introduce new regulations for the control of emissions from all large combustion sources [16].

In the *CSFR*, pollution levels are among the highest in Europe. The extensive use of coal by the country's energy industry has led to extremely high and concentrated levels of sulfur dioxide (SO_2) emissions. Emissions of SO_2 per capita are roughly 50 per cent higher than in Poland or Hungary. Other environmental problems include water pollution -- half of the drinking water does not even meet the government's own standards -- and forest depletion. During the recent governmental and economic restructuring of the country, new legislation covering air pollutants and other environmental problems has been adopted. However, efforts to implement environmental regulations and economic incentives have been held up by inter-ministerial conflicts and by uncertainties about Federal/Republic jurisdiction.

Measures relating to international trade

Trade policies in the three countries under consideration have undergone a rapid liberalisation. Tariff reductions, the elimination of many quantitative restrictions and improved transparency during the last few years have significantly changed the trading environment. While some controls remain, exchange rate policies based on market forces have been adopted and internal convertibility allows domestic operators to sell and buy foreign currencies for trade operations at a unified exchange rate.

In December 1991, the EC signed Association Agreements with Poland, the CSFR and Hungary, covering the movement of goods and services, capital and workers. Under the agreements, which entered into force on 1 March 1992, the EC will abolish all barriers to industrial imports within five or six years, while the three Central European countries will have until the year 2000 to do so. There are special provisions for the steel and textile industries and agriculture. The EFTA countries signed a free trade agreement with the CSFR in March 1992. Similar agreements with Hungary and Poland are presently being negotiated in concertation with the EC Association Agreements.

In *Poland*, trade liberalisation has included establishing internal convertibility of the zloty, lowering the weighted average tariff from 18.3 to 5.5 per cent and abolishing the state monopoly on foreign trade. Low tariffs, long suppressed demand for foreign goods, and the removal of various quantitative restrictions led to a sharp rise in imports, in particular of consumer goods. In August 1991, Poland revised its tariff schedule and import duties were raised to a level similar to those at the start of the transformation programme [17]. The new schedule is based on the so-called combined nomenclature of the EC, which specifies that the tariff level on a particular product depends on the country and region of origin, as stipulated in GATT regulations.

In *Hungary*, trade protection is rapidly being dismantled. Average tariffs were reduced to 13 per cent from 16 per cent in 1991 with tariff reductions on 600 items. There is political commitment to further lower tariffs to an average of 8 per cent by 1997. However, tariff protection for certain products, including electrical machinery, clothing and plastics, has been increased. Much of the protection that Hungarian industry enjoyed through "natural" trade barriers (preferential purchasing by government and preferential exports to the CMEA, quotas and licence restrictions) has been swept away. Several other trade barriers are also receiving attention. For instance, the global quota on selected consumer goods was increased to about US$650 million for 1991.

The *CSFR* has also taken a number of measures to liberalise its trade regime. Quotas on imported goods have been virtually eliminated. Tariff levels were reduced a weighted average of 5 per cent. In addition, the monopoly status of the Foreign Trade Organisations has been eliminated. Since the beginning of 1991 all registered enterprises can legally engage in foreign trade. While in 1988 there were only 50 organisations with foreign trading rights, by the end of 1991 around 5 000 producers were directly involved in international trade.

As in Poland, some of the recent liberalising trade measures appear to be subject to reversal. At the end of 1990, the CSFR introduced transitory surcharges of 20 per cent on imports of mainly consumer goods. About half a year later the surcharges were reduced to 15 per cent and their elimination is anticipated. However, recent tariff reforms raised the average tariff level to 6 per cent, and the new schedule is more discriminatory than before.

Measures relating to foreign investments

Foreign investment has a key role to play in the economic restructuring process. Benefits to the economy flowing from foreign direct investment (FDI) include reducing government domestic debt, providing employment, developing foreign markets and substituting for some imports, and increasing domestic competition. Foreign investment is also conceived as a major pillar in privatisation as it improves the capability and efficiency of privatised enterprises by introducing modern technology and management, accountancy and marketing methods, and promoting more rapid re-structuring than would be possible without foreign investment (see also chapter II.F on international investment in Part 3 of this report).

In *Poland*, foreign investment inflows have been less than expected. In the competition among PIT countries to attract foreign investment, Poland has some advantages (such as its large domestic market and the richest natural resources endowment), but also a number of handicaps. Several of the latter are related to the policy context: unstable bureaucracy, unclear ownership status for real estate, uncertainties surrounding tax policies, and the hostile attitude of extreme political forces.

According to the latest statistics, the total amount of joint ventures and direct acquisitions of Polish firms amounted to US$670 million by October 1991 (since then several large contracts in the automotive sector have been signed). The most dynamic developments in the area of foreign investment concern joint ventures. By the end of June 1991, 4 850 licenses for the formation of companies with foreign participation had been issued, 2 130 of which were joint ventures. Apart from the manufacture of apparel and plastic goods, there are relatively few joint ventures in the manufacturing industry sector. They operate mainly in activities such as services, foreign trade, and wholesale of consumer goods.

Several measures have been taken to attract foreign investment in Poland. Recent legislation removes, at least formally, earlier provisions concerning the maximum share foreign investors were allowed to hold in Polish enterprises. In July 1991, a new law went into effect that enables foreign investors to transfer all their profits out of the country. To further facilitate foreign investment, accounting standards are being brought into line with those of the EC.

Hungary has experienced a boom in foreign direct investment. While before 1989 there was relatively little foreign investment, in 1990 inflows amounted to US$900 million, and then rose to US$1.46 billion in 1991. Inflows into Hungary are over 50 per cent of the total of FDI going to the CEECs. It is the most important source of privatisation funds for large state-owned enterprises (80-90 per cent); and about one half of the FDI inflow has gone to purchase state enterprises. With the collapse of domestic investment, FDI was 15 per cent of gross investment in 1990, and it is estimated to have reached over 20 per cent in 1991. It has concentrated in manufacturing industry (half of the FDI stock end-1990, two-thirds of inflows for the first three quarters of 1991), mainly in machinery industry, automobiles and food processing industry.

Reasons for Hungary's success in attracting foreign investments include its political stability, its advance on other CEECs in the transition to a market economy, relatively clear ownership and privatisation plans, and the provision of a relatively "western" commercial and business infrastructure. Procedures for setting up foreign investments are simple, and there are generous and transparent corporate tax incentives for foreign investors. Since 1989, foreign partners may own 100 per cent of an enterprise, and may purchase existing enterprises. Since 1991 there has been simple company registration with the Court of Registration with a minimal 1 million forints.

In the *CSFR*, foreign direct investment activity has generally lagged behind that of Hungary and Poland, and only recently has started showing signs of rapid expansion. The bulk goes to Czech enterprises: so far they have attracted about 90 per cent of all FDI in the CSFR. In August 1991, there were nearly 3 000 joint ventures with foreign partners registered, which was more than twice as many as were registered nine months earlier. This amounted to a total capital outlay of CSK 10 billion, about two thirds of which was in manufacturing industry. Germany and Austria are the two major investors in the CSFR. At the end of 1991, they accounted together for over 60 per cent of total foreign direct investment in the Federation.

The regulatory framework for foreign direct investment in the CSFR has largely been put in place and is rather liberal, although registration procedures and approval processes are still relatively cumbersome. Remaining obstacles to foreign investment stem from specific features of the broader economic and political environment such as uncertainty concerning the future of the Federation, deficiencies in the "business infrastructure", and the high levels of business risk during the transition period. Tax provisions are slightly more generous to joint ventures than to domestic enterprises, but the CSFR provides fewer tax incentives than Poland or Hungary. There is the possibility of two-year tax holidays on a discretionary basis, and further measures are under consideration.

NOTES AND REFERENCES

1. This section of the report concentrates exclusively on trends and policies in the countries of central and eastern Europe that participate in the OECD "Partners in Transition" (PIT) programme: Poland, Hungary and the Czech and Slovak Federal Republic.

2. See also OECD (1991), *Industrial Policies in OECD Countries: Annual Review*, Paris.

3. See OECD (1992), *OECD Economic Outlook No.51*, Paris, June.

4. For en elaboration of these arguments, see OECD (1992), *Industry in Poland: Structural Adjustment Issues and Policy Options*, Paris.

5. OECD (1992), *OECD Economic Outlook No.51*, Paris, June.

6. OECD (1992), *Industry in Poland: Structural Adjustment Issues and Policy Options*, op.cit.

7. Official statistics, however, overstate the decline in volume of output. Only units with more than 50 employees are currently included in official production data, and private sector activities and small firms are measures poorly. Although new and small firms operate predominantly in services and trade, there is evidence that an increasing share of manufacturing industrial production comes from small private firms.

8. OECD (1992), *OECD Economic Surveys : the Czech and Slovak Federal Republic*, Paris.

9. See OECD (1992), "Bank Restructuring in Central and Eastern Europe: Issues and Strategies", *Financial Market Trends*, No. 51, February.

10. OECD (1992), *OECD Economic Surveys : Poland*, Paris.

11. OECD (1991), *OECD Economic Surveys : Hungary*, Paris.

12. See also OECD (1992), *Employment Outlook*, Paris, July.

13. OECD (1992), *Science, Technology and Innovation Policies: Hungary*, Paris.

14. OECD (1992), *Science, Technology and Innovation Policies: Czech and Slovak Federal Republic*, Paris.

15. This survey was conducted by the OECD and the World Bank in February - April 1992. It was aimed at the 1 000 largest manufacturing, mining, and construction companies based in North America and Western Europe. The preliminary results were presented during the "International Conference on Privatisation, Foreign Direct Investment, and Environmental Liability", organised in May 1992.

16. International Energy Agency (1992), *Energy Policies, Hungary -- 1991 Survey*, OECD, Paris.

17. OECD (1992), *OECD Economic Surveys : Poland*, Paris.

MAIN SALES OUTLETS OF OECD PUBLICATIONS
PRINCIPAUX POINTS DE VENTE DES PUBLICATIONS DE L'OCDE

ARGENTINA – ARGENTINE
Carlos Hirsch S.R.L.
Galería Güemes, Florida 165, 4° Piso
1333 Buenos Aires   Tel. (1) 331.1787 y 331.2391
                     Telefax: (1) 331.1787

AUSTRALIA – AUSTRALIE
D.A. Book (Aust.) Pty. Ltd.
648 Whitehorse Road, P.O.B 163
Mitcham, Victoria 3132   Tel. (03) 873.4411
                   Telefax: (03) 873.5679

AUSTRIA – AUTRICHE
Gerold & Co.
Graben 31
Wien I   Tel. (0222) 533.50.14

BELGIUM – BELGIQUE
Jean De Lannoy
Avenue du Roi 202
B-1060 Bruxelles   Tel. (02) 538.51.69/538.08.41
               Telefax: (02) 538.08.41

CANADA
Renouf Publishing Company Ltd.
1294 Algoma Road
Ottawa, ON K1B 3W8   Tel. (613) 741.4333
                   Telefax: (613) 741.5439
Stores:
61 Sparks Street
Ottawa, ON K1P 5R1   Tel. (613) 238.8985
211 Yonge Street
Toronto, ON M5B 1M4   Tel. (416) 363.3171
Les Éditions La Liberté Inc.
3020 Chemin Sainte-Foy
Sainte-Foy, PQ G1X 3V6   Tel. (418) 658.3763
                   Telefax: (418) 658.3763

Federal Publications
165 University Avenue
Toronto, ON M5H 3B8   Tel. (416) 581.1552
                   Telefax: (416) 581.1743

CHINA – CHINE
China National Publications Import
Export Corporation (CNPIEC)
16 Gongti E. Road, Chaoyang District
P.O. Box 88 or 50
Beijing 100704 PR   Tel. (01) 506.6688
                   Telefax: (01) 506.3101

DENMARK – DANEMARK
Munksgaard Export and Subscription Service
35, Nørre Søgade, P.O. Box 2148
DK-1016 København K   Tel. (33) 12.85.70
                   Telefax: (33) 12.93.87

FINLAND – FINLANDE
Akateeminen Kirjakauppa
Keskuskatu 1, P.O. Box 128
00100 Helsinki   Tel. (358 0) 12141
                   Telefax: (358 0) 121.4441

FRANCE
OECD/OCDE
Mail Orders/Commandes par correspondance:
2, rue André-Pascal
75775 Paris Cedex 16   Tel. (33-1) 45.24.82.00
Telefax: (33-1) 45.24.85.00   or (33-1) 45.24.81.76
                   Telex: 640048 OCDE

OECD Bookshop/Librairie de l'OCDE :
33, rue Octave-Feuillet
75016 Paris   Tel. (33-1) 45.24.81.67
            (33-1) 45.24.81.81

Documentation Française
29, quai Voltaire
75007 Paris   Tel. 40.15.70.00

Gibert Jeune (Droit-Économie)
6, place Saint-Michel
75006 Paris   Tel. 43.25.91.19

Librairie du Commerce International
10, avenue d'Iéna
75016 Paris   Tel. 40.73.34.60
Librairie Dunod
Université Paris-Dauphine
Place du Maréchal de Lattre de Tassigny
75016 Paris   Tel. 47.27.18.56
Librairie Lavoisier
11, rue Lavoisier
75008 Paris   Tel. 42.65.39.95
Librairie L.G.D.J. - Montchrestien
20, rue Soufflot
75005 Paris   Tel. 46.33.89.85
Librairie des Sciences Politiques
30, rue Saint-Guillaume
75007 Paris   Tel. 45.48.36.02
P.U.F.
49, boulevard Saint-Michel
75005 Paris   Tel. 43.25.83.40
Librairie de l'Université
12a, rue Nazareth
13100 Aix-en-Provence   Tel. (16) 42.26.18.08
Documentation Française
165, rue Garibaldi
69003 Lyon   Tel. (16) 78.63.32.23
Librairie Decitre
29, place Bellecour
69002 Lyon   Tel. (16) 72.40.54.54

GERMANY – ALLEMAGNE
OECD Publications and Information Centre
Schedestrasse 7
D-W 5300 Bonn 1   Tel. (0228) 21.60.45
                   Telefax: (0228) 26.11.04

GREECE – GRÈCE
Librairie Kauffmann
Mavrokordatou 9
106 78 Athens   Tel. 322.21.60
               Telefax: 363.39.67

HONG-KONG
Swindon Book Co. Ltd.
13-15 Lock Road
Kowloon, Hong Kong   Tel. 366.80.31
               Telefax: 739.49.75

ICELAND – ISLANDE
Mál Mog Menning
Laugavegi 18, Pósthólf 392
121 Reykjavik   Tel. 162.35.23

INDIA – INDE
Oxford Book and Stationery Co.
Scindia House
New Delhi 110001   Tel.(11) 331.5896/5308
               Telefax: (11) 332.5993
17 Park Street
Calcutta 700016   Tel. 240832

INDONESIA – INDONÉSIE
Pdii-Lipi
P.O. Box 269/JKSMG/88
Jakarta 12790   Tel. 583467
               Telex: 62 875

IRELAND – IRLANDE
TDC Publishers – Library Suppliers
12 North Frederick Street
Dublin 1   Tel. 74.48.35/74.96.77
               Telefax: 74.84.16

ISRAEL
Electronic Publications only
Publications électroniques seulement
Sophist Systems Ltd.
71 Allenby Street
Tel-Aviv 65134   Tel. 3-29.00.21
               Telefax: 3-29.92.39

ITALY – ITALIE
Libreria Commissionaria Sansoni
Via Duca di Calabria 1/1
50125 Firenze   Tel. (055) 64.54.15
               Telefax: (055) 64.12.57
Via Bartolini 29
20155 Milano   Tel. (02) 36.50.83
Editrice e Libreria Herder
Piazza Montecitorio 120
00186 Roma   Tel. 679.46.28
               Telefax: 678.47.51
Libreria Hoepli
Via Hoepli 5
20121 Milano   Tel. (02) 86.54.46
               Telefax: (02) 805.28.86
Libreria Scientifica
Dott. Lucio de Biasio 'Aeiou'
Via Coronelli, 6
20146 Milano   Tel. (02) 48.95.45.52
               Telefax: (02) 48.95.45.48

JAPAN – JAPON
OECD Publications and Information Centre
Landic Akasaka Building
2-3-4 Akasaka, Minato-ku
Tokyo 107   Tel. (81.3) 3586.2016
               Telefax: (81.3) 3584.7929

KOREA – CORÉE
Kyobo Book Centre Co. Ltd.
P.O. Box 1658, Kwang Hwa Moon
Seoul   Tel. 730.78.91
               Telefax: 735.00.30

MALAYSIA – MALAISIE
Co-operative Bookshop Ltd.
University of Malaya
P.O. Box 1127, Jalan Pantai Baru
59700 Kuala Lumpur
Malaysia   Tel. 756.5000/756.5425
               Telefax: 757.3661

NETHERLANDS – PAYS-BAS
SDU Uitgeverij
Christoffel Plantijnstraat 2
Postbus 20014
2500 EA's-Gravenhage   Tel. (070 3) 78.99.11
Voor bestellingen: Tel. (070 3) 78.98.80
               Telefax: (070 3) 47.63.51

**NEW ZEALAND
NOUVELLE-ZÉLANDE**
Legislation Services
P.O. Box 12418
Thorndon, Wellington   Tel. (04) 496.5652
               Telefax: (04) 496.5698

NORWAY – NORVÈGE
Narvesen Info Center – NIC
Bertrand Narvesens vei 2
P.O. Box 6125 Etterstad
0602 Oslo 6   Tel. (02) 57.33.00
               Telefax: (02) 68.19.01

PAKISTAN
Mirza Book Agency
65 Shahrah Quaid-E-Azam
Lahore 3   Tel. 66.839
       Telex: 44886 UBL PK. Attn: MIRZA BK

PORTUGAL
Livraria Portugal
Rua do Carmo 70-74
Apart. 2681
1117 Lisboa Codex   Tel.: (01) 347.49.82/3/4/5
               Telefax: (01) 347.02.64

SINGAPORE – SINGAPOUR
Information Publications Pte. Ltd.
41, Kallang Pudding, No. 04-03
Singapore 1334   Tel. 741.5166
                        Telefax: 742.9356

SPAIN – ESPAGNE
Mundi-Prensa Libros S.A.
Castelló 37, Apartado 1223
Madrid 28001   Tel. (91) 431.33.99
                        Telefax: (91) 575.39.98
Libreria Internacional AEDOS
Consejo de Ciento 391
08009 – Barcelona   Tel. (93) 488.34.92
                        Telefax: (93) 487.76.59
Llibreria de la Generalitat
Palau Moja
Rambla dels Estudis, 118
08002 – Barcelona
       (Subscripcions) Tel. (93) 318.80.12
       (Publicacions) Tel. (93) 302.67.23
                        Telefax: (93) 412.18.54

SRI LANKA
Centre for Policy Research
c/o Colombo Agencies Ltd.
No. 300-304, Galle Road
Colombo 3   Tel. (1) 574240, 573551-2
                        Telefax: (1) 575394, 510711

SWEDEN – SUÈDE
Fritzes Fackboksföretaget
Box 16356
Regeringsgatan 12
103 27 Stockholm   Tel. (08) 23.89.00
                        Telefax: (08) 20.50.21
Subscription Agency-Agence d'abonnements
Wennergren-Williams AB
Nordenflychtsvägen 74
Box 30004
104 25 Stockholm   Tel. (08) 13.67.00
                        Telefax: (08) 618.62.36

SWITZERLAND – SUISSE
Maditec S.A. (Books and Periodicals - Livres
et périodiques)
Chemin des Palettes 4
1020 Renens/Lausanne   Tel. (021) 635.08.65
                        Telefax: (021) 635.07.80

Librairie Payot
Service des Publications Internationales
Case postale 3212
1002 Lausanne   Tel. (021) 341.33.48
                        Telefax: (021) 341.33.45

Librairie Unilivres
6, rue de Candolle
1205 Genève   Tel. (022) 320.26.23
                        Telefax: (022) 329.73.18

Subscription Agency - Agence d'abonnement
Naville S.A.
38 avenue Vibert
1227 Carouge   Tél.: (022) 308.05.56/57
                        Telefax: (022) 308.05.88

See also – Voir aussi :
OECD Publications and Information Centre
Schedestrasse 7
D-W 5300 Bonn 1 (Germany)
                        Tel. (49.228) 21.60.45
                        Telefax: (49.228) 26.11.04

TAIWAN – FORMOSE
Good Faith Worldwide Int'l. Co. Ltd.
9th Floor, No. 118, Sec. 2
Chung Hsiao E. Road
Taipei   Tel. (02) 391.7396/391.7397
                        Telefax: (02) 394.9176

THAILAND – THAÏLANDE
Suksit Siam Co. Ltd.
113, 115 Fuang Nakhon Rd.
Opp. Wat Rajbopith
Bangkok 10200   Tel. (662) 251.1630
                        Telefax: (662) 236.7783

TURKEY – TURQUIE
Kültur Yayinlari Is-Türk Ltd. Sti.
Atatürk Bulvari No. 191/Kat. 13
Kavaklidere/Ankara   Tel. 428.11.40 Ext. 2458
Dolmabahce Cad. No. 29
Besiktas/Istanbul   Tel. 160.71.88
                        Telex: 43482B

UNITED KINGDOM – ROYAUME-UNI
HMSO
Gen. enquiries   Tel. (071) 873 0011
Postal orders only:
P.O. Box 276, London SW8 5DT
Personal Callers HMSO Bookshop
49 High Holborn, London WC1V 6HB
                        Telefax: (071) 873 8200
Branches at: Belfast, Birmingham, Bristol, Edinburgh, Manchester

UNITED STATES – ÉTATS-UNIS
OECD Publications and Information Centre
2001 L Street N.W., Suite 700
Washington, D.C. 20036-4910 Tel. (202) 785.6323
                        Telefax: (202) 785.0350

VENEZUELA
Libreria del Este
Avda F. Miranda 52, Aptdo. 60337
Edificio Galipán
Caracas 106   Tel. 951.1705/951.2307/951.1297
                        Telegram: Libreste Caracas

Subscription to OECD periodicals may also be placed through main subscription agencies.

Les abonnements aux publications périodiques de l'OCDE peuvent être souscrits auprès des principales agences d'abonnement.

Orders and inquiries from countries where Distributors have not yet been appointed should be sent to: OECD Publications Service, 2 rue André-Pascal, 75775 Paris Cedex 16, France.

Les commandes provenant de pays où l'OCDE n'a pas encore désigné de distributeur devraient être adressées à : OCDE, Service des Publications, 2, rue André-Pascal, 75775 Paris Cedex 16, France.

10-1992